Hypnotic Investigation of Psychodynamic Processes

Photograph by René Bergermaier

Milton H. Erickson, MD (1901–1980) Ernest L. Rossi, PhD

Hypnotic Investigation of Psychodynamic Processes

by MILTON H. ERICKSON

The Collected Papers of
Milton H. Erickson on Hypnosis
Volume III

Edited by Ernest L. Rossi

IRVINGTON PUBLISHERS, INC., New York

Library of Congress Cataloging in Publication Data

Erickson, Milton H.
Hypnotic investigation of psychodynamic processes.

(The collected papers of Milton H. Erickson on hypnosis; v. 3)
Bibliography: p.
1. Hypnotism. 2. Subconsciousness. I. Rossi, Ernest Lawrence. II. Title.
RC495.E714 vol. 1. 616.8'916'208s [616.8'916'208]
ISBN 0-8290-0544-7 79-15939

Printed in the United States of America

Foreword

This series of Milton Erickson's papers contains a fascinating array of original contributions related to every phase of hypnotic theory and practice. The papers contain stores of invaluable data that can be productively mined by researchers and clinicians for treasures useful in hypothetical structuring and experiment, as well as in catalyzing psychotherapy. Dr. Erickson is perhaps the most creative and imaginative contemporary worker in the area of hypnosis and his inspired writings in this series rank among the enduring classics in the field.

Lewis R. Wolberg, M.D.
Clinical Professor of Psychiatry,
New York University School of Medicine

Emeritus Dean, Postgraduate Center
for Mental Health

Acknowledgments

The Editor wishes to acknowledge the assistance and suggestions of many colleagues and members of the American Society of Clinical Hypnosis in the preparation of these volumes. In particular: Marian Moore, Robert Pearson, Florence Sharp, and Andre Weitzenhoffer. Significant editorial and secretarial skills have been contributed by Margaret Ryan.

The following journals and publishers have generously permitted the replication of papers in these volumes:

American Journal of Clinical Hypnosis, American Journal of Psychiatry, American Medical Association, American Psychiatric Association, American Psychological Association, Appleton-Century-Crofts, *Archives of Neurology and Psychiatry, British Journal of Medical Psychology, Bulletin of the Georgetown University Medical Center, Diseases of the Nervous System, Encyclopaedia Britannica,* Family Process, Harper and Row, Paul B. Hoeber, Inc., *Journal of Abnormal and Social Psychology, Journal of Clinical and Experimental Hypnosis, Journal of Experimental Psychology, Journal of General Psychology, Journal of Genetic Psychology, Journal of Nervous and Mental Disease, Journal of the American Society of Psychosomatic Dentistry and Medicine,* Journal Press, Julian Press, Macmillan Company, Medical Clinics of North America, Merck, Sharp and Dohme, *Perceptual and Motor Skills,* Physicians Postgraduate Press, *Psychiatry, Psychoanalytic Quarterly, Psychosomatic Medicine,* W. B. Saunders Company, Springer Verlag, William Alanson White Psychiatric Foundation, Williams and Wilkins, and Woodrow Press.

Contents

Editor's Preface

These four volumes of Milton H. Erickson's selected papers have been collected for clinicians and researchers who wish to explore in depth the work of one of the most seminal minds in the history of hypnosis and psychotherapy. When Erickson began publishing his studies in the early 1930s, hypnosis was in a curious position: most investigators agreed that hypnosis had played a central role in the early studies of psychopathology and our first efforts at psychotherapy, but the authoritative approaches associated with its use were supplanted on the one hand by the seemingly more sophisticated approaches of the psychoanalytic schools, and on the other hand by experimental psychology.

The situation might have continued in just this manner, with hypnosis regarded as nothing more significant than a colorful curiosity in our therapeutic past. Into this situation, however, came the accident that was Milton H. Erickson. He was an accident of nature born with a number of congenital sensory-perceptual problems that led him to experience the world in ways so different that his acute mind could survive only by realizing at a very early age the relativity of our human frames of reference. To these early problems was added the rare medical tragedy of being stricken by two different strains of polio at the ages of 17 and 51. His efforts to rehabilitate himself led to a personal rediscovery of many classical hypnotic phenomena and how they could be utilized therapeutically.

Erickson's experimental and therapeutic explorations with the hypnotic modality span more than 50 years. His successful rejuvenation of the entire field may be attributed to his development of the nonauthoritarian, indirect approaches to suggestion wherein subjects learn how to experience hypnotic phenomena and how to utilize their own potentials to solve problems in their own way. The contents of these four volumes can be best understood as working papers on a journey of discovery. There is little that is fixed, final, or permanently validated about them. Most of these papers are heuristics that can stimulate the mind of the reader and evoke the awe of discovery, the potentials for which are unlimited in the dimension of human consciousness.

The problem of how to present these papers in the best order could have been solved in many ways. A simple chronological order seemed unsatisfactory because the record of much of Erickson's earliest work was published only at a later date. Many papers dealing with the same theme which should obviously be grouped together were published in different phases of his career. Because of this the editor decided to make a balanced presentation wherein each volume identifies a major area of exploration with appropriate sections wherein the papers are presented in an approximation of chronological order.

Each of the first four volumes of this series contains a number of unpublished papers selected by the editor from several boxes of manuscripts entrusted to him by Erickson for this purpose. A companion volume, in preparation, will contain only previously unpublished lectures and hypnotic demonstrations by Erickson throughout his career. Many of these exist in various forms of neglect and deterioration all over the world wherever he gave his numerous presentations. The editor is currently assembling as many of these as can be accurately transcribed and reviewing them with Erickson for his elucidating commentaries. So subtle are his approaches that even a detailed study of his demonstrations often leaves the investigator without a full understanding of what Erickson is doing. Because of this the editor would like to take the occasion of the publication of these four volumes to make an appeal to whomever is in possession of previously unpublished records of Erickson's work to make them available to us for possible inclusion in this companion volume. It is only through such cooperation that we can all grow together.

Ernest L. Rossi

I. General and Historical Surveys of Hypnotism

The papers of this section are all of a general nature and were written by Erickson between 1934 and 1967. The paper entitled "Hypnotism" from the *Encyclopaedia Britannica* (Fourteenth Edition, 1954) is representative of a range of his contributions to the *Britannica* as well as *Collier's Encyclopedia* from 1946 through 1960. These papers survey the historical development of hypnosis, the common misconceptions of its nature, the phenomenon of hypnosis, and a host of major issues about its induction and utilization. Of particular note is how Erickson has explored, from the very beginning of his career, the naturalistic explanations of hypnosis, completely eschewing any tendency to the mystical and miraculous.

A person's life history of experiential learning forms the repertory of associations and mental skills that can be evoked as "hypnotic phenomena" and channeled into desirable therapeutic responses. Even the concept of the "unconscious" is given pragmatic treatment in relation to hypnosis in the paper, "The basis of hypnosis: Panel discussion on hypnosis" (1959). Erickson verbalizes it as follows: "In hypnosis we utilize the unconscious mind. What do I mean by the unconscious mind? I mean the back of the mind, the reservoir of learning. The unconscious constitutes a storehouse." Although this view may appear naive in its simplicity, it is the essential basis for understanding the profound complexities of the second part of this volume, which deals with psychodynamic processes and many of Erickson's innovative hypnotic approaches to the unconscious.

1. A Brief Survey of Hypnotism

Milton H. Erickson

HISTORICAL SKETCH

Hypnotism, or the artifically enhanced state of suggestibility resembling sleep, has been known for many centuries. In ancient days, however, there was neither understanding of it nor appreciation of its nature, and it was attributed to the powers of darkness and magic. It is well known that ancient conjurers, magicians, and fakirs, particularly among the Hindus, practiced various forms of hypnotism. Even in the present day Hindu fakirs are peculiarly adept in this procedure, as observers of their art will attest. The ancient magicians in the time of Genghis Khan also practiced group suggestion and hypnosis in order to obtain visual and auditory hallucinations, of which practices Marco Polo has given several somewhat unsatisfactory accounts.

The first practice of suggestion as a therapeutic measure, although it was not recognized as such at the time, began with Mesmer, whose period was from 1734 to 1815. Because of his development of the art the word *mesmerism* was adopted as a descriptive term. Mesmer's practice of suggestion therapy consisted in the use of "the natural qualities of animal magnetism" which could be induced to manifest themselves in people, trees, or any chosen object. In establishing his clinic Mesmer appears to have had an unusual appreciation of clinical psychology. He had beautifully decorated apartments, illuminated carefully with subdued lights, the rooms filled with the odor of incense, and the walls covered with velvet hangings. In addition, there were usually the gentle tinkle of running water and soft, faint music. His patients waited as a group in a large treatment room, which he would enter elaborately gowned. He administered therapy by gently stroking the arms and ailing parts of the patients, thereby "transferring" to them the healing qualities of "animal magnetism." Often, as would be expected, he achieved satisfactory and even startling results with patients who had been abandoned by orthodox physicians. During his career he discovered that the "quality" of "animal magnetism" could be transmitted to inanimate objects and that patients coming in contact with those articles would experience a cure of their ills. Critical observers at his clinic saw patients sent out to touch "magnetized"

Reprinted with permission from the *Medical Record* for December 5, 1934 trees, thereby becoming healed. However, it was noticed that patients were cured even though they touched the wrong tree. Consequently the opinion developed that Mesmer was a charlatan and there was no realization of the psychological truths of this therapy. Despite the unfortunate reputation Mesmer received, many physicians visited his clinic and acquired valuable ideas and information.

The next great figure in hypnotism was John Elliotson. He was born in 1791, studied medicine at Edinburgh, and in 1817 was appointed assistant physician at St. Thomas' Hospital, where he aroused much antagonism because of his liberal and radical attitudes toward the practice of medicine. He was one of the first men in England to approve of Laennec's stethoscope, thereby incurring great ridicule for having accepted the "silly fad." In 1837 he was appointed professor of the practice of medicine at the University College in recognition of his outstanding clinical ability. At about the same time he began his researches in hypnotism, or "mesmerism" as it was called. He practiced it on patients, received much condemnation for this, and in 1846 for this reason was made the victim of a bitter attack by the *Lancet.* Unfortunately, Elliotson believed in phrenology, clairvoyance, and odyllic forces with the consequence that his researches in hypnotism were placed in a similar category. Nevertheless, he had a wide practice and left a great many records of bona fide cures.

Elliotson was succeeded as the champion of "mesmerism" by James Esdaille (1808-1859), who began his work in India, stimulated in the study of hypnotism by reading Elliotson's reports. Under governmental protection he succeeded in the application of hypnotism to medical cases, and was instrumental in the founding of a hospital for this express purpose. Before he left India, he had utilized it in thousands of minor and in about 300 major operations. Records of these cases are still available to the scientifically curious. Despite the protection of the government, he was subjected to much persecution by his fellow-practitioners.

Following Esdaille came James Braid, an English surgeon who was born in 1795 but who did not take up the study of hypnotism until 1841. At that time he witnessed a "mesmeric trance" and was loud in his denunciation of the entire scene as a fraud. By chance he was induced to make a medical examination of the subject, following which he became intensely interested in the phenomenon and devoted himself to a thorough investigation of the manifestation. It was due to the researches of Braid that hypnosis was placed on a scientific basis, and his coining and application of the terms *hypnotism* and *hypnosis* to the phenomenon instead of the misnomer of *mesmerism* facilitated its acceptance by the medical profession. In the course of his investigations Braid reached the conclusion that hypnotism was wholly a matter of suggestion, which constituted the first attempt at a scientific and psychological explanation.

He made a detailed study of the technique of hypnosis and the various phenomena obtained in trances. He was a prolific writer and left extensive treatises which are surprisingly modern in their conceptions. Since Braid, various other well-known clinicians have been interested in the subjects, particularly Charcot, Liébault, Bernheim, and Heidenhain. More recent scientific leaders who studied hypnosis are G. Stanley Hall, William James, Morton Prince, Sir William Crookes, and Pierre Janet.

METHODS OF HYPNOTIC TRANCE INDUCTION

The methods employed in inducing hypnotic trances vary widely among hypnotists. A good operator varies the details of his technique from subject to subject, fitting it to the peculiarities of each personality. Mesmer's method was to put his hands upon the shoulders of the patient and then to stroke the arms downward to the fingers. In addition, he made various passes and gentle, soothing contacts with his hand over forehead and the part to be healed. Esdaille usually put his subjects in a darkened room and told them to sleep, and then made passes without contact over the entire body. Braid customarily had his subjects look at some bright object and instructed them to relax and to fall asleep. Later he modified his technique to that of the direct verbal method in which repeated suggestions of fatigue and sleep were given. As a result of the present-day scientific understanding of the phenomenon, the direct verbal suggestion technique has become the more common. Drugs also may be utilized to produce hypnotic states, but the results are unsatisfactory since the narcotic effects frequently interfere with trance manifestations. Drugs which may be used are paraldehyde, barbital compounds, and amytal.

Usually the best method of inducing a trance consists in placing the subjects in a relaxed and comfortable position, giving them at the time a few brief explanations in order to relieve any misapprehensions and at the same time afford them some idea of what is about to happen. Then, suggestions are given in a carefully graduated form to the effect that they are getting tired and more tired, that they are getting sleepy and more sleepy, and that they will gradually go into a light sleep and thence into a deeper and deeper sleep. The period of time required varies with every subject, some taking less than one minute to go into the deep sleep for the first time and others requiring hours of effort. Once the subject is asleep the same manner of technique is utilized to elicit any of the characteristic manifestations of the trance state. Repeated suggestions to the effect desired are given until the subject responds. The trance is usually terminated by the request to awaken, but occasionally it becomes necessary to arouse subjects slowly by suggesting wakefulness in the same manner that sleep was suggested.

EXPLANATORY ASPECTS

There are a number of questions concerning hypnosis that must be mentioned since they arise at every discussion of the topic. In the first place many ask, "Is it harmful?" A study of the scientific literature reveals no good evidence of harm inflicted, or any very logical theoretical possibility of injury other than that which might accrue from ordinary personal contact in the waking state (Erickson, 1932).

Nevertheless, many unscientific writers, some of whom frankly confess their inexperience with hypnosis, are emphatic in their denunciation of it, basing their attacks upon medieval conceptions of the phenomenon. Earnest, thoroughgoing students, however, seriously question the possibility of harm. In the author's experience, in which some of his subjects have been hypnotized from 300 to 500 times each over a period of years, no harmful effects have been noted. Nevertheless, hypnotism is not a matter for superficiality and carelessness, but should be utilized only by capable and trained workers even as are other complex and difficult techniques.

The second question is, "What would happen if you could not awaken the subject?" The experience of capable investigators who have questioned this possibility, as well as the author's, indicates that such a likelihood could not occur. It is possible, and occasionally happens, that subjects are so comfortable in the hypnotic sleep that they are unwilling to awaken, but if the operator allows a subject to sleep despite commands to awaken, it would indicate merely his ignorance of proper hypnotic technique. Subjects can always be awakened by a series of suggestions paralleling those which put them to sleep. Further, even if the subjects did continue to sleep, as soon as they were left alone the hypnotic sleep would spontaneously change into a natural sleep—an important though little appreciated fact. This is also true for sleep states induced by posthypnotic suggestion. As for the question of what would happen if the hypnotist suddenly died or left the subject in a deep trance, there would occur one of two possible things. Either the trance sleep would lapse into a natural sleep or the subject, becoming aware of the absence of the hypnotist and sensing the loss of contact with him, would awaken spontaneously to ascertain the nature of the situation. Essentially, hypnosis is a relationship between two people, and when one of them is removed from the situation, the phenomenon then ceases because there can no longer be the cooperation necessary between the two.

But there is another and indirect implication of these questions which deserves an answer. This is the assumption that the sudden and absolute removal of the hypnotist or his unwillingness to awaken the subject would wreak irreparable harm. This idea is a continuance of the ancient superstitition of "strong mind/weak will" arising from the mistaken idea that hypnotism in some subtle, occult fashion altered the very being of the subject, thereby giving the hypnotist unlimited power and control over the entranced person. This power had then to be relinquished formally and personally or otherwise the subject would be psychically crippled. Fortunately, the light of present-day psychological knowledge as well as experimental findings exposes the absurdity of such ideas.

Another problem which arises is the question of whether or not an unscrupulous hypnotist could make use of the art for malicious and criminal purposes. Briefly, the answer obtained by careful and thorough investigators is negative. Suggestions leading to antisocial acts or even to mere improprieties are rejected, and if pressed upon them, the subjects will invariably awaken with a disturbed and uneasy feeling and usually become uncooperative regarding further hypnosis. In unusually cooperative subjects when this is attempted there will be a seeming compliance with the suggestion but it will be executed in such a fashion as to defeat its purpose. The subject instructed to stab the first comer will pick up a strip of rubber or some such harmless object and simulate the act. If given a real dagger, the stabbing will be done slowly and carefully in empty space or else not at all. Authentic reports to this effect are given in the literature. In the author's experimentation his siblings were used as subjects, since there was a possibility that the realtionship offered greater opportunities for positive findings and at the same time would enhance the value of negative ones. The results of repeated attempts to induce them to commit various improprieties can be summed up best in the uneasy and worried remark of one sister in the trance state, who said in her effort to explain her utter unwillingness to do as asked, "Well, if you want me to do that, you can wake me up and let me do it while I'm awake." The same and additional experiments were repeated on friends and acquaintances, all with negative results. Schilder and Kauders (1927), after extensive experience, have declared that hypnotism is a dubious aid for antisocial purposes.

The author's own experience indicates that the loss of environmental orientation in trance states constitutes an actual obstacle to the misuse of the art.

Also in this regard there should not be an oversight of the significance of the actual social contact of two personalities in the hypnotic situation. With this in mind there is the realization that harmful results may be attributed more properly to such social contact rather than to the hypnosis per se. Further, when it is considered that the hypnotist must implant his suggestions in the vast aggregate of mental reactions and patterns accumulated throughout the subject's lifetime, the great difficulty of causing extensive changes and alteration of behavior and personality reactions is apparent. Indeed, what marvels of mental catharsis and psychotherapy could be achieved were it possible to establish significant and meaningful alterations of personality reactions by a few suggestions given in a time-limited situation.

A fourth question is, "What is hypnotism? Some mystic occult magical thing based upon the overwhelming influence of a strong personality upor a weak will and accompanied by the emanation of a secret power?' Actually, of course, it is not this. On the contrary, it is a psychological phenomenon as little understood as most psychological phenomena. It requires no unusual personality or strong will on the part of the hypnotist or weak will or feeble intellect on the part of the subject. Any person willing to learn the psychological principles involved can perform hypnosis. It is purely a matter of technique, a technique of convincing and persuasive suggestion similar to that utilized every day in ordinary commercial life for quite other purposes. Just as anyone may be a hypnotist, so may anyone be a subject, whether man or woman, old or young, excluding only the extremes of age and those of too pronounced mental abnormality. The best subjects are the highly intelligent, highly sensitive people with good control of their mental faculties, while those of lesser endowments are more difficult and less satisfactory to work with and are limited in their performance.

What hypnosis actually is can be explained as yet only in descriptive terms. Thus it may be defined as an artificially enhanced state of suggestibility resembling sleep wherein there appears to be a normal, time-limited, and stimulus-limited dissociation of the "conscious" from the "subconscious" elements of the psyche. This dissociation is manifested by a quiescence of the "consciousness" simulating normal sleep and a delegation of the subjective control of the individual functions, ordinarily conscious, to the "subconsciousness." But any understanding of hypnosis beyond the descriptive phase is purely speculative.

THE PHENOMENA OF HYPNOTISM

The phenomena of hypnotism vary in degree and variety with every subject, depending, of course, upon the innate endowments of the person. Furthermore, all phenomena do not necessarily occur in every subject, but manifest themselves only as a rule, some subjects failing to show this or that particular characteristic.

First of all, hypnosis is a result of cooperation. Without full cooperation between the subject and hypnotist there can be no hypnotism. Unwillingness to be hypnotized, admitted or concealed, signifies the failure of the essential cooperation, and consequently a trance does not and cannot occur. This necessity for cooperation constitutes a further indication of the improbability of inflicting harm upon the subject and also exposes the fallacy of the belief that one can be hypnotized surreptitiously.

As the subject goes into a hypnotic sleep, the field of consciousness narrows and external stimuli, except those given by the hypnotist, lose their significance. Ultimately the subject loses contact with the external world except for the operator. Essentially, the "consciousness" is in a state of sleep, while the "subconsciousness" is left in control and in rapport with the hypnotist. This rapport, which constitutes a fixed phenomenon of hypnotic trances, may be defined as a state of harmony between the subject and hypnotist, with a dependence of the former upon the latter for motivating and guiding stimuli, and is somewhat similar to the "transference" of the psychoanalytic situation. It enables the hypnotist to remain in full contact with the subject while to the rest of the world the hypnotized person remains an unresponsive object. This rapport may be transferred by the command of the operator to any designated person, and subjects who distrust the hypnotic state but permit hypnosis may spontaneously retain rapport with anybody they wish as they go into the trance.

Another phenomenon is the marked suggestibility occurring in the trance. Any suggestion not objectionable to the subject will be accepted and acted upon. Thus he will become paralyzed, anaesthetic, deaf, blind, hallucinated in all spheres, accept as the truth any variety of suggestions, and act upon them provided they are not objectionable. If they are offensive, there is a failure of cooperation and the suggestions are without effect.

A fourth phenomenon which characteristically appears without direct suggestion is catalepsy, which resembles cerea flexibilitas. In this state the subject's arm may be lifted and it will remain fixed in any position. The subject appears to be unable to move the arm, nor does he seem to experience any sense of fatigue. Some experimental work done in this regard suggests that there is a definite lessening of the sense of fatigue, permitting the performance of work actually past the point of normal capacity (Williams, 1929; Nicholson, 1920).

A fifth feature of the trance is that of posthypnotic suggestion. While in the trance state subjects may be given a suggestion to be performed or acted upon at a designated time after awakening, and they spontaneously—as they think—respond in the designated fashion with no realization of why they do so. In this phenomenon lies the greatest therapeutic advantage of hypnosis, since thereby the subjects can be given suggestions to guide their later conduct.

A sixth characteristic of hypnosis is amnesia. The subject's recollection of events occurring during the trance is approximately inversely proportional to its depth. One who has been in a profound trance has a complete amnesia for all events, suggestions, and experiences occurring therein, even though he has walked down the street, talked to friends, and eaten a meal. However, this amnesia may not remain total, since the subject may at a later date recall everything spontaneously as if in a dream. But for practical purposes there is essentially an actual amnesia.

Still other manifestations, similar in nature, are automatic writing and crystal-gazing. The activity involved in these is perhaps one of the best "proofs" of the existence of a "subconscious mind." They afford a wide avenue of approach to experimental studies and to therapeutic and exploratory measures.

Finally, there can be induced in trances by means of posthypnotic suggestions a state of somnambulism wherein the subjects appear to be normally awake. They may perform all the routine duties of daily life or successfully cope with any chosen situation, but they do so in a trance state and upon awakening have no recollection of any events which occurred. In appearance and nature this somnambulistic state is an experimental equivalent to the states of dissociation in dual personalities met in psychiatric practice. It differs only in being benign, time-limited, and wholly dependent upon definite suggestions from the hypnotist.

APPLICATION OF HYPNOTISM

Hypnosis has a definite value in the practice of medicine, which was shown very early in its history, and as medical men acquire a better understanding of psychology, its value will probably increase. In general practice the technique can be utilized to quiet and reassure the patient and to establish that desirable state of rapport between physician and patient connoted by "the bedside manner." In Europe, particularly in Germany and France, it has been used to some extent as a direct surgical aid in both major and minor procedures. In certain patients it can be used as a substitute for drugs in producing anaesthesia, and since the time of Esdaille it has been used repeatedly for this purpose. It has the advantage over anaesthetics of affording the patient peace of mind, a sense of security and confidence, and it has no afteraffects. However, even at the present day its application in the field of surgery should be limited properly to the minor field until the general medical practitioner as well as the laity have a better understanding of psychological manifestations. It has also been used successfully in obstetrics and undoubtedly would be used much more if there were not such a misapprehensive, fearful attitude toward it. A primary objection to its use by the medical man, remediable by proper study of the practice, is the difficulty experienced in inducing and maintaining trances. No hypnotists know for a certainty whether or not they are going to succeed with a particular subject at a given time or whether their technique for the occasion will be sufficient for the maintenance of the trance. But this is more fortunate than otherwise, since the therapeutic and medical application of hypnosis should not be taken lightly or left in the hands of the dilettante.

In the field of psychological medicine, however, hypnosis offers a unique approach to many mental problems and difficulties. Its value lies in the fact that it allows the physician to approach directly the subconsciousness of the person with its disturbing conflicts. It often serves as a gateway through his resistances and allows indirect approaches to many difficulties which otherwise could not be attacked. Further, induced states of dissociation can be established, exploratory measures developed, and vital information obtained which otherwise would be inaccessible both to the patient and to the therapist. Also of paramount importance is the fact that the hypnotized patient is in a receptive state for psychotherapy. The difficulty involved in getting patients to accept therapeutic suggestions directly constitutes the greatest obstacle in psychotherapy. Hypnosis renders the person receptive. Indeed, as has been mentioned before, it is a state of enhanced suggestibility. Consequently, by means of hypnotism it is possible to implant therapeutic ideas upon the "subconsciousness" and to have them take effect when endless numbers of suggestions given in the waking state would be given no heed or even actively resisted. Thus the patient accepts hypnotic suggestions and acts upon them without conscious awareness and without building defense reactions. In so doing he allows them to become a valid part of his mental patterns, all the more so since fundamentally, if not immediately, he does desire aid against his conflicts. By this means patients can be given new mental equipment wherewith to deal with their difficulties, a new equipment which does not have to pass the protective scrutiny of their "consciousness." At the same time dissociated experiences and amnesic material are rendered available for reassociation and reorganization. Nevertheless, hypnosis is not to be looked upon as panacea nor is it to be discarded because it has definite limitations. On the contrary, it is a valuable addition to the medical armamentarium, most particularly to that of the psychiatrist.

Perhaps the most fertile and productive application of hypnotism is in the sphere of experimental psychology. More and more laboratories are becoming interested in the peculiar and significant problems which hypnosis renders available for study. This rapidly increasing interest in experimental hypnotism both in this country and abroad may be taken as an indication of a growing realization of the fruitfulness of hypnosis as a field of scientific research. It constitutes almost a virginal territory for psychological investigations, and it appears to offer a good approach to an understanding of many mental mechanisms which have hitherto defied comprehension.

2. Hypnosis: A General Review

Milton H. Erickson

The history of hypnosis is as old as that of the human race. The most primitive of savages, both ancient and modern, were aware of this striking psychological manifestation, and it was utilized in the mystic rites of their medicine men to produce fear and to intensify belief in the supernatural and the occult. With this long historical past of supernaturalism and mysticism, coupled with its own startling, inexplicable, and bewildering phenomenology, it is not astonishing that the general public's attitude toward hypnosis has been and still is one of misunderstanding, antagonism, and actual fear, and that the first development of any scientific interest did not occur until the last half of the 18th century.

These first scientific beginnings in the study of hypnosis began with Anton Mesmer about 1775, from whose name has derived the term *mesmerism* still in current usage. Mesmer's use of hypnosis began with his discovery that selected types of medical patients responded satisfactorily to a stroking of their arms and ailing parts and suggestions of sleep. Mesmer attributed these therapeutic results to the transferring to the patients of a "quality" of "animal magnetism," and he developed the theory that animal magnetism was some peculiar cosmic fluid with healing properties. Despite Mesmer's excellent intuitive knowledge of clinical psychology, as evidenced by his elaborate clinic in which he employed colored lights, incense, music, and rich draperies to impress his patients and establish in them a receptive state of mind, he had no realization of the psychological nature of his therapy. Nevertheless, he treated successfully large numbers of patients on whom orthodox medical procedures had failed, but unfortunately his personality and the mystical character of his therapy served finally to bring him unjustly into disrepute. However, many physicians had visited his clinic during the height of its success and had learned unwittingly one of the first lessons in the then unknown art of psychotherapy—specifically, the importance of clinical psychology.

Since Mesmer there has been a succession of outstanding men who became interested in hypnosis and utilized it successfully in medical practice, giving it an increasingly more scientific foundation and validity. Elliotson, the first man in England to use the stethoscope, became interested in hypnosis about 1817, employed it extensively, and left

---

Reprinted with permission from *Diseases of the Nervous System*, Jauary, 1941, Vol. II, No. 1.

excellent records of its therapeutic efficacy in selected cases. Esdaille, stimulated by Elliotson's case reports, became an ardent advocate of mesmerism, as it was then called, and actually succeeded in interesting the British government in building a hospital in India, where he used it extensively on all types of medical patients, leaving many excellent records of major and minor surgery performed under hypnotic anesthesia.

The initiation of a psychological understanding of the phenomenon began in 1841 with James Braid, at first an opponent and then later a most ardent investigator and supporter. It was he who invented the term *hypnosis,* recognized the psychological nature of hypnotic sleep, and described many of its manifestations, devising methods whereby to test their validity.

Since Braid there has been a constantly increasing number of clinicians first and psychologists later, among them many outstanding scientists, who have contributed greatly to an establishment of its scientific validity and opened it as a field of scientific investigation and therapeutic endeavor. The result now is that during the past 20 years there has been a progressively rapid increase in the amount of attention given to hypnosis as a problem of significant scientific interest by the medical profession, particularly psychiatrists, and by psychologists in university laboratories.

Unfortunately, particularly among the psychologists, there is still a tendency to develop research along the outmoded concepts and techniques of the 19th century. Thus, in a recent paper by a psychologist, the statement was made that the experimental technique was based entirely on Braid's original methods, and in another paper thc declaration was that Forel's technique and criteria of fifty years ago had been used implicitly. Thus, while interest in hypnosis as a scientific problem has advanced, it is still in its infancy and needs development in terms of present-day understandings and concepts of personality and interpersonal relationships.

General questions always arising when hypnosis is mentioned concern its possible detrimental effects upon the hypnotic subject, the possible antisocial use of hypnosis, the character of the relationship between the hypnotist and the subject, the controllability of the hypnotic state, and the relationship of hypnotic sleep to physiological sleep.

To all of these questions one may make a comprehensive reply by stating simply that the hypnotic state is essentially a psychological phenomenon, unrelated to physiological sleep, and dependent entirely upon full cooperation between hypnotist and subject; neither is it injurious or detrimental to the subject in any way, nor can it be used for antisocial or criminal purposes. Each of these statements is based upon extensive, carefully controlled experimental investigations too numerous to cite, and conducted by many investigators. References, however, will be listed at the conclusion of this paper.

The general mistaken belief is that hypnotists exercise some remarkable power over their subjects, that hypnosis is a matter of dominance and subservience, of strong mind over weak will, and that hence all manner of undesirable results may obtain. Actually, of course, hypnosis depends upon full cooperation between hypnotist and subject, and without willing cooperation there can be no hypnosis. Furthermore, the hypnotic subject can be both hypnotist and subject, and more than one hypnotist has been hypnotized in turn by his own subjects to further the development of experimental work. Because of the absolute need for cooperation, subjects cannot be hypnotized against their will or without their knowledge, nor can subjects be kept in a trance without their cooperation. Nor can cooperative subjects be left in a trance an unreasonable length of time without their full understanding and cooperation. In brief, hypnosis and every use made of the trance state necessarily depends upon full and ready cooperation with adequate and direct understanding on the part of the subject of what is desired.

Another fact of importance is that there can occur no detrimental effects from repeated trances, even over a period of years. This fact has been confirmed by the experience of hypnotists who have been interested in this possibility and by the experience of subjects who have been hypnotized hundreds and even thousands of times. In addition, when one considers the difficulty in producing wanted therapeutic changes in the personality by hypnosis, the possibility of effecting unwanted changes becomes remote and most unlikely.

The best hypnotic subjects are normal people of superior intelligence, and any really cooperative person can be hypnotized. Maladjusted, hysterical, feebleminded, or psychotic persons are usually difficult to hypnotize, although there are many exceptions. For this reason hypnosis as a therapeutic measure is often difficult to apply despite full cooperation.

Concerning the technique of the induction of hypnotic trances, this is a relatively simple matter requiring primarily time, patience, and careful attention to and consideration for the subjects, their personalities, and their emotional attitudes and reactions. Properly, there is no set form or pattern to follow, just as there is no set form for a good bedside manner. One needs the respect, confidence, and trust of a subject, and then one suggests fatigue, a desire for sleep and rest, an increasing feeling of sleep, and finally a deep sound restful sleep. These suggestions are given repetitiously, with gradual progression from one to the next, always with careful reassurance of the subjects as they make response to them. The making of passes, the use of crystal balls, the staring into the subject's eyes, and various other mystical procedures belong to vaudeville or ancient history. One simply, persuasively, and patiently suggests sleep of a restful character until the subject does sleep, and then the subject is instructed to remain asleep until all reasonable purposes are accomplished. There should be no forcing or rushing of subjects, and every effort should be made to enable the subjects to appreciate any physical feeling they have suggestive of sleep. This simple technique can be learned by anyone, and anybody who has been hypnotized can employ it to hypnotize others, given cooperation and the patience to make use of it. As for awakening the subject, one can suggest an arousal directly, or give the subject suggestions to the effect that he is slowly and progressively awakening, repeating these suggestions until the subject is fully awake.

Once the trance state has been induced, there will become manifest various general phenomena characteristic of hypnosis, though not all are necessarily manifested by each individual subject. Foremost is the condition termed *rapport,* in which the hypnotic subjects respond only to the hypnotist. In the deep trance they are seemingly incapable of hearing or seeing anything unless so instructed by the hypnotist. However, this rapport may be transferred to others by appropriate suggestions by the hypnotist.

A second phenomenon is *catalepsy.* As a result of the hypnosis, there develops in the subjects an increase in muscular tonus so that there seems to be the same condition as exists in the stuporous catatonic patient manifesting flexibilitas cerea. Thus, the subject's hand, raised up in the air by the hypnotist, is held in that position apparently without fatigue until the hypnotist either puts it down or instructs the subject to lower it.

Amnesia constitutes another phenomenon of interest. Particularly after a deep trance the subject tends to have a profound amnesia for everything that occurred in the trance situation. This amnesia is subject to control, since the hypnotist can suggest the recovery of the memory of some or all items of the trance experience, or the subject may deliberately set himself the task of remembering everything. This phenomenon is most inconstant and uncertain, depends upon many individualistic and situational factors. In an experimental procedure the amnesia can be demonstrated to be as resistant to all nonhypnotic forces and as profound as amnesias developing pathologically.

Suggestibility is, of course, a primary feature of hypnosis, and is necessarily present. However, there is always a need, if serious and satisfactory purposes are to be achieved, to give suggestions in accord with the subject's understandings and desires, although in the type of hypnosis practiced on the vaudeville stage, ridiculous and undignified suggestions can be given. In the experimental psychological laboratory any number of behavioral responses can be suggested and subjected to study, such as suggestions of amnesia, recovery of memories, hallucinations, delusions, anesthesias, deafness, blindness, identifications, disorientation, etc. In the medical situation suggestions relating to the problem in hand can be given, such as the suggestion to recall a forgotten troublesome traumatic life experience, or the suggestion to avoid or to meet adequately some difficult problem.

However, regardless of the suggestibility of the subject, there is frequently a primary need to give suggestions indirectly rather than directly and dogmatically as if hypnotic suggestions were miraculous in effect.

Another common phenomenon is the capacity for visual hallucinations often described as "crystal-gazing." Essentially, this is the result of suggestions to the effect that the subject visualize various scenes and memories. This phenomenon is of great significance in investigative and experimental work upon legitimate psychological and medical problems. The ability, called forth by hypnotic suggestion, to reconstruct a visual image of a past and even forgotten experience is often of great service in psychological research and in psychotherapeutic procedures.

Automatic writing, long known but mystically regarded, is often easily elicited in the hypnotic state. It is essentially the act of writing without any awareness of the fact. Such writing is comparable in its processes to the unwitting mouthing and chewing the absorbed mother does when she spoon-feeds her baby. This automatic writing can be elicited without hypnosis, during hypnosis, and after hypnosis, and the context of the writing represents usually material of which the subjects are not consciously aware and which they often reject as not theirs, or as meaningless to them. In the psychological laboratory or in the psychotherapeutic situation such automatic writing is of great value in the study or analysis of behavior and in the eliciting of important but otherwise unavailable information.

Posthypnotic suggestion, or the giving of suggestions to the hypnotized subjects to be acted upon at some later time when they are awake, constitutes another most interesting phenomenon. By this measure the hypnotic subject's behavior can be directed and controlled subsequent to the trance state, but only to a reasonable and acceptable degree. Thus the subjects may be told to perform a certain act at a given time in the future, and at that time they do as instructed, usually without awareness that they are doing so, or, if they are aware of their conduct, without any understanding of why they are so doing. Rather they think they are acting spontaneously since there is an amnesia for the posthypnotic instructions. In this way effective therapeutic suggestions can often be given.

The scientific applications of hypnosis are as yet only in the developmental stage. The persistence of unsound mystical beliefs and mistaken fears about hypnosis, now fortunately being discarded rapidly, have hampered and delayed its scientific growth. Also, much of the serious study made of hypnotic phenomena has been based upon concepts of hypnosis developed long before present-day understandings of dynamic psychology and psychiatry. Furthermore, many of the efforts made to study hypnosis scientifically in psychological laboratories have omitted all clinical personality considerations relating to the hypnotic subject as a person and have attempted unfortunately to deal with hypnotic manifestations as didactic academic items unconnected with a human personality. With the present rapid increase of recognition by psychologists of dynamic and personality factors and forces, there is developing a new and more fruitful trend in the study of hypnotic behavior, and the psychologists are now beginning to discard the old belief that hypnosis transforms a person into some strange, passive, dominated new creature. Instead they are beginning to realize that hypnosis can be used and should be used to elicit the natural and innate behavior and reactions of the subject, and that through such a measure human behavior can be studied in a controlled scientific manner.

Primarily, the greatest field of application for hypnosis is in the study and analysis of human behavior and disturbances in behavior. By means of the hypnotic trance it becomes possible to suggest to the subject any chosen form of behavior and response and thereby have literally a laboratory in which to synthesize and analyze any desired pattern of behavior. For example, the problem of amnesia can be treated as a laboratory investigation by creating, removing, and reestablishing an amnesia and slowly and systematically studying the psychological processes and mechanisms involved in such mental processes. Similarly, one can through hypnosis duplicate in a subject the symptomatic manifestations of personality disturbances and emotional stresses and have an opportunity to study such problems in laboratory form in a manner similar to the laboratory study of medical problems and procedures before application is made to an actual patient. Instead of speculating vaguely and attempting to deduce uncertainly the consequences of a patient's complexes and conflicts, necessarily of unknown character, one can build up in a hypnotic subject a complex or conflict of known character and then have the direct opportunity of studying its results and consequences upon the subject with a view to determining the psychological sequences and interrelationships of the various manifestations and their significances to the personality.

The usefulness of hypnosis to medicine lies in two fields of application, that of research and that of psychotherapy. In relation to both fields its usefulness relates primarily to behavior problems, emotional disturbances, minor forms of psychopathology, and the neurotic or psychoneurotic illnesses which confront the general practitioner on every hand. However, its applications are greatly restricted, aside from the need for special laboratory situations for research and selected types of patients for psychotherapy, by the general public's misapprehensions concerning hypnosis, the irrational fears entertained about it, and the primary need for unlimited time and effort if effective results are to be obtained. Too often, in both fields of application, unsatisfactory results are obtained because of the tendency to regard hypnosis as a miracle producer and to substitute dogmatic emphatic hypnotic suggestion for a laborious, time-taking, systematic procedure of experimental investigation or of psychotherapeutic reeducation. It is not a miracle worker, even though its results sometimes seem to be miraculous. Rather, it is an effective measure by which one can slowly, carefully, and thoroughly elicit, as a result of careful suggestions, forms of behavior, emotional reactions, insights, and understandings which would be impossible or nearly so in the ordinary waking state in which the subject's attention to a chosen field cannot be so completely secured and rigidly fixed as it can be in hypnosis.

Unfortunately for the development of adequate research in medical applications of hypnosis, most of such investigators are psychologists untrained in clinical medical and psychiatric aspects of personality disorders. However, as psychologists become increasingly aware of the personality implications of hypnotic research, such problems as amnesia will cease to be studied entirely in terms of statistical evaluations of nonsense syllables learned and forgotten and approached more frequently in terms dynamic behavior reactions peculiar to the personality of the hypnotic subject, who in turn will be recognized as a human being and not treated, as is the tendency of psychologists today, as a passively responsive laboratory instrument.

As for direct psychotherapeutic use of hypnosis, aside from the problems imposed by public mistrust and the need to select suitable patients, there is also the problem of avoiding the too common errors in psychotherapy of forcing the suggestions upon the subject. Rather than hypnotically treating patients suffering from a phobia for doorknobs by telling them in the trance to forget their phobia, to overcome it, to realize its foolishness, one tries instead by hypnosis to elicit indirectly and adequately the story of the genesis of that phobia and to build up in these patients anew their own forgotten and repressed pattern of normal behavior toward doorknobs. One does not try to force upon the patient a new pattern of normal doorknob behavior, but rather to reestablish the old, unused, and forgotten pattern of behavior the patient had previous to the development of his phobia. One may temporarily relieve symptoms, but medicine is interested in a cure by complete removal and not in symptomatic relief. But such methods are slow and laborious, hence only those wishing to spend adequate time and effort should try them.

Recent clinical work (Bass, 1931; Beck, 1936; Bramwell, 1921; Brickner & Kubie, 1936; Erickson, 1932, 1933, 1934, 1935, 1937a, 1937b, 1938a, 1938b, 1939a, 1939c, 1939d; Erickson & Erickson, 1938; Erickson & Kubie, 1930, 1939; Huston et al, 1934; Luria, 1932; Platonov, 1933;

Schilder & Kauders, 1927) has shown the possibilities and fruitfulness of hypnosis in approaching the problems of personality disturbances and psychoneurotic illnesses, and it is this field of medicine in which hypnosis can contribute greatly—and unquestionably will—as increasingly adequate recognition is given to the value of hypnosis.

3. Hypnotism

Milton H. Erickson

"Hypnotism" and "hypnosis" are the terms applied to a unique, complex form of unusual but normal behavior which can probably be induced in every normal person under suitable conditions and also in persons suffering from many types of abnormality. It is primarily a special psychological state with certain physiological attributes, resembling sleep only superficially, and characterized by a functioning of the individual at a level of awareness other than the ordinary state, a level of awareness termed, for convenience in conceptualization, unconscious or subconscious awareness.

When hypnotized, or in the hypnotic trance, the subject can think, act, and behave as adequately as, and often better than, he can in the ordinary state of psychological awareness, quite possibly because of the intensity of his attention to his task and his freedom from distraction.

He is not, as is commonly believed, without willpower or under the will of the hypnotist. Instead, the relationship between the hypnotist and subject is one of interpersonal cooperation, based upon mutually acceptable and reasonable considerations. Hence, the subject cannot be forced to do things against his will, but rather he can be aided in achieving desired goals. However, frequent failures in hypnotic therapy of patients disclose limitations of hypnosis in accomplishing even desired goals, and the more extensive and reliably controlled experimental studies discredit the possibility of utilizing hypnosis for antisocial purposes.

The history of hypnosis is as ancient as that of sorcery, magic and medicine, of the armamentarium of which practices it formed a part. Its scientific history began in the latter part of the 18th century with Franz A. Mesmer, a Viennese physician who used it in the treatment of psychiatric patients. However, because of his mistaken belief that it was an occult force, which he termed "animal magnetism," that flowed through the hypnotist to the subject, he was soon discredited; but mesmerism, as it was named after him, continued to interest medical men. Extensive use was made of it by outstanding clinicians without any real recognition of its nature until the middle of the 19th century, when James Braid, an English physician, became interested, recognized its psychological nature, studied

---

Reprinted with permission from *Encyclopaedia Britannica,* 14th edition, © 1954 by Encyclopaedia Britannica, Inc.

its phenomena, and coined the terms *hypnotism* and *hypnosis* to name it. Thereafter many scientifically trained men worked on the problem, but only after World War I was much significant progress made. World War II gave added impetus to the study of hypnosis, greatly extended its recognition and use, and freed it from many of the superstitions, fears, and taboos that had hampered its scientific acceptance and investigation. However, because of its inexplicable character and the fascinating, startling nature of its phenomena, it remained subject to exploitation by charlatans and misconceptions by well-intentioned but insufficiently trained and experienced experimenters.

HYPNOTIC TECHNIQUE

Popular beliefs still ascribe much superstitious significance to ritualistic magical devices such as stroking of the body, the use of "hypnotic crystals," the "eagle eye," and "willpower." Actually the important consideration in inducing hypnosis is a willing, cooperative, relaxed subject to whom a trusted hypnotist can persuasively and repetitiously suggest that he will become tired and sleepy, that his eyes will close, that he will lose progressively his interest in external events and become more and more completely absorbed in a feeling of being in a state of sleep in which he can function at a level of unconscious awareness. The length of time required to induce a trance differs greatly with subjects, and the time spent should be in reasonable accord with the importance of the hypnotic work. Thus, for an exhibitionistically inclined subject on the vaudeville stage, a few minutes may suffice, while hours might be required for a scientifically oriented study or for hypnotic therapy.

Another essential consideration in the technique of investigative or therapeutic work is the utilization of the subject's own patterns of response and capacities rather than an attempt to force upon the subject by suggestion the hypnotist's limited understanding of how and what the subject should do. The failures in hypnotic therapy and experimental work often derive from dealing with the subject as an automaton expected to execute commands in accord with the hypnotist's understanding, to the exclusion of a recognition of the subject as a personality with individual patterns of response and behavior.

HYPNOTIC PHENOMENA

Hypnotic phenomena will differ from one subject to another and from one trance to the next, depending upon the depth of the trance, since hypnosis is a phenomenon of degrees ranging from light to profound trance states. There are, however, certain basic manifestations, the extent and clarity of which may vary in accord with circumstances. Foremost among these is rapport, which signifies the limitation of the subject's awareness to what is included in the hypnotic situation. Usually the subject responds spontaneously only to stimuli from the hypnotist who may limit or direct the subject's state of awareness as he wishes. However, in response to personality needs or the demands of the situation, the subject may remain in contact with part of or even all the circumstances surrounding the trance. Rapport can then be discovered experimentally by investigating the rigidity of the subject's responsive patterns to the entire situation.

Catalepsy is another manifestation, properly tested only indirectly since direct tests often serve to effect a suggesting of it. This is a peculiar state of muscle tonus and balance which permits the subject to maintain postures and positions for unusually long periods of time without appreciable fatigue responses.

Suggestibility, or a state of remarkable receptiveness to suggestions, is a striking characteristic. However, the suggestions must be acceptable to the subject, and rejection of them can be based upon whims as easily as upon sound reasons. By the acceptance of suggestions, and acting upon them, subjects can become deaf, dumb, blind, hallucinated, disoriented, or anaesthetized, or they can manifest any type of behavior regarded by them as reasonable and desirable in the given situation. The process is esentially the vivification of memories, ideas, and understandings so effectively that they are subjectively experienced as external events rather than as internal processes, with a consequent endowment of them as reality experiences. This is the feature of hypnosis most often abused, since most persons will allow themselves to be imposed upon to provide entertainment even when not hypnotized and the same general tendency exists in the hypnotic subject.

A most fascinating manifestation is that of posthypnotic behavior. By this is meant the execution, at some later time, of instructions and suggestions given during a trance and intended to become a part of the pattern of some later activity. Thus, for example, subjects may be instructed to read a certain chapter in a chosen book at a specified later time—hours, days, months, and even years later—and at that time they perform the act without really understanding consciously why they do so. In this type of phenomenon lies probably the greatest medical and experimental value of hypnosis, since it permits a direction and a guidance of behavior, but only in terms of the patterns of response belonging to the individual.

The forgetting of things or the development of amnesias for minor memories is an everyday occurrence. In hypnosis, however, there occurs an amnesia of an extensive character which can be induced at will or become manifest spontaneously. The amnesia usually includes all the events of the trance state, but it can be altered by instruction to include any desired experience. It is a reversible phenomenon, may be induced or abolished as desired by the hypnotist and also by the subject should there arise adequate personal motivation to alter a state of hypnotic amnesia. It is a useful tool both in therapy and in experimental work.

Conversely, hyperamnesia, an ability to remember transcending the everyday ability to remember the past, is found. Thus, in the trance state, the subject can remember vividly long-forgotten, even deeply repressed experiences, recount them fully and still have a complete amnesia for them when aroused from the trance state. This ability is remarkably useful in both therapeutic and experimental work, since it permits the recovery of memories otherwise unavailable, and hence the exploration of the experiential past of the subject.

A phenomenon of the profound trance of extreme interest is somnambulism. The subjects, seemingly awake in a state of ordinary awareness, behave, within reasonable limitations, as if they were not hypnotized, but actually they are in deep trance and capable of manifesting any desired hypnotic behavior within their personal capabilities. Experience and training are often required even to recognize the somnambulistic state, and even more experience is required to induce it and to utilize it scientifically, particularly in therapy as well as in experimental work.

Regression, or a return to earlier and simpler patterns of behavior, characterizes all trances and can be utilized and enhanced to a remarkable degree. In the ordinary trance there tends to occur a significant literalness of a childlike character in the subject's understandings, the handwriting and other motor activities are childlike, and emotional attitudes reflect those of an earlier age level.

Experienced utilization of this phenomenon can result in the development of an effective amnesia for all experiences and learning subsequent to a chosen age level and the revivification of the actual patterns of behavior, responses, and understandings of the selected age level. Highly significant therapeutic and experimental work has been done in this regard, especially when regression characterized by revivification of past patterns of behavior has been employed rather than a less satisfactory procedure wherein the subject is permitted to limit his regression to his current understandings of what probably constituted his past.

There are two other phenomena which are of particular interest but which are essentially modifications and elaborations of those manifestations already described. One is crystal-gazing, which does not necessarily require an actual crystal and which consists of a clear vivid visualization of memories and ideas as if they were current reality experiences. The other is automatic writing, in which the subjects write without conscious volition and often without conscious knowledge of the fact that they are writing.

Both these phenomena are of great value in experimental and therapeutic work, since they provide unusually effective methods for the recovery of the experiential past and for an integrative understanding of the self.

Autohypnosis is entirely possible, but it is a sterile procedure, despite various overenthusiastic claims. Even among the Balinese, who practice autohypnosis extensively, it is a social manifestation limited to established traditional and ritualistic activities. It can, however, be of value when practiced under the supervision of an experienced hypnotist who can guide the activities of the autohypnotic subject.

RELATED QUESTIONS

Certain questions are always asked by the general public about hypnosis. Among these is the possibility of employing hypnosis to commit crimes. The best scientific studies deny this possibility, therapeutic experience discredits it, and the only positive evidence is that investigators have induced subjects to pretend to commit crimes, but a pretense is not a reality. Experimenters have also been able to induce subjects to perform minor antisocial acts in a limited experimental situation, but waking subjects will do the same; hence, the findings cannot be regarded as of hypnotic origin only.

Concerning harmful effects, no well-experienced hypnotist has ever reported any. Occasionally, an amateur may hypnotize a subject suffering from a personality disorder and elicit hysterical behavior, but this derives from the personality problem and not from hypnosis.

Can people be hypnotized against their will or without their knowledge? As previously stated, hypnosis always requires cooperation on the part of the subject, but sometimes this cooperativeness is well concealed behind a superficial attitude of unwillingness, with a consequent distortion of the true situation. Additionally, a trance state cannot be maintained without the subject's awareness of the fact, or full cooperation and genuine acceptance of the situation. Then, too, there is the age-old question about the possibility of not being able to arouse the hypnotic subject from the trance state. This actually cannot occur. Occasionally, the amateur may have difficulty in arousing the subject who insists upon remaining in a trance, but this is easily corrected with a little experience in handling subjects.

In any scientific field as undeveloped as hypnosis, no definitive statement can be made of its values. However, the history of its development warrants the definite assertion that it is a significant and valuable instrument in the study of human behavior and in the therapy of selected types of personality disorders.

4. The Basis of Hypnosis: Panel Discussion on Hypnosis

Milton H. Erickson

In opening the discussion on hypnosis I would like to give you some background for understanding its usefulness in the general practice of medicine. Perhaps the best way to approach the subject would be through that phase of medicine which constitutes a good share of your practice—the role of psychological forces in human behavior. An illuminating specific example is that of the combat veteran who jumped down the stairway in his hurry to get home from the college he was attending and fractured his ankle badly. He walked home but came back three weeks later for physical examination because his foot was so swollen and because it made funny grating noises when he walked. Examination showed a stocking anesthesia, not only superficially but deep. The X-ray films showed a comminuted fracture of every bone in his ankle.

INFLUENCE OF PSYCHOLOGICAL FORCES

How did this man manage to do a thing like that, without any help or any instruction whatever? It seems incredible, but all of you in the practice of medicine discover that patients can make use of their psychological forces to rule out, govern, or control physiological phenomena.

Another instance of psychological force influencing physiological behavior concerns the businessman whose firm is operating well. He is making a profit; he is successful, but he worries. He has imaginary worries. He can think of dozens of things which can happen to him or his firm. What does he do with these worries? He punctures holes in his duodenal or gastric mucosa.

There is the housewife who worries about various things and develops severe headache. There is no question about the severity of her headache; it is very real, although its cause may be quite imaginary. One of the most striking examples of this sort of thing is a 15-year-old boy I once saw who was put in a boarding school. He resented it terrifically, and he had a very

---

Transcribed from a presentation before the Annual Meeting of the Washington Academy of General Practice, Longview, Washington, May 13, 1959. Reprinted with permission from *Northwest Medicine,* October, 1959.

strong feeling of rejection. What did he do about it? He developed ulcerative colitis, an expression of his resentment. These psychological forces are tremendously important.

EXPERIENTIAL LEARNING

The next thing I wish to call to your attention is the matter of the experiential learning that we all absorb during a lifetime of experiences. Little children practice walking and getting up and sitting down, lying down, rolling over, using every muscle and action of their extremities and torso. They get acquainted with the various parts of their bodies and learn the full extent of their capabilities. They learn these things so thoroughly that years later, when they are full-grown adults and have forgotten the process through which they learned their actions they will respond promptly when a mosquito lands on any part of their body. Say that the mosquito lands on a shoulder. Without any thought, without any analysis, without recognition that it is on the right shoulder, and even if the left hand happens to be in the pocket, a person can, with great speed and accuracy, withdraw the left hand from the pocket and swat the mosquito at the instant of its biting. How did the body learn this accuracy of movement?

Little children learn first to eat with their fingers. Later they take a spoon. At first they bite the spoon and probably scatter food over themselves and everything around them. Eventually they learn to measure all movements so that they can put the spoon in the mouth.

Children learn to twist their faces, to twist their shoulders, to wriggle their feet. When they first try to write script, they are apt to twist their bodies and wriggle their feet. Gradually they learn to do it with their right hand. You all once went through this phase, and if at that time someone had been curious, they could have discovered that, without one bit of practice, you could have written with your left hand, without going through all of the original learning practice. In fact, one who never has had any such training can with a pencil held in the toes, write just as legibly as any doctor can. This is true because of the transference of learning. Human beings, once they have learned anything, transfer this learning to the forces that govern their bodies.

UTILIZING THE UNCONSCIOUS MIND

In hypnosis we utilize the unconscious mind. What do I mean by the unconscious mind? I mean the back of the mind, the reservoir of learning. The unconscious mind constitutes a storehouse.

You can be in physiological sleep, lying on your back, and you can dream that, instead of lying on your back, you are walking through the house or that you are talking to a friend working in the yard. You can smell the flowers, listen to the birds, feel the breeze, and enjoy the conversation with your friend. Everything is utterly perfect and real because your unconscious mind allows this elaboration in a dream. The real truth is that you are in bed between the sheets. During the dream you may sit down in the garden chair. At that particular moment you probably turned over and rested your back against the mattress. That was the time when in your dream you leaned against the back of the garden chair. The great secret here is that the unconscious mind can deal with the reality of the bed mattress and blend with it the reality of eye memories or mental images of any kind.

What one does is primarily to get the patient interested in ideas, memories, understanding, or a concept of any kind. As the patients deal with these they can develop understanding. I will give a demonstration. I will hold up this notepad and tell you to keep looking at it. Actually, all you receive from this particular object is a visual image. You keep looking at it, but you will notice that I put it on the table and you can conceive seeing it right there. However, you still have the visual image and visual memory in your mind. You could project the visual image in the air exactly where it was—where the actual object was before. This is exactly what you do in your dream. You project memories of objects and ideas so that you can talk to a friend in the garden.

Understanding of this projection of memories is important to the understanding of hypnosis. This particular phenomenon can be defined as a state of ordinary awareness, but it is devoted primarily to the consideration of ideas in themselves, with full attentiveness to the idea. This differs from our conscious attention, which is directed only to reality. As I speak to you, you are aware that you are sitting in this room and listening to me, that I am holding a microphone, that there are lights above you, that there is someone to the left and someone to the right of you, someone in front of you, and someone behind you. All these observations are relevant to listening to me in the ordinary state of conscious awareness. You tend to orient to reality and to give your attention in a diffuse way.

In the state of hypnosis, as in the state of conscious awareness, you give your attention but you give your attention to selected ideas. Your mind is open to these ideas. For example, if I were to ask anyone of you what you wore on your third birthday, you would look at me and say: "That was a long time ago. How could I possibly remember it? It really is not important, and why should I remember it?" You would reject the task of recalling because of attendant circumstances and your appraisal of the difficulty. In the hypnotic state the subject is susceptible to ideas and accepts them. Under hypnosis you would accept the idea that what you wore on your third birthday is simply part of the birthday. You did have a third birthday, which is an historic fact. Furthermore, you did wear clothes, and furthermore, on that third birthday there was a momentous combination of one-time experiences. In the trance state you could start thinking in terms of those realities. Hypnosis, therefore, is essentially a state of receptiveness to ideas and the appraisal of their inherent values and significance. The subject may either accept or reject the idea but can respond to the idea in terms of experiential learning.

TRANCE INDUCTION

Concerning the phenomenon of hypnosis I should mention the matter of trance induction. There are many ways of inducing a trance. What you do is to ask patients primarily to give their attention to one particular idea. You get them to center their attention on their own experiential learning. You could suggest levitation to them and could have them lift a hand higher and higher. You could have them close their eyes bit by bit. Either of these things tends to direct their attention to processes which are taking place within them. Thus you can induce a trance by directing patients' attention to processes, to memories, to ideas, to concepts that belong to them. All you do is direct the patients' attention to those processes within themselves.

There are different levels of trance behavior. These vary with the individual patient and vary with the need of the situation. A light trance, a medium trance, or a deep trance may be induced. You must vary the trance according to the patient's needs.

Another thing I should mention is the matter of hypnotizability. Who is hypnotizable? Any normal person is hypnotizable but not necessarily by you or by me or by Dr. Bryant or by Dr. Hershman. Every patient has the right to go into a trance in accord with his or her own choice of the operator. One hundred percent of normal people are hypnotizable. It does not necessarily follow that 100 percent are hypnotizable by any one individual. A mentally ill patient can be hypnotized, but it is difficult. The feebleminded person can be hypnotized, but it is difficult. Various types of neurotics can be hypnotized, but again, some of them are difficult subjects. It depends on the situation and on the motivation of the patient. The personal relationship established between the operator and the subject is of great importance. When you hypnotize patients you are asking them to pay attention to ideas or to any parts of reality pertinent to the situation. The patients then narrow their attention down to the task at hand and give their attention to you.

INCREASED MUSCLE TONICITY

One of the first phenomena is that of increased muscle tonicity. A result of this factor is that you can lift the arm and have it stay in a position indefinitely. In a sense this is a psychological laboratory activity, but it is sometimes very useful in the practice of medicine. Sometimes you want patients to lie quietly in bed because it aids their recovery. I recall reading about a burn case in England where the patient as a result of hypnosis stayed in the same position for three weeks. He did this at his own voluntary muscular level so that a pedicle skin graft could take. It is a very useful thing to be able to produce this muscle tonicity for three weeks so that a patient can stay in an awkward position.

ALTERED SENSE OF TIME

Another thing is the matter of a sense of time. Under hypnosis the patient is paying attention to ideas and memories in fields of attitude and understanding. Time has a different subjective value. For example, all of you know that five minutes of acute pain seem like an endless period, and yet an afternoon spent visiting with friends seems very, very short. Subjective time is a tremendously important thing, and you want your patients to experience pain as briefly as possible. You want them to experience pleasure for long periods of time. Cancer patients, for example, suffering acute pain should have that pain cut down in subjective time values, and they should have a period free from pain greatly exaggerated subjectively. You cannot alter the clock, but you can alter the way the patient feels about it. There are many things you can do in altering patients' feelings toward themselves so far as pain is concerned. Sitting in a dental chair, for instance, can be made to seem only about one minute when actually it was an hour.

IDEOMOTOR ACTIVITY

Another thing is the matter of ideomotor activity. All of you have been in the back seat of a car when you thought the driver should put on the brake, and you have automatically tried to put on the brake with him. You have released your foot from the floor only to start shoving it down again.

Have you ever tried to feed a baby and opened your own mouth? You opened your mouth when you thought the baby would open his mouth. This was the idea of motor activity, and you attempted to carry it out. I have had polio and I know something about it. When you put into a trance patients who have recovered from polio but lost a tremendous amount of muscular movement, you ask them to remember what the movements were like. By this means you give them the idea of what the movement is. You can do a great deal of good in the matter of correction of polio handicaps in this way.

IDEOSENSORY BEHAVIOR

There are many fields in which to utilize hypnosis. Ideosensory behavior is another phenomenon. By this I mean the idea of sensory experience, the idea of sensation. Perhaps one of the best illustrations of this is the fact that after a dental appointment you may scratch your face out in thin air well away from the actual skin of your face. You do it that way because it does not feel right—it feels different.

What do you want patients to do if they have suffered a serious injury of the head? You want them to have numbness of the head or you want them to have anesthesia or you want them to have analgesia. You give them the idea of a particular sensory state because, you see, all hypnotic phenomena derive from learnings that you experience in everyday life. Did you ever go to a suspense movie with a severe headache or a severely painful corn, and did you get interested in the movie until you forgot all about the pain?

Right now, what about the anesthesia you have? You have anesthesia of various parts of your body, and you use it every day. You have forgotten the shoes on your feet, the glasses on your face, the collar on your neck. You recognize them very promptly when you pay attention to them. By inducing sensory changes in the patient you bring about these changes by utilizing the experiential learning of their everyday life.

POSTHYPNOTIC SUGGESTION

Another phenomenon is the matter of posthypnotic suggestion. By this I mean a suggestion given here, now, today, to be carried out at some future time. The anesthesiologist may see patients the night before the operation, induce a trance, and suggest to the patients that they will get through the operation very nicely. He can relieve the fear and anxiety, and correct the insomnia that the patients may have. The next day the patients undergo the operation, and the anesthesiologist has already suggested that they will recover from the anesthesic. "I would like you to have good physiologic sleep. I would like to have you feel very comfortable. I would like to have you make a very nice recovery postoperatively." Your patient can accept that suggestion and have a good postoperative recovery.

You can use posthypnotic suggestion in another way. Suppose you have a patient who is going to have a baby. You teach her to go deeply into a trance and you find out what kind of delivery she wants to have. Does she want to participate in it? Does she want to have a sense of feeling with absence of pain? Just how does she want it? Would she want to see the baby immediately? Would she like to be discussing things in a friendly fashion with her obstetrician? You have her in a trance today. Six months later she will carry out your posthypnotic suggestions and participate in the birth of her baby free from pain, or have it with as much pain as she would like to have.

REGRESSION

Another possibility with hypnosis is regression. By this I mean reestablishment of long-forgotten memories. A 50-year-old man can remember what he wore on his third birthday and he can tell you what he ate for breakfast that morning. Sometimes experiences can be verified through old records and things that have been recorded in baby books, the family Bible, and such places. Somnambulism is another useful effect of hypnosis. By somnambulism we mean the profound hypnotic state in which the patient presents the appearance of being wide awake. I mentioned prior obstetrics hypnosis, where the patient can participate and visit and chat and be alert and aware of everything that is going on during her delivery, but feel only the amount of pain she wishes to experience. In somnambulism the patient can look as though she is wide awake. Actually, she is in a cooperative hypnotic situation. A patient in this room could be aware of the audience or of as many of the people in the audience as she wished to know about.

Autohypnosis is another phenomenon, but it is considerably more difficult. It is useful, but induction is difficult and instruction in autohypnosis actually belongs in an advanced course.

In the induction of an hypnotic trance, one induces suggestions and primarily gives the suggestions in an indirect fashion. You should try to avoid as much as possible commanding or dictating to your patient. If you wish to use hypnosis with the greatest possible success, you present your idea to patients so that they can accept and examine it for its inherent value.

ABLATION OF MEMORY

Hypnosis can involve the matter of ablation of memory as well as recall. You can forget a man's name with instant ability. Have you ever been introduced to someone, exchanged the usual courtesy, repeated his name, and immediately said to yourself, "Now what was his name?" and been embarrassed because you forgot it so quickly? Sometimes you wish to hypnotize patients and help them forget. You may want patients to forget pain. You need to do this when you wish to control the pain experienced by cancer patients. You might wish to teach them how to experience a pain and then how to forget it so that they can spend the remaining days of their lives without having to look forward to anticipated pain. You want them to forget it so that each time the pain occurs they can forget that they ever had pain. In this way they can spend the remaining days of their lives in contact with their families.

CONCLUSION

Hypnosis can be useful to you, and with it you will be able to help the patients you see. You can understand it and you can help your patients to understand it by understanding the normal psychological phenomena we have been discussing. Hypnosis simply utilizes these normal reactions and the experiential learnings that are common to all of us.

II. Psychodynamic Processes: Hypnotic Approaches to the Unconscious

The following sections deal with classical hypnotic phenomena such as amnesia, age regression, automatic writing, and literalness as well as the mental mechanisms involved in understanding what the Freudians describe as "psychopathology." In this work Erickson was responding to the *Zeitgeist* that surrounded him in his professional appointments in the 1930s and 1940s. Many of his colleagues and coauthors, such as Kubie, Hill, Huston, and Shakow at this period, were either psychoanalysts or strongly oriented toward Freudian concepts. While Erickson was able to use hypnosis to validate certain psychoanalytic conceptions of psychodynamics, he never identified himself as a partisan of any psychoanalytic school. Indeed, to this editor he often decried what he felt was a premature limitation and rigidification of our understanding of human nature in the belief system of most "true believers" of any "school."

In the papers of these sections we see Erickson at his best—he utilizes his unique version of the "field approach" to explore the human psyche in open and semi-structured situations, frequently with observers present, to allow serendipity in the form of spontaneous unconscious responses to manifest itself in a manner that could be observed and understood.

Section 1: Amnesia

INTRODUCTION

The papers on amnesia in this section are of two categories: (1) clinical endeavors to recover lost memories, and (2) theoretical and empirical expositions on the nature of normal and hypnotic processes of amnesia.

The first two papers on clinical endeavors to recover lost memories introduce us to the difficulties involved and the highly individualized approach that is required in dealing with repressed contents. These papers illustrate the potpourri of hypnotic approaches that Erickson uses to recover amnesic material. So complex are the psychological processes involved that we rarely have any idea at the time of just which approach will be successful with a specific patient—or, indeed, why a particular approach was successful while many others were not. Again we are brought to the realization that the characterization of hypnosis as a process of "manipulation and control" is a caricature of what is more often in actual practice a process of "hope and seek."

Other related questions concerning the nature of hypnosis and consciousness itself are raised in the paper on "The investigation of a specific amnesia." Since the subject in this experiment could not initially find access to the amnesic material on either the "conscious" or "subconscious" levels, Erickson hits upon the inspiration of evoking a "third level of consciousness" that would "emerge from the depths of her mind" to guide her in the process of automatic writing. What is taking place here? Is Erickson using a specious concept somehow to circumvent repression by "fooling" the Freudian censor, or are there, in fact, multiple levels of consciousness that can be used to reflect one another in the hyman psyche? It is currently a psychological cliche to say that we all have "multiple levels of awareness," but how can we specify, activate, and utilize these levels more exactly? We have seen a fascinating expression of these multiple levels of awareness in Erickson's hypnotic work with Aldous Huxley (see Volume One of this series), and we will see still more in his case of the February Man (reported in Volume Four), where he utilizes the therapeutic device of evoking a trance within a trance. Is this analogous to the fairly common experience of dreaming a dream within a dream? Are such processes real in the sense of expressing different levels of consciousness, or are they semantic persiflage? The editor has previously outlined the various processes and phenomenology of self-reflection that occur in the dream state. While no answers were provided, the empirical terrain was at least described and examined (Rossi, 1972b).

It is obvious that we know these matters on only descriptive, inferential, and anecdotal levels. We have as yet no objective and systematic method of investigating multiple levels of awareness, even with the use of hypnosis. What young investigator will come along and shed some revolutionary light on these matters? The problem is fundamental—as fundamental as understanding the basic dynamics of self-reflection and the nature of consciousness itself.

The last three papers in this section represent at least three decades of Erickson's efforts to write a comprehensive, theoretical paper on amnesia. The first version, "Clinical and experimental observations on hypnotic amnesia" (circa 1950), was not published at the time because Erickson felt it was still too tenuous a formulation. The second version, "The problem of amnesia in waking and hypnotic states" (circa 1960s), was originally planned as a joint effort with Andre Weitzenhoffer, but it languished in an uncompleted form in Erickson's files. This editor finally synthesized the essential views and case material of these two versions in a third form that was finally published in 1974 as "Varieties of hypnotic amnesia." It was felt by the editor that the background of observations and thinking recorded in the two earlier, unpublished versions were worth publishing here as a record of the development of Erickson's views; they contain a wealth of observations that may be of value to other researchers investigating the processes of amnesia as they occur in hypnosis and everyday life.

5. The Investigation of a Specific Amnesia

Milton H. Erickson

Specific amnesias are an everyday occurrence. Their study and analysis offer a wide field of therapeutic and theoretical interest through the understanding they afford of the mechanisms of repression and the means of removing, overcoming, or circumventing repressive forces. Psychoanalysts have written much on the subject, particularly in regard to the rôle of affect and the utilization of free-association techniques in the recovery of the forgotten word or name or whatever the amnesia may be. Recently the problem of a specific amnesia was presented to the author for investigation and recovery of the forgotten material. In achieving the desired results, use was made of the various psychological techniques of free association, hypnosis, automatic writing, crystal-gazing, and dream activity. The complexity of psychological phenomena, the successful use of disguise mechanisms, the apparent though perhaps artificial sublevels of consciousness, and the peculiar behaviour of the affect encountered all invite speculation and give rise to problems for investigation.

The subject in this experiment was a young girl studying for her doctorate in psychology. She came to the author in October, stating that on the previous Christmas she had presented a gift to a young man in whom she was much interested. The identity of this gift she had forgotten, possibly because she had later considered it not entirely suitable. She refused to give any additional information, insisting that only the nature of the forgotten object interested her, and she suggested that the very scantiness of information given be considered a part of the experimental situation.

For two weeks previously she had been trying unsuccessfully to recall the forgotten material. She was advised to continue for another week, which she did without success, reaching the conclusion that she would have to write a letter of enquiry to her friend. (The significance of this conclusion will become apparent later.) Having failed in her efforts, she now wished the author to take charge of the problem.

Free association was the first technique employed, but her conscious unwillingness to reveal anything of a personal nature rendered this means futile. Accordingly it was discarded in favor of hypnotism, since she had been trained previously for experimental hypnotic work. In the use of this technique the subject was hypnotized and awakened repeatedly

Reprinted with permission from *The British Journal of Medical Psychology,* 1933, Vol. XIII, Part II.

throughout the course of the investigation in accordance with the needs of the immediate situation. All trances were of the profound, somnambulistic type characterized by dissociation and an apparently complete amnesia for trance suggestions and experiences.

In the first trance she was asked to give free associations. She did this readily, producing many nonidentifying associations, but she persisted in her waking refusal to give additional pertinent information. When asked in the trance state to name the gift directly, she manifested strong emotional tension and declared that she was unable to do so, that it had been forgotten completely. Since apparently no progress could be made by this method, she was given posthypnotic suggestions to the effect that when she awakened she would talk freely in generalities about the gift and suddenly name it. This succeeded in all but the naming of the object. The attempt was repeated in a second induced-tranced state, with the additional suggestion that she would interrupt her general remarks to declare impulsively, "It was a (name)." These instructions were obeyed to the crucial point, when she became emotional, seemed surprised, and complained of sudden mental blankness. Questioning revealed that she did not even have the feeling of "something on the tip of her tongue."

A third trance state was induced, in which she was given posthypnotic suggestions to perform automatic writing upon awakening. In her writing she was to give various descriptive details and finally the identity of the gift. Meanwhile, she was to engage the author in an animated conversation as a means of absorbing her attention away from her writing. However, nothing definitely descriptive was written, and when it came to the point of writing the name of the gift, her hand moved more and more slowly while she twisted and squirmed on the chair, complained of feeling tired, and protested about the hopelessness of the experiment. When the probable nature of the complaints and protests was mentioned, she showed good insight but declared herself to be unable to control her emotions. She was shown her automatic writing, of which she had been unaware. She exhibited surprise, then eagerness expressed in the enquiry, "Did I write the name?", and finally disappointment when she noted her failure. The procedure was repeated, using more forceful suggestions, but with no better results.

A slight variation was made in the technique. Posthypnotic suggestions were given to the subject to write automatically and in mixed order the letters contained in the name of the object. An excessive number of consonants was obtained. The procedure was repeated, with instructions to write automatically the letters of the alphabet, underlining those which were significant. As before, an excess of consonants resulted. In both attempts marked affective disturbance was noted, but the particular letters could not be determined. When shown her production, the subject exhibited, as before, surprise, eagerness, and disappointment.

These failures indicated a need for a still further change of technique.

While in a state of profound hypnotic sleep the subject was given the suggestion that she could reveal indirectly the information desired with neither "conscious" nor "subconscious" realization of what she was doing. To this end she was instructed to continue in a state of deep hypnosis, thereby "dissociating" her "conscious mind" and leaving it in a state of quiescence. At the same time, by means of her "subconscious" mind she was to engage the author in an animated conversation. Thus, with both "conscious" and "subconscious" minds engaged, a "third level of consciousness" in a response to hypnotic suggestion would "emerge from the depths of her mind" and would express itself by guiding her hand in automatic writing, of which she would be aware neither consciously nor subconsciously.[1] On the first trial, in accordance with this instruction, she wrote vaguely descriptive material concerning the gift. Further suggestion was given to the effect that the "third level of consciousness" could now write the significant information, but in such disguised fashion that its true meaning would not be apparent. The sentence illustrated in Figure 1 was obtained. As she wrote the word *box,* she became emotionally disturbed and complained of feeling tired, uncomfortable, and "funny," but this behavior disappeared as she completed the sentence. She was shown the sentence in both the trance and waking states, but denied seeing any pertinent meaning in it and declared that it was not her handwriting, substantiating her contention by writing the same sentence in her normal waking state, as illustrated in Figure 2. Another trance was induced and the same instructions were given to her with the addition that the word *box* would influence her hand to write the exact identity of the gift, but in such guise as to lead both herself and the author astray. Obeying these instructions while conversing vivaciously in a deep trance state, her hand automatically wrote in a hesitant fashion the sentence illustrated in Figure 3. As she wrote the second, third, and fourth words she exhibited much emotion, sighed, flushed, squirmed, and complained of feeling "funny."

Figure 1.

She also expressed a skepticism toward whatever the author was trying to do, declaring that he must be trying to make her do something—what it was she did not know, but she did know that she could not do it.[2] When

[1]The author assumes no responsibility for the validity of these concepts, and the trance state of the subject probably accounts for her acceptance of them, but at all events they served the purpose.

[2]The subject appeared to have a rather limited understanding of the whole situation when in the trance state.

shown what she had written, she read it listlessly, declaring that it had no meaning for her and insisting that it was not her handwriting. Awakened, she likewise disowned the writing but she read the sentence with great interest and recalled for the first time that she had contemplated giving a cigarette case but had changed her mind. All associations became blocked at this point, and she was insistent that the experiment be discontinued as hopeless. However, her insight into the whole situation soon rendered her attitude more favorable.

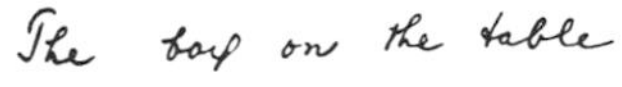

Figure 2.

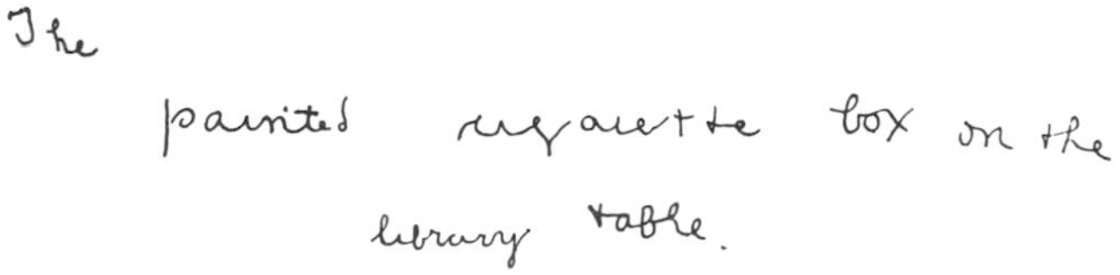

Figure 3.

Because of the subject's affective state, another change in technique was made by asking her to attempt crystal-gazing. In the crystal she saw herself walking down the street, entering a jewelry store in which she inspected cigarette cases, and then continuing down the street and entering a department store, whereupon she immediately lost sight of herself in the crowd. She saw herself next leaving the store with a small package under her arm. She took the package to her room and placed it in a bureau drawer. In response to further suggestions she watched herself prepare the gift for mailing, but each time that she was about to catch sight of the gift, her crystal image would turn in such fashion as to occlude her line of vision. All suggestions to the contrary were without effect other than that she was able to give the rough dimensions of the article, which had not been possible previously. Further variations of the crystal-gazing were without results. Finally she was rehypnotized deeply and given posthypnotic suggestions to the effect that she would dream that night about the gift but would not verbally identify it in her dream. The next morning, however, she could recall the dream and in so doing would recall the name of the gift.

Early the next day, with a complete amnesia for the posthypnotic suggestions, she related that she had awakened during the night in the midst of a dream about the forgotten article. She had recounted this dream to herself on the possibility that the author might be interested. In the morning, however, she recalled dreaming but not the dream content. Instead she suddenly recalled having a letter in her strong box thanking her for the present, and she felt herself forcibly impelled to read the letter. She did this and discovered that the object was a box of paints. She was shown the automatic writing illustrated above, and she exclaimed, "How different it looks now!"

The discovery of the identity of the gift did not end the problem, but gave rise to new and interesting aspects. A week later the subject complained that she was unable to recall her dream and that she felt a strong desire to know what it was. She asked that hypnosis be utilized in the securing of this lost memory. Much the same procedure was followed in this regard as had been used in attempting to recover the nature of the gift. All attempts were failures, however, until she was given suggestions disorienting her temporally. When these suggestions had been accepted, she was told that it was the night of her dream and that she was actually in the midst of her dream. As she relived the dream, she was instructed to give an account of it to the author, and thus a verbatim report was obtained. The dream was: "There was a group of people in a place. It takes place in a hospital—hospital people. I'm telling them about the procedure, telling them about the results, telling them we got the name of the gift, but I don't tell them what the gift was." She was awakened with instructions to remember the dream. This she did, and expressed her pleasure, until suddenly she declared in great surprise, "I've forgotten the name of the gift now." She was urged to try to recall the gift, but after much effort and numerous attempts at free association she failed. She repeated the dream content in an effort to reawaken her associations, but even this failed. A trance state was induced and she was told to recall the name of the gift after awakening. When aroused from the trance, she promptly declared, "Why, I remember it now. It's a box of paints." After a general conversation she was casually questioned about her dream content, and to her profound amazement she discovered that again she had forgotten the dream completely. Repeated investigations disclosed that she could not keep the identity of the gift and the dream content in her mind simultaneously. Finally, in the waking state in which she could recall the name of the gift, she was casually informed of the dream content. Following this she was able to remember both.

Four days later she complained to the author that she had been trying daily to write a letter to her friend in accordance with her regular custom, but that she could not do so. She had forced herself repeatedly to sit at her desk and begin the letter, but found herself unable to write more than a line or two before her thought processes became blocked and she felt emotionally disturbed and compelled to do something else. She was given the plausible explanation that the affect originally causing the repression had not been dissipated but had subsequently attached itself to the dream content, later to the identity of the gift, and finally, when both of these repressions had been circumvented, the affect had attached itself to the idea of a letter to her friend. After listening to this explanation the subject declared, "I understand now. Now I can write my letter."

Contact was maintained with the subject following this experience, but no unusual occurrence came to either her or the author's attention.

Because of the clinical interest aroused, attention may be called here to a consideration of the automatic writing. The word *box* was markedly displaced in the first sentence, which is suggestive of some unrecognized purpose. A similar displacement of the significant words in the second sentence enhances the possibility that this measure is a purposeful though unconscious means of self-betrayal. This conclusion is substantiated further by noting the relatively smaller size of the letters *e* and *d* in the word *painted*. The scrawling of the word *cigarette* appears superficially to be a clever method of distracting attention, but the account of the motivation suggests a deep and significant symbolism for it as well as for the other two words.

The peculiar behavior of the affect at the termination of the experiment, resulting in the alternate repression of the identity of the gift and of the dream content, with subsequent attachment to the related concept of the letter, suggests a strong conflict and an unwillingness or an unreadiness to accept the symbolic significance of the ideas concerned.

Not until the above report had been drafted into its final form for publication and submitted to the experimental subject for criticism was it possible to secure an account of the motivations for her repression. Fortunately she had kept a daily journal of her thoughts during the entire time of the amnesia, and from this and her elaborations of this journal the motivations were obtained. Minor and incidental points as well as elaborations of the symbolism are omitted for personal reasons.

For five years the subject, S., had been in love with M., a man belonging to another race and culture, artistic in nature and extremely idealistic, puritanical, and conventional in attitude. She had planned to marry him at the expiration of another year. Her own philosophy of life at the time was very similar to his. In the month of September preceding the amnesia she met C., a man of her own race and culture and whose personal philosophy was the antithesis of M.'s. A warm friendship rapidly developed between S. and C., with the consequence that she felt strongly inclined to relinquish her former teachings and ideals and to accept C.'s broader and freer ideals of life. Yet to do so would be essentially a negation of what she had considered to be the final principles of personal life and a destruction of her worthiness in the eyes of M., whom she loved. As she considered this problem, she realized that any independence for herself could evolve only from a deliberate choice on her part between these opposing personal philosophies. Yet she dared not choose C., although critical thinking suggested such a choice, because to do so would be to overthrow the conventional and idealistic precepts of her past teaching. To choose M. would mean the hampering of her intellectual and emotional nature. She hoped that something would happen which would force her to recognize her fundamental inclinations, because she knew that she lacked the courage to face the decision deliberately. It was then that the amnesia developed as one of the indications of her conflict. At first she considered the amnesia inconsequential, but soon she began to feel that it symbolized her choice, and she felt a compulsive need of discovering the nature of this amnesia in order to know its meaning, and yet she feared to know its meaning. Upon the recovery of the memory she immediately understood the rationale for the selection of the forgotten object. In purchasing the Christmas gift she had first inspected cigarette cases, thereby establishing an associative value. C. possessed a beautiful antique painted box which he used as a cigarette container. The one man, artistic and idealistic, was easily symbolized by the box of paints, while the other man possessed a painted box of practical personal use. With the recovery of the forgotten identity she sensed its import but dared not recognize it. To rob it of its meaning a second problem had to be created—namely, the amnesia of the dream. When this problem was solved, she still had the fundamental question to face, but could not do it, and so a second amnesia of the gift occurred. When finally forced to remember both the dream and the gift, she realized that she had made her choice and sat down to write a letter to M., thereby formulating her ideas and definitely committing herself. However, she could not do this until, with the aid of the author, she forced herself to recognize the affective features of the whole situation.

In summary, the problem investigated was an attempt to recover the content of a specific amnesia of the entity of a Christmas gift without the aid of supplementary information. Techniques of free association alone, free association and direct questioning in hypnosis, automatic writing, and crystal-gazing were tried without success. Finally, by means of a specious argument concerning the existence of a third level of consciousness and the permission to use disguise mechanisms, the forgotten material was actually obtained, but in such guise that its true significance was not recognized. Then by means of dream activity a situation was created whereby the subject, without assuming the responsibility, could circumvent the repression. Following this a conflict state developed, characterized by the alternate repression of two ideas, and was ultimately resolved by the attachment of the affect to a related subject, from which it was eventually dispelled. The motivation of the amnesia was not learned until months later, when the subject disclosed its origin to lie in an emotional conflict concerning two men.

6. Development of Apparent Unconsciousness During Hypnotic Reliving of a Traumatic Experience

Milton H. Erickson

A general experimental project, to be reported later in its entirety, was undertaken to investigate the possibility of exploration by means of hypnosis of the psychic development of a patient recently recovered from an acute psychotic episode of a schizophrenic reaction type.
The method employed consisted of an attempt to have him relive his past life as completely as possible in a special state of hypnosis.

METHOD

The experimental procedure consisted of training the patient to enter profound somnambulistic hypnotic trances, during which, by means of a series of hypnotic suggestions, he was disoriented completely and then reoriented to an earlier period of his life. When thus reoriented, by the employment of carefully worded systematic suggestions and questions, he was induced to relive past events in a chronologically progressive fashion, describing them in detail to the experimenter as if they were in the course of actual development in the immediate present. An attending stenographer recorded in full the entire course of the experimental events, including the descriptive material. In every instance for which adequate data were available from sources other than the patient himself, it was found that events of the distant past were relived and recounted by the patient with remarkable vividness and with richness and accuracy of detail.

In this connection mention should be made of the fact that neither detailed questioning in the normal waking state nor instruction to recall fully these past events in a state of ordinary deep hypnosis served to secure the same degree of accuracy and amount of detail as did the procedure of reorientation. Furthermore, even after the patient had relived an experience while reoriented to that period of his life, such

Reprinted with permission from the *Archives of Neurology and Psychiatry*, December, 1937, Vol. 38, pp. 1282-1288.

completeness of recall could not be secured without resort to posthypnotic suggestions worded in such fashion as to bridge the temporal gap between the actual present of the experimental situation and the chronological period to which the patient had been reoriented. The following example illustrates such posthypnotic suggestion: "This thing that has just happened to you and which you have told me about is important. You are to remember it fully and completely for the rest of your life, so that ten or even twenty years from now, it will be as fresh in your mind as it is now."

EXPERIMENTAL RESULTS

Study of the experimental findings disclosed an incident of peculiar interest, illustrative in an unusual fashion of psychosomatic interrelationships. This incident concerned the development of what appeared to be a state of unconsciousness as the patient relived the experience of a homicidal assault which had occurred two years previously, when he was 17 years old. All previous information concerning this assault consisted of the statement by the patient that he had been "taken for a ride" and beaten so badly that hospitalization had been necessary. He seemed to have complete amnesia for all informative details of this experience, including even the name of the hospital. Extensive and persistent questioning in the ordinary deep hypnotic trance, as well as in the normal waking state, secured only unimportant items, despite the fact that he seemed to be cooperating to the limit of his ability.

When the day of this event was reached in the hypnotic reliving of his past life, the patient expressed his fears over his employment as a police informer, vividly portraying intense anxiety concerning threatened criminal vengeance, and his entire behavior and appearance were suggestive of a most harried state of mind. When the hour of 4 P.M. was reached in his reexperiencing the events of this day, he relived, with marked intensity of feeling, the scene of his being ordered into an automobile by two men whom he knew to be criminal characters and his fearful behavior during the course of a long drive, during which he pleaded piteously with his abductors in a terrified fashion. Finally, he reenacted his forced acceptance of a bottle of pop from the criminals, fearfully and hesitantly drinking from an imaginary bottle. As he swallowed, he grimaced, mumbled that it tasted bitter, asked if it was poisoned, and dodged and cowered as if evading a blow. His entire appearance continued to denote intense terror. Shortly after completing the act of drinking, he belched and suddenly looked bewildered. His pupils, which previously had been fluctuating constantly in size, became widely dilated, and fine lateral nystagmus developed. He then rubbed his eyes, complained that he could not see plainly, said that everything was getting dark and that he was dizzy, and began shaking his head as if to throw off something or to rouse himself. Questioning by the experimenter elicited the information that the patient felt himself becoming sleepy. It was noted that his speech, previously clear, was now thick and indistinct and that his appearance had changed from that of terror to that of somnolence.

At this time the patient was sitting on a couch, and every few seconds the experimenter had been testing him for the presence of catalepsy as an index of his continuance in the hypnotic state. After about two minutes of decreasing activity, during which the patient shook his head more and more slowly and mumbled with increasing inarticulateness, his eyes closed, despite his apparent effort to keep them open. Suddenly he gave a short, gasping grunt and collapsed, sprawling inanimately over the couch. Immediate examination by the experimenter disclosed complete loss of hypnotic rapport, with absence of the catalepsy which hitherto had been consistently present. Physically, there were sagging of the lower jaw and marked atony of the muscles of the legs and arms. Also, the patellar and pupillary reflexes, which are consistently present during hypnotic states, were absent. The respiration and pulse, which had been greatly increased during the state of terror, had decreased somewhat during that of somnolence. Now they were found to be markedly diminished in rate and so weak and faint as to be barely perceptible. In brief, the patient presented every appearance of being unconscious. However, before the blood pressure and accurate counts of the pulse and respiration could be taken, the patient seemed to be recovering. He stirred slightly and moaned, and catalepsy returned slowly. Shortly he opened his eyes and, after staring vacantly around, weakly closed them again. It was noted that the pupils were still widely dilated, that fine nystagmus was present, and that the eyes were not focused. The patient licked his lips repeatedly, moaned for water, and weakly rubbed his forehead, grimacing with pain as he did so. He paid no attention to the experimenter's insistent questions, "What's the matter? What's happening?" except to say, "It's dark, dark." This was followed by a second collapse, of slower onset than the first but apparently of the same character, with the same physical findings except that the respiration was deep and labored while the pulse was slow and firm. Repeated attempts were made by the experimenter to arouse the patient, but he remained unresponsive for several minutes. Finally, catalepsy returned, and the patient opened his eyes and stared about unseeingly. Nystagmus was absent, and the pupils were somewhat dilated but responsive to light. He twisted his head about, moaned, rubbed his neck as if it were painful, rubbed his forehead gently, grimacing as if with pain, and shivered constantly. Again, he licked his lips repeatedly and kept moaning for water. No response was made to the experimenter's insistent questioning except the monosyllables "light" and "woods." Now and then he put his hands to his ears, rubbed them feebly and mumbled, "buzzing."

Soon the patient seemed to recover to a considerable degree, and he again became fairly responsive to the experimenter's inquiries, which concerned the events he was reliving. There followed a relatively inadequate account, as compared with his initial communicativeness, of lying in a ditch alongside a road through a woods, of being cold, wet, and uncomfortable, and of suffering from intense thirst, roaring in the ears, headache, and a painful, bleeding wound on his forehead, from which he went through the act of wiping blood in a gingerly fashion. He also declared that it seemed to be morning.

From then, he recounted in a fragmentary fashion the experience of being picked up by some men and taken to a hospital. The reliving of the next two days was also disjointed and inadequate, but that of subsequent events was complete, during the course of which the name of the hospital was obtained.

The total time required by the patient to relive this entire experience, which had actually extended over a period of two and one-half days, was slightly more than four hours.

Later, inquiry was made at the hospital named by the patient, and the information was obtained that on the morning of the day specified by him he had been found lying in a confused, semiconscious state in a ditch beside a road leading through a woods, suffering from exposure and a contused laceration of the forehead, and that he had seemed not to recover full consciousness for nearly two days. In addition, inquiries made of the police force for which he presumably had acted as informer verified his account of such employment and served to identify one of the criminals whom he had described as a well-known police character having a record of being involved in several homicides and as one on whom the patient had informed. Also, the police records disclosed that the patient had made his usual morning report on the day of the assault but had failed to make his evening report and had not been heard from since.

The entire experimental project was interrupted by external circumstances for more than a year. On resumption it was repeated in its entirety, including the incident already reported. The records obtained were compared with those of the first investigation and were found to be essentially identical, including all the findings contained in this report. The same descriptive details, the same sequences, the same physical manifestations, and even the same fragmentary utterances and gaps in the reexperiencing of the events were found. About five months later, in an endeavor to check certain aspects of the major project, the experimenter again had the patient repeat this event, among others. Again, the record obtained was identical with that of the first and second investigations, and the time required for each repetition ranged from three to four hours.

After each experimental session in which this experience was relived, the patient awakened from the hypnotic state with complete and persistent amnesia for everything that had taken place during the trance. However, he complained bitterly in each instance of severe headache, overwhelming fatigue and weakness, and extreme general discomfort; he was tremulous physically and unstable emotionally. All this he attributed to the hypnosis, although he readily admitted that previous hypnotic work had left no aftereffects. In addition, he became antagonistic and hostile toward the experimenter and the idea of further hypnotic work, and special effort, in one instance extending over a month, was necessary to secure continued cooperation.

COMMENT

One of the first considerations in determining the significance of the experimental findings is the validity of the entire investigational procedure. In this regard the reports in the literature disclose that hypnosis can be employed to arouse dormant associations and to recover amnesic material otherwise inaccessible (Erickson, 1933), and that it often makes possible an exceedingly vivid and complete recollection of apparently totally forgotten events. Furthermore, recent experimental work by Platonov and Prikhodivny (1930), among others, has indicated that regression in a hypnotic state to an earlier period of life is possible, with the reestablishment of its corresponding patterns of behavior uninfluenced by subsequently acquired skills. Other experimental work demonstrates the possibility of producing in the hypnotic state significant personality-situation changes of an objectively measurable character (Huston et al, 1934; Erickson, 1935). In the light of these facts, the practicability and validity of the major project as an experimental method become more readily apparent and serve to suggest the reliability of the findings reported here. In addition there is the confirmation from the hospital where the patient was treated of the facts of his injury and of his confused mental state, which he had duplicated in the experimental situation. The hospital report also served to indicate the possibility, apart from emotional considerations, of a traumatic basis for the general amnesia manifested by the patient for the original experience in the normal waking state and in the simple deep hypnotic trance. Additional confirmation of the reliability of the experimental findings may be found in the identity of the results obtained on repetitions a year and nearly a year and a half later. Such identity suggests both the intrinsic completeness and the credibility of the date.

The possibility of reliving past experiences as a dynamic process is becoming increasingly recognized, and the validity of the phenomenon has been repeatedly demonstrated in both psychiatric and psychoanalytic experience. Perhaps the best example that may be taken from normal life to illustrate the type of findings obtained in this experiment is the relatively common occurrence of the vivid dreaming of a long-past event as a current experience. In such dreams often no modifications may be found of the dream responses and behavior which should derive from the dreamer's experiences subsequent to the original dreamed-of occurrence, and this despite the fact that the course of the dreamer's life may have been such as to modify or to change completely his capacity to respond in the fashion depicted in the dream. Thus, the adult may dream vividly of being a child in all respects, without the dream responses and behavior reflecting the maturity of his actual status. Such a dream, however, is a spontaneous occurrence; thus it differs from the patient's experience in this investigation, which was the outcome of deliberate experimentation.

The reliving of this patient's experience did not take place in the usual sense in which it is observed in psychiatric and psychoanalytic practice, since it occurred at a "subconscious" level in a peculiar state of hypnosis which precluded any subsequent conscious recollection and since it involved an experience for which the patient had, and continued to have, essentially total amnesia.

The regression to the earlier period of life at which this experience originally occurred, occasioned by the hypnotic suggestions for reorientation, apparently functioned in such fashion that all experiences subsequent to that event, including even development of the amnesia, were eliminated by hypnotic dissociation from the patterns of response which were manifested in the experimental situation. Thereby, revival of the experience with its associated responses was permitted as if it were in the course of actual development. Once this process had been initiated by the evocation of readily accessible memories, the recovery of each item functioned in itself as an aid in recovering additional material in its original chronological order, thus constituting a continuous progression to completion of sequential activity. Hence there would be aroused in proper order and relationship the concomitant psychic and somatic activities with their corresponding alterations and adjustments of the mental and physical states, the entire process being directed by the originally established patterns of response.

The apparent state of unconsciousness developed in the patient raises immediately the question of psychosomatic interrelationships. It is unfortunate that the exigencies of the experimental situation, including the emphasis on the project as a whole, resulted in failure to secure more adequate data concerning his physical state. However, every item of such information which was secured, including the startling clinical effect of the patient's appearance, strongly suggests that he was actually unconscious.

More particularly is this indicated by the absence of the pupillary and patellar reflexes, the changes in pulse and respiration and the loss of muscular tonus, all of which are unaffected by the hypnotic state, except muscular tonus, which may be slightly increased (Bass, 1931). Further confirmation of the possibility that actual unconsciousness was produced may be found in the familiar phenomenon of a faint produced by purely psychic stimuli and, more closely parallel with this experiment, in the faint that has been known to result from a terrifying dream.

Likewise the aftereffects of which the patient complained in each instance after the reliving of his experience are highly suggestive that the processes involved had been of such character as to produce definite somatic and physiological changes which were not limited to the experimental hypnotic state but persisted into the following waking condition. Further evidence for the possibility that marked changes in the functioning of the body can result from psychic factors may be found in a report made before the American Psychiatric Association in May 1936 on the experimental production of deafness in the hypnotic state and published two years later in greater detail (Erickson, 1938a, 1938b).

The temporal abridgment in the experimental situation of the probable period of unconsciousness signifies possibly a qualitative as well as a quantitative difference, to be attributed to the fact that the experimental state of unconsciousness arose from mental and physical states of developing in response to internal stimuli, in contrast to the external factors involved in the original experience.

A question may be raised concerning the reason that the patient, on becoming unconscious in the trance state and thus disrupting the hypnotic condition, did not recover consciousness in the normal waking state. Aside from the fact that the entire process was conditioned by hypnosis, the parallel phenomenon is frequently observed of recovery from sudden traumatically induced unconsciousness marked by reorientation to the situation immediately preceding the trauma.

In conclusion, mention may be made of the clinical psychiatric effects of the hypnotic reliving of the patient's traumatic experience. Unfortunately, a complete study of these changes was not made at the time, but certain clinically significant alterations of behavior occurred. After the first hypnotic reliving, despite the fact that no apparent change in his conscious amnesia was detected, the patient showed complete loss of his phobic reactions to visiting the city where he had been a police informer, although, as was learned on questioning, he did not revist his former haunts, rationalizing this failure with a casual explanation of lack of time. After the second and third experiences in reliving, no apparent trace of any of his fears remained, and he revisited his former haunts with every evidence of pleasure. Some months later, during a casual conversation, he reminded me that he had once told of being taken for a ride without being able to remember many of the details. He then added that he had recalled more of that experience "a few days ago," stating that "Whitey and another guy picked me up on Washington Street about four o'clock one afternoon and took me for a ride. They drugged me, conked me, and shoved me in a hospital—I think it was in Providence—they were after me for squealing on them. They said they'd get me, but they didn't." This was all he seemed to recall, and he told it casually, with no manifestation of the affective strain and tension previously much in evidence. The marked contrast between his original fearful, hesitant manner of telling what he remembered and this casual, unconcerned elaboration of the story suggests that a definite emotional catharsis had resulted from the hypnotic procedure, even though the entire process had occurred at a level below conscious awareness.

CONCLUSIONS

The specific conclusion to be derived from this report may be stated as follows:

Significant psychosomatic changes culminating in the development of, and recovery from, an apparently definite state of unconsciousness were produced in a patient during the hypnotic reliving of an amnesic traumatic experience. More general conclusions are:

1. Hypnosis can be employed to produce significant personality-situation changes, as evidenced by the definite psychic and somatic effects produced by the reorientation to, and the reliving of, a past experience as a current process.
2. The procedure of hypnotic reorientation to a past event makes possible the reliving of that experience as if in the course of the actual original development, thus excluding the modifying effects of the perspective and the secondary emotional reactions which obtain in the normal waking state and permitting revival of the experience in a more sequential order and in greater detail than is possible in the normal state.
3. Amnesia, even when associated in origin with the physical conditions of trauma to the head and possible narcosis, need not preclude recovery of the major memory images.

7. Clinical and Experimental Observations on Hypnotic Amnesia: Introduction to an Unpublished Paper

Milton H. Erickson

Hypnotic amnesia is a much more complex phenomenon than is commonly realized. The general tendency is to look upon it as a relatively simple, definite manifestation comparable if not identical with forgetting as ordinarily experienced, and controlled and regulated by hypnotic suggestions with almost the same ease and effectiveness as one can govern vision by opening or closing the eyes, or by turning the light on and off in a light-proof room. Extensive experience, however, discloses that, while hypnotic amnesia does derive from the trance state and is characterized by a functional loss of ability to recall or to identify past experiences, it constitutes a form of dynamic behavior quite different from ordinary forgetting. It resembles the latter superficially and primarily in the final end results—namely, the inaccessibility of memories. Because of this one point of resemblance there is a general tendency to investigate hypnotic amnesia by procedures primarily suitable for a study of learning and forgetting behavior. In such studies there is an oversight of the fact that hypnotic amnesia, which permits subjects to forget in a moment's time their name, age, and similar items of fact ordinarily impossible to forget, cannot be tested adequately by a procedure devised to test the retention of nonsense syllables. At best, such investigative measures can be employed to test the effects of hypnotic amnesia upon the retention of nonsense syllables, but a determination of such effects in relation to a chosen, limited form of behavior does not constitute a study of hypnotic amnesia as a phenomenon in itself.

Experiments may also be devised in which subjects are permitted to undergo certain experiences while in the trance state. Then, either with or without instructions to forget those experiences, subjects are awakened and tested directly or indirectly for any memories they may have of the events of the trance period. In such an experimental procedure it is assumed that any unusual decreases or inaccessibilities of the memories of the hypnotic experiences derive simply, directly, and immediately from the hypnotic state itself, from any suggestions to forget that may have been given or from a combination of both factors. Also, it is assumed that

---

Unpublished manuscript, circa 1950s.

any decreases that are found constitute evidence of an actual process of forgetting as a simple, unitary, specific phenomenon and that any immediate failure to show such decreases in memory signifies the ineffectiveness of the effort to secure hypnotic amnesia.

In other words, in this type of experiment the basic assumptions are that hypnosis in and of itself may be an entirely adequate genetic factor for the development of an amnesia, that such an amnesia necessarily develops readily and immediately, that it may be elicited by simple suggestions to that effect, and that any amnesia developed is necessarily a sufficiently stable manifestation to resist explorative measures despite the fundamental suggestibility of the hypnotic subject upon which the amnesia itself is based.

Another unfortunate assumption in this type of procedure is that a test procedure can be elaborated, controls established, and time limits set for the evocation of investigative results without adequate realization that reliable experimental results do not depend upon the completion of an experimental procedure, however well devised, that does not make full provision for the nature of the phenomenon under investigation.

Additionally, these general assumptions favor the continuance of the misconception of hypnotic amnesia as analogous to ordinary forgetting. They permit an oversight of the fact that the hypnotic state is a result of a dynamic, purposeful interplay of personality forces, and they do not make provision for the probability that any derivative or outcome of the hypnosis is also of a dynamic, purposeful character not comparable to the progressive, sequential processes of psycho- and neurophysiological functioning basic to forgetting as commonly experienced.

Consequently, experimental studies that have been based upon limited and inadequate assumptions and understandings and that have failed to make provision for a phenomenon quite different from ordinary forgetting have led to conflicting and confusing though occasionally informative findings. For example, reports have been made of no amnesia, of a partial or incomplete amnesia, of a profound amnesia, of an intentional or an unwitting simulation of amnesia, and of results similar in effect to amnesia such as blocking and repression.

Despite these contradictory investigative findings and the frequent uncertainty and unreliability of hypnotic amnesia as it is encountered both experimentally and clinically, experience discloses it to be a definite and significant trance phenomenon, exceedingly complicated in its manifestations, sometimes difficult to discover and to recognize and always difficult to test satisfactorily. It resembles ordinary forgetting in certain superficial aspects, and this resemblance can be greatly enhanced by a careful choice of hypnotic suggestions in inducing it. It is much more likely to seem to resemble or to parallel various forms of psychodynamic behavior seen in everyday life and to duplicate in many regards psychopathological states, from which it seems to differ mainly in the degree to which it can be manipulated and controlled rather than in its form, structure, and associated developments.

In addition to the difficulties caused by the complexity of hypnotic amnesia, there is another experimental difficulty of primary importance to investigative procedures—namely, the inherent contradictions of the total experimental situation. Stated simply, the total situation requires that an amnesia be suggested to a subject in a highly suggestible state. This suggestion of an amnesia is then followed by a second suggestion—direct, implied, or inherent in the test procedure—that the subject recover the amnesic material. Hence, the findings obtained are more likely to be a measure of the relative strength of the two opposing suggestions rather than a measure of the extent of the hypnotic amnesia originally induced.

Nor can this inherent contradiction be circumvented easily, since the amnesia is an induced phenomenon, more or less sharply defined as an experience, and not the outcome of progressive processes of behavior as is ordinary forgetting. For example, the induction of hypnotic amnesia for learned nonsense syllables, followed by the task of learning a new set of nonsense syllables actually inclusive of some of the presumable amnesic syllables, does not constitute a satisfactory experimental situation. In undertaking the new task the subjects, if they cooperate fully, are at liberty to do anything that can aid their performance—and this may include in their understanding the recovery of any memories or associations that might help in the new task. Hence the greater rapidity of learning for the amnesic syllables is not necessarily a measure of the incompleteness of the hypnotic amnesia; it may equally well be a measure of the degree to which the subjects were to abolish the amnesia in their effort to perform the new task.

Another important consideration, definitely related to the problem of suitable experimental conditions, lies in the highly significant role played by associations—whether chance, incidental, relevant, or irrelevant—in permitting the recovery of amnesic material. Although this is fairly well recognized generally, it is often overlooked in experimental settings. The following account is an example of ordinary forgetting that discloses the readiness with which amnesic barriers may be overcome by an item of experience serving to arouse associations related to the forgotten data.

A college graduate, in anticipation of a visit with his senior-year roommate whom he had not seen for 15 years, was led to discover a 20-year-old college directory in which, at the end of his freshman year, he had placed a checkmark opposite the names of all his college mates whom he knew well. To his amazement he could call to mind very few of them. Repeated efforts during the next two weeks permitted the recovery of a few more identities. Upon the arrival of the guest, and before there had been any exchange of reminiscences, the directory was produced. To the man's astonishment he discovered at once, and with no help other than the mere presence of his former roommate, that a wealth of recollections came flooding back, and he was able to recall a large number of the forgotten identities.

Two weeks after the departure of his friend he again looked through the directory, only to discover that he had again forgotten nearly all of the names, retaining only a few more than he had originally recovered by himself.

This chance observation led to several experimental investigations under controlled conditions of a similar problem. The subjects were chiefly psychiatrists who had formerly worked in the same mental hospital. They were tested separately and together for their recollection of the names of former ward patients, among which were listed names unfamiliar to them. The results obtained in each instance confirmed those of the original observation. Furthermore, similar observations and experimental inquiries that yielded comparable results have been related to the author by a number of associates.

Discussion of the above observations is hardly necessary. They serve to emphasize the importance, in a memory-searching situation, of realities and associations, even those remotely connected with the amnesic material, in permitting a recollection of otherwise inaccessible memories. In the same vein they show that the removal of those associations—as in the above instances, mere physical removal of the person constituting the source of associations—is sufficient to reestablish the amnesia in large part.

Hence in any study of hypnotic amnesia there is a need to be most appreciative of the possible removal of an established amnesia through the force of associations unintentionally established by an experimental setting, with a consequent misinterpretation of test results. Since hypnosis and presumably its derivatives are based upon dynamic interpersonal relationships, the significant effectiveness of associations may be of primary importance in maintaining or abolishing an induced amnesia.

Also pertinent to the importance of associations in the accessibility and utilization of past learnings is the following example from the field of animal psychology. Although it bears more upon the problem of learning than upon amnesia, it effectively illustrates that something well learned can become meaningless when encountered out of context, thus giving an effect comparable to a failure of recognition and such as may occur in amnesia.

This example relates to the teaching of a series of tricks to the family dog. By force of circumstances this teaching and all performances of the tricks occurred in a basement room, although the dog had the run of the entire house. One day, long after the dog had not only learned the tricks well but would perform them spontaneously in anticipation of a food reward, visitors asked for a demonstration. The dog was called into the living room, a crust of bread was offered, and the usual commands were given. The dog gave every evidence of wanting the bread but seemed to have no understanding of the commands or of what was wanted, despite patient, repeated efforts. When everyone went down to the basement, the sight of the bread crust was sufficient to elicit repeated spontaneous performances of all her tricks without commands being given. Even after having eaten the bread, she performed readily upon commands from anybody without further reward. Upon return to the living room the dog again seemed unable to understand commands, nor did the offer of food do more than elicit restless, hungry behavior. Giving her small morsels didn't help, but another trip to the basement resulted in an adequate performance. Finally, after repeated commands and offering of food and much restless puzzled behavior by the dog, she finally began to understand the familiar command of "Roll over." She responded by racing to the basement, performing the task, and then racing back for the food reward, repeating this behavior at every new command.

While this behavior cannot legitimately be called an amnesia, certain of the results were comparable to those that would derive from an amnesia. Furthermore, when it is realized fully how extensively hypnotic amnesia depends upon associated circumstances and conditions of a limited character, the possible parallel with this example becomes apparent and serves to demonstrate the need, in any experimental study, to make adequate provision for possible association factors.

This brief discussion of the difficulties involved in the experimental study of hypnotic amnesia is not intended to be exhaustive or to define all of those problems for which provision must be made if satisfactory findings are to be obtained. Rather, the immediate purpose of this discussion is to direct attention to certain general considerations that seem to be of basic importance in such studies as a preliminary to a report of the author's clinical and experimental studies of hypnotic amnesia. The objective of these studies was primarily an extensive observation of the general characteristics, forms, and varieties of hypnotic amnesia, rather that an attempt to define presumably possible behavior in terms of a precisely controlled situation. By such observational studies it was felt than one might obtain a more extensive knowledge of the possible manifestations of hypnotic amnesia, which could then more readily permit the devising of experimental situations offering better provision for the nature of the phenomena under study and for a more precise definition of the behavior elicited.*

*Editor's Note: Erickson's examples in this unpublished paper were edited and assimilated into the last paper of this section, "Varieties of hypnotic amnesia," coauthored by the editor in 1974.

8. The Problem of Amnesia in Waking and Hypnotic States

Milton H. Erickson

In the experience of this author, which extends over 40 years, amnesia as a phenomenon of hypnosis is of three varieties—all of which have their counterparts in the ordinary state of conscious awareness. The primary differences between hypnotically induced amnesias and those of everyday life are that the former can be intentionally controlled or directed by others, while those of daily life are not easily amenable to external direction but are dependent upon processes within the person for their manifestation.

Yet, in many ways the development of hypnotic and waking amnesias occurs in much the same way; both types can be spontaneous and directly or indirectly suggested. However, hypnotic amnesias can be determined deliberately and controlled extensively, but not necessarily completely, by someone else. Perhaps the best way of clarifying this subject of hypnotic amnesia, which is much debated and even denied as a phenomenon of actual occurrence by a few critics of hypnosis, is by discussing the various types.

SPONTANEOUS AMNESIAS: WAKING AND HYPNOTIC

Perhaps the best examples of spontaneous amnesias of the waking state are those that occur frequently in the experience of most people. One example is the experience of being introduced to someone, shaking hands and acknowledging the introduction by repeating the person's name, and a moment or so later wondering desperately what that person's name is. Another common experience is asking directions when intent on reaching a certain destination, repeating the directions as they are given, only to wonder a few minutes later at which intersection to turn and whether to turn right or left.

Then there is that common occurrence where a professor carefully specifies to an attentive class the day, the hour, and the room in which the final examination of the course is to be given, only to find members of the

Unpublished manuscript planned with André Weitzenhoffer, circa 1960s.

class a few minutes later in the hallway wrongly debating the hour, the day, and the room specified. This rapidly teaches instructors to say, as a preliminary remark, "Now write this down carefully," before giving such vital information. Even so, students highly interested in the course and fully expectant of a high grade will discover their need later, perhaps by the time they reach the dormitory, to consult their notes in order to know what instructions they had been given.

In all three examples the primary element is something quite different from lack of attentiveness. In the first instance the social gathering is of primary importance—not some stranger's name, no matter how attentively received. In the second instance the reaching of the destination, not the precise noting of distances, is of primary importance. Similarly, in relationship to the predicament of the students the final completion of the course is important, not the hour of the exam, which is usually different from the class hour; not the day, which has no bearing upon the course; not the specified room, which so often is not the regular classroom. We tend to spontaneously forget the parts or details of a situation when we are fixated or motivated by the total Gestalt or major goal of that situation.

Still another type of peculiar and spontaneous waking amnesia is that encountered when asking directions from a stranger for a specific goal well known to that stranger. For example, the author was riding in a car with some colleagues when we arrived at a small town. Our general information was that the meeting we were to attend was being held in a hall across the street from St. Mary's Church. Noting a woman who had just concluded an animated conversation with a gas station attendant, our driver stopped at the curb and, as the woman reached the sidewalk, asked her if she knew where St. Mary's Church was. She answered promptly, "I certainly do. I go there for Mass every Sunday. Just drive straight ahead for exactly one mile, and at the top of the hill there, turn right. It's right near the corner." Our driver thanked her, whereupon she asked curiously why we were going there at that time in the evening. The driver explained that we were attending a medical meeting in a building opposite the church. She replied, "Oh, yes, I know that medical building, but it's not straight across from the church. It's about two houses further down." She was thanked, and our driver drove on two blocks, then stopped the car and declared, "Something is wrong. She was too explicit, too precise, so completely certain in each statement. I'm going back to that gas station and get correct directions."

The gas station attendant was told precisely the directions the woman had given. The man looked puzzled, then his face cleared and he laughed and said, "My wife gave you exactly the right directions, only she must have forgotten she was downtown and not at home. You're headed in the right direction now, but at that stoplight one block down, turn right, go about three blocks, and at the top of the hill you'll see it—the only church there." His directions were correct.

What brings about such an occurrence? *There is a dominance of a well-established item of memory that takes precedence over the incidental, immediate realities of the situation which are spontaneously forgotten* so that a response is made accurately in terms of the well-established memory belonging to a totally different situation. More than once the author has experimentally inquired for directions to the location of a landmark familiar to him. Upon receiving explicit instructions, the author has carefully repeated them with an introduction such as, "Now let's see, we are at the corner of 7th and Wall Street and. . . ." Not infrequently the informant has remarked in astonishment, "Oh, no! I told you the way I usually think. I just forgot for the moment that I was *here,*" and then corrects the previous instructions.

Numerous other instances of spontaneous waking amnesia could be cited, varying in type, but the above should be sufficiently common experiences to establish the reality of this phenomenon. Also, the amnesia can be experimentally elicited without the use of suggestion by evoking processes occurring within the person.

Yet another example of spontaneous everyday amnesia comes to mind. This is best exemplified by the sudden, dismayed remark, "I was just about to say something very important to you. I know it was important—it's been on my mind for an hour—and just as I was about to say it, someone slammed the door, and for the life of me I can't remember it." And they do not, though perhaps an hour, a day, a week, or even months later the specific communication will be inexplicably recalled, perhaps in a dream, perhaps by another sudden slamming of a door, or the occurrence of some specific stimulus evocative of that intended communication. *Here the amnesia is evidently due to the loss of an important associative connection caused by an outer interruption that momentarily distracts the person and "breaks his train of thought."* Then, too, there is the somewhat compable experience of leaving a room and entering another on a specific errand with the frustrating realization that the purpose in mind has vanished upon arrival in that room. One can puzzle and puzzle and not recall, but often a return to the original room and/or a resumption of the interrupted task brings a flash of recollection, which is then laboriously kept in mind while the trip to the other room is successfully repeated. *Here the amnesia is due to a break in important, momentary environmental associative connections because of a sudden loss of the support that the outer situation contributes to the memeory item.*

Both of these last two types of spontaneous waking amnesia can be deliberately induced by the simple expedient of speaking to subjects on some topic unrelated to their thinking or intentions. As they become aware of their amnesia, they might remark exasperatedly, "Now you've broken my train of thought and I can't remember what I was going to say or do." But again, the process is experienced as occurring within the self, not actually induced by the other person except incidentally. Also, in both of these last two types one can often aid the amnesia victim by saying, for example, "You just came out of the kitchen," or "you were just doing (such and such interrupted task) . . ." whereupon, by some inner process, the "broken train of thought" is reestablished.

Yet there are those persons who, for reasons not clear to this author, disclaim the phenomenon of hypnosis as no more than complaisant behavior or as "role-playing," and that the "amnesia" of this so-called hypnosis is nothing more than an "as-if pretense." In other words, the claim of these critics is that a nonexistent phenomenon (hypnosis) so alters the behavior of people that they cannot manifest the same behavior (amnesia) under hypnosis that they spontaneously manifest in the ordinary waking state.

In this author's experience there can be developed in a person a special state of awareness that is termed, for the sake of convenience and historical considerations, *hypnosis* or *trance.* This state is characterized by the subject's ability to retain the same capacities possessed in the waking state and to manifest these capacities in ways possibly, though not necessarily, dissimilar to the usual actions of conscious awareness. *Trance permits the operator to evoke in a controlled manner the same mental mechanisms that are operative spontaneously in everyday life.*

Thus, certain hypnotic subjects may develop without instruction a totally spontaneous amnesia because of an interruption of the ordinary state of awareness by the establishment of a different state of awareness (due to hypnosis, drugs, shock) with no associative connections to the ordinary state of awareness. On arousal from this special state and return to the usual state of consciousness there will frequently be an amnesia for the events that transpired during the special state [see the "state-bound" theory presented in the next paper]. One might consider the hypnotic state marked by a total amnesia—a phenomenon this author has found can last for 40 years—as an intrustion of a special state of awareness into the ordinary state to which it has no relationship or associative connections. It is similar to the common situation in life when one may drive automatically through heavy traffic so intently interested in a conversation with a companion that the arrival at the destination becomes a total surprise, and there is no recollection of having stopped at red lights or of being delayed at police-patrolled intersections. The only proof of competent driving is the safe arrival without a citation. *The absorbing conversation was a special state that precluded any memory of irrelevant details of the situation in which it took place.*

These examples indicate that there can be separate states of awareness that develop spontaneously in ordinary life: they are independent of each other, and can give rise to a total amnesia. If this can occur spontaneously, why then should there be any doubt that similar situations can be set up psychologically in order deliberately and intentionally to evoke hypnotic amnesias?

In addition to total spontaneous hypnotic amnesia there may be a partial spontaneous amnesia in which the recollections are unclear and vague, such as, "You had me read something—maybe it was a book—I'm not even sure it wasn't writing—something about something blue." A year later the subject—without further hypnosis, but upon being reminded of something we did last year—might very well reply, "Oh, yes, something about a book or writing, maybe something about a color." This has occurred whether or not the person was used as an hypnotic subject in the meantime.

There can also occur a spontaneous selective amnesia in which only certain events are remembered—just as in the ordinary waking state some people always remember either the pleasant or the unpleasant aspects of past occasions, but not the total event.

In subsequent trances, however, a full recollection of the previous trances could occur, but again and again the same selective spontaneous amnesias and the same spontaneous recollections would also occur. Repeated efforts have failed to discover the reasons for such selectiveness, since the amnesia involves minor, unimportant matters as frequently as it involves major matters.

Another item of interest is the inconstancy of spontaneous amnesia as a phenomenon. Only a few subjects consistently develop a spontaneous amnesia. The great majority of such subjects are likely at times to have spontaneous recall either immediately or later. There seems to be no known way of predicting in advance what will occur in any individual trance situation or for any particular subject. The same is true of subjects showing spontaneous selective amnesia and partial amnesia as is true of those showing complete spontaneous amnesia. They may manifest on one occasion a complete spontaneous amnesia; at another time only partial amnesia is present; at still other times an immediate or delayed recall, either partial or complete, will appear.

Predictions as to trance outcome can be made only at a statistical level for repeated trances in the same subject. However, continued experience with a single subject often provides minimal cues that, when perceived by the sensitive operator, can lead to fairly accurate predictions.

DIRECT SUGGESTIONS FOR AMNESIA

Amnesia resulting from direct suggestion is a phenomenon that occurs in everyday life most commonly in relation to children, though it also occurs in relation to adults. One of the most typical examples involving children would be the case of the child who comes dashing into the house to complain bitterly about a violent disagreement with a favorite playmate and is told casually but sagaciously by the parent, "Oh, forget it and go out and have a good time with Milly." An hour later, when the child is questioned at length, one frequently discovers that the child reacted literally as told and even looks blankly as the playmate relates the quarrel. Upon hearing the story retold, there is often a slow recovery of the forgotten quarrel.

A typical example of this type of amnesia among adults is the situation that occurs within a social group dining out in a restaurant. When the tab arrives, one of the group usually says, "Oh, forget it, *boys*. This is on me." Then, if the group goes for a social hour after the dinner to the home of someone other than the man who paid the bill, the various guests can be casually asked, "Who paid for the dinner?" Frequently the answer is, "I was going to, and so was everybody else, but I just don't remember who did. I only know I didn't pay the bill." However, if the wives present are asked, they invariably remember (they are not one of the *boys)*. Also significant is the fact that if the social gathering is held at the home of the man who paid the bill, the dinner host is usually remembered without fail.

In teaching nurses, social service workers, postgraduate psychology students, medical students, interns, and residents in psychiatry, a certain experiment has been conducted repeatedly both verbally, and by mimeographed material. The procedure is simple. One selects 10 or 20 items of any subject matter judged to be of equal value. All of these items are explained in equal detail, but to the explanation of some items there is added the casual statement, "This is just for your general knowledge, so you can forget about it now."

This can also be carried out in written form, using mimeographed sheets with that parenthetical statement appended to the chosen item. The experiment can then be repeated in many different ways: using different groups of subjects and altering the choice of item for each group; repeating the same procedure both verbally and with mimeographed material; and by using different sets of comparable items, with one item always marked by that casual admonition. Tests given on the various series of the items always show a higher percentage of failure on the item carrying the instruction to forget it for both instances of verbal or mimeographed presentation.

A comparable experiment was conducted in which the casual statement was appended parenthetically to one item: "This is for your general information, and now that you know it you might as well remember it." Tests given some three months later yielded higher percentages of recall on this item. This experiment was repeated many times with different groups of subjects, always with similar results.

It was also observed that if the tests were given too close together in time, the admonition to forget or to remember would be remembered from the previous occasion. Under these circumstances the admonition to forget had an opposite effect and the one to remember led to even higher percentages of remembering. Over the long period of years during which the author taught, there was adequate opportunity in which to space these experiments over relatively long intervals.

Still another type of direct suggestion witnessed by the author on more than one occasion concerns a group of teenagers at a local hangout. A police officer, sensing something about to happen, authoritatively says, "All right, boys, break it up and move along." More than once the author has subsequently questioned one of the dispersed gang and received the resentful reply to the effect that they were planning some fun when the cop came around and spoiled their plan. When asked what the proposed fun was, quite frequently a surprised look followed by one of resentment developed, and the answer given was, "I just got so damn mad that I forgot what it was."

Interviews with teenagers who have a tendency toward delinquency have frequently elicited the complaint, "We were just minding our own business planning something when Old Baldy [the high school principal] came along and said, 'No loitering in the corridor. Just forget what you're about to do and go to your respective classes.'" Asked what had been planned, the reply would be, in effect, "It was plenty sharp, but Old Baldy got me so mad that I can't remember."

In the ordinary state of awareness, then, direct suggestion can be given to elicit amnesias. In this author's experience, however, such suggestions are most effective if given in a casual, nonrepetitive fashion and under circumstances involving some form of increased emotion. Too frequent a repetition of the word *forget* will usually have the opposite effect. Thus, when the following conditions were present and mimeographed material was given to the subjects, the opposite of what had been admonished would occur: The item chosen for them to forget was prefaced by the statement, "This item you may forget if you wish, since it is only for your general information," followed by the material chosen for them to forget. The admonition was repeated at the end of the test. Repetition of the instruction to forget produced a better recollection of it than of the other "neutral" items. In this way direct suggestion to forget in the ordinary waking state can be effective—particularly if it is given in a casual manner.

Moreover, such forgetting is characterized by considerable difficulty in recall. The person usually "puts it out of mind," and when told to remember "that which is forgotten," responds with a blank and wondering look. However, if the material that is amnesic is identified in part, there is an immediate and complete recall often followed by the explanation, "Do you know, that slipped my mind completely."

In hypnosis the matter of direct suggestion to forget is of another character. It can be given directly, emphatically, and repetitiously as a specific instruction rather than as an incidental, casual admonition or suggestion. Furthermore, the amnesia that develops is effective in both the trance state as well as posthypnotically. For example, a female subject may be told to forget what she had eaten for breakfast that morning. As she accepts the suggestion, she can then be questioned by naming a variety of possible foods, among them those she actually did have for breakfast. She may reject each one readily, or she may thoughtfully consider each one and recall previous occasions on which certain items were eaten. But those of the morning's breakfast are not recognized. They do not "come to mind" when mentioned as they do in the waking state. Additionally, the duration of the directly suggested amnesia can often be easily determined, and its recovery can be made contingent upon any chosen cue or even a minimal nonpertinent stimulus at some later time. This is not true of the forgetting that occurs in the waking state.

Then, too, such a recovered memory can be hypnotically abolished immediately upon a direct request—almost an absurdity in the waking state. It can also be abolished by minimal nonpertinent posthypnotic cues which can be repeated indefinitely. Such amnesias are dependent upon external stimuli rather than upon inner associative processes.

INDIRECT SUGGESTIONS FOR AMNESIA

A remarkable anecdote taken from a clinical case history best illustrates indirectly suggested hypnotic amnesia. A rather paranoid patient of the author's kept his Monday appointment, stating in belligerent, obscene, and profane language that he wanted no further nonsensical efforts at psychotherapy. He wanted a deep hypnotic trance induced without any further evasion or delay.

The author's response, as the patient seated himself in a chair, was to lean back comfortably in his own chair and in a soft voice, slowly, gently offer suggestions of increasing relaxation, fatigue, sleepiness, and the development of a deep, sound hypnotic trance.

Irately the patient leaned forward with his hands on his knees, scornfully denounced the author as being idiotic in using "that soft, gentle voice of yours," and demanded instantly that a strong authoritarian technique be used. Unconcerned, the author continued his "soft, gentle technique" uninterrupted by the continuously repeated demands of the patient for the next 50 minutes. Then the author glanced openly at the clock and sat up to dismiss the patient. Bitterly the patient commented on another "wasted hour," declaring that the whole procedure was a total failure and that he could remember everything the author had so stupidly said. At this point the author said, in the same gentle, soft voice, "Naturally you heard everything I said here in the office, and you remember it here in the office. You are sitting within six feet of me, and so here in the office you remember everything I said. Your next appointment will be the usual hour on Wednesday." Still in a rage the patient left after a few more caustic remarks.

The next Wednesday he was carefully met in the waiting room, not the office. In a puzzled manner he asked, "Did I keep my Monday appointment?" The author replied, "Naturally, if you kept your appointment on Monday, you would remember it!"

He then explained that on Monday he had found himself sitting in his car outside his apartment, trying to remember if he had just come back from the university or from the author's office. He did not know how long he sat there debating with himself, but he was sure it was a long time. Finally he looked at his watch and realized that it was definitely more than an hour later than the scheduled appointment. Again he asked if he had kept his appointment, and the same reply was given.

The author led the way into the office, and as the patient stepped over the threshold into the office, he declared irately, "I did too keep my Monday appointment, and you wasted the whole hour and charged me for it, with that soft, gentle technique!" He had much more to say and did so emphatically. When he finished, the author casually remarked, "There's a magazine in the other room I want you to look at." Obediently, the patient followed the author out of the office, only to repeat in full the foregoing scene, with the author giving the same replies. Upon reentry of the office, the behavior of a few minutes before was repeated. The same casual comment about a magazine was again made, and upon returning to the waiting room there was yet another repetition of the amnesic behavior.

A return to the office elicited the same response a third time, but as he concluded the patient added in astonishment, "Why this is the third time I've remembered keeping my Monday appointment!" Instantly the author replied, "Naturally, here in the office you remember."

The patient then became interested in his out-of-the-office amnesia and promptly stepped out of the room. Hesitantly he paused and with embarrassment turned around to remark, "I can't understand why I found myself walking backward toward your office. But I am puzzled to know if I kept my Monday appointment." He was invited to come into the office, and he immediately declared, "I wasn't backing into your office. I was going out to see if I could remember out there if I kept my Monday appointment, but I didn't. Now I'm going to back out of the office and see what happens."

This he did, and just outside the door he asked, "Will it be all right if I come in now? I'm curious about my Monday appointment." He was invited to enter and immediately said, "I remember everything in here—why that's what you said! 'Here in the office you can remember everything!' And I thought you weren't hypnotizing me, and I was mad at you because I thought you were failing me. But you must have put me in a trance and given me a posthypnotic amnesia. I wonder if it still works." With that he stepped outside the office, turned around, looked at his watch, and said, "I guess I'm about twenty minutes late. All the way here I've been trying to remember if I kept my Monday appointment."

He was invited into the office, developed full recollection, and said, "That settles it. I apologize for my rudeness last Monday. And I do have a posthypnotic amnesia outside this office. You must have thought me some kind of fool bouncing back and forth, forgetting out there, remembering in here, then forgetting out there again. From now on you do therapy on me any damn way you want to. It's plain you know more about me than I do."

Since then the patient has developed a complete amnesia for the entire matter. Several times he has inquired if the therapist thought hypnosis would be of any value, and he has readily acceded to the author's negation. From that day on steady therapeutic progress was made.

Hypnotic amnesias can be given time limits that are not possible in the ordinary waking state. An example is that of a student repeatedly hypnotized during the author's senior year in medical school. This subject was unable to develop a spontaneous amnesia, but he could develop amnesia upon direct suggestion. He had sought hypnotherapy by the author, who at that time was working under the joint supervision of the departments of psychology, psychiatry, and pharmacology and a psychiatrist-lawyer, all of whom acted as his sponsors to prevent the Dean of the College of Liberal Arts from expelling him for daring to deal with the black art of hypnosis.

This particular student was seeking therapy for stuttering. It was discovered that in the trance state he spoke fluently. A posthypnotic suggestion for a total amnesia of all trance experiences was offered as an experimental measure and out of curiousity following the first few trances, during which an effort had been made to secure a history of his stuttering. No therapeutic progress was made with the patient, but he was insistent upon continuing and expressed a willingness to be an experimental subject for the author to compensate him for the hoped-for therapy.

Accordingly, because of the author's interest in hypnotic amnesia, the following direct suggestions were offered: That he develop a complete amnesia for all trance experiences; that he visit the author socially once a week for the remainder of the month; and that he develop a deep trance each time he talked fluently.

Two more social visits occurred, and upon opening the door the student spontaneously developed a deep trance, awakening only as he left the author's apartment. On each of these visits he offered the information that he had not been stuttering since he had been instructed to have a waking amnesia for trance experiences.

On the last visit, while in a profound trance, he was told that the author was leaving Madison for an internship in Colorado and thus might not see him again for a period of a year—perhaps many years—and since an amnesia for his trance experiences seemed to correct his stuttering, he might as well continue to maintain that amnesia for all hypnotic work. Additionally, he was given the posthypnotic suggestion, "On the occasion of our next meeting, no matter where or when, as we greet each other with a handshake, you will immediately develop a profound trance state so that I can ask you a few questions." To this he readily agreed.

Approximately nine years later the author called upon another hypnotic subject who was then the city editor for a daily paper in Madison. As the author was about to enter the editor's office, his former stuttering patient came rushing out on an assignment, recognized the author at once, extended his hand in greeting, and developed a deep trance state. A hasty social visit with him occurred, and he explained that he was a reporter for the paper and on a rush assignment. Special inquiry elicited that he had maintained his amnesia and that he had not stuttered in the past nine years. He was told to "keep up the good work" and to continue his amnesia.

During the visit with the editor, mention was made of meeting Jimmy just before entering the office. The editor remarked, "I didn't know you knew him. He is our prize reporter, and I just sent him out on a big story that has to be covered fast." The author then asked the editor if Jimmy stuttered. The editor was astonished by the question and stated, "In the five years he has worked for me, he has never stuttered, and I know him thoroughly. He's my prize man. Did you know him before?" An evasive reply was made, and the editor was asked if his wife was still as opposed to hypnosis as she had been nine years previously. He replied, "Oh, yes, Nan never got over her prejudices, but now and then I call at Herb's office [Herb was a classmate of the author's and was Nan's brother], and he puts me in a trance to relax me. You know, being the city editor is not the most relaxing job you can have, especially when big news stories break fast." Just why or how a posthypnotic amnesia served to effect a correction of stuttering is completely inexplicable. But then, much psychopathology is also completely inexplicable.

This is not the only case. Another Wisconsin student had sought out the author, explaining that he was a bad stutterer and that he hoped hypnosis could be used to correct it. He had undergone much speech therapy in various schools but without any good effect. In fact, he felt that his condition had worsened, and he was having much difficulty in his premedical course work. All of this constituted a serious handicap for him, and he earnestly pleaded for at least a trial at therapy. He was told that the author was leaving Madison within two weeks to take up his internship and had barely time to teach him how to go into hypnosis. Upon his insistence, however, hypnosis was attempted, and he was found to be an easy somnambulistic subject with complete spontaneous amnesia. He was deeply hypnotized on four occasions, and each time he talked fluently in the trance state. Because of the author's clinical ignorance as to what to do in the way of therapy, the following suggestion was offered: That since he really knew how to forget his trance experiences when in the state of conscious awareness, and since he could talk fluently in the trance state, he might undertake to spend the summer putting his stuttering into his unconscious mind and replacing it with the fluent speech of the trance state, all the while maintaining his total amnesia of trance experiences.

Some 13 years later a patient walked into the author's office bearing a letter of referral from this former premedical student, stating that he had failed in his psychoanalytic therapy of the patient but that hypnotherapy might be of value. This was the author's first knowledge of what had become of that premedical student. A few years later, when lecturing at a psychoanalytic institute, one of the psychoanalysts came up and introduced himself. It was the former premedical student. Inquiry was made about the progress of the patient referred, and the author cautiously inquired why he had referred that patient. The analyst stated that he had long followed the author's publications and that his own frustration with the patient had led him to wonder if another type of therapy might be of value.

Since the analyst was speaking fluently, he was even more cautiously asked if he and the author had ever met before. He replied with a laugh that the author probably would not remember, but the last year the author had been in medical school, he had consulted with him about a bad stammer with which he had then been afflicted. The author effected to recall vaguely and asked if his analysis had corrected the stammer. The astonishing reply was, "No, it just naturally disappeared that summer." Thereupon he was asked what his own psychoanalysis had revealed about the past in relation to the stammering. The reply was made, "That was one area of my life that has been completely blacked out, and I'm not really interested in ever learning anything at all about it." He was asked if this was an emotionally based attitude. He answered, "Well, it might be, but I haven't stuttered since that summer. During my analysis I became curious about it, but nothing ever came through."

As if to change the subject, the author asked what interest the analyst had in hypnosis. His reply was that he was entirely content with psychoanalysis and did not have any interest at all in hypnosis except that for some unknown reason he was extremely interested in the author's publications and that he had continued to read them during the time of his analysis despite his analyst's objections. He had never withheld this fact from his analyst, but neither of them had ever uncovered the source of his peculiar interest in the author's, and only the author's, publications on hypnosis. Thereupon he introduced the author to his analyst, who remarked, "I've often wanted to meet you since John always violated my instructions in relation to you and your writings. What is the relationship between the two of you?" My reply was simply, "Well, we both were at the University of Wisconsin at the same time one year, and we are both interested in human behavior." Since then, despite other referrals and some casual meetings at conventions, nothing further has developed.

One can only futilely speculate on what did occur in this particular patient—not only therapeutically, but also in relation to the significance of the hypnosis, the spontaneous amnesia, and the remarkable known persistence of that amnesia from 1928 to the time of our last meeting in 1958. It also gives rise to a number of questions concerning psychoanalysis as an exploratory,, investigatory, or evocative modality, since the man underwent three years of "therapeutic" psychoanalysis and two years of "controlled" psychoanalysis without recall of his hypnotic experiences.

9. Varieties of Hypnotic Amnesia

Milton H. Erickson and Ernest L. Rossi

This paper is a condensation and synthesis of three unpublished efforts by Milton H. Erickson during the years 1936 to 1970 to illustrate his studies of hypnotic amnesia in clinical and naturalistic settings. The complexity of hypnotic amnesia, long recognized by Erickson as a result of such studies, has become established fact during the ensuing years of controlled laboratory investigations. There still remains a stark contrast between the results obtained in clinical and laboratory settings, however. A recent interview (Cooper, 1972) of the research literature on hypnotic amnesia summarizes this problem by stating, "What needs yet to be done is to systematize and carefully record the important factors in the clinical situation, and then study their influence in a clinical laboratory setting; that is, a laboratory setting in which the clinical factors are maximally operative (p. 252)."

As a contribution to recording "the important factors in the clinical situation" a number of Erickson's original studies illustrating the varieties of hypnotic amnesia will be presented together with some of his innovations in producing amnesia. These studies were chosen because they illustrate the complex behavior that may result from investigative work where the clinician is able to explore and utilize the individuality of each patient to enhance the development of hypnotic amnesia. They disclose interesting mental phenomena which are usually overlooked in the usual experimental situation. These phenomena may also account for some of the unreliable findings of the typically standardized and statistical approach, where the significance of individual differences and the psychodynamics of each individual trance situation are presumably neutralized or controlled rather than directly utilized, as they can be in the clinical situation.

A case will then be made for conceptualizing hypnotic amnesia in clinical practice as "state-bound." We will conclude with a summary of the very important place of amnesia in hypnotherapy.

Reprinted with permission from *The American Journal of Clinical Hypnosis,* April, 1974, Vol. 16, No. 4.

AMNESIA FLUCTUATING IN TIME AND PLACE

Amnesia by Distraction

Example 1. This first example centers about a subject who had often been used for demonstration purposes and who occasionally delighted in deliberately recalling past hypnotic experiences to prove that there was no such thing as hypnotic amnesia. One morning Erickson found him relating to Erickson's secretary a detailed account of the hypnotic demonstration in which the subject had been used the previous evening. Erickson's appearance somewhat embarrassed him, but he was immediately reassured that Erickson would be most interested in discovering how adequately he could recall those events. Thereupon, directing his full attention to Erickson, the subject proceeded to give a remarkably complete account of the entire demonstration. During his running narrative Erickson's secretary, without the subject's knowledge, took complete notes. Several days later Erickson gave the typewritten account to the subject with the request that he read and correct it. As was discovered later, he understood Erickson's request to mean merely that he was to proofread a manuscript, a task he had often performed for Erickson. After reading for several minutes he suddenly remarked, "This is most interesting." Since Erickson could not understand his comment, he made no reply. The subject continued his reading and then expressed the wish that he could have seen the demonstration and that he would like to know who the subject was. Not fully comprehending these remarks, Erickson evasively replied that it was just one of his hypnotic subjects.

On a subsequent occasion he was handed the same manuscript to read, but he immediately recognized it as one he had already read. Upon Erickson's insistence, however, he reread it, remarking that it was sufficiently interesting to be worth reading a second time, but he was obviously rather curious about Erickson's insistence. This same procedure was repeated on several more occasions, but it succeeded only in arousing his curiosity as to Erickson's purpose. He even advanced the idea that Erickson was trying indirect suggestion on him so that he himself might give a similar demonstration sometime. At no time did he become aware that it was an account of his own hypnotic experience.

On a still later occasion Erickson rehypnotized him deeply and questioned him about what had happened to him in reference to that specific demonstration. He immediately manifested a full understanding of the total situation and simply explained that after his narration of that experience he had forgotten it completely at a conscious waking level. Hence he had been able to read the typewritten account with the full conscious belief that it concerned someone else. When asked if that amnesia at a conscious level of awareness would persist in the future, he replied that it probably would unless Erickson gave him instructions to the contrary.

No such instructions were given, and, although the subject has since spontaneously recalled various experiences of subsequent trances, this particular amnesia still persists. Nor has additional reading of the account done more than remind him of his previous readings.

To summarize, a hypnotic subject recalled in detail a prolonged hypnotic experience and described it adequately to others. Subsequently he developed a spontaneous amnesia, not only for the hypnotic experience itself, but also for the conscious waking experience of recalling and verbalizing it. This amnesia persisted, and even the record of his performance aroused no memories. Nevertheless, in a new trance state full understanding was found, but in the subsequent waking state the amnesia was again present.

A spontaneous amnesia together with full recall of trance events in another trance constitutes the classical evidence for hypnotic amnesia; there is a continuity of memory from one trance to another and from one awake state to another, but there is an amnesia between trance and awake state. What is unusual in this account is the fact that the subject apparently had a full memory of all trance events in the awake state until he developed a spontaneous amnesia at a later time.

The relevance of this example of hypnotic amnesia developing at a later time, after a full recall of all trance events had taken place in the awake state, for experimental work is obvious. The typical research design testing for hypnotic amnesia immediately upon trance termination misses the spontaneous and suggested amnesias that develop at a later time.

Erickson, in fact, makes it a routine practice not to talk to the patient about trance events immediately upon awakening. The trance state persists for a few moments after the appearance of wakefulness. Questioning during this period frequently permits full recall. Erickson typically engages the patient in casual conversations, anecdotes, and shaggy dog stories very remote from the hypnotic experience for a while after trance termination to effect an *amnesia by distraction.* Alternatively Erickson will sometimes "rush" a patient out of the office to avoid talk about trance. He will distract and do just about anything he can to make the waking situation very different from the trance situation and thus promote amnesia.

Amnesia by Indirect Suggestion

Example 2. Another example illustrating the development of a suggested amnesia at a later time and place after the subject had actually rehearsed all trance events in the awake state is as follows:

A professional psychologist related to Erickson her history of failing to go into a deep trance with a number of different hypnotherapists. She claimed that an amnesia for all trance events would be a satisfactory criterion of trance depth. She very much wanted to be surprised by her amnesia. Erickson acknowledged her story with the compound waking suggestion, "You haven't failed this time since we haven't started yet." This is a favorite approach with Erickson: The suggestion contained in the first half of the sentence, "You haven't failed this time," tends to be accepted when associated with the obvious truth of what follows, "since we haven't started yet."

Erickson then proceeded to fixate her attention: "You haven't looked at this glass paperweight before, therefore you don't know what effect it will have on a deep trance." This is another compound suggestion: This time an obvious truth is in the first half of the sentence, with a suggestion implying deep trance in the second half. Erickson then proceeded with a typical induction which included a 20-minute period during which the psychologist was instructed to go deeper all by herself. Immediately upon awakening the dialogue went as follows:

Subject: I was in a pretty deep trance, but I remember everything.
Erickson: Isn't that all right?
Subject: I expected an amnesia.
Erickson: When?
Subject: Immediately.
Erickson: Is it necessary that it happen immediately? Won't you be surprised when you find it has happened?

Thus Erickson implied the possibility of a later amnesia by the indirect suggestions contained in his questions. His last comment, "won't you be surprised . . ." is an effort to utilize her expressed wish to experience a surprise.

The psychologist then verbalized all trance events to prove she had no amnesia and actually rehearsed them on her long drive home from Arizona to California. On arriving home she began writing a letter to Erickson stating she still recalled all trance events but left the letter unfinished when she went to bed. The next morning she awakened with an amnesia for all trance events, even though she recalled that she had been to Arizona to visit Erickson.

It will be noted that while this was a suggested amnesia, it was indirectly suggested. This type of indirectly suggested amnesia is vastly more effective for clinical purposes than the baldly asserted direct suggestions used in most experimental work *(e.g.,* the Stanford Hypnotic Susceptibility Scale, Form A, uses the following direct suggestions: "You will have difficulty in remembering; you will have no desire to try to recall . . ."). When such direct suggestions had been used in this patient's previous hypnosis work with other therapists, they were conspicuously ineffective in producing amnesia.

The reason for the greater effectiveness of indirect suggestions may be formulated as follows: In most trances some consciousness is invariably present in the form of an observer attitude; the subject is in part lost in the experience, but in part the ego is quietly observing what is happening, just as it can in dreams (Rossi, 1972 a, b).

When a direct suggestion for amnesia is given, the observing ego takes note of it, just as it quietly takes note of most direct suggestions. Having noted the suggestion, the ego later has the power of choice as to whether or not the suggestion shall be carried out. When the subject has this awareness of a suggestion, he can debate with himself regarding its merits and decide about carrying it out. When a suggestion is made indirectly, however, even the observing ego tends to miss the fact that a suggestion has been given. With little or no awareness of the suggestion there is little or no ability to debate and negate it. Indirectly administered suggestions are programmed more easily into preconscious or unconscious levels and can then emerge more naturally in the patient's ordinary course of behavior.

Amnesic Material in Dreams

Example 3. This example concerns a graduate nurse who was hypnotized on many occasions and invariably had a spontaneous amnesia for all trance events. Even the reading of a full stenographic account of her trance behavior would not awaken a sense of recognition for the items described. Upon being rehypnotized, she would disclose a full recollection of the hypnotic experience, but upon awakening the amnesia would again become manifest.

One day this subject approached Erickson and reported that she had a most interesting dream and proceeded to give an adequate account of a previous hypnotic demonstration before a group. Full notes made of her dream and subsequently compared with the stenographic account of that demonstration proved the correctness of her dream account.

Uncertain as to her purpose in such a communication, Erickson inquired cautiously as to the possible relationship of this dream to hypnosis. She explained that she always dreamed quite vividly for some nights following hyponotic trances, but this was the first occasion on which she had had so extensive and interesting a dream. Further questioning disclosed her to be entirely sincere in her belief that her account was only a dream and that Erickson would naturally be interested in it for psychiatric reasons. Asked why she knew her account to be a dream and not the recovered memory of a forgotten trance, she explaiend that dreams are characterized by a quality of unreality. This unreality permitted unreasonable things to occur. And in her dream she and Erickson had been alone in a large room in which there had suddenly and inexplicably appeared an inconstant audience which came and went, or grew large or small for no apparent reason, and which sometimes included people she knew definitely could not have been at a hypnotic demonstration.

No effort was made to explain that these peculiarities of the audience, as the stenographic account itself disclosed, really resulted from the hypnotic suggestions she had been given.

For some time the subject was encouraged to report her dreams. Further investigation disclosed that in the trance state she had an adequate understanding of her dreams as indirect recoveries of trance memories. However, specific hypnotic instruction had to be given for her to recall in the waking state both the trance experience and the dream revival of it before she could go through a slow process of fusing them into a single understanding.

In summary, this hypnotic subject developed spontaneous amnesia for trance experiences but spontaneously recovered that amnesic material in the form of dreams. She thus had a complete amnesia for one experience (trance) and a full awareness of an entirely different kind of an experience (dream) with an identical content.

Example 4. Another subject was found who reviewed in her dreams many events of the trance session. She was aware, however, of the nature of her dreams and purposely utilized dream activity to overcome hypnotic amnesia. Her explanation was that she had an intense curiosity about what occurred in trance, but her hypnotic amnesia had constituted an effective barrier until she spontaneously dreamed about a trance session and recalled the dream the next morning. In reviewing the dream she became aware that it was a valid recollection of trance events. Thereafter, whenever she wished to know what she had done in a trance state, she circumvented the hypnotic amnesia by dream activity.

Further investigation disclosed that her dreams were much less extensive than the first subject's, and that the dream content related only to those things of most interest to her. When this was pointed out to her by having her read a complete stenographic account which contained much material she did not recall, she responded that night with a more extensive dream. In this dream she recovered approximately all of the details of another trance experience.

The behavior of these subjects who circumvented hypnotic amnesia by dream revivals is most informative. It strongly suggests that neuro- and psychophysiological processes of normal sleep can be employed as a medium by which to gain access to experiences not available to the waking state. Hence, the assumption seems justified that extensive neuro- and psychophysiological processes are involved in hypnosis and in hypnotic amnesia.

Amnesia by the Displacement and Distortion of Memories

Example 5. This example concerns an investigation of suggested hypnotic amnesia in an informal setting. The subject, in a deep trance, was instructed that after awakening he was to smoke a special Russian cigarette which would be furnished at a given cue. Upon lighting the cigarette he was to join enthusiastically in the general conversation with those present. Upon finishing the cigarette he was to extinguish the butt and then develop a complete amnesia for all occurrences between the giving of the cue and the discarding of the cigarette.

This sequence of events developed as intended, and notes were made of the subject's behavior and the topics of conversation. For some minutes after disposing of his cigarette the subject seemed to be self-absorbed. These few minutes of self-absorption may be understood as a spontaneously generated posthypnotic trance (Erickson & Erickson, 1941), which was required for the profound neuropsychological changes to effect the suggested amnesia. Then, suddenly, he joined in the conversation of the group. Shortly the topic of smoking was raised, the subject was questioned about his habits, and then, in a progressive and systematic fashion, he was questioned more and more closely about the events of the presumably amnesic period.

At first no evidence of any recollections could be secured from him, but after some 30 minutes of insistent questioning with extensive use of the notes made, particularly those relating his expressed opinions on controversial topics, the subject suddenly began to recover his memories of the entire period. When an adequate recall finally had been obtained, he was asked to account for his previous failures to recognize items that had suddenly become familiar. He proceeded by offering various rationalizations and then began to insist, with obvious sincerity, that he had not experienced amnesia at all. He claimed he had merely simulated it by evading questions, misunderstanding remarks, and by deliberate suppression. Checking these assertions against the notations that had been made of his actual behavior, however, suggested the probability of a retrospective falsification.

The experiment was then apparently discontinued, and more than an hour was spent in casual conversation on other topics. Finally references were again made to the events of the amnesic period. It was immediately apparent that the subject was confused by such references, and he was again amnesic for the entire period between lighting and extinguishing his cigarette. This second amnesia also included the questioning that led to the breakdown of the original amnesia and all his assertions and rationalizations about it.

The subject now believed that on another occasion three months earlier, in a different social group (that included only one of the present group) and under entirely different circumstances, he had smoked a Russian cigarette while discussing the conversational topics about which he had just been questioned. Extensive inquiry about this new belief disclosed that the content of the amnesic experience had been displaced in time and setting; it had been interpolated into an older and different experience. In this new belief the subject could not be shaken.

In summary, this subject developed an extensive amnesia, recovered the amnesic material under mass social stimulation, and then unaccountably developed another amnesia that included both the original material and the associated experience of recovering it. He then recovered the original amnesic material through a total displacement of it onto an entirely different past experience.

On the surface this subject's amnesia sounds a bit like hypnotic "source amnesia" (Evans & Thorn, 1966), wherein the subject can recall material learned in trance but forgets that he learned it under hypnosis. Source amnesia has been frequently contrasted in the recent research literature with the more conventional "recall amnesia." In one unusually protracted period of naturalistic observation Erickson explored the dynamics of both recall and source amnesia; he made an extensive effort to discern exactly what happens to the amnesic material and some of the factors effecting its recall.

Example 6. This man, 25 years old, of superior intelligence and decidedly capable as a hypnotic subject, had been used on many occasions for both experimental and demonstration purposes. After extensive experience he developed the firm belief, expressed privately to others rather than Erickson, that hypnotic amnesia was entirely a matter of voluntary suppression of memories and of deliberate redirection of attention to other thoughts. In support of this conviction he frequently recalled and related secretly to his friends accounts of his trance experiences. Chance discovery by Erickson of this practice suggested the possibility of naturalistic investigation of hypnotic amnesia free from the handicaps and limitations of an artifial laboratory setting and the distortion of results that might arise from purposeful cooperation by the subject.

Accordingly, arrangements were made with his friends to report in detail to Erickson any of the subject's accounts of his trance experiences. These could then be checked against the original complete stenographic record usually made of this subject's hypnotic work, sometimes without his knowledge. Most of the 23 observers who participated in this study were college-educated, and in addition the majority were trained in psychology, medicine, or psychiatry.

The findings obtained by this procedure varied greatly as a function of the associative situations, the subject's relation to the observers, and the intrinsic interest the subject had in the trance experiences. Time itself did not seem to be important, and the type of material, whether emotional or nonemotional, did not seem to have any remarkable effect. For convenience the results will be discussed under seven headings.

1. Recall of trance events dependent upon associative situation.

While often a remarkably complete account of a hypnotic session could be obtained, it was found that the completeness of this depended upon certain factors. The closer the subject was to the trance situation in the matter of associations, the more extensive was the account. The most extensive accounts were obtained by observers present or believed by the subject to have been present at the time of the trance, and when the subject was interviewed in the actual physical setting in which the trance state had been induced and the trance behavior elicited. An account secured in the same room where the trance had taken place was more complete than one secured in a similar room. The same building permitted a more adequate account than a totally different physical setting; similarly, observers actually present during the trance were given more complete accounts than those not present. Time itself, within reasonable limits, did not seem to be a significant factor. Furthermore, an account elicited in the physical setting of the trance situation by an observer present at that time could not be secured in the same detail subsequently by the same observer if the questions were repeated in a situation other than the trance setting. Yet, upon return to the trance setting the same observer could obtain a repetition of the first detailed account. Repeated efforts served to confirm this observation.

2. Variation in recall with different observers.

Accounts given to different observers separately often varied extensively in details. When a repetition of an account was called for in the presence of two or more observers to whom the account had already been related separately, there was usually a recovery of still further material but without awareness that more was being related. Occasionally, however, the account would be definitely abbreviated and the subject would not remember details previously related to one or the other or both of the observers separately. The subject was not aware of these discrepancies. There were frequently omissions which seemed to be definitely associated with one or another of the observers. In the presence of certain persons the subject seemed to be unable to recall certain items readily accessible in the presence of other persons.

3. Substitution of detailed partial accounts for total recall.

Another frequent finding was the substitution of an extremely detailed recollection of minor details for a comprehensive account of the total trance events with no realization by the subject that other activities had occurred. For example, a remarkably vivid detailed account was given of a checker game with no apparent evidence of awareness of the wealth of other activities that had preceded and followed the checker game.

4. Telescoping of two or more events or sessions.

Often the events of several different trance sessions, separated by as much as a period of a week, would be recounted as the narrative of one single trance session. Especially was this true when the trances had been induced in the same general physical setting. For example, in telescoping into a single account the events of two separate trances, the subject described his activities in relation to two persons. His account of the actual activities was accurate in all details, except for the fact that one of the two persons had left the hospital a week before the other had arrived, hence his account placing them together in the same room was obviously inaccurate. Confronted with this fact the subject slowly realized its truth but nevertheless continued to "remember clearly" making certain remarks to one of them and making other remarks to the other sitting in an adjacent chair. Checking of the original records disclosed that he had made the remarks he claimed and that he did remember correctly the chairs which had been occupied and their relative positions. Despite earnest effort on his part he was not able to reconcile his "memories" with his knowledge of the actual facts. This distressed him seriously and resulted in an apparently total amnesia for both the trance sessions. Numerous instances of this occurred repeatedly.

5. Failure to distinguish between hallucination and fact.

Another distortion of marked interest was the substitution of hypnotically suggested hallucinations for factual items. A typical example was when a footstool was presented to the subject while in trance with much elaborate description as a rocking chair which was finally offered him as his seat for the rest of the session. Near the close of the session care was taken to offend him slightly as a measure of arousing antagonism that would tend to preclude the development of hypnotic amnesia. This was followed shortly by insistent commands that he develop a total amnesia for all events of that session. Some days later, with much pleasure, he related to his friends an adequate account of the entire session with the one major inaccuracy that the footstool was described as an actual rocking chair, an understanding from which he could not be shaken.

Similarly, in another trance session he was induced to hallucinate a colleague of Erickson's entering the room, borrowing a book, and then leaving. Subsequently, in recounting the events of the trance, he related this as a factual occurrence. The measure of repeating this procedure by having him hallucinate various colleagues who were on vacation at the time led to several more instances of hallucinatory experiences reported as factual occurrences. Confronted by this fact on one occasion he became distressed and confused, offered various rationalizations, and finally developed an apparently total amnesia for the trance events and for the waking experience of having given an account of them.

Much later he was again hypnotized and inquiry made into one such instance. The subject recalled the whole experience and the original suggestions. He was distressed by Erickson's detailed knowledge of his posttrance behavior, but cooperated by explaining that at the time he had related the story to his friends, he had believed fully in its truth. When they confronted him with the facts, he had at first been very much puzzled and was unwilling to think about the matter further, and then forgot the entire thing. He explained further that as he now viewed the matter, the hallucination had been so clear and vivid that he had, in the original trance, forgotten all about the experience of having the hallucinations suggested to him. Hence, in relating the trance events to his friends he had not recalled those original suggestions because they were doubly forgotten—that is, forgotten in the original trance state and then forgotten a second time in consequence of the hypnotic amnesia.

6. *Persistent amnesia for certain trance experiences.*

Although the subject demonstrated an ability spontaneously to recover memories of many trance experiences, sometimes all of those belonging to a single trance session, there were numerous instances where he failed to recover certain memories. On these occasions simple or leading questioning would serve to assist him materially in recovering the forgotten items. However, there were many instances of persistent amnesia for certain trance events that did not yield to any of the measures employed to facilitate recall. Even relating the amnesic material to the subject would not elicit recognition from him. Some of this persistent amnesic material was emotional in character, but just as frequently it seemed to be entirely neutral.

The only measure that was at all effective in these instances was rehypnosis and questioning about the forgotten material. Invariably he would readily recall it in the trance state. After awakening and relating the events of this second trance, he might gain access to the previously inaccessible memories. Sometimes, however, he would remember all of the trance events except those concerning the previously inaccessible memories, and thus there would continue a persistent, conscious amnesia despite his ability under hypnosis to recover all forgotten material.

7. *Development of amnesia after full recall while awake.*

Another frequent observation was that after having awakened and related his memories of a trance session, he would spontaneously develop an amnesia for both the trance events and the fact of having related them. An illustrative instance of this phenomenon with another subject was reported above as Example 1.

Structured Amnesia (Amnesia by Reorientation in Time)

Example 7. While Erickson was carrying on an experimental study, a 27-year-old female interne volunteered her services as a hypnotic subject. Her offer was tentatively accepted with the explanation that the experiment might require too much of her time and hence preclude her participation. An appointment was made to meet her in the laboratory where she could avail herself of books to pass away time until Erickson's experimental work permitted him to see her. She kept the appointment and read until Erickson was free. She then proved to be a most capable subject, and in the hypnotic trance full arrangements were made with her to report regularly at the laboratory for the experimental work, which would continue over a period of many weeks. At that time and on all subsequent occasions she was instructed to have a posthypnotic amnesia for all events of the trance sessions.

She kept all appointments, usually arriving about a half-hour early and devoting the waiting period to study. *When the time came to hypnotize her, use was made of a posthypnotic cue to induce the trance while she was reading. When the experimental work was completed, she was always returned and awakened carefully at the same desk where she did her reading and waiting for the experimental session to begin.*

Then one day in the staff dining room mention was made of a new hypnotic subject with whom Erickson hoped to work. Immediately she burst into an infuriated tirade, the burden of which was that a long time ago she had volunteered her services, that she had been put off with an evasive answer by Erickson, and that no effort of any sort had been made to utilize her services which she had offered in good faith. She declared that the least Erickson could have done was to offer her some explanation of why he did not consider her worthwhile as a hypnotic subject. Since this outburst of temper was not understood, and since another hypnotic session was scheduled for that afternoon, no explanation was offered her. Furthermore, it was considered undesirable to give her an explanation because it might interfere with the experiment in progress.

That afternoon she appeared at the laboratory at the proper time, was decidedly short in her greeting of Erickson, and continued to read the book she was studying. However, at the posthypnotic cue she developed a deep trance, and the experimental work was continued. No effort was made to explore the situation. For an additional two weeks she was seen regularly for experimental work. During this period of time she continued to be unfriendly and resentful in her attitude toward Erickson in social situations.

When the experiment was completed, however, inquiry was made in the trance state concerning her outburst of temper and her unfriendly attitude toward Erickson. Her explanation was simple. She stated that she had no unfriendly feeling or resentment toward Erickson while she was in the trance because she knew that she was participating in the experiment. However, when she was awake she knew nothing at all about the experiment or the fact that she was contributing, hence she believed fully in the waking state that her offer had been disregarded. Therefore, she was left in the uncomfortable position of believing in the waking state that she was not acceptable as a hypnotic subject, and there was nothing she could do to correct this misunderstanding because of the posthypnotic suggestion of amnesia for all trance events. When she was asked what she wished Erickson to do, she stated that she felt all explanation should be postponed until the experimental work was completed, since, obviously, Erickson felt it unwise to apprise her of the actual situation. She was asked if she wished Erickson to give her a full explanation upon the completion of the experiment or if it would be better to let events follow the natural course of development. After thinking this over, she suggested that the latter course might be the better to follow. She was again dismissed in the usual way.

Her unfriendly attitude toward Erickson continued for another two weeks, when again she lost her temper in another situation similar to the first. With many apologies Erickson attempted to explain the total situation to her. She was most critical of the explanation and rejected it completely. She declared that she knew that she had never been hypnotized, and she explained her regular appearances in the laboratory as resulting from her self-imposed course of study. The only significant admission secured from her was the statement that she felt she had gained very little from her studies despite the great amount of time she had spent, and she explained Erickson's invariable presence there as coincidental and as not related to her.

When finally it became apparent that no amount of argument or discussion could correct her understandings, a suggestion was offered that a trip to the laboratory and an examination of the experimental records might serve to prove to her that she had been acting as a subject. She denounced this suggestion as a futile, useless proposal but finally consented to examine Erickson's records. These she was shown in full detail. Thus, she was forcibly convinced that she had been acting as a subject over a period of many weeks. However, as she explained, this knowledge, while acceptable as factual, did not give her any feeling of inner conviction that she had been a subject. She then asked that she be hypnotized so that she could learn if she could be hypnotized. She also suggested that use be made of hypnotic suggestion to convince her of the facts of the total situation.

She was promptly hypnotized and then instructed to abolish the posthypnotic amnesia and to recall in chronological order the entire course of events for which she had developed an amnesia. Upon awakening a casual conversation was initiated during which she was reminded of her temper outbursts. Then she was asked to give an account of any memories that she might recover. To her great amazement she experienced a sudden flow of recollections and associations, which she related in detail. These were discussed fully with her.

The reason for this deep experience of hypnotic amnesia will be lost on the uninitiated reader who does not understand the significance of the italicized material in the second paragraph. This italicized procedure was instrumental in effecting a carefully "structured hypnotic amnesia." The literature on hypnotic amnesia generally classifies two basic types according to the manner in which they are generated—spontaneous and suggested. Erickson is here utilizing a third way of generating hypnotic amnesia: *The structured amnesia is effected by awakening the subjects in a manner that reorients them to the exact place, time, and associative content of consciousness where they were when they entered trance.* The total situation is so structured that the trance period falls into a lacuna between two events structured to be so identical that consciousness does not recognize them as two and is thus amnesic for all that occurred between them. Erickson (1964) has described it as follows: "This measure of reorientation in time by reawakening trains of thought and associations preceding trance inductions, in this author's experience, is far more effective in inducing posthypnotic amnesia than direct forceful suggestions for its development. One merely makes dominant the previous thought patterns and idea associations [p. 299]." Because the subject may have a feeling of duration or the passage of time (Erickson, Haley, & Weakland, 1959), even though amnesic for events, it would seem that the more general term *structured amnesia* is a more accurate description than *reorientation in time*.

AMNESIA BY INTERRUPTING THE SPONTANEOUS POSTHYPNOTIC TRANCE

This category is another of Erickson's original methods of evoking hypnotic amnesia. It is mentioned here only for the sake of completeness but will not be illustrated since it has already been adequately described (Erickson & Erickson, 1941). In brief, Erickson has established that the execution of a posthypnotic suggestion spontaneously evokes a brief hypnotic trance while the posthypnotic act is taking place. If subjects are interrupted and prevented from executing the posthypnotic act, they remain in trance, and this posthypnotic trance can be utilized to interpolate new hypnotic work. Subjects are then allowed to complete the original posthypnotic act and then awaken with a spontaneous amnesia for the interpolated events.

THE ALTERNATION OF HYPNOTIC AND NATURAL AMNESIA

Example 8. A patient under therapy for a personality problem was found to have an extensive amnesia for a significant life experience. Exploration in the hypnotic state finally elicited a complete account of that experience, as was subsequently verified. When she was awakened from the trance, however, she continued to be amnesic for that experience and also for the fact of having recovered the memory of it while in the trance state. This occurred despite the fact that in the trance state she had reacted to the recovered material with much emotional intensity.

When progress of the therapy permitted, systematic suggestions enabled her to recover her memories of that trance experience in full. She gained access to the details of the forgotten experience, but she recovered that amnesic material as an account of what she had recollected in the trance rather than an actual memory from the past. She recognized the trance experience as unquestionably true, and she was able to add further details about it while in the waking state, but it still had no vital meaningful significance to her except as a recent trance experience of recalling something she knew to be true but which she could not recognize emotionally as really belonging to her past life.

Rehypnotized, she again recalled the past experience as a vital occurrence in her life and was greatly distressed emotionally by it. Reawakened, she had an amnesia for this second trance but recalled having been awakened from the first trance and recollecting the experiences belonging to it. Her problem then became, as she verbalized it:

> What I have really got to do now is to remember that it happened when it did and not remember it just as something I remembered about when I was in a trance. Right now, it's just something that I recall remembering about even though I really know that it must all have happened. But knowing that it must have happened doesn't make that experience mean anything to me. It's just like reading something about yourself that you know is true but which you have just completely forgotten. In the

> trance, I knew it did happen, that's why I cried so. But now when I'm awake, all of it is just something that I remembered in the trance, and that's all it is.

When further therapeutic progress had been made, it became possible for the patient to recall the forgotten experience while in the waking state and to react to it emotionally as she had originally in the trance state. This waking recollection, however, was accompanied by a spontaneous amnesia for all developments centering around recall in the first trance. There was thus a spontaneous alternation of hypnotic and natural amnesia.

Subsequent to her recovery, rehypnosis disclosed her to have a full understanding of all that had occurred. She now reported her feeling that only the waking account had been of sufficient importance to warrant recalling. The two previous trance recollections were regarded simply as preparatory measures in which she had been enabled to assemble all of the forgotten data and to prepare herself for a waking recollection.

This is a frequent finding in hypnotic therapy. Amnesic memories may be recovered in the trance state and reacted to at the time, but the total experience of this does not carry over into the waking state. When, subsequently, the patient recovers the amnesic material in the waking state, preliminary trance activity becomes unimportant to the personality and is not recollected. As one patient explained:

> It's like baking and serving a cake. You remember doing that, but you never bother to remember about studying the recipe, mixing the batter and that sort of thing. All of that's very important, probably even more important than serving the cake, but you just remember that you served the cake that you baked. It's the same way when it comes to remembering forgotten things in a trance. When you had me remember while I was asleep those things I had forgotten, I suppose I was just getting them in order, and arranging them, and getting all set so that when the right time came when I was awake I could give them out. Then, when I remembered them when I was awake, just getting them ready to remember wasn't important any more so I just forgot about what I did in the trance just like you forget which bowl you mix an important cake in.

To summarize this account briefly, the patient originally had an amnesia of spontaneous origin for a traumatic experience. In hypnosis the factual data were recovered, but the patient awakened with no recollection of the trance work. When the amnesia for the trance activities was abolished in another trance, she recovered the factual memories of the past experience and recognized their validity, but found that they lacked all meaningfulness to her as a personality. When she later recovered in the waking state the same amnesic material as a personally meaningful past experience, she developed a secondary amnesia for those previous trance activities in which she had first recalled the amnesic material. In clinical practice it is frequently found that a spontaneous amnesia develops for trance work after the memories originally recovered in trance are integrated in the conscious personality.

That hypnotic amnesia and amnesia as naturally experienced are two entirely different phenomena is strongly indicated by the observations reported in this example. There can exist simultaneously, but totally independently of one another, two types of amnesia for the same items of fact. The abolition of one of the two amnesias had no effect upon the other, and each had to be recovered as a separate experience. This is an observation of much significance in relation to many failures of hypnotic psychotherapy. It is not enough simply to recover amnesic material in trance. Such trance work is often only preparatory to the full integration of the material by the conscious personality in the awake state.

THE "STATE-BOUND" NATURE OF HYPNOTIC AMNESIA

Taken together these clinical and naturalistic investigations stongly suggest that hypnotic trance is an altered *state* of consciousness and amnesia, in particular, is a natural consequence of this altered state. Recent research in "state-dependent learning" lends experimental support to the general view of all amnesias as being "state-bound." We can now understand hypnotic amnesia as only one of a general class of verifiable phenomenon rather than a special case. Fischer (1971) has recently summarized the relation between state-dependent learning and amnesia as follows:

> Inasmuch as experience arises from the binding or coupling of a particular state or level of arousal with a particular symbolic interpretation of that arousal, experience is state-bound; thus, it can be evoked either by inducing the particular level of arousal, or by presenting some symbol of its interpretation, such as an image, melody, or taste.
>
> Recently, some researchers had 48 subjects memorize nonsense syllables while drunk. When sober, these volunteers had difficulty recalling what they had learned, but they could recall significantly better when they were drunk again. Another scientist also

> observed amphetamine-induced excitatory, and amobarbital-induced, "inhibitory," state-dependent recall of geometric configurations. His volunteers both memorized and later recalled the configurations under one of the two drugs. However, while remembering from one state to another is usually called "state-dependent learning," extended practice, learning, or conditioning is *not* necessary for producing "state-boundness." On the contrary, a single experience may be sufficient to establish state-boundness.
>
> Déjà vu experiences and the so-called LSD flashbacks are special cases of the general phenomenon of state-boundness. Note that neither focal lesions nor molecules of a hallucinogenic drug are necessary for the induction of a flashback—a symbol evoking a past drug experience may be sufficient to produce an LSD flashback.
>
> It follows from the state-bound nature of experience, and from the fact that amnesia exists between the state of normal daily experience and all other states of hyper- and hypoarousal, that what is called the "subconscious" is but another name for this amnesia. Therefore, instead of postulating *one* subconscious, I recognize as many layers of self-awareness as there are levels of arousal and corresponding symbolic interpretations in the individual's interpretive repertoire. This is how multiple existences become possible: by living from one waking state to another waking state; from one dream to the next; from LSD to LSD; from one creative, artistic, religious, or psychotic inspiration or possession to another; from trance to trance; and from reverie to reverie [p. 904].

We would submit that hypnotic trance itself can be most usefully conceptualized as but one vivid example of *the fundamental nature of all phenomenological experience as "state-bound."* The apparent continuity of consciousness that exists in everyday normal awareness is in fact a precarious illusion that is only made possible by the associative connections that exist between related bits of conversation, task orientation, etc. We have all experienced the instant amnesias that occur when we go too far on some tangent so we "lose the thread of thought" or "forget just what we were going to do," etc. Without the bridging associative connections, consciousness would break down into a series of discrete states with as little contiguity as is apparent in our dream life.

It is now a question of definition and further empirical work as to whether these states are discrete and different in mental content alone or whether more gross physiological indicators can be used in defining them.

A drug obviously introduces a physiological change that may or may not be measurable with current techniques. With hypnotic trance the case is more equivocal. The case is further complicated by the fact, as Fisher indicates above, that once an altered state is produced, "symbolic" associations alone are sufficient to reinduce it.

How can we reconcile this special state theory of hypnotic trance with the many informative experimental studies which support the alternative paradigm (Barber, 1972) of hypnosis as a "responsive waking state" that is not discontinuous or essentially different from normal ordinary consciousness? In many of his papers Erickson (1939e, 1952, 1966) has emphasized that deep or really satisfactory trance experience is dependent upon the ability to subordinate and eliminate waking patterns of behavior. To achieve this end Erickson evolved many new techniques of induction and stressed the need for careful "hypnotic training" whereby the individuality of each subject was carefully taken into account to maximize the presence of involuntary or autonomous behavior in trance with as little participation of waking patterns as possible. Erickson rarely gives therapeutic suggestions until the trance has developed for at least 20 minutes, and this only after hours of previous hypnotic training.

In actual practice it is admittedly difficult if not impossible to eliminate *all* waking patterns. This is particularly true in the typical experimental study, where standardized instructions and direct suggestions are utilized with little or no extensive hypnotic training directed to the elimination or at least the mitigation of waking patterns in trance. The presence of many verbal, sensory, perceptual, and psychodynamic associations common to both the trance and waking situation in most experimental studies bridges the gap between them and further reduces their discontinuity. We would therefore submit that the alternative paradigm, which views the trance and waking conditions as more or less continuous, with no evidence of a "special state of trance," is correct in evaluating the typical experimental situation. It does not, however, adequately conceptualize those clinical situations where the skill of the therapist together with the needs of the patient interact to produce the striking discontinuities between trance and the normal state of consciousness that are so suggestive of special state theory.

The issue is analogous to the heated controversy about the fundamental nature of light as continuous (waves) or discontinuous (bundles) that plagued physicists of the past generation. In practice it has been found helpful sometimes to think of light as waves and other times as bundles. The most adequate conceptualization, however, is through mathematical symbols that cannot be meaningfully related to in terms of everyday associations on the verbal and imagery level. Likewise in clinical practice it may be helpful to conceptualize and stress those antecedent and mediating variables that promote discontinuity between trance and waking state, while in experimental work there may be more theoretical interest in dealing with the continuities.

UTILIZING AMNESIA IN HYPNOTHERAPY

The practical problem of coping with the bridging associations between trance and waking state takes us directly to Erickson's utilization of amnesia to facilitate the effectiveness of hypnotherapeutic suggestion. As implied in our earlier discussion of the superiority of indirect over directly administered suggestions, the basic problem of securing reliable results from suggestions is to "protect" them from the doubting, debating, and potentially negating effects of the patient's conscious sets and attitudes. Patients are patients because of the erroneous and rigid sets that govern their maladaptive behavior. By administering suggestions indirectly so they are not recognized by consciousness, the suggestions are able to enter the patient's preconscious and/or unconscious and are there utilized in an optimal manner for the patient's overall development. Hypnotic amnesia is thus a convenient approach for coping with consciousness and protecting therapeutic suggestions from the limitations of the patient's conscious sets. Hypnotic amnesia effectively breaks the bridging associations between the trance and waking situation and thus seals hypnotic suggestions from the potentially negating effects of the patient's conscious attitudes (Erickson, 1954).

Section 2: Literalness

INTRODUCTION

The two previously unpublished papers of this section on literalness reveal another facet of the hypnotic state. The first paper, "Literalness: An experimental inquiry," was a part of Erickson's early systematic investigations which sought to distinguish between the waking and the hypnotic states with particular focus on the nature of hypnotic realities. This experimental study typifies Erickson's characteristic approach by stimulating or disguising the important variables in a problem situation, thus making the actual primary variables appear as a minor and incidental part of another major, attention-getting activity.

The second paper emphasizes the subtlety of the phenomenon of literalness and its significance as a means of evaluating a patient's mental state and receptivity to therapeutic suggestion in dealing with the neurosis. A patient experiencing literalness is presumably responding to the exact meaning of the stimuli directed to him. The literal response thus takes place without the mediating influence of reflective thinking; the ego's function of critical evaluation tends to be omitted. From this point of view literalness becomes an excellent *indirect* indicator of the existence of trance and the presence of a receptive, suggestible state within the patient.

10. Literalness: An Experimental Study

Milton H. Erickson

A form of experimental inquiry, simple in character and effective in eliciting remarkably different results from waking and from hypnotized subjects, has been carried on over a period of more than 25 years on many hundreds of subjects. The experiment was based originally upon the observed literalness of hypnotic subjects when responding to instructions, questions, or suggestions. Such literalness of response is decidedly infrequent in everyday living—when it does occur then is suspect of being a deliberate play, as it often is. Innumerable persons were asked in the ordinary waking state such questions as: "Do you mind telling me your name?" "Do you mind standing up?" "Do you mind reading this?" (handing them a card bearing a typed sentence such as, 'This is a nice day.')" "Do you mind taking a step forward?" "Do you mind sitting in this other chair?" The usual response received from subjects in the ordinary waking state—whether friend, acquaintance, or even a total stranger—was almost always an acquiescence to the *implication* of the question, not a simple reply to the actual question. Thus, the awake subject would actually say his name, stand up, read the card, or whatever. In exceptional cases the response might be a challenging, "Why should I?" or an obvious rejection such as "I don't want to," or an ignoring of the request, usually with a questioning or doubting facial expression.

Comparable questions with dozens of hypnotic subjects led almost invariably to a simple verbal affirmative reply *without any movement to acquiesce to the behavioral implications of the inquiry*. This was particularly true with somnambulistic subjects, somewhat less so with medium subjects, and slightly less so with subjects in the light trance. On rare occasions the reply would be complete inaction, explained upon request by the statement that they were comfortable as they were or that there was no need to do so. On the other hand, the waking subject would explain a negative response with the challenging, "Why should I?" or "I don't want to," or "It doesn't make sense to do that."

These repeated findings suggested the possibility of establishing the fact of a recognizable difference between waking and hypnotic behavior *without corrupting the experimental investigation by disclosing to the subjects that an experiment was being performed by a testing of specific behavioral responses or by asking for deliberate simulation of behavioral*

Unpublished manuscript, circa 1940s.

responses or any other intentional or planned distortion of experimentally elicited responses.

With the formulation of this experimental inquiry, the project was carried out with many hundreds of subjects in the ordinary waking state. These subjects fell into one of the following categories:

(1) Those who had never been hypnotized and never were subsequently by the experimenter.
(2) Those who had never been hypnotized, were used as subjects, and subsequently were hypnotized and used as subjects.
(3) Those who had been hypnotized previously and were used as subjects, sometimes first in the waking state, and next in the trance state, and equally often by a reversal of this order of procedure.
(4) Those who had been tested on the same occasion for both types of behavior, sometimes first in the trance, sometimes first in the waking state.
(5) Those who had been tested in one or the other states first on a separate occasion with a following completion of the inquiry at a later date.
(6) Those who were tested singly or in group situations, under both private and public circumstances, and in group situations where all present were hypnotic subjects but not necessarily all in a trance at the time.

The age distribution ranged from four to 80 years, and age was not found to be a factor. The sex distribution was essentially equal, and no sex differences were found. The subjects employed included Japanese, Chinese, Filippino, Hindu, Hawaiian, Indian, Negro, Caucasian, and such ethnic groupings as native Americans, Mexicans, Venezuelans, Scandinavians, Germans, English, French, etc. The one thing in common was that they understood English, some less well than others, but all subjects gave comparable results.

The educational levels ranged from grade school to doctoral degrees. Psychiatric patients, some of whom were psychotic but most of whom were neurotic, were employed. The results from this group were comparable to those from subjects not receiving psychiatric care. There were also inmates of penal institutions, but none of these varied from the ordinary population except for a greater number showing challenging noncompliance. Of these, more males than females were tested, but there were no recognizable differences except that there was less open aggressiveness on the part of the women.

As would be expected, total strangers were the most uncooperative. For example, a total stranger approached in an airport and asked, "Would you mind standing up?" could readily reply, "And what business is it of yours if I sit down or stand up?" The social ice thus engendered could easily be broken by the plausible statement, "I'm a physician, and my hobby is visually comparing sitting and standing heights, and if you ask people informatively, they invariably sit higher and stand higher instead of more naturally." Such an explanation usually led to ready compliance with the implications of the original request, but since the response was actually to the explanatory statements, it would not be included in the experimental results except as a rejection.

In the early years of the experimental study exact records were kept of age, sex, education, occupation, hypnotic history or sophistication, and experimental setting, but as the data accumulated it became progressively apparent that the important factors in the experiment were (1) the state of ordinary waking awareness and (2) the existence of a hypnotic state. The results were enhanced by increasing depths of the trance state.

In all about 4,000 subjects were employed, of whom approximately 1,800 were in a hypnotic state. The greater number of nonhypnotic subjects arises from the fact that many subjects were employed who never became hypnotic subjects. However, it must be borne in mind that these two groups, nonhypnotic and hypnotic, are not mutually exclusive, since many subjects were used for both hypnotic and nonhypnotic experimentation. The reason for this was that behavioral differences between waking subjects and hypnotic subjects were found to be directly in accord with the existing state of awareness at the actual time of the experiment, whether hypnotic or waking. Previous experience with hypnosis had no bearing on the results. Subjects showing the typical waking response would subsequently manifest the typical hypnotic response, then again the waking response, and then again the hypnotic. The exceptions were those who were sophisticated in hypnotic behavior. Thus, a physician used first as a hypnotic subject gave the characteristic response and later the usual waking response. Shortly after the waking test he exclaimed in a startled fashion, "Doesn't that beat all? I was caught by the very test I use myself to see if my patient is in a trance." (Comment will be made on this later.)

Undoubtedly a major factor in the success of the experimental study was the fact that the test was always used as an extremely minor part of some other attention-commanding task. Thus there was no opportunity or occasion for direct critical thinking or analysis. For both hypnotic and nonhypnotic subjects, with the exception of total strangers, there was the implication that the experimental request was preliminary to some other more important task that was expected to follow.

The method of procedure was essentially the same for both waking and hypnotic states in a great variety of situations and under many different sets of circumstances. Also, the actual experiment was not always carried out by the experimenter but would be done at his secret request by a colleague who did not know the purpose. Perhaps the best example to illustrate the procedure is the following: At a lecture gathering, topic unannounced, the request would be made quietly of various people, "Would you mind telling me your name?" or "Would you mind standing up for a moment?" or "Would you mind sitting in that other seat?"

A lecture on therapy for the neuroses might then be presented with carefully calculated remarks leading to the introduction of the subject of hypnosis. This would lead to an offer to demonstrate hypnosis with several volunteers. Upon the induction of a trance, precisely the same questions would be put to the subjects as had been put to the members of the audience in the waking state. This would be done in a manner inaudible to the audience, and then the same questions would be directed to members of the audience not previously so questioned. Then the questions would be repeated to the subjects, this time so as to be audible to the audience.

Immediately the audience would become aware that the affirmative verbal response of the hypnotic subjects without responsive action was markedly different from the possibly wondering but silent responsive behavior of the waking subjects, who had promptly acted upon the implications of the questions rather than verbally offering a simple yes or no, as had the hypnotic subjects.

It was soon learned that even after this had been demonstrated, unexpected repetitions with the audience would elicit either complete or partial execution of the implied response before there would be realization of what was happening and consequent self-conscious inhibition of the acquiescent behavior.

It was also learned that somnambulistic subjects in full visual and auditory rapport with the audience could describe what waking persons did when so spoken to but did not apply that understanding to their own conduct when so addressed.

Nor did it invalidate findings to let the audience observe the behavior of both waking and hypnotic subjects without discussing it and then call upon observers who had been employed as waking subjects to act as hypnotic subjects. While they had observed behavior of others in both waking and trance states, and had so responded themselves in the waking pattern before trance induction, they had drawn no understandings or inferences of a governing character from what they had observed. In the trance state, they gave hypnotic responses, but in subsequent waking states, they continued to give waking responses. Nor did intellectual sophistication of hypnotic subjects serve to alter their characteristic behavior, but repetitions and instructions in the trance state would institute the waking pattern of behavior.

As the experiments continued over the years, it was progressively confirmed that by making the experimental inquiry an incidental, minor, and hence unnoticed part of a larger activity, there could be a study of behavior in either the waking or the hypnotic states without the response in the one state of awareness influencing the behavior in the other state of awareness. Situations reasonably expected to lead the subjects to become sophisticated and thus to inhibit the natural response failed to do so completely. For example, the physician cited above, as well as other subjects subsequently employed repeatedly, invariably made a partial response before self-consciously inhibiting the waking responsive behavior. Yet, the physician continued to use this measure as a means of determining the presence of a trance successfully and knowingly.

THE RESULTS

The following table does not give the total number of responses, since tabulation was discontinued when the consistency of results had been repeatedly noted. The experiment was continued as a testing measure with the hope of securing data on other aspects of hypnotic behavior, and the noting of data not in accord with that already recorded was not laborious. In other words, a greater proportion of variant responses were recorded than of the single positive results. This fact in no way significantly alters the overwhelming character of the positive data.

***FIRST-TIME RESPONSES*[1]**

Waking State		***Hypnotic State***	
	Light Trance	**Medium Trance**	**Deep Trance**
3,000	**350**	**300**	**250**

***SECOND-TIME RESPONSES*[2]**

Waking State		***Hypnotic State***	
	Light Trance	**Medium Trance**	**Deep Trance**
1,800[3]	**350**	**300**	**250**

[1]All first-time waking subjects included subjects used subsequently as trance subjects. Their number is disproportionately large since a good number refused to be hypnotic subjects and could not be tested a second time in the trance state.

[2]Both types of subjects were employed for repetitions of the experiment, but data thus secured was only confirmatory of the original results obtained; hence the results of multiple trials were not included in this experiment.

[3]This figure is doubled in value, however, since all hypnotic subjects were tested for the second time in the waking state on the assumption that their hypnotic response might alter their waking response.

The experimental results may be classified as follows:

WAKING STATE

1. Acquiescence by executing the implied request	95%
2. Challenge (Why should I?; Is it necessary? etc.)	3
3. Rejection (by ignoring or a direct negation of the implied action)	2

HYPNOTIC STATE

Light Trance:

1. An utterance of "no" or a negative shaking of the head.[4]	80
2. The question of "Do you want me to?" or a comparable inquiry.	12
3. Answer of "I don't want to" or its equivalent.	3
4. Hesitant, sluggish, inadequate effort to acquiesce to implied question.	3
5. Slow, uncertain, but actual acquiescence.	2

Medium Trance:

1. An utterance of "no" or a negative shaking of the head.	90
2. The question of "Do you want me to?" or a comparable inquiry.	1
3. Answer of "I don't want to" or its equivalent.	2
4. Hesitant, sluggish, inadequate effort to acquiesce to implied question.	1
5. "Can't."	1

Deep Trance:

1. An utterance of "No" or a negative shaking of the head.	97
2. The question of "Do you want me to?" or its equivalent.	2
3. No response.	1

Occasionally a light- or a deep-trance subject would say, "Can't," and an occasional deep subject would say, "I don't want to," "I'm fine," or a comparable response.

Special further experimental study was conducted with a large number of both types of subjects to determine the effect of repeated experimental trials—as before, these trials were an incidental part of a much larger activity. It was learned that the experimental procedure could be repeated indefinitely, the only adverse result being that the waking subject became

[4]Meaning, "No, I do not mind . . ." telling one's name, changing seats, standing up, or whatever the request.

too alertly interested or annoyed. There was no such effect upon the hypnotic subject unless the questions were put in rapid succession too many times. Then there would be acquiescence.

Direct sophistication by explanation of their behavior to subjects with no instructions concerning the response they were then to make resulted in a voluntary, usually embarrassed inhibition of the usual response in the waking subject and an effort to duplicate the hypnotic subject's precisions of literal response. Unless fully attentive and alert, however, waking subjects tended to make their natural response. This was not so with the hypnotic subjects, who continued with their own typical response until definitely instructed otherwise. Then they would easily and naturally respond in the same manner that characterized the unsophisticated waking response. It was also learned that sophistication of the hypnotic subject could come from long, continued hypnotic work, particularly when the subject in a trance studied the hypnotic behavior of other subjects.

The experiment had been set up originally as an incidental part of a major activity for the purpose of concealing the fact that a specific item of behavior was under study. This helped to avoid the distortion or falsification of responses that results from a realization that one's behavior is under scrutiny. When a large number of results had been obtained, a study was made including only the pertinent matters as the total experiment. Very quickly the waking subjects became aware that the question and their response constituted a vital issue, and efforts at repetition led to a variety of conflicting, uncertain, and inconsistent results. For the hypnotic subject this rigid limitation had little or no effect until too many repetitions aroused a definite interest in the purposes being served by such repetition. Even in this connection there was a significant difference between waking and hypnotic subjects in that the waking subjects inhibited their natural responses while the hypnotic subjects did not become inhibited. Instead they became curious about the experimenter's purposes asking, "Tell me why you ask," or assuming that acquiescence was desired and making a corresponding ready response with no inhibitory reactions.

In other words the predominant natural response to such an inquiry, as "Do you mind standing up, stating your name," etc. was an acquiescence by subjects in the waking state to the behavior implied by the question. In the hypnotic state the responsive behavior was of another character entirely. Most often the question itself was answered negatively, thereby implying positive willingness to acquiesce to the implied action of the question if and when such request were made explicitly.

Even variations of the predominant responses were of a totally different character, ranging from a direct refusal of an act regarded as possible in the waking state to the recognition of a physical inability to act in the trance state.

Repeated experience with the same experimental situation in both the waking and the trance states did not alter the natural response of each state of awareness. Direct sophistication of the subjects had the effect of inhibiting the natural response in the waking state with some degree of self-consciousness. Both sophistication by direct enlightenment or by permitting long-continued, interested study of hypnotic behavior in the self and others had the effect of making the hypnotic-state response identical to the unsophisticated waking response—again, a difference of behavior for the two states of awareness.

Nor has this finding been restricted to this experimenter's studies. He has encountered various colleagues who have themselves noted this literalness of response to questions and have used comparable questions as clinical tests for determination of the presence of the hypnotic state.

This general difference between waking and hypnotized persons in the meaningfulness of communications has been noted in many other regards and has led to the general admonition to offer suggestions to the hypnotic subject with clarity and meaningfulness. Operators must be aware of what they are actually saying.

11. Literalness and the Use of Trance in Neurosis

Milton H. Erickson and Ernest L. Rossi

E: The conscious mind already has its own set ideas about the neurosis. It has its fixed, rigid perceptions that constitute a neurotic set. It's very difficult to get people at the conscious level to accept an alteration of their general thinking about themselves. You use the trance state so that you can get around the self-protection which the neurosis provides on an unrecognized level. The neurotic is self-protective of the neurosis.

R: How does trance get around that self-protective aspect of neurosis?

E: The *literalness* of the trance state causes the patient to have a new pattern of listening. He listens to the words in the trance state rather than to the ideas.

R: The therapeutic words that the therapist says?

E: Yes. The patient gets those individual words and can hear the therapist say, for example, "you . . . don't . . . want . . . to . . . smoke." In the ordinary waking state he only hears, "You . . . don't." He feels that is condemnatory, as if he is being attacked. So he becomes defensive and is unable to hear the rest of the sentence.

R: So trance gives the patient a chance to hear your entire message, to hear exactly what you are saying without screening out any elements.

E: Without screening and without lifting or activating defense mechanisms. When you hear a *pleading tone in the patient's voice,*—for example, when he says, "I just can't stop smoking . . . ," that is a signal to make use of his unconscious by letting him go into trance because consciously he cannot listen to you.

R: He has a pleading tone because his conscious mind is distressed?

E: Yes. When you hear this conscious distress——

R: That means consciousness is in a weak position relative to the forces of neurosis, and it needs help.

E: Yes, it needs help, and that help can be given so much more easily and directly in trance. You drop the patient into a trance state and you say, "You came to me, you stated your problem as 'I don't want to smoke,' [spoken as a weak plea] and you have a lot of feeling in your voice. A lot of meaning in that tone of your voice. You put it there. It's your

Dialogue between Milton H. Erickson and Ernest L. Rossi, 1973.

meaning. Now think it over and recognize the meaning that you put there." That begins his inner recognition, "I don't want to *smoke!* [spoken firmly and with conviction] rather than a plea of distress.

R: You let him think quietly at that point in trance?

E: That's right.

R: And then does he talk to you about what conclusion he came to? What's the next step?

E: Patients' reactions vary tremendously. Some will ask, "Have I got the strength?" rather than making a piteous plea. Another will ask, "What approach should I take?" "Will I get fat?" etc. The answer to the last question is, "You don't want any problem." You see, that's a very comprehensive statement.

R: Because that statement is made in the trance state, it helps free the patient from "any problem."

E: Yes. "What you really want is the comfort of enjoying not smoking." That helps him focus on *comfort* as he gives up smoking rather than looking for other problems.

R: You give the patient an alternative that is better than the problems.

E: *An alternative that you have defined in such general terms:* "You don't want any problem. You want the enjoyment that is rightfully yours."

R: A general suggestion given in a positive way.

E: But it seems so specific when you listen to it.

R: Because the patient applies it to specifics (such as the things he wants to enjoy) within himself.

E: Yes. You make general statements that a person can apply to specifics within his own life.

R: This is a general approach that could be applicable to a great variety of neurotic problems.

E: That's right!

Section 3: Age Regression

INTRODUCTION

Erickson began his studies of hypnotic age regression while still a student working with Clark L. Hull at Wisconsin University in 1924. Erickson identified the first two fragments of this section as having been written in that period, although some of the raw data that appear pertinent to the experimental study of the second fragment (performance data on the Otis Self-Administering Tests of Mental Ability) bears dates in August, 1931, when he was working at Worcester State Hospital. From these fragments it is evident that the genuineness of hypnotic age regression as a phenomenon was one of his major preoccupations in this period.

The primary value of these two fragments lies in Erickson's detailed outline of his newly developed technique of an extended and fairly indirect approach to the evocation of hypnotic age regression. This outline, which is presented in the second fragment, is a model of his careful considerations in the evocation of all genuinely experiential hypnotic phenomena. It is not the operator's direct "command" that evokes a genuine age regression, but rather the careful evocation of relevant psychological processes of associations within the subject.

The second paper in this section, "Past weekday determination in hypnotic and waking states," confirms Erickson's interest in establishing the authenticity of the experiential aspects of age regression during this early period in his life. In it he describes his approaches and results during two periods of studying age regression. Although these studies do not measure up to current experimental standards in the use of controls and statistical presentation, they do present a colorful picture of the first stages in isolating the relevant experimental variables dealing with a fascinating psychological phenomenon. In general both articles make the point that "the waking subject is restricted to his general conscious concepts of how to function intellectually, while the hypnotic subject responds in a totally different way based on real-life experiences and the reactivated memories of such experiences."

The next paper, "On the possible occurrence of a dream in an eight-month-old infant," is an important empirical observation that gives us an estimate about the early appearance of dreams in infants, which could have implications for age regression studies. What is the earliest age from which the experience of hypnotic age regression could obtain valid memories?

The last paper in this section, "The successful treatment of a case of acute hysterical depression by a return under hypnosis to a critical phase of childhood," is an illustration of Erickson's innovative approaches to age regression and the value of this approach in therapy. As is typical of his work, one gains a vivid impression in this paper of the exploratory-clinical nature of his work, wherein he systematically applies just about all the useful approaches he knows to meet the needs of each unique, individual patient.

12. Age Regression: Two Unpublished Fragments of a Student's Study

Milton H. Erickson

FRAGMENT ONE: THE CONCEPT OF AGE REGRESSION

The psychiatric concept of regression, originally developed by the psychoanalytic school of thought, has proved a most useful measure in the classification and evaluation of various forms of behavior, both normal and abnormal. Psychiatrically, regression may be defined loosely as the tendency on the part of the personality to revert to some method or form of expression belonging to an earlier phase of personality development. The use of this concept, however, has remained largely on the descriptive level at which it originated, chiefly because it relates to data obtained in the main observation of a post hoc character. Hence there has been little opportunity to evaluate this concept except by the method of relative comparisons of observational material.

Another difficulty involved in the evaluation of the concept lies in the fact that its application must remain individualistic, since the varying degrees of development among different personalities and among the various aspects of the same personality may render precisely the same mode of expression regressive for one individual, progressive (in the sense of being the opposite of regressive) for another, or regressive in relation to certain aspects of the personality and not regressive in relation to certain other aspects. Then, when it is taken into consideration that the "degree of development" upon which the concept of regression is fundamentally based is in itself a vague, speculative concept, the difficulty of evaluating regression directly becomes all the more apparent. Hence there arises the question of the advisability of approaching the problem by qualitative and quantitative measures of some of the mental processes that presumably are involved in regressive phenomena.

In this regard, since regression consists of the reestablishment of a form of self-expression or behavior belonging to an earlier phase of development, a likely approach would seem to be any experimental procedure that would serve to reestablish individuals in an earlier period of their lives in such a fashion that the reestablishment would constitute a reorientation not based on memories or recollections as such—with their consequent and, for experimental purposes, distorting perspectives—but a reorientation in the past as an immediate actuality with its evocation of corresponding attitudes and behavior.

That such an experimental reorientation can be achieved satisfactorily is

---

Written between 1924 and 1931.

a serious question despite the fact that the psychological and psychiatric literature is replete with instances of such spontaneous occurrences on what is known as a functional basis and many of which were of a reversible character, permitting the person to live alternately in the chronological present or in the immediate present of the reestablished past.

Further, experimental psychological work, particularly in the field of hypnotism, has shown that mental states can be induced that are unrelated to immediate reality but are, so far as can be determined, actual reactivation of mental states previously experienced and uninfluenced by mental patterns acquired subsequent to the original experiences. Examples may be found in the restoration of the original awkwardness and uncertainty in skilled acts, the evocation in deep hypnosis of long-lost skills and knowledge, and the reestablishment of previous attitudes and behavior contrary to that required by the chronological present.

In the observtional and experimental work that has been done, however, the validity of the findings could be judged only by the method of relative comparison—that is, by a comparison of the established attitudes and behavior of the chronological present with the attitudes and behavior elicited in the presumed reactivation of the past. By such a method the conclusions drawn are, at best, only inferential.

Theoretically, the ideal approach to the problem would be the recording of all essential data regarding the experimental subject and then, at a suitable subsequent time, activating the original situation in which the data were collected. However, the length of time requisite to eliminate factors of simple memory and immediate relationships to the chronological present render such a procedure impractical.

FRAGMENT TWO: AN INDIRECT APPROACH TO AGE REGRESSION

My initial efforts to induce age regression by the traditional approach of direct suggestion gave inconsistent results. Although age regression could be readily induced by direct suggestion, the subject's general behavior was usually characterized both by remarkable accuracies and gross errors. The fidelity with which various minute details of behavior in a given situation for a specified age were often portrayed, however, suggested that the errors and inconsistencies were the result of inadequacies in the technique of hypnotic suggestion. Accordingly, an indirect technique of suggestion for this experiment was then worked out through a trial-and-error method on a number of hypnotic subjects. As a measure of avoiding possible coaching effects, none of these subjects was used subsequently in the experiment itself. Instead, four other subjects were employed, three female and one male. All were college graduates; all were unaware of the nature or purpose of the experiment; and all were able to develop profound somnambulistic trances because they had been thoroughly trained to do so in connection with other experimental work. In addition, confirmatory data were obtained on another subject, a recovered mental patient who had been reoriented by the experimental technique to the period of his acute illness; for this time there was an adequate psychometric record by which the validity of his reorientation might be tested.

The indirect approach to age regression that was used with these subjects consisted of four stages:

1. The allotment of enough time for both the induction of the trance state itself and for reorientating the subject to the desired age level. A minimum of 20 minutes was allowed for each of these processes. Contrary to general opinion, the induction of a sound, consistent, and firmly established trance or the execution of difficult, complicated hypnotic suggestions are not matters of simple, prompt obedience to emphatic hypnotic commands, but rather the results of a profound psychophysiological process requiring time for the organization and development of patterns of response and behavior. Particularly is this so when subjects are called upon for difficult, complex performances.

2. The giving of suggestions in accord with a definite pattern of presentation that has been found clinically to be effective. This consisted in first giving the suggestions vaguely and indefinitely, so that the subjects became rather uncertain and confused about exactly what was wanted and meant and definitely desirous of receiving any further understandings that might be offered to them. There followed then a repetition of the suggestions more and more clearly, concisely, and insistently until the subjects had a clear understanding of them and had accepted them, as indicated by the subjects' general behavior and responses. This done, the suggestions were again repeated over and over, but this time in broad, general, inclusive terms to preclude the subjects from taking exception to, or resisting, any of the suggestions, thus emphasizing the commands and yet leaving the subjects free to react fully and completely despite any inadequacy of the suggestions themselves. While this was being done, the next series of suggestions was introduced in vague, general terms. There was thus an interweaving of suggestions, permitting a slow, gradual, virtually unnoticeable progression from one type of suggestion to the next. This served to promote the shifting from one mental attitude to another—an essential basis for the experiment.

3. The giving of a series of suggestions to secure the following sequence of effects upon the subjects:

(*a*) general state of emotional indifference and unconcern;
(*b*) general state of confusion and uncertainty;

(*c*) general slowness, uncertainty, and blocking of memories, particularly those for the events of the current day, week, and month;
(*d*) general state of disorientation for person, place, and time;
(*e*) development of a definite amnesia for the events of the current day, week, and month;
(*f*) development of an amnesia for the events of the past year, the year before that, etc., and a forgetting even of the existence of those years;
(*g*) the realization that "time is changing" and "everything is changing," that soon the subjects, completely forgetful of all those stated years, will *feel* themselves to be of a specified age, then *believe* themselves to be of that age, and then *know* that they are exactly so old, while at the same time they will realize that the current year actually belongs to the remote future—as, indeed, do all the years subsequent to their specified age year;
(*h*) the subjects' realization that soon they will find themselves in a pleasant situation at the specified age, knowing all those things they should know—not less, not more—experiencing the feelings that all people know they have, possessed of the interests and desires rightfully theirs, being themselves and just themselves and enjoying their rightful span of specified years;
(*i*) finally the realization that they are of the specified age, feeling, thinking, knowing, and experiencing all those things rightfully theirs, just as they experienced and enjoyed those feelings and things not only today but yesterday and last week, and just as they will tomorrow and the next day and next week, and that now they are to open their eyes, ready and willing to pick up a pencil and to do whatever they are asked to the very best of their ability and as rapidly and thoroughly as they can.

4. The repetition of the entire procedure of suggestion for each age level tested for from 8 to 18 years, and the limitation of each experimental session to the investigation of a single age level.

EXPERIMENTAL PROCEDURE

Upon being hypnotized and reoriented in accord with the technique described, each subject was given one of the four forms, A, B, C or D, of the Higher Examination of the Otis Self-Administering Tests of Mental Ability. A time period of 20 minutes was allotted to each for the test performance. The order of administration of the various forms of the test, together with the order of suggestion of the various age levels, was systematically random to secure an irregular succession both of test forms and of age levels without there being a sequence of identical forms or of successive years.

At the expiration of the allotted time the subjects were reoriented and suggestions were given for an amnesia of the entire experience. At a later date—perhaps the next day, perhaps the next week—they were again approached with the request to contribute an hour or two for some hypnotic work the experimenter was planning. The time actually required for the experiment averaged between 25 and 30 hours per subject. The experimental sessions were spread over a period of five to six weeks, for the purpose of confusing any spontaneous memories and to impede any deliberate organization of test performances. In addition, from time to time the tests were given in the simple trance state to safeguard still further against spontaneous memories or deliberate systematization of responses.

When the experimental aspect of the problem had been completed, the subjects were asked (through an associate of the experimenter's, to avoid possible hypnotic effects) to perform in the waking state, item by item, the tasks already accomplished without their apparent knowledge in the trance state. Upon their consent they were given a detailed description of what was desired in terms embodying essentially the same points as had the hypnotic instructions. This was done as a measure of giving them the same type of cues as had been given in the trance state. Once these complete instructions had been given, the subjects were found to be unwilling to listen to repetitions for further test performances.

As an additional control measure a group of six nonhypnotic subjects, comparable in training and intelligence to the experimental subjects, were asked to perform the same experimental task at a waking level. They were given the same full instructions as had been given the experimental subjects for the control series. The entire series of tests was not performed, however, because some of the control subjects were found to be unable to perform the task, while others governed their performance by arbitrary standards serving to establish the exact extent of their performance for any specified age level.

EXPERIMENTAL RESULTS AND SUMMARY

The data as finally obtained included complete experimental and control results on three hypnotic subjects, nearly complete data on a fourth, confirmatory data from a single age regression on an additional hypnotic subject, and control data on six nonhypnotic subjects, adequate in character but incomplete in quantity because of the significant character of the first test performance by those subjects.

In addition to the experimental results many clinical observations were also made.All of them contributed significantly to the experimental findings, serving to clarify and to explain them and to give a better realization of the actual effects of the hypnotic suggestions and of the general problems to be met in this type of hypnotic experimentation. However, for this report these will not be given except in general outline.

A summary of the findings of this investgation may be given briefly in the following paragraphs:

1. A total of four hypnotic subjects in a deep trance, reoriented to earlier age levels and subjected to intelligence tests, gave evidence of a definite approximation of the mental patterns of the specified age levels. Three of the four subjects were reoriented to the age levels of 8, 9, 10, 11, 12, 14, 16, 17, and 18 years, and two of these to the additional years of 13 and 15. One subject was reoriented only to the age levels of 8, 10, 12, 14, 16, and 18. For these subjects the results obtained both in general behavior and in test performance were appropriate to the age levels suggested to them. Their performances on the test were straightforward and serious; it was taken always at face value, and the entire allotted period of 20 minutes was invariably utilized to the utmost. There was a distribution of correct and incorrect answers and of omitted questions appropriate to the various suggested age levels: For the earlier ages there were frequent evidences of juvenile misunderstandings and approximations in various of the wrong answers. There was no evidence of any carrying over of memories from one test situation to another. The same subjects gave right and wrong answers to the same question, in keeping with appropriate age levels.

2. Of the same subjects asked to perform under normal waking conditions the task already completed in the hypnotic state, two actually made an attempt somewhat similar to their trance performance. A third, through a process of specious reasoning, gave a highly systematized adult performance, and when asked to perform the task again, but in a different fashion because of the falsity of his first attempt, found it too difficult. A fourth subject, on whom the trance data were incomplete, found the task entirely too difficult to be done in the waking state, despite repeated conscientious attempts. The results obtained on the first two subjects resembled the trance findings only in the mental age as derived from the test scores. The performance of each subject was entirely that of an adult, in full awareness of his adult mental state, seeking to limit his adult performance to a lesser one that was presumably appropriate to a specified age level. In no instance did there seem to be any recognition or understanding of what the task actually implied—namely, behavior appropriate to the specified age level. In brief, the test performance under the control conditions was characterized wholly by adult behavior; responses were systematically calculated and organized in accord with a full adult conception of what might constitute the lesser performance appropriate to the specified age level. To this end the subjects arbitrarily restricted the amount of time used of the allotted 20 minutes to a period of three to eight minutes for the earlier age levels. Similarly, the number of questions answered at each age level was arbitrarily limited by the individual subject and systematically increased for each higher age level. In addition, all answers were correct; there seemed to be no realization on the part of the subjects that mistakes might and would be made at the various age levels. Also, there was little or no omission of specific questions because of their difficulty, except as a process of deliberate calculation, but there were mass omissions of questions for the sole purpose of limiting the total quantity of the performance. In brief, in the control examinations the subjects arbitrarily limited the time and quantity of their performance in accord with their adult understanding of what might be accomplished at a specified age limit. There was no effort to attempt either the behavior or the test performance appropriate to the specified age level.

3. The performance of the nonhypnotic control subjects was characterized by the same type of adult behavior as had been shown by the hypnotic subjects in their waking control performance, and the findings obtained, both as to method and actual results, were essentially comparable.

4. This experiment led to an attempt at testing the experimental results by reorienting a recovered mental patient to the time of the height of his acute mental illness more than a year previous, at which time a complete psychometric record had been obtained. Psychometric examination upon reorientation served to secure results in remarkable agreement with those actually obtained more than a year previously. For example, on the Otis Intermediate Test administered originally, his mental age was found to be seven years, ten months; on the same test, upon reorientation to that period, his performance scored seven years, eleven months.

Likewise his ratings on the Stanford-Binet, the Army Alpha, and various performance tests showed similar remarkable agreement. In addition a psychometric examination made previous to the reorientation experiment disclosed his normal mental age to be 13 years, 6 months.

13. Past Weekday Determination in Hypnotic and Waking States

Milton H. Erickson and Allan H. Erickson

Since the mid-1920s, when the senior author first became interested in hypnotic age regression, periodically there has been propounded the proposition that any intelligent college student can readily and easily calculate the day of the week for any given past date. At the time researchers uncritically accepted this assumption[1] as proof that any correct identification of the weekday by subjects who had been age-regressed hypnotically was not evidence of the reestablishment of earlier understandings and patterns of behavior. In this regard the senior author had repeatedly regressed hypnotic subjects in age, had then asked them what day of the month it was, and had received an immediate answer. Without further pause they would be asked what day of the week it was, and an immediate reply would be given which, in the majority of instances, was correct. This had been regarded by the senior author as a significant finding that tended to validate age regression as a genuine phenomenon, particularly when numerous inquiries of fellow students in the normal waking state had disclosed a definite inability to perform such a task.

Thus, students in the awake state would be asked, "On what day of the week did your second, last [third, fourth, fifth] birthday come?" Or, "On what weekday did Christmas [New Year's, Fourth of July, Valentine's Day] come two [three, four, five] years ago?" A correct answer to this type of question was found to be a rarity. The usual answer was, "I just do not know" or "I'd have to work that out." Some accepted the question as an interesting problem and actually tried to devise calculation methods to determine the answer. On the whole, however, practically all failed in their calculations, so that a correct answer by a correct method was as much a rarity as was a correct spontaneous answer. Among the correct spontaneous answers were some invalidated by personal referents such as, "That's easy, my birthday that year was the day after Thanksgiving, so it would be Friday." Sometimes a special event would permit a correct answer for a certain birthday. Thus, there might be a correct answer such as, "My birthday is exactly three weeks before Christmas. Last Christmas

---

Unpublished manuscript written with Allan Erickson, 1962.

[1] An experimental demonstration of the incorrectness of this assumption is presented in the Appendix by Allan Erickson.

was on a Sunday because I had to go to work on a new job the next day, so my birthday last year was on Sunday." Even so, they would be confused and uncertain as to the date of the week for the preceding and the subsequent birthdays.

FIRST STUDY

The senior author proceeded to regress a series of 10 hypnotic subjects to various age levels. The usual procedure of an orientation backward in time through the years was employed, thereby effecting a blanket amnesia for all events subsequent to the preselected past time. If time permitted, at least four different past ages were selected. The experiment was not done for publication but simply to discover if there were sufficient grounds for studying hypnotic regression as a valid phenomenon. The periods of time preselected were intentionally described to the subject as "this nice day in summer [fall, winter, or spring], and you are about 17 [11, 9, or 7 years old]. These specific ages were not used for each subject but serve merely to indicate the type of age range. For each subject the separate regressions were done in random fashion: The first regression might be to the youngest age level, the next might be to the oldest, and the order of the next two might be from the lesser to the greater or vice versa. The selection of season of the year followed a random pattern, too: A subject might be regressed to a childhood summer, for example, with subsequent regressions to spring, winter, and fall for other age levels.

In determining the year to which the subject was regressed, the point of time of orientation was made the subject's responsibility by employing such seemingly definitive descriptions as, "And now it will soon be your 16th birthday," or, "You are now 13 years old and school will soon begin again." Thus, a birthday early in January (there were no preliminary questions for such determinations) might compel the subject to orient to the preceding year in accordance with his definition of the word *soon*. Or the subject might be instructed, "And now it is such a nice day, right in the middle of the summer just before you go into the 8th grade." A follow-up question might be, "I wonder if it is going to rain today. What do you think?" An answer might then lead to such spontaneous dialogues as follows:

Patient: I hope not 'cause Daddy is going to take us fishing.
Therapist: Does your Daddy always take you fishing?
Patient: No, but he promised to take us fishing today because it is Willie's birthday tomorrow and we go to church on Sunday, so he has to take us today.

Thus, the weekday would be an indirect spontaneous disclosure.

Or the question of "What do you think you will do today?" might elicit the following dialogue:

Patient: Oh, it's visiting day and I got to go visit my Daddy.
Therapist: Why is that?
Patient: My Daddy and my Momma don't live together no more, and every Saturday I have to go visit him.

Such spontaneous disclosures were not infrequent at lower age levels, but when questioned for the day of the month the subjects usually did not know it. Occasionally, when the subject was queried at an early age level for the month of the year, a reply of the following character would be received: "It's July—no, it was July last week, and now it's August."

Frequently no weekday identification could be secured at the lower age levels. Instead, the subjects would state that they didn't know what weekday it was or would offer several questioning guesses. When they were then questioned, "What day do you think it is?" the confident answer would be, "It's 'painting' day [or 'story' day or 'practice' day], and inquiry would disclose that once a week some activity in school would be emphasized. This finding was frequently encountered among the senior author's fellow students in the waking state, who more than once, when asked the day of the week, would reply, "Let's see, I went to chemistry class [mathematics, physics, etc.] today. That's a Monday-Wednesday-Friday course, and it was my second class this week in Chemistry—so it's Wednesday." Subsequently the author encountered a similar identification of weekdays in his fellow medical students. The weekday nomenclature was replaced by courses being taken as the identification. Thus Saturday ceased to be Saturday; it became Dermatology Clinic day. Years later the senior author's medical students did the same thing. More than once he received a telephone call: "Is Eloise [the post office name of the Wayne County General Hospital and Infirmary on the outskirts of Detroit, Michigan] Day tomorrow, or the next day?" Frequently, the hospital staff replaced Wednesday with "Staff Day," to which one would orient temporarily by "day before" or "day after Staff." Hence the early regression-state-identification of weekdays in terms of events was accepted at the time, with increasing evidence of its validity in subsequent observation of human behavior.

At the older age level regressions, especially from twelve upward, there tended to be two types of reply. Thus the senior author might say hesitantly to the subject, "Uh, let's see, oh, what day is it today?" To this the subject was likely to respond (1) with a statement that he didn't know, hadn't noticed, had been too busy to pay attention to the calendar, or (2) immediately with a specific weekday or day of the month. If the subject gave a specific weekday, the author would get further information with the remark, "Oh, I meant the day of the month!" If initially the subject gave the day of the month, the author would ask for the day of the week. At the older age levels this type of reception was misleading as to the author's actual purposes and served to get additional data by which doubly to confirm or to disprove the responses given.

The same measure employed at younger age levels disclosed that both items of information were difficult to secure; some subjects tended to remember the day of the week, while others remembered the day of the month. It then became necessary to ask for other data, such as, "What are you going to do today?" when a reply indicated that it was the 13th of April at their regressed age of eight. Then if the answer was "go to church," one could test the validity of the reply. If the answer was "go to school," this would be followed by "And the next day? And the day after that?" If either of these two questions was answered, "Oh, stay home like every time," the inference of Saturday would be warranted. Or one can inquire about yesterday and the day before. If both questions are answered by a statement of school attendance and a question about tomorrow, and if the next day also elicits an answer of school attendance, the inference is warranted that the day of the month given is a Tuesday, Wednesday, or Thursday. However, other comparable check questions, or the technique of reorienting the subject to a month earlier or three weeks later, will serve to yield check data. It was early discovered that the answer, "I stayed home the next day and the next day and then I went to school again," does not necessarily mean that the subject is speaking of a Saturday or a Sunday. It might signify an absence from school because of illness or a holiday.

Many of the subjects at the upper age levels failed to identify the weekday or the day of the month. But this was found to be true in the ordinary school and college population and, for that matter, in medical school as well. And who has not encountered adults asking both the day of the week and the day of the month? Inquiry and observation over the years have disclosed a definite unreliability in weekday and month day identification deriving from legitimate interests, not only from neurotic conflicts.

As a consequence of all these special inquiries, the senior author felt satisfied with the results. He had learned that approximately two out of three age-regressed hypnotic subjects could give accurately the weekday or its equivalent for some past day in their life history and that this ability was apparently directly correlated with the age level to which they had been regressed. The lower age levels appeared to have more identification labels based on activity (e.g., "painting day" or "story day"), while the person in the waking state gave responses of another character altogether. Since the senior author was primarily interested in the subjective and emotional meaningfulness to the subject of regression experiences, rather than in the absolute validity of objective factual reporting, this inquiry was dropped as having served its purpose in establishing the validity of age regression in many instances.

SECOND STUDY

In the late 1930s, while the senior author was conducting hypnotic research in relation to the past emotional experiences of psychotic patients at Wayne County General Hospital, the same adverse criticism as to the superior ability of age-regressed subjects verus nonregressed subjects to recall past week and month days was encountered anew. Recalling the original study, a second comparable inquiry was made on a new population of students of medicine and psychology, secretaries, nurses, social service workers, staff physicians, and even psychiatry patients, including some people who were actively psychotic. This study varied in that past dates for both the 20th and 19th centuries were used. The responses elicited were (1) rejections of the task, (2) failure when attempted, and (3) two correct answers to the weekday identity of the past 20th-century date. These correct answers happened to be from two chess experts, but both of them failed to identify the 19th century dates. They had forgotten, along with all subjects except one psychology student, that 1900 was not a leap year. (A surprising number of the subjects did not recall this fact about 1900 and even challenged the senior author regarding it.)

The hypnotic subjects, who were often tested in the presence of critics, gave correct answers in a definite majority of instances. Since there were more female subjects in the hypnotic group than in the waking group, the secondary criticism that the inquiry with the waking group might not be valid because of the large number of women in that group was invalidated.

In neither the first nor the second study were the age-regressed subjects asked to identify a weekday of a date preceding their birth—such inquiries were considered undesirable. Since the purpose of utilizing hypnosis as an experimental procedure was to examine the meaningfulness of the subjects' past, personal, experiential realities, to request information preceding their birth would have been a falsification of the emotional content inherent in the hypnotic state.

The criticism may be leveled that these two inquiries were separate in kind for the waking as opposed to the hypnotic groups. The waking group was presented with a mathematical problem, whereas the hypnotic group was presented with a problem contingent upon subjective experiences. That it can be solved only on a mathematical basis is, however, the prevalent waking assumption. The senior author's experience is that the *waking subjects are restricted to their general conscious concepts of how to function intellectually, while hypnotic subjects respond in a totally different way based on real-life experiences and the reactivated memories of such experiences.* The waking subjects approach the problem as a cognitive one, requiring time and careful calculation, whereas the age-regressed hypnotic subject utilizes reactivated personal associations in an immediate and spontaneous manner.

APPENDIX

A college class of algebra students was given the following problems to test the assumption that any college student could calculate the day of the week for any given date of the past.

First Problem

Given: What day of the week it is today.
Find: What day of the week it was x years ago, where x is approximately 20 years ago (x is a whole number of years).

Second Problem

Given: What day of the week it is today.
Find: What day of the week it was x years ago, where x is approximately 75 years ago (x is a whole number of years large enough to make the day sought fall in the 19th century).

Total number of people attempting to solve the problems: 39

Results
24.8

(*1*) Number of people who got both problems entirely correct using a correct method: 1
(*2*) Number of people who got first problem entirely correct using a correct method: 14
(*3*) Number of people employing a correct method in solving the problems (some minor mistakes): 15

(*4*) Number of people who knew 1900 is not a leap year: 1
(The one person who got the problem correct.)

(Note: The one person who did get the correct answers was an A student in an intermediate algebra course in college.)

The final algebra grades of the students who got the correct answer through a correct method to the first problem are as follows:

A = 3
B = 4
C = 2
D = 4
F = 1

Time Requirements

Number of minutes required by the one student who got both answers correct to calculate the problems:	5½
Average number of minutes required by the students who got the correct answer to the first problem but the wrong answer to the second problem ($N = 13$):	13½
Average number of minutes required by the 15 students to work the problem through a correct method without regard to answer:	15½

From these results it is evident that most students in a college algebra class cannot quickly and easily calculate the day of the week or any given past date.

14. On the Possible Occurrence of a Dream in an Eight-Month-Old Infant

Milton H. Erickson

The age at which dreams first play a part in the psychic life of the individual is unknown. Various careful studies have reported that dreams may occur even before the development of speech, but the weight of evidence has been inferential in character and based upon sleep disturbances for which purely physiological, as distinct from psychic, activity might as readily be postulated. With the development of speech, however, definite evidence of dreaming by very young children has been obtained, their utterances while asleep disclosing their sleep disturbances to have an unmistakable psychic content, as is shown so clearly in recent observations of dreaming in a two-year-four-month-old baby (Grotjahn, 1938).

Pertinent to these considerations is the following brief note reporting an instance in detail which suggests strongly that a dream with definite psychic and affective content may occur even at the early age of eight months. The attendant circumstances are given in full since they suggest a possible background for the development of affective desires which might in turn give rise to dream activity.

> For a period of months a father was in the habit of playing with his infant daughter regularly just previous to her 6 P.M. feeding, and much pleasure was taken in inducing her to laugh and in watching her extend her legs, flex her arms over her chest, and turn her head from side to side as she laughed. The infant had developed a definite attitude of expectation for this specific play activity.
>
> When she was exactly eight months old, external circumstances caused the father to be absent from home one evening and the next. Returning at midnight the second evening, he paused at her bedroom door. He could see her clearly outlined in the moonlight, lying quietly in her crib, breathing deeply and sleeping soundly. As he was about to turn away, she moved restlessly, extended her legs, flexed her arms over her chest, turned her

Reprinted with permission from *The Psychoanalytic Quarterly*, July, 1941, Vol. X, No. 3.

> head from side to side, laughed merrily, took another breath and laughed again. This was followed by general relaxation and a continuance of the deep, quiet, breathing, nor did she arouse when her father entered, but continued to sleep as he tucked her more securely under the covers.

To say that an infant of eight months could have a dream of definite psychic content and with affective components seems questionable, but even more questionable would be any attempt to postulate a physical discomfort which would disturb sleep and result, at that age, in an expression by laughter. Likewise questionable could be any attempt to draw conclusions about so young a child experiencing affective deprivation so strongly that resort would be had to a dream satisfaction. Yet in this instance such an inference seems plausible. In any event the observation is noteworthy in relationship to the problem of dream life, and it is hoped that other observers may report similar instances.

Since making this original observation, another of similar character has been made.

As they were returning late one night, the parents heard the baby, then 13 months old, laughing merrily. Entering her bedroom immediately, they found the child apparently sound asleep. Before they had an opportunity to touch her, however, the child again laughed merrily, and this laughter was immediately succeeded by a third peal, following which the infant continued to sleep so soundly that even the changing of her diaper did not arouse her.

That this type of behavior occurred in relation to a pleasing psychic content or experience on the order of a dream seems to be a reasonably plausible and legitimate inference.

At the age of 23 months, this same child became much concerned over a rather extensive abrasion of the knee suffered by her older sister as a result of a fall on the pavement—an accident discussed by all of the children in the family and their playmates. Several nights later, after she had been sleeping about three hours, she suddenly began to cry. Upon being picked up, still crying, she sobbed, "Po' Kaka [Carol]. Kaka bad bump. Kaka hurt. Kaka cry." Efforts to reassure her verbally failed, as did an attempt to show her that Carol was sleeping quietly. She continued crying, adding, "Kaka fall down. Kaka hurt knee." She seemed still to be asleep and unresponsive to all reassurances. Accordingly she was aroused completely. Thereupon she repeated her remarks, but with much less grief in her voice, and she seemed to be very greatly bewildered and puzzled by the sight of Carol sleeping quietly in bed, as if she could not reconcile a dream content with the actual sight of her sleeping sister. She then proceeded to discuss the matter, and the impression derived from her fragmentary remarks was that she was trying hard to explain the situation to her parents. Following this she returned readily to bed and slept comfortably the rest of the night. In this instance there can be no doubt of the occurrence of an actual dream based upon a previous experience.

15. The Successful Treatment of a Case of Acute Hysterical Depression By a Return Under Hypnosis to a Critical Phase of Childhood

Milton H. Erickson and Lawrence S. Kubie

EVENTS WHICH LED TO THE ATTEMPT TO TREAT A DEPRESSION BY HYPNOSIS

An unusually capable 23-year-old woman had been employed in a mental hospital for several months. Toward the end of this period she developed a progressively deepening depression. Later it became known that she had continued to discharge her duties fairly well for some weeks after a certain upsetting event; but that as time passed she had become increasingly disinterested and ineffectual in her work, slowly discontinuing all social relationships, and spending more and more time in her secluded room. At this point in her illness she ate only in response to her roommate's pleading, sobbed much of the time, occasionally expressed a wish to die, and became blocked and inhibited in speech whenever any effort was made to question her about her difficulties. During the latter part of this phase the patient's symptoms became so acute that her relatives and friends sought psychiatric help.

The patient was seen by several psychiatrists, some of whom diagnosed her condition as the depressive phase of a manic-depressive psychosis. A psychoanalyst and one of the authors, Dr. Erickson, believed it to be an acute reactive depression. Later evidence, which became available only as the story developed, indicated that it was a typical "hysterical depression," that is, a depression reaction growing out of a definite hysterical episode.

Several consultants were in favor of commitment. To this, however, the family of the patient would not consent, insisting that some form of active psychotherapy be at least attempted. Accordingly, sympathetic and persuasive encouragement was tried. The patient responded to this sufficiently to appear slightly less depressed and to return to her work in a

---

Reprinted with permission from *The Psychoanalytic Quarterly,* October, 1941, Vol. X, No. 4.

feeble and rather ineffectual fashion; but she remained unable to discuss her problem.

This slight amelioration of her symptoms was sufficiently encouraging to warrant further efforts, yet, was far from sufficient to free her from the danger of a relapse into deeper suicidal depression. Furthermore, the threat of commitment still hung over her head; therefore, with many misgivings the suggestion was made that she attempt psychoanalytic treatment. She showed some interest in this idea, and despite the fact that it is unusual to attempt analysis in the midst of a retarded depression, for a period of about a month she was encouraged to make daily visits to an analytically trained psychiatrist.

During this month, except for the fact that the analytic hour seemed to help the patient to make a better adjustment during the rest of the day, she made little progress, produced no free associations, related only a few fragmentary parts of her story, and usually spent the hour in depressed silence with occasional futile efforts to say something, or in sobbing as she declared that she did not know what awful thing was wrong with her or what awful thing had happened to her. Toward the end of the month she began to show signs of relapsing into an acute depression of psychotic intensity so that commitment seemed imperative.

In spite of these discouraging experiences the family again asked that before resorting to commitment some other therapeutic measure be attempted. The suggestion that hypnotic therapy might be of value was accepted by her relatives, and plans were made for this *without the patient's knowledge.* At this point the patient's problem was referred to Dr. Erickson with the following story which had been pieced together by the various psychiatrists from the accounts of the patient's roommate, of her relatives, of a man in the case, and in small part, of the patient herself.

CLINICAL HISTORY

The patient was the only daughter in a stern, rigid, and moralistic family. Her mother, of whom she always stood in awe, had died when the patient was 13 years old. This had had the effect of limiting her social life somewhat, but she had an unusually close friendship with a neighbor's daughter of her own age. This friendship had continued uneventfully from childhool until the patient was 20 years old, three years before the date of the patient's illness.

At that time the two girls had made the acquaintance of an attractive young man with whom both had fallen in love. Impartial toward them at first, the young man gradually showed his preference for the other girl, and presently married her. The patient responded to this with definite disappointment and regret but quickly made an adjustment which seemed at the time to be unusually "normal," but which in view of later developments must be viewed with some suspicion. She continued her friendship with the couple, developed transitory interests in other men, and seemed to have forgotten all feelings of love for her friend's husband.

A year after the marriage the young wife died of pneumonia. At the loss of her friend the patient showed a wholly natural grief and sorrow. Almost immediately thereafter the young widower moved to another section of the country, and for a time dropped out of the patient's life completely. Approximately a year later he returned and by chance met the patient. Thereupon their former friendship was resumed, and they began to see each other with increasing frequency.

Soon the patient confided to her roommate that she was "thinking seriously" about this man, and admitted that she was very much in love with him. Her behavior on returning from her outings with him was described by the roommate and by others as "thrilled to the skies," "happy and joyous," and "so much in love she walks on air."

One evening, after some months, she returned early and alone. She was sobbing, and her dress was stained with vomitus. To her roommate's anxious inquiries the patient answered only with fragmentary words about being sick, nauseated, filthy, nasty, and degraded. She said that love was hateful, disgusting, filthy, and terrible, and she declared that she was not fit to live, that she did not want to live, and that there was nothing worthwhile or decent in life.

When asked if the man had done anything to her, she began to retch, renewed her sobs, begged to be left alone, and refused to permit medical aid to be summoned. Finally she yielded to persuasion and went to bed.

The next morning she seemed fairly well, although rather unhappy. She ate her breakfast, but when a friend who knew nothing of these events casually asked about the previous evening's engagement, the patient became violently nauseated, lost her breakfast, and rushed precipitously to her room. There she remained in bed the rest of the day, sobbing, uncommunicative, uncoöperative with a physician who saw her, essentially repeating the behavior of the previous evening.

During that day the man tried to call on her. This precipitated another spell of vomiting; she refused to see him. She explained to her roommate that the man was "all right," but that she was nasty, filthy, disgusting, and sickening, and that she would rather kill herself than ever see that man again. No additional information could be obtained from her. Thereafter a telephone call or a letter from the man, or even the mention of his name, and finally even a casual remark by her associates about their own social contacts with men, would precipitate nausea, vomiting, and acute depression.

To a psychiatrist the man stated that on that evening they had gone for a drive and had stopped to view a sunset. Their conversation had become serious, and he had told her of his love for her and of his desire to marry her. This confession he had long wanted to make, but, he had refrained even from hinting at it because of the recency of his wife's death and his knowledge of the depth and intimacy of the friendship that had existed between the two girls. As he had completed his confession, he had realized from the expression on her face that she reciprocated his feelings, and he had leaned over to kiss her. Immediately she had attempted to fend him off, had vomited over him in an almost projectile fashion, and had become "just plain hysterical." She had sobbed, cried, shuddered, and uttered the words "nasty," "filthy," and "degrading." By these words the man had thought she referred to her vomiting. She refused to let him take her home, seemed unable to talk to him except to tell him that she must never see him again, and to declare that there was nothing decent in life. Then she had rushed frantically away.

Subsequently, all efforts on the part of friends or physicians to talk to the patient about these events had served only to accentuate the symptoms and to evoke fresh manifestations.

PREPARATION FOR AN INDIRECT HYPNOTIC INVESTIGATION

Many hints from this story induced the investigator not to attempt to hypnotize the patient simply and directly. In the first place there was the fact that she had rejected every overt sexual word or deed with violent vomiting and with a paralyzing depression which practically carried her out of contact with those who had attempted to help her. She rejected the man so completely that she could not hear or mention his name without vomiting; this reaction to men had become so diffused that she could not accept the ministrations of male physicians, but reacted as though they meant to her the same kind of threat her suitor had represented. She had been able to accept him only in a spiritualized and distant courtship, or when she was protected by the presence of her friends. It was evident that she would far too greatly fear direct hypnosis ever to submit to it.

She was moreover too deeply entrenched in the refuge of illness to fight energetically for health. She had no resources with which to struggle against her anxiety and depression, but at any signal she collapsed deeper into illness. This gave warning that in the preliminary phases of treatment one would have to work completely without her cooperation, either conscious or unconscious, without raising the least flurry of anxiety, without making a single frightening or disturbing allusion to her trouble, if possible without her even knowing that she was being inducted into treatment—and most important of all, without her feeling that the therapist (the hypnotist) was directing his conduct toward her at all. Whatever was going on in her presence must seem to her to relate to someone else. Only in this way could the treatment be undertaken with any hope of success. It should be recalled that even the passive, quiet, wordless, almost unseen presence of an analyst had been too great an aggression for the patient to accept, an intolerable erotic challenge, with the result that after a month she had sunk deeper into depression.

Accordingly, arrangements were made to have the patient's roommate confide to the patient that for some time she had been receiving hypnotic psychotherapy. Two days later the psychoanalyst approached the patient and asked her, as a favor to him in return for his efforts on her behalf, to act as a chaperone for her roommate in her regular hypnotic session with Dr. Erickson.

This request he justified by the explanation that she was the only suitable chaperone who knew about her roommate's treatment; the nurse who usually chaperoned the treatment was unavoidably absent. The patient consented in a disinterested and listless fashion, whereupon he casually suggested that she be attentive to the hypnotic work, since she herself might sometime want to try it.

By asking the patient to do this as a favor for him, the analyst put her in an active, giving role. By suggesting to her that she listen carefully because she herself might want similar help some time, he eliminated any immediate threat, at the same time suggesting that in some undefined future she might find it useful to turn to the hypnotist for therapy.[1]

THE FIRST HYPNOTIC SESSION

Upon entering the office, the two girls were seated in adjacent chairs, and a prolonged, tedious, and laborious series of suggestions was given to the roommate, who soon developed an excellent trance, thereby setting

[1]These two points are of special interest to analysts who are accustomed to demand of their patients an awareness of their illnesses and of the need for treatment, and an acceptance of the therapeutic relationship to the analyst. While this is a valid basis for therapeutic work with many of the neuroses, it is an impossible goal in dealing with many neurotic characters and with those neuroses which are accompanied by severe affective disturbances, and with psychoses. Analysts who become too completely habituated to their own method may delude themselves with the idea that their passivity is pacifying, and may overlook the extent to which it may be an assault in terms of the patient's unconscious emotional reactions. The approach described above, therefore, is an illustration of a method whereby, under appropriate circumstances, these difficulties can be circumvented.

an effective example for the intended patient. During the course of this trance suggestions were given to the roommate in such a way that by imperceptible degrees they were accepted by the patient as applying to her. The two girls were seated not far apart in identical chairs and in such a manner that they adopted more or less similar postures as they faced the hypnotist; also, they were so placed that the hypnotist could inconspicuously observe either or both of them continuously. In this way it was possible to give a suggestion to the roommate that she inhale or exhale more deeply, so timing the suggestion as to coincide with the patient's respiratory movements. By repeating this carefully many times, it was possible finally to see that any suggestion given to the roommate with regard to her respiration was automatically performed by the patient as well. Similarly, the patient having been observed placing her hand on her thigh, the suggestion was given to the roommate that she place her hand upon her thigh and that she should feel it resting there. Such maneuvers gradually and cumulatively brought the patient into a close identification with her roommate, so that gradually anything said to the roommate applied to the patient as well.

Interspersed with this were other maneuvers. For instance, the hypnotist would turn to the patient and say casually, "I hope that you are not getting too tired of waiting." In subsequent suggestions to the roommate that she was becoming tired, the patient herself would thereupon feel increasing fatigue without any realization that this was because of a suggestion which had been given to her. Gradually it then became possible for the hypnotist to make suggestions to the roommate, while looking directly at the patient, thus creating in the patient an impulse to respond, just as anyone feels when someone looks at one while addressing a question or a comment to another person.

At the expiration of an hour and a half the patient fell into a deep trance.

Several things were done to ensure her cooperation in this trance and its continuance and to make sure that there would be opportunities to use hypnotic treatment in the future. In the first place the patient was told gently that she was in a hypnotic trance. She was reassured that the hypnotist would do nothing that she was unwilling to have him do and that therefore there was no need for a chaperone. She was told that she could disrupt the trance if the hypnotist should offend her. Then she was told to continue to sleep deeply for an indefinite time, listening to and obeying only every legitimate command given her by the hypnotist. Thus she was given the reassuring but illusory feeling that she had a free choice. Care was taken to make sure that she had a friendly feeling toward the hypnotist, and for future purposes a promise was secured from her to develop a deep trance at any future time for any legitimate purpose. These preliminaries were time-consuming, but they were vitally necessary for safeguarding and facilitating the work to be done.

It was obvious that the patient's problems centered around emotions so violent that any therapeutic exploration would have to be carried out in some wholly "safe" fashion without provoking the least trace of guilt or fear. Such "safe exploration" meant dealing with everything in such a way that the patient could escape all painful implications. The first maneuver was to lead the patient back to a childhood devoid of childhood pain.

Accordingly, emphatic instructions were given to the patient "to forget absolutely and completely many things," carefully omitting to specify just what was to be forgotten. Thus the patient and the hypnotist entered into a tacit agreement that some things were best forgotten—that is, best repressed. Permission also was thereby given to the patient to repress them without naming them. The exploratory process which lay ahead would be faciliated by this permission to repress the more painful things, since automatically it would be applied to those which were most troublesome.[2]

Next the patient was systematically subjected to a gradual disorientation for time and place, then gradually reoriented to a vaguely defined period in childhood lying somewhere between the ages of 10 and 13. The technique used is described in some detail in studies on the hypnotic induction of color blindness and of hypnotic deafness (Erickson, 1938a, 1939e). The hypnotist suggests first a state of general confusion as to the exact day, carrying this over step by step to include the week, the month, and the year. Then this is elaborated toward an intensification of a desire to recall certain unspecified things that had occurred in previous years, which also are left indeterminate. The process is a slow one and involves jumping from one confusing idea to another until out of the state of general confusion the patient develops an intense need for some definite and reassuring feeling of certainty about something, whereupon she becomes only too glad to accept definite reassurance and definite commands.

In reorienting the patient toward the age period between 10 and 13, the hypnotist was careful to be extremely dogmatic in tone of voice but equally vague and indefinite as to his precise meaning. The suggestions were given to the patient as though talking to someone else rather than directly to her. She was not told that she herself had to seize upon some meaningful event in those three years.

The years from 10 to 13 were chosen with the idea that they just preceded her mother's death and that they must have included the period of onset of her menstruation and therefore have meant the critical turning

[2]Here again is an interesting and significant departure from analytic technique, in which the implicit and sometimes explicit challenge is to break through every repression. The rigidity with which this axiom of analytic technique is applied may account for some analytic failures; it may also be an example of conflict between research and therapeutic purposes.

point in her general emotional life and in her psychosexual development. Since nothing was known in detail about her life, the exact period of time to which she would finally become reoriented was left to the force of her own experiences.

She was at no time asked to name and identify specifically the age to which she became reoriented in the trance. By allowing her to avoid this specific detail, she was compelled to do something more important—namely, to speak in general terms of the total experience which those years had meant.[3]

Presently in her trance the patient showed by the childishness of her posture and manner, as well as by the childishness of her replies to casual remarks, that she had really regressed to a juvenile level of behavior. She was then told emphatically, "You know many things now, things you never can forget no matter how old you grow, and you are going to tell me those things now just as soon as I tell you what I'm talking about." These instructions were repeated over and over again with admonitions to obey them, to understand them fully, to be prepared to carry them out exactly as told; she was urged to express and affirm her intention to carry through

[3]The search back toward reliving an earlier period in the life of a hypnotic subject occurs in either of two ways. First there can be a "regression" in terms of what the subject as an adult believes, understands, remembers, or imagines about that earlier period of her life. In this form of "regression" the subject's behavior will be a half-conscious dramatization of her present understanding of that previous time, and she will behave as she believes would be suitable for her as a child of the suggested age level. The other type of "regression" is far different in character and significance. It requires an actual revivication of the patterns of behavior of the suggested earlier period of life in terms only of what actually belonged there. It is not a "regression" through the use of current memories, recollections, or reconstructions of a bygone day. The present itself and all subsequent life and experience are as though they were blotted out. Consequently, in this second type of regression the hypnotist and the hypnotic situation, as well many other things, become anachronisms and nonexistent. In addition to the difficulties inherent in keeping hypnotic control over a total situation, this "deletion" of the hypnotist creates an additional difficulty. It is not easy for the hypnotist to enter into conversation with someone who will not meet him until 10 years hence. This difficulty is overcome by transforming the hypnotist into someone known to the patient during the earlier period, by suggesting that he is "somone whom you know and like and trust and talk to." Usually a teacher, an uncle, a neighbor, some definite or indefinite figure belonging to the desired age period is selected automatically by the subject's unconscious. Such a transformation of the hypnotist makes it possible to maintain contact with the subject in the face of the anachronism mentioned above. Unfortunately many investigators of "hypnotic regression" have accepted as valid that type of "regression" which is based upon current conceptions of the past; and they have not gone on to the type of true regression in which the hypnotic situation itself ceases and the subject is plunged directly into the chronological past.

all of these suggestions. This was continued until her general behavior seemed to say, "Well, for what are we waiting? I'm ready."

She was told to relate everything that she knew about sex, especially in connection with menstruation, everything and anything that she had learned or been told about sex during the general period of this hypnotically reestablished but purposely undefined period in her childhood. It is fair to call this an "undefined period in her childhood" because three or four years is indeed a long time to a child, and from among the many and diverse experiences of those years she was at liberty to select those things which were of outstanding importance. Had she been confined to a more restricted span of time, she could have chosen inconspicuous items. Leaving her to select from within a certain braod but critical period in her life forced her to choose the important and painful items.

Up to this point the hypnotic procedure had been systematically planned, with the expectation that any further procedure would depend upon the results of these preliminary maneuvers.

To these instructions the patient reacted with some fright. Then in a tense and childlike fashion she proceeded obediently to talk in brief disconnected sentences, phrases, and words. Her remarks related to sexual activity, although in the instructions given to her emphasis had been laid not upon intercourse but upon menstruation. The following constitutes an adequate account:

> My mother told me all about that. It's nasty. Girls mustn't let boys do anything to them. Not ever. Not nice. Nice girls never do. Only bad girls. *It would make mother sick.*[4] Bad girls are disgusting. I wouldn't do it. You mustn't let them touch you. You will get nasty feelings. You mustn't let them touch you. You will get nasty feelings. You mustn't touch yourself. Nasty. Mother told me never, never, and I won't. Must be careful. Must go good. Awful things happen if you aren't careful. Then you can't do anything. It's too late. I'm going to do like mother says. She wouldn't love me if I didn't.

Many of the remarks were repeated many times in essentially identical wordings. Some were uttered only once or twice. She was allowed to continue her recitation until no new material was forthcoming, except the

[4]The phrase, "It would make mother sick," may have had much to do with her illness: Mother had had intercourse and died. Her friend, who was a mother substitute had had intercourse and died. The same thing was about to happen to the patient. Mother has said it, and it must be true. It is a child's passive acceptance of logic from the image with which it has become identified.

one additional item that this moralistic lecture had been given by the mother on several occasions.

No attempt was made to introduce any questions while she was talking, but when she had ceased she was asked, "Why does your mother tell you these many things?"

"So I'll *always* be a good girl," was the simple, earnest, childlike reply.[5]

Although it was clear, almost from the start, that the patient's passive and submissive dependence upon the mother's commands would have to be broken, it was equally evident that the image of the dead mother played a role in her life which overshadowed that of any living person and that this idolized superego figure could not be dislodged from its position by any direct frontal attack. For this reason the hypnotist's stratagem was to adopt a point of view as nearly identical with the mother as he could. He had first to identify himself entirely with this mother image. Only at the end did he dare to introduce a hint of any qualifying reservations. Therefore he began by giving the patient immediate and emphatic assurance: "Of course you *always* will be a good girl." Then in a manner which was in harmony with the mother's stern, rigid, moralistic, and forbidding attitudes (as judged from the patient's manner and words), each idea attributed to the mother was carefully reviewed in the same terms, and each was earnestly approved. In addition the patient was admonished urgently to be glad that her mother had already told her so many of those important things that every mother really should tell her little girl. Finally, whe was instructed to "remember telling me about all of these things, because I'm going to have you tell me about them again some other time."

The patient was gradually and systematically reoriented in terms of her current age and situation in life, thereby reestablishing the original hypnotic trancc. However, the earlier instructions to "forget many things," were still in effect, and an amnesia was induced and maintained for all of the events of the hypnotically induced state of regression. This was done in order to soften the transition from those early memories to the present because of the intense conflict which existed between the early maternal commands and her current impulses.

She was prepared for the next step, however, by being told that she would shortly be awakened from her trance and that then she would be asked some questions about her childhood which she was to answer fully.

[5]Here is an important bit of profound, unconscious psychological wisdom. The commands had been repeated incessantly in the patient's mind, whether or not in reality they had been repeated as incessantly by the mother. This repetition, which is the essence of all neurosis (Kubie, 1939), must occur because of the resurgent instinctual demands. Hence the patient indicates in the word *always* her continuing secret insurrection against a continuing prohibition, and therefore her ever-present state of fear.

To have asked her in her ordinary waking state about her sexual instructions would have been merely to repeat the severe aggressions of all of her previous experiences with psychiatrists; but by telling her during her trance that questions about her childhood would be asked, she was prepared to take a passive intellectual attitude toward the demand, and to obey it without consciously admitting its connection with her present problems.

As a further preparation for the next step she was told that the nature of the questions to be asked of her would not be explained to her until she had awakened, and that until then it would suffice for her to know merely that the questions would deal with her childhood. Here again the hypnotist was governed by the basic principle of making all commands as general and nonspecific as possible, leaving it to the subject's own emotional needs to focus his remarks.

Finally, technical suggestions were given to the patient to the effect that she should allow herself to be hypnotized again, that she should go into a sound and deep trance, that if she had any resistances toward such a trance she would make the hypnotist aware of it *after* the trance had developed, whereupon she could then decide whether or not to continue in the trance. The purpose of these suggestions was merely to make certain that the patient would again allow herself to be hypnotized with full confidence that she could if she chose disrupt the trance at any time. This illusion of self-determination made it certain that the hypnotist would be able to swing the patient into a trance. Once she was in that condition, he was confident that he could keep her there until his therapeutic aims had been achieved.

Upon awakening, the patient showed no awareness of having been in a trance. She complained of feeling tired and remarked spontaneously that perhaps hypnosis might help her, since it seemed to be helping her roommate. Purposely, no reply was made to this. Instead she was asked abruptly, "Will you please tell me everything you can about any special instructions concerning sexual matters that your mother may have given you when you were a little girl?"

After a show of hesitation and reluctance, the patient began in a low voice and in a manner of rigid primness to repeat essentially the same story that she had told in the earlier regressive trance state, except that this time she employed a stilted, adult vocabulary and sentence structure, and made much mention of her mother. Her account was essentially as follows:

> My mother gave me very careful instruction on many occasions about the time I began to menstruate. Mother impressed upon me many times the importance of every nice girl protecting herself from undesirable associations and experiences. Mother made me

> realize how nauseating, filthy, and disgusting sex can be. Mother made me realize the degraded character of anybody who indulges in sex. I appreciate my mother's careful instruction of me when I was just a little girl.

She made no effort to elaborate on any of these remarks and was obviously eager to dismiss the topic. When she had concluded her account of her mother's teachings, they were systematically restated to her without any comment or criticism. Instead they were given full and earnest approval, and she was told that she should be most grateful that her mother had taken advantage of every opportunity to tell her little daughter those things every little child should know and should begin to understand in childhood.

Following this an appointment was made for another interview a week hence, and she was hastily dismissed.

During the course of the following week no new reactions were noted in the patient by her roommate, and the general trend of her depressive behavior continued unchanged.

THE SECOND HYPNOTIC TRANCE

At the second appointment the patient readily developed a deep trance and at once was instructed to recall completely and in chronological order the events of the previous session. She was asked to review them in her mind silently, then to recount them aloud slowly and thoughtfully but without any elaboration.

Such silent review of a hypnotically repressed experience is a necessary preparation. It ensures completeness of the final recall. It avoids uneven emphasis on separate elements in the recollection and distorted emphasis which the subject subsequently would feel the need of defending. It permits an initial recall in silence without any feeling that in remembering facts the subject is also betraying them to someone else. This facilitates the reassembling of painful elements in the subject's memories. Finally, when the subject is asked to tell aloud that which has just been thought through in silence, it becomes a recounting of mere thoughts and memories, rather than the more painful recounting of actual events. This also helps to lessen the emotional barriers against communicating with the hypnotist.

As the patient completed this task, her attention again was drawn to the fact that her mother had lectured her repeatedly. Then she was asked, "How old were you when your mother died?" She replied, "When I was thirteen." Immediately the comment was made with quiet emphasis,

"Had your mother lived longer, she would have talked to you many more times to give you advice; but since she died when you were only thirteen, she could not complete that task, and so it became your task to complete it without her help."

Without giving the patient any opportunity either to accept this comment or to reject it, or indeed to react to it in any way, she quickly was switched to something else by asking her to give an account of the events which had occurred immediately after she had awakened from her first trance. As she completed the account, her attention was drawn to the repetitive character of her mother's lectures, and the same careful comment was made on the unfinished character of her mother's work.

It will be recalled that on the first day of hypnotic work the patient was brought back to an early period in her childhood, and in this pseudoregression, she was asked to give an account of the sexual instructions her mother had given her. Then through a series of intermediate transitional states she was wakened, and in her waking state she was asked to give an account of the same instructions, but with an amnesia for the fact that she had already told any of this to the hypnotist. In the second hypnotic treatment up to this point the patient was promptly hypnotized, and the posthypnotic amnesia for the first hypnotic experience was lifted so that she could recall all of the events of her first trance. Then she was asked to review the material which she had discussed immediately after awakening from the first trance—in short, her conscious memories of her mother's puritanical instructions. By reviewing in a trance both the events of her previous trance and the events that had occurred immediately on her waking from this trance, a direct link was established between the childhood ides and affects and those of the previous week's adult experience. Thus the two could be contrasted and compared from her adult point of view.

The patient then was reoriented to the same period of early childhood. She was reminded of the account she had given before and was asked to repeat it. When she had done so, in terms essentially identical with those she had used in her original account, similar approving remarks were made, but this time so worded as to emphasize sharply the fact that these lectures had all been given to her in her childhood. When this seemed to be impressed upon her adequately, the suggestion was made quietly that as she grew older, her mother would have to give her additional advice, since things change as one grows older. This idea was repeated over and over, always in conjunction with the additional suggestion that she might well wonder what other things her mother would tell her as she grew older.

Immediately after this last suggestion the patient was brought back from her pseudochildhood to an ordinary trance state. She was asked to repeat her account of the remarks she had made in the waking state. She was urged to take special care not to confuse the words she had used when fully awake with the words of the account she had given in the first pseudochildhood trance state, even though the ideas expressed were essentially the same and even though she had both accounts fresh in her mind. This request constituted a permission to remember now in an ordinary trance the events of the second pseudochildhood trance, since this had been merely a repetition of the first, but the fact that there had been a second trance of this kind would not be recalled. Instead the two trances would be blended into a single experience.

As before, the purpose of these devices was to bring gradually together the child's and the adult's points of view. Into her childhood perspective an element of expectation and of wondering had been introduced by the comment that as she grew older, her mother would have had more to teach her. This now was ready to be brought to bear upon the adult version of her mother's instructions, which she had also given.

The blending of the two experiences served an additional technical purpose. In the first place repetitions are necessary under hypnosis, just as they are in dream analysis or in the recounting of experiences by patients under analysis in general. Without repetitions one cannot be sure that all of the material is brought to expression; moreover, allowing the subject under hypnosis to recall both the original version and the various repetitions as though they were a single occasion actually gives the subject something to hold back—namely, the fact that there were two or more experiences. This seems to satisfy the subject's need to withhold something, by giving her something unimportant to withhold in return for the important fact which is divulged. This the hypnotist can well afford to do, just as one can allow a baby to refuse to give up a rattle when he has already given up the butcher's knife. The baby is satisfied and so is the parent.

As the patient concluded this task, her attention was drawn again to the period of her life in which her mother's lectures had been given, the repetitions of these lectures, their incompleteness, the unfinished task left to a little girl by her mother's death, and the necessity to speak to a child in simple and unqualified language before she is old enough for more complex adult understanding. Every effort was made to impress each of these specific points upon her, but always by the use of terms as general as possible.

Without giving the patient an opportunity to develop or elaborate these points, the suggestion was made that she might well begin the hitherto unrealized and unrecognized task of continuing for herself the course of sexual instruction which her mother had begun but had been unable to finish because of her death. She was urged that she might best begin this unfinished task by speculating earnestly and seriously upon what advice her mother would have given her during the years intervening between childhood and adolescence and between adolescence and adult womanhood. As she accepted this suggestion, it was amplified by additional instructions to take into consideration all intellectual and emotional aspects, all such things as physical, psychological, and emotional changes, development and growth, and most important to give full consideration to the ultimate reasonable goals of an adult woman, and to do so completely, fully, freely, and without fail, and to elaborate each idea in full accord with the facts appropriate to herself.

Immediately after this instruction was given, the patient was told that upon awakening she should repeat all of the various accounts she had given in this hypnotic session, preferably in their chronological order, or else, if she chose, in any other comprehensive form which she preferred. Thereupon she was awakened.

The patient's waking account was decidedly brief. She slowly combined everything which she had said into a single, concise story. Significantly, she spoke in the past tense: "My mother attempted to give me an understanding of sex. She tried to give it to me in a way that a child such as I was could understand. She impressed upon me the seriousness of sex; also, the importance of having nothing to do with it. She made it very clear to me as a child."

This account was given with long pauses between each sentence, as though she was thinking profoundly. She interrupted herself several times to comment on her mother's death and on the incompleteness of her instruction, and to remark that had her mother lived, more things would have been said. Repeatedly she said, as if to herself, "I wonder how mother would have told me the things I should know now."

The examiner seized upon this last remark as a point for terminating the session, and the patient was dismissed hastily. No attempt was made to guide her thoughts beyond the urgent instruction to speculate freely upon the things her mother would have told her and which she now needed to know. She was told to return in one week.

During this week the patient showed marked improvement. Her roommate reported "some crying, but of a different kind," and none of the previous depressed behavior. The patient seemed rather to be profoundly self-absorbed, absent-minded, and puzzled; much of the time she wore a thoughtful and sometimes bewildered expression. No attempt was made to establish any contact with the patient during the week.

THIRD HYPNOTIC SESSION

Promptly upon her arrival for the third session the patient was hypnotized and instructed to review rapidly and silently within her own mind all of the events of the two previous sessions, to recall the instructions and suggestions which had been given to her and the responses she had made, to include in her review any new attitudes which she might have developed and to give full and free rein to her thinking, and finally to summarize aloud her ideas and conclusions as she proceeded with this task.

Slowly and thoughtfully, but with an appearance of ease and comfort, the patient proceeded to review these events freely, briefly, and with no assistance. Her final statement summarized her performance most adequately:

> You might say that mother tried to tell me the things I needed to know, that she would have told me how to take care of myself happily and how to look forward confidently to the time when I could do those things appropriate to my age, have a husband and a home and be a woman who has grown up.

The patient was asked to repeat this review in greater detail, in order to be sure that toward both her childhood and adult years she had achieved suitable adult attitudes. As these instructions were repeated slowly and emphatically, the patient became profoundly absorbed in thought, and after a short while she turned with an alert, attentive expression, as if awaiting the next step.

Instruction was given that when she awoke she was to have a complete amnesia for all three sessions, including even the fact that she had been hypnotized, with the exception that she would be able to recall her first stilted, prim, waking account. This amnesia was to include any new and satisfying understanding she had come to possess. She was told further that upon awakening she would be given a systematic review of her sex instruction as the hypnotist had learned about these matters from her, but that because of the all-inclusive amnesia this review would seem to her to be a hypothetical construction of probabilities built by the hypnotist upon that first waking account. As this occurred, she was to listen with intense interest and ever growing understanding. She would find truths and meanings and applications understandable only to her in whatever was said, and as those continued and developed, she would acquire a capacity to interpret, to apply, and to recognize them as actually belonging to her, and to do so far beyond any capacity that the hypnotist might have to understand.

At first glance it would seem strange to suggest repression of insight as one of the culminating steps in a therapeutic procedure. In the first place it implies that much of the affective insight may either remain or again become unconscious without lessening its therapeutic value. Secondly, it protects the subject from the disturbing feeling that anyone else knows the things about her which she now knows, but which she wishes to keep to herself; hence the importance of the suggestions that she would understand far more than the hypnotist. Thirdly, by looking upon the material as a purely hypothetical construction of probabilities by the hypnotist, the patient was provided with an opportunity to recover insight gradually, in a slowly progressive fashion, as she tested this hypothetical structure. Had the same material been presented to her as definite and unquestionable facts, she might again have developed sudden repressions with a spontaneous loss of all insight. If that occurred, the investigation would have had to be undertaken afresh. On the other hand, where a certain measure of repression is ordered by the hypnotist, it remains under his control, because what the hypnotist suppresses he can recover at will. Thus her degree of insight remained under full and complete control by the hypnotist, so that he could at any time give the patient full insight or prepare her for it again. Finally, by depriving the patient temporarily of her new and gratifying insight, a certain unconscious eagerness and need for further knowledge was developed which assisted in the ultimate recovery of full insight.

When these instructions had been repeated sufficiently to effect a full understanding, the patient was awakened with an amnesia for all events except the stilted, prim account which she had given at the end of the first therapeutic session. Reminding her of that account, the hypnotist offered to speculate upon the probable nature and development of the sex instructions which she had been given. He proceeded to review all the material she had furnished in general terms that permitted her to apply them freely to her own experiences.

Thus the patient was given a general review of the development of all the primary and secondary sexual characteristics: the phenomenon of menstruation, the appearance of pubic and axillary hair, the development of her breasts, the probable interest in the growth of her nipples, the first wearing of a brassiere, the possibilities that boys had noticed her developing figure and that some of them may have slapped her freshly, and the like. Each was named in rapid succession without placing emphasis on any individual item. This was followed by a discussion of modesty, of the first feelings of sexual awareness, or autoerotic feelings, of the ideas of love in puberty and adolescence, of the possible ideas of where babies came from. Thus without any specific data, a wide variety of ideas and typical experiences were covered by name. After this, general statements were made as to the speculations that might have passed through her mind at one time or another. This again was done slowly and always in vague general terms, so that she could make a comprehensive and extensive personal application of these remarks.

Shortly after this procedure was begun, the patient responded by a show of interest and with every outward manifestation of insight and of understanding. At the conclusion the patient declared simply, "You know, I can understand what has been wrong with me, but I'm in a hurry now and I will tell you tomorrow."

This was the patient's first acknowledgment that she had a problem, and instead of permitting her to rush away, she was promptly rehypnotized and was emphatically instructed to recover any and all memories of her trance experiences that would be of use. By stressing in this way the fact that certain of those memories would be valuable and useful to her, the patient was led to view all of them as possibly useful, thus withdrawing her attention from any conflicting feelings about those memories. This assists in their free and full recovery by the patient. She was told that she should feel free to ask for advice, suggestions, and any instruction that she wished, and to do so freely and comfortably. As soon as this instruction had been firmly impressed, the patient was awakened.

Immediately, but with less urgency, she said that she wanted to leave but added that she would first like to ask a few questions. When told that she might do so, the patient asked the hypnotist to state his personal opinion about "kissing, petting, and necking." Very cautiously and using her own words, approbation was given of all three, with the reservation that each should be done in a manner which conformed with one's own ideals and that only such amorous behavior could be indulged in as would conform to the essential ideals of the individual personality. The patient received this statement thoughtfully and then asked for a personal opinion as to whether it was right to feel sexual desires. The cautious reply was given that sexual desire was a normal and essential feeling for every living creature and that its absence from appropriate situations was wrong. To this was added the statement that she would undoubtedly agree that her own mother, were she living, would have said the same thing. After thinking this over, the patient left hastily.

THERAPEUTIC OUTCOME

The next day the patient returned to declare that she had spent the previous evening in the company of her suitor. With many blushes she added, "Kissing is great sport." Thereupon she made another hurried departure.

A few days later she was seen by appointment and held out her left hand to display an engagement ring. She explained that as a result of her talk with the hypnotist during the last therapeutic session, she had gained an entirely new understanding of many things, and that this new understanding had made it possible for her to accept the emotion of love and to experience sexual desires and feelings, and that she was now entirely grown up and ready for the experiences of womanhood. She seemed unwilling to discuss matters further, except to ask whether she might have another interview with the hypnotist in the near future, explaining that at that time she would like to receive instruction about coitus, since she expected to be married shortly. She added with some slight embarrassment, "Doctor, that time I wanted to rush away. . . . By not letting me rush away, you saved my virginity. I wanted to go right to him and offer myself to him at once."

Sometime later she was seen in accordance with her request. A minimum of information was given her, and it was found that she had no particular worries or concern about the entire matter and was straightforward and earnest about her desire to be instructed. Shortly afterward the patient came in to report that she was to be married within a few days and that she looked forward happily to her honeymoon.

About a year later she came in to report that her married life was all she could hope for, and that she was anticipating motherhood with much pleasure. Two years later she was seen again and was found to be happy with her husband and her baby daughter.

SUMMARY AND DISCUSSION

For special reasons the treatment of this patient had to be approached with many precautions. The circumstances of her illness made a direct approach to her problem (whether by a man or a woman) dangerous because such an approach invariably caused an acute increase of her panic and of her suicidal depression. She could be treated, if at all, only by creating an elaborate pretense of leaving her problems quite alone, without even letting her realize that any therapy was being attempted, without acknowledging the development of a relationship between the patient and the physician, and without open reference to the experiences which had precipitated her illness.

For these reasons the treatment was begun by pretending to treat someone else in her presence, and, through this means she was slowly and gradually brought into a hypnotic state in which her own problems could be approached more directly.

From this point on the treatment proceeded along lines which are the reverse of the usual psychoanalytic technique. Some points seem to be worthy of special emphasis.

Instead of depending solely upon memory to recover important experiences out of the past, the patient under hypnosis was translated back to a critical period of her childhood, so that in that state she could relive or revive the general quality of the influences playing upon her, but without recapturing the details of specific scenes and episodes. Instead of stirring them up and making them conscious, there was a deliberate effort to avoid the induction of any feelings of guilt or fear. Similarly, instead of insisting upon total conscious recall, persmission was freely granted to the patient to forget painful things, not only during but also after the hypnotic treatment. Underlying this permission to forget was the confidence that even those facts which were consciously forgotten could be recovered during the hypnosis when needed for therapeutic use, and that their therapeutic efficacy would continue even during the posthypnotic repression.

The hypnotist's attack on the patient's rigid superego was interesting from various points of view. Particularly noteworthy, however, was the fact that the attack on the superego began with a complete support of all the most repressive attitudes which the patient attributed to her dead mother. It was only by forming a bond in this way between himself and the mother that he was able later slowly to undermine the rigidity of this repressive figure and thus to penetrate the patient's tense and automatic defenses of her mother's dictates. Another significant point is the method used by the hypnotist to help the patient silently assemble her ideas before communicating them. This seemed to assist materially in reducing the patient's fear of remembering presumably because it is not as difficult to recall embarrassing things which one can keep to one's self as it is to bring them to mind with the knowledge that one must confess them at once; moreover, once such things have been reviewed in thought, it becomes easier to talk of the thoughts than it would have been to talk of the events themselves. This two-stage method of recalling and assembling data before communicating it might have its usefulness in analysis as well.

A point at which the work of the hypnotist coincides closely with that of the analyst is in the use of repetitions in many forms and at each age level investigated. This use of repetitions is quite similar to what is found to be necessary in analysis as well.

In understanding the course of this treatment and of the patient's recovery, there are many gaps in the material, gaps which could be filled in only by conducting a treatment of this kind in a patient who had been under a fairly prolonged analysis.

There are many questions we would like to have answered. Was the basis of the mother's overwhelming authority primarily affection or hostility and fear? Were the dead mother and the dead friend equivalent? If the hypnotist had said instead that he was the dear friend, and that as the dead friend he encouraged and approved of her love-making with the dead friend's husband (an equivalent of a mother telling her that she could make love to her father), would this impersonation of the friend by the hypnotist have freed the patient from guilt feelings and from her hysterical depression without the induced regression to childhood? What was the mechanism of the cure? Was the hypnotist equated to her mother, and thus enabled to remove the mother's taboos? Or was the fiancé at first a surrogate father until the hypnotist took over the father's role, thus removing it from the man and thereby making it possible for the patient to have an erotic relation with the man without a barrier of incest taboos? What was the role of her orality and its significance in relationship to the vomiting? In general, what was the role of all those basic facts of her early life, which must have determined the patient's relationship to her parents and to people in general?

The answers to these gaps in information is challenging, both from a theoretical and from a factual point of view. The knowledge of these facts is indispensable for an understanding of the structure of the illness and the dynamics of the recovery. But the fact that recovery could take place so quickly and without hospitalization, in face of the fact that there were so many things which the hypnotist never discovered and that the patient did not know, also has its important theoretical consequences. It faces us with the question: if recovery can take place with the gain of such rudimentary insight, what then is the relationship between unconscious insight, conscious insight, and the process of recovery from a neurosis?

Section 4: Automatic Writing and Drawing

INTRODUCTION

The papers in this section on automatic writing and drawing are all representative of Erickson's favorite field approach, wherein he partially structures a situation that permits the unconscious to express itself in an observable form. While the investigations that gave rise to these papers were all oriented toward validating classical Freudian concepts of mental mechanisms and the unconscious, we can already see the occasional appearance of some of the basic phenomena that would later lead to the utilization of Erickson's work as a foundation for an entirely different model of psychodynamics: the double-bind.

Although at the time of these investigations, in the 1930s, no one had yet heard of the double-bind model (Bateson et al did not formulate it until the 1950s), Erickson's structuring of the field situation and his own choice of words in describing it in protocol I of the first paper of this section ("The experimental demonstration of unconscious mentation by automatic writing," 1937) are such that the actual phenomena under consideration could be interpreted as supporting either the psychoanalytic or the double-bind models. Thus, when Erickson told the subject ". . . *that she was to write something in full conscious awareness of what she was writing, that her writing was to be clearly legible to everyone present, but that in writing it, her unconscious would so guide her hand that she would in actuality write something beyond that which could be read either by herself or by the others present,*" he is structuring an ambiguous situation that permits either the Freudian unconscious or the Batesonian metalevel of a double-bind to come into operation.

When the subject responded to these ambiguous instructions with, "You say words, but they don't make sense," Erickson reports that this was "a flippant reply not in keeping with the serious, general tone of the discussion." The full significance of this flippant remark did not appear until later, when the subject cleverly wrote "thirty" in longhand but attached to it in an ambiguous way the numeral 8. In this way it was ostensibly to be read as "thirty," but it could also be read as "38." Thus "words don't make sense," but a shift from a mental set for written numbers ("thirty") to a numerical set ("30") is required to decode the number 8.

Saying something and then commenting on it through the use of gesture, vocal dynamics, or a flippant remark is a typical means by which a metalevel is manifested in the double-bind model. Thus, to an ambiguous and double-binding set of instructions presented by Erickson, the subject responded with a double-bind reply. As Erickson describes the situation, "By replying in this way she consciously neither accepted nor rejected the instructions, but left herself free to react to the instructions as she chose. Consciously she accepted the task; but at the same time, by this flippant attitude, she shifted onto her unconscious the guidance of her response."

This process by which "she shifted onto her unconscious the guidance of her response" is also the essence of the model of hypnotic responsiveness that the editor later developed in association with Erickson during the 1970s (stages 3 and 4 of the microdynamics of trance and suggestion, presented in Volume One of this series). Thus, we see in this simple empirical situation at least three possible models of explanation, each formulated about a generation apart, all contending for validation. Since the models are not mutually exclusive, they can each perhaps have their own value in facilitating *creative* responses in different experimental and therapeutic situations—"creative" in the true sense that neither the experimenter/clinician nor the subject/patient can predict just what response will be generated.

16. The Experimental Demonstration of Unconscious Mentation By Automatic Writing

Milton H. Erickson

For the most part our knowledge of psychological processes has been achieved through clinical observations. That such knowledge is valid is readily admitted, but its confirmation by other methods is essential. For this reason the application of experimental procedure is a desirable means of retesting conclusions reached clinically. In this way hypotheses may be subjected to direct tests from which the extraneous forces inevitable in clinical situations may be excluded. In an effort to develop methods for this sort of laboratory investigation, the experimental procedures reported here were undertaken.

PROTOCOL I

During an evening gathering of about ten college people a discussion arose about hypnotism and the role of the unconscious in conscious actions. The writer claimed that people could perform an act consciously which would express fully all of their conscious purposes, but which could simultaneously have another unconscious meaning, and that by appropriate measures this unconscious meaning could be brought fully into consciousness. This gave rise to much argument, and presently one of the subjects of the writer's earliest experiments with hypnotism volunteered her services.

In casting about for some act which could be regarded fully so that no doubts might arise, the suggestion was made that the subject be asked to write something, thus making the performance tangible. Accordingly, the subject was told *that she was to write something, in full conscious awareness of what she was writing, that her writing was to be clearly legible to everyone present, but that in writing it her unconscious would so guide*

Reprinted with permission from *The Psychoanalytic Quarterly,* October, 1937, Vol. VI, No. 4.

her hand that she would in actuality write something beyond that which could be read either by herself or by the others present. To these instructions a flippant reply was given, not in keeping with the serious general tone of the discussion, namely, "You say words, but they don't make sense."

There followed further discussion about what should be written. The author proposed that all present should guess the length of time that it had taken a member of the group to move a certain article in the room. The guesses ranged from two seconds to half a minute, the subject alone venturing the absurd estimate of "two to three minutes." Each one defended his own guess warmly, but the subject was peculiarly insistent upon her accuracy. After some general argument the author suggested to the subject that she write her *unconscious guess* as to the length of time involved. She protested emphatically that her conscious and unconscious guesses would be the same, and that there was no point in writing it down since she had already put it into words and defended it orally. However, in response to the author's insistence she began to write. As she set pencil to paper, she looked startled and declared emphatically, "It wasn't either—it was at least two minutes." She then proceeded to write rather slowly and in the uncertain, juvenile script shown in the illustration. Again as she wrote she said, "It wasn't either, I know it was at least two

minutes, nearer three." When finished, she was asked if she knew what she had written. She replied, "Yes, I know, but it isn't so." She was promptly told not to say aloud what she had written, and the paper was passed around with the injunction that each should read it silently.

When all had examined it, the subject was asked what she had written. She replied, "I wrote 'thirty seconds,' but that isn't right because it was at least two minutes, if not three." After scanning the writing again, the author asked if the group accepted her statement of what she had written. Some reexamined the writing but all agreed that it read "thirty seconds." The subject was reminded of the original discussion about hidden unconscious meanings and asked if she was sure she had read it correctly. To this she replied, "As soon as I started to write, I knew I was going to write 'thirty seconds.' I knew that that was wrong, but my hand just went ahead and wrote it." Again she was asked if she was sure she had read her writing correctly. She replied, "Well, you will have to admit that that's a *t* and an *h* and an *i*. Look at that *r*—you can't mistake that, or the *t*. It just has to be thirty. You have all the letters there. I admit the writing is bad, but you try holding paper on your lap when you write and your writing won't be so good either. I'm sure that that *s* is an *s*." Here the subject asked several of the group individually if they, too, felt certain of the identity of the *s*. Finally accepting their reassurances, she continued, "That's a period after *c*, which makes the abbreviation for seconds. 'Thirty sec.' is what it reads, with seconds abbreviated, but my handwriting would be better if I had a better place to put the paper." Again the author asked, "But really, haven't you written something more? Can't you read something more than just 'thirty sec.?' She scanned the paper carefully, as did the other members of the group, but all insisted that the writing clearly and legibly read "thirty sec." The subject continued to insist that she knew what she was going to write immediately upon the initiation of the act of writing, and that she had written exactly what was in her mind.

She was then requested to answer the following questions *by means of automatic writing*, as a method of securing unconscious responses directly. The questions and the answers obtained by the automatic writing are given verbatim:

Q. Does this writing read "thirty sec."?
A. Yes.
Q. Does the writing have any additional meaning?
A. Yes.
Q. Can it be read?
A. Yes.
Q. Has anybody read the writing correctly?
A. No
Q. Is "thirty sec." the correct reading?
A. No.
Q. Is something omitted in reading "thirty sec."?
A. Yes.
Q. Will you write that which has been omitted?
A. Yes.
Q. All right, write what has been omitted.
A. 8 [written as a numeral].
Q. What does the writing really read, then?
A. 38 sec. [in numerals.]

Immediately after writing the last reply, the subject picked up the original writing and declared, "Yes, it does read *38*, only I didn't realize that *y* was written as an *8*. I can see it now. I wasn't thinking of numbers and I was sure that *thirty* was wrong. Yet I knew that the *t* and the *r* were plain, and I was sure the *s* was an *s*. I can see the *8* now, but I couldn't before even though I know now that I wrote it. I was so sure you were wrong when you acted as if I had written something I didn't know about."

The subject was then asked to write automatically the replies to the following questions, which are given verbatim with their answers:

Q. Do you recall the instructions I gave you about combining conscious and unconscious activity?
A. Yes.
Q. Is this writing your demonstration of this?
A. Yes.

Summary of Protocol I

The main steps in this observation can be summarized as follows:

1. A general discusssion of the question of whether a single act can simultaneously express both a conscious and an unconscious meaning and purpose.
2. The decision to test this through automatic writing.
3. An offer to serve as the "test animal" by a woman who had frequently been subjected to hypnosis by the experimenter.
4. The request made that clearly and consciously she should write something which contained a concealed double meaning.
5. Her flippant retort.
6. The execution of this order: while she is thinking and saying "two to three minutes," she writes out in script "thirty sec." in such a way that the *y* conceals the number *8* and can also be read to mean "38 seconds."
7. This is done so cleverly that at first no one except the experimenter consciously recognizes the presence of the concealed figure *8*.
8. When asked to describe *aloud* what she had written, the subject insists that she has written "thirty seconds." When asked to describe this *by automatic writing,* the subject writes "38 sec.," thus indicating that on an unconscious level she was fully aware of the little joke with which she had carried out the experimenter's request, although on a conscious level she had no knowledge of it.

Discussion

In the above experiment two types of behavior attract attention. The first of these is the subject's flippant and ambiguous reply when given her instructions. By replying in this way she consciously neither accepted nor rejected the instructions, but left herself free to react to the instructions as she chose. Consciously she accepted the task; but at the same time by this flippant attitude she shifted onto her unconscious the guidance of her response.

To support this shift another simple technique of self-distraction was employed: the grossly exaggerated guess which she made about the time. Although of the others present none guessed more than a half a minute, the subject insisted that the action had taken two to three minutes. Thus she placed herself at variance with the entire group and gave herself a conscious issue to battle over. As a result, as she began to write, she was concerned not with the identity of *what* she was writing, but rather with the problem of her correctness.

Then, after she had completed her writing, and her defenses against full conscious awareness were threatened again as the experimenter asked her to examine her writing, she rendered this dangerous procedure harmless by isolating the individual letters one from another. Even so the irregularity of the *y* raised a pressing problem. From this she extricated herself by stressing the difficulty of writing on paper held in her lap (in itself a valid rationalization) and then furthered this distraction by raising an immediate and insistent doubt concerning the identity of the letter *s*, thereby displacing to safer territory the doubt properly centering about the *y*. This was followed by still further distraction of her attention to the period and to the abbreviated form of the word. Having thus identified the two parts, she was able again to identify the phrase as a whole, avoiding as she did so any other possibility. Thus, with the irregularity of the critical letter *y* explained plausibly by the physical difficulties of writing, and its identity bounded on both sides by clearly identified letters, any critical conscious consideration of its meaning was precluded.

When she was pushed still further to search for hidden meanings in what she had written, the emotions involved in the unconscious purpose to keep her little joke to herself were expressed as an anxiety concerning the experimenter, later described as the feeling, "I was so sure you were wrong."

Finally, mention must be made of her use of two different types of written symbols, the word form and the numerical form, to express a unitary thought. The tendency for one pattern of thinking to persist, and the difficulty in shifting to another type, are generally recognized. The task imposed on the subject of this experimentation implied the simultaneous performance of two different types of mental activity, one of which would be obvious and attention-compelling and thus able to establish a pattern of mental activity that could obscure and inhibit the recognition of the other. Hence the written production began with a word and ended with a word, with the numerical symbol secreted in a part of the first word, although when seen in isolation it is easily recognizable.

Thus by writing the phrase "thirty-eight seconds" with the eight as a numerical symbol forming the *y* of the word *thirty*, by apparently failing to understand instructions, by developing minor affects of a mild anxiety, by rationalizing realities, and by employing techniques of self-distraction and mixing together two different types of symbolic expression, she was able to execute consciously an act which in itself was fully expressive and complete, but which simultaneously possessed an additional unrecognized significance at another level of mentation. By a technique of automatic writing this hidden meaning was revealed by the subject, who only then could recognize it consciously.

PROTOCOL II

A 22-year-old girl, a college graduate and member of the staff, had been one of those present when the previous experiment had been performed. She was interested in the possibility of independent unconscious thinking and asked to be hypnotized and to be taught automatic writing as a possible means of identifying some of her own inner conflicts. After some discussion an appointment was arranged, and that very evening an attempt was made to hypnotize her.

She was exceedingly resistive, and finally it became necessary to pretend to abandon the attempt. The hypnotist feigned interest in a radio program and somewhat discourteously ignored her request that he try again. She became resentful at this and retaliated, perhaps, by going into a spontaneous sleep. As soon as she was sleeping soundly, she was roused gently, and then by slowly graduated suggestions she was led into a fairly deep hypnotic sleep. In this state a domineering type of suggestion was employed, and she was literally forced to walk about, to change her position, and to manifest catalepsy, in order to induce a deeper trance.[1]

During these procedures casual mention was made of automatic writing—a few general remarks, followed by a vague hint that she herself might sometime do automatic writing. Then, after further and more explicit discussion, a definite suggestion was made that she write automatically at once. She was seated at a desk and instructed to dream of pleasant things of long ago, and told that as she did this her hand would automatically write some simple unemotional statements. She complied

[1]The domineering type of suggestion employed here is used reluctantly and only under special circumstances such as this. This is not the place for a full discussion of the relationship of the technique employed to the underlying unconscious fantasies which the subject brings to the hypnotic experience. Empirically, however, it has been found necessary at times, when dealing with subjects who consciously approach the experience with enthusiastic cooperation but with exceptionally intense unconscious resistances, to subject them to this type of exercise before undertaking any steps relating to the experiment itself.

fairly readily, showing the typical juvenile script of automatic writing, and wrote, "The lady washed my hair," followed by, "Cats and dogs fight."

When it was observed that her writing was legible and her arm movements free, she was given the further suggestion that after awakening, whenever the experimenter rapped on his desk or chair, she should automatically write the sentence, "'Twas a dark and dreary night." She was also instructed to write legibly, easily, rapidly, and without paying any conscious attention to her hand.

The subject was wakened, and subsequently eight times during the course of the evening she was induced to write the phrase, "'Twas a dark and dreary night," in response to eight separate tapping signals. Some of these were done while she was awake, but with her attention distracted. Some were done while she was again in a state of hypnotic sleep. At the end, under hypnosis, she was instructed to remember nothing of the entire complicated activity of the evening except the fact that she had been in a trance—once. It was this command which became the storm center around which the experiment focused.

Several times during the course of these observations, when questioned as to the number of times she had written the posthypnotic phrase, the subject became confused and had made varying mistakes. It was evident, however, that she was always struggling against a too-compliant acquiescence to the suggestions which had been given her under hypnosis. The same attitude was indicated now at the end of the experiment.

For some minutes she was allowed to sleep quietly, after which she was awakened and a casual conversation was resumed. Suddenly this was interrupted in order to ask, "How many times have you been in a trance this evening?" She looked puzzled and then very slowly and very thoughtfully replied, "three times, maybe four, but I wouldn't know how many because *all I want to say is 'once'* and I can't figure out why I should want to say 'once.'" The remark was made casually, "Well, if you want to say numbers and are interested in saying numbers, just say the first number that comes into your mind." She replied with unwonted alacrity, "Thirty-five." The experimenter had expected her to say "eight," thus completing her rejection of the general instructions for amnesia which she had begun in her statement about the number of times she had been in a trance. Although she had wanted to reply "once" in obedience to my instructions, she actually had answered "three to four."

She was asked, "Why did you say, 'thirty-five'?" She answered, "I don't know. That was the first number that came to my mind that seemed to be right." Asked, "Why is it right?" she answered, "It just seems that way." "Has it any meaning?" "Well, all numbers have meaning, and I presume you would say then that thirty-five has a meaning." The experimenter wrote the number 35 and asked her to look at it carefully and to tell what it meant. She looked confused and puzzled, kept glancing at the number and then at the experimenter as if she could not understand what was meant. Finally she declared that the request was meaningless to her: "I just can't understand what you mean." Her whole manner suggested that she was blocked and unable to think clearly. In silence the experimenter wrote clearly on the paper, "7 plus 1 equals 8, which is the reason for saying 35." She still looked at it as blankly as a schoolchild struggling helplessly with a problem in arithmetic, and when told to think that over carefully, she smiled in an amused fashion, read it aloud, and said, "That doesn't mean anything to me. What has seven plus one equals eight got to do with thirty-five? There isn't any connection." Here again she seemed to show the pseudo-stupidity of a frightened schoolchild whose unconscious affects have got in the way of the thinking processes. She was asked, "Does your unconscious know what that means?" She replied, "I don't know, maybe it hasn't got any meanings."

The suggestion was given that her hand write automatically. She looked rather puzzled, picked up the pencil, and then glanced up for a cue. She was asked, "Does your unconscious understand that sentence?" She continued to look at the experimenter with a puzzled expression while her hand wrote freely in typical automatic script, "yes." When she had finished writing, the pencil dropped to the paper and she became aware that her hand had written. She looked at the word "yes," spelled it out, and asked, "What does that mean? Why did my hand write that?" The experimenter suggested, "That is the answer to my question," to which she replied, "What question?" The question was repeated, "Does your unconscious understand that sentence?" She again looked at "yes," grasped its relationship to the question, but still looked puzzled as to its meaning. Then she was asked, "Has that statement anything to do with the instructions given you in the last trance?" Again she wrote "yes," while still studying the experimenter's face as if she did not understand what he said. As before she became aware of having written "yes" only as her pencil dropped on the page. She promptly inquired, "What does all this mean?" This query was answered with the further question, "Has it got anything to do with something you have done?" Again the automatic writing answered "yes."

The following series of questions was then asked, to each of which the subject replied with automatic writing, each time showing bewilderment and an inability to understand as she watched her hand write. The manner of asking each question was to address it to her hand as if it were a third person which will explain the reference to the subject herself as "she."

Q. You have written a sentence a number of times for me?
A. Yes.
Q. You know how many times you have written it?
A. Yes.

Q. Could you tell me how many times?
A. Yes.
Q. Would *she* know?
A. No.

There the subject interrupted to declare, "That isn't so. I know how many times I wrote it. Look, here I wrote it three times, and there once, that makes four, and here are two more, and there's another, no, that's the same one, no, here's that one—one, two, three, four, five, six, seven," pointing each time, "seven times I wrote it. You can see for yourself." In making this count, and pointing each time, she had moved her hand repeatedly back and forth over the eighth writing without noticing it, although it was fully as plain as the rest of the writing.

Again addressing the subject's hand:

Q. That's the right count for her, isn't it?
A. Yes [a pause, and then in fainter characters and less clearly formed letters], for her.

As the subject read this she demanded, "What does that mean, 'for her'? I'm the only one that's writing—'for her'—Oh yes, that's what you just said when you spoke."

Q. Shall we tell her?
A. No [pause], not yet.

Here the subject read this reply aloud wonderingly, repeated "not yet," then in a tone of marked affect demanded, "Say, what's going on here?" Then apologetically, "Oh, I beg your pardon, Dr. Erickson, I didn't mean that, I'm sorry."

Q. It's all right, isn't it?
A. Sure!

Here the subject read her answer aloud saying, "Sure? Why, Dr. Erickson, I wouldn't answer you like that, I don't mean to be impolite. You know that, don't you? I didn't write that."

Q. Was that number a chance selection?
A. No [written in large characters with pencil pressed heavily].
Q. Has that number the same significance as the answers you have been writing? [pointing to the previous answer, "No, not yet."].
A. Yes [written emphatically].

Q. What do you think when I write [suiting the action to the word] "7 plus 1 equals 8 which is the reason for saying 35?"

As this was written, she declared, "I just got a wild desire to snicker, and I don't know why. You are so serious, and it seems so silly." But as she was making this statement, her hand was writing automatically, "You know too much," concluding the writing by banging the pencil down to form a period. This attracted her attention, and she read it over and over in an abstracted, puzzled fashion, glancing up from time to time, trying to speak but apparently blocking each time, glancing down at the writing immediately each time that the words failed to come.

After some patient waiting:

Q. Has that [pointing to the written equation] got anything to do with the instructions given in the last trance?
A. [Verbally] Last trance, why, I can't remember—last trance, which one—what happened—I—I——

Here she was interrupted by her hand again banging the pencil on the desk, and she became aware consciously that she had written, "You are too wise." She read it aloud, glanced at the experimenter, repeated it, and said, "Why, my hand must mean you—that's impertinent.—Just like this is [pointing to the "You know too much"]. I don't mean to be disrespectful—it isn't me—it's my hand [a pause]. Why, you and my hand are talking to each other—what are you talking about—tell me—tell me." Here the subject became so insistent that the experimenter was forced to yield.

Q. Would you like to know?
A. Yes [pause], tell her.
Q. Will you tell her?
A. No [pause], you.

During this questioning the subject watched her hand in a fascinated fashion and seemed greatly puzzled by the replies her hand was giving.

Q. How many times have you written, "'Twas a dark and dreary night"?
A. [Verbally] I wrote it seven times—but what has that got—oooh, ooh, I wrote it eight times—I forgot—you told me when I was asleep to forget everything—I only forgot part—I remember now—I wrote it here [searching the paper and identifying the writing correctly] see seven and one more, that makes eight, just like you said, but what has that got to do with thirty-five?

Q. Will you tell her?
A. No—you [automatic writing].
Q. I will tell her, but you fill in my explanation.

My explanation was: "Look at thirty-five—you see three, five." Here the subject interrupted, "Oh, I see it now. You told me to forget everything in the last trance and you rapped on the desk and I wrote and I remembered that I wrote it—I didn't forget it and I wanted to tell you that. I still remembered that I had written it eight times but I only remembered writing it seven times, if you get what I mean, and when you asked me to give a number, I thought I was just giving any number. But now I can see that I was telling you eight times, and I was worried that you wouldn't understand, and when you wrote 'seven plus one equals eight which is the reason for saying thirty-five' I knew you understood, and I thought you were too smart. No, that isn't what I said, I wrote 'you are too wise,' but I meant too smart. I just told you thirty-five because that meant eight times. I can see it just as plain now."

The subject then stated that as she had written the two "impertinent" statements, she had had a "wild desire to snicker" but had controlled herself for fear of giving offense, and that this desire had been replaced by a sense of elation and satisfaction.

Summary of Protocol II

1. Request of a young female graduate student to be hypnotized and to be taught automatic writing.
2. Unsuccessful effort to hypnotize her.
3. Pretense of abandoning this effort.
4. Spontaneous sleep.
5. Spontaneous sleep converted into hypnotic sleep.
6. Forceful deepening of hypnotic sleep with induction of vigorous activity.
7. First automatic writing, consisting of irrelevant phrases while daydreaming.
8. Posthypnotic suggestion to write a special posthypnotic phrase whenever a tapping signal was given.
9. At this point the subject was put through a complicated series of maneuvers, some of them while awake but under the guidance of a posthypnotic suggestion, some of them under superinduced repetitions of the hypnotic state. During the course of these complicated tests, on eight occasions she wrote down the posthypnotic test phrase in response to the tapping signal.
10. Finally, while asleep, she was given the suggestion that she

should remember nothing of the entire evening's experience except the fact that she had been in a hypnotic trance once. The obedience to this command was used as the experimental test situation.

11. Quiet sleep for several minutes, then awakened.
12. Asked how often she had been in an hypnotic state, she struggled against the suggestion (10), but acknowledged that she had a strong impulsion to say "once" although she knew it was more than that.
13. Finally came the number test with a concealed double meaning. When asked to say the first number she thought of, she said "thirty-five" and could give no reason for saying it.
14. Series of steps by which the point was made clear to the hypnotist and to the subject that 35 was an elliptical and secretive method of writing, "three plus five equals eight," to indicate the number of times which she had written the posthypnotic phrase. During this phase the patient's replies were divided so completely as almost to indicate a split into two organized egos, her conscious ego and the unconscious pseudo-ego organized around her automatic writing hand.

Discussion

For a definite reason these somewhat rambling observations were made without a carefully prearranged program. Their immediate goal was simply to demonstrate experimentally, and beyond any possible doubt, the fact that consciously chosen words, thoughts, and acts can mean more than one thing at a time: their conscious or manifest content on the one hand, and a latent, unconscious content on the other. Thus in these experiments what has long been known to be true for dreams is shown to be true for other human psychic processes. The more significant ultimate purpose of these random observations, however, was to seek out ways in which the technique of hypnotism and more particularly of automatic writing could be used for experimental purposes, and to suggest specific problems to which they might be applied. The experiments give rise therefore to various somewhat heterogenous reflections.

1. In the first experiment one is struck by the versatility of the unconscious with respect to the methods it employs in order to dissimulate its purposes. The technique illustrated in the first protocol offers an opportunity to study the relationship between specific types of normal or neurotic characters and the various methods of unconscious dissimulation which different neurotic types habitually employ.

The development of such a study in relation to the personality as a whole necessitates a simultaneous study of the subject by psychoanalysis.

2. In the first experiment devices are used unconsciously which are familiar to us chiefly in humor. It would seem, therefore, that humorlessly and quite without conscious comic intent the unconscious can use irony, punning, and the technique of the puzzle. In short, the techniques of conscious humor are an earnest and serious matter in unconscious psychic processes. This is always particularly disconcerting when weighty and significant problems are treated by means of unconsciously chosen representatives and devices which to our conscious judgments seem ridiculous and trivial. This has been observed repeatedly in dream analysis, and it is clearly demonstrated here in automatic writing and hypnosis. There are few findings in the field of psychoanalysis, or its experimental study through hypnotism, which excite more skepticism than does this observation.

3. In the second experiment described above two other interesting facts are presented for consideration:

a. The seemingly unmotivated elation which arose when the subject put over a secret and unconscious defiance suggests a mechanism for certain types of elations in patients.

b. The particular kind of block in thinking which was produced during the course of the experiment is strongly reminiscent of thinking difficulties observable in schoolchildren. There is a hint here that the further elaboration of this type of investigation may be of use to educators in the problems of some children who, despite good native gifts, fail in academic studies.

In conclusion we may say that these experiments demonstrate not merely the coexistence of hidden meanings in conscious acts, but also carry the promise of usefulness for an experimental attack on many significant problems. It is obvious, however, that all such work demands a close collaboration between those familiar with experimental work in the field of hypnosis and those familiar with the psychoanalytic technique. For adequate development of the applications of such experiments to the problems involved in understanding psychic dynamisms, it would be advisable to have the subjects under psychoanalytic study in order to observe fully their reactions to the experimental procedure, to determine the influence of the experiment upon the subject, and to throw light on analytic theory and its applications.

17. The Use of Automatic Drawing in the Interpretation and Relief of a State of Acute Obsessional Depression

Milton H. Erickson and Lawrence S. Kubie

No matter how accurate any body of scientific theory may be, its confirmation by the use of some technique other than that on which the theory first rested is always valuable. This is the most convincing way of ruling out the misleading influence of possible undetected methodological fallacies. With this in mind the following case is reported in detail because, by means of a nonpsychoanalytic technique, it illustrates a certain type of symbolic activity which is comparable in character to that studied by psychoanalysis in dreams and in psychotic states, and because of its clear demonstration of certain of the dynamic relationships which exist between conscious and unconscious aspects of the human psyche. Finally, it is reported because of our interest in this general type of technique as a means of uncovering unconscious material, and because of the challenge this may offer to certain phases of psychoanalytic technique (Erickson, 1937b).

HISTORY

A 24-year-old girl attended a clinical demonstration of hypnosis for a class in psychology at the university. At this demonstration particular emphasis was laid on the phenomenon of automatic writing and on the integrated functioning of subconscious processes as a seemingly independent entity in the total psyche. Afterward she inquired at length about the possibility of acquiring the ability to do automatic writing herself, and whether it was probable or even possible that her own unconscious might function in a coordinated, integrated fashion without her conscious awareness. Affirmative replies were given to both inquiries. Thereupon, as the explanation of her interest she volunteered the statement that during the preceding month she had become unhappy and uneasy in all

Reprinted with permission from *The Psychoanalytic Quarterly,* October, 1938, Vol. VII, No. 4.

her relationships for some unknown reason, and that she was becoming increasingly "worried, unhappy and depressed" despite the fact that she knew of no personal problem that could trouble her seriously. She then asked if she might try automatic writing through which her unconscious, acting independently, could give an account of whatever was troubling her. She was told that she might try this plan if she were really interested, and she responded that first she would like to have a formal psychiatric review of her life.

Accordingly, on the next day she was interviewed at length. The more important data obtained in this interview may be summarized as follows:

1. She was an only child, idolized by her parents, as they in turn were by her, living in what seemed to be a very happy home.
2. Her adjustments to college had been excellent until the preceding month, when her work had begun to suffer seriously in consequence of the sudden development of "worry," "concern," "fear," "unhappiness," and "horrible depression," which persisted almost continuously and for which she knew no cause whatever.
3. Recently she had been impelled to read some psychoanalytic literature and had found the subject of symbolism "most interesting and fascinating," but "silly," "meaningless," and "without any scientific validity." When asked for the references, she replied, "Oh, I just thumbed through a lot of books and journals in the library, but the only thing that interested me was symbolism."
4. For a month, and only since reading about symbolism, she had noted the development of a habit of "scribbling," "scratching," "drawing pictures and lines" when telephoning, studying, sitting in the classroom, or merely idling. She did this in an abstracted manner, usually without noting what she was doing, and thought of it merely as a sign of nervousness, of a desire to do something, but what this might be she did not know. She added that it was a "jittery" habit, objectionable because it "dirtied" the walls of telephone booths, the tablecloths in restaurants, and clean paper in her notebooks. (Throughout the interview the patient constantly demonstrated this "habit" most adequately, and it was obvious that she was not aware that she was doing so. Only at the close of the interview did she notice her scribbling, and remarked, "Well, I guess I have demonstrated that jitteryness better than I described it.")
5. Finally, the only personal problem which troubled her consciously was the fact that her three years at college had slowly and gradually separated her from her most intimate girlhood friend,

in spite of that girl's regular weekend visits to the patient's home. The patient felt "lonely" and "resentful" about this, and said that during the preceding few weeks this angry feeling had increased until it had become an "uncontrollable resentment" over the loss of her friend. Nor was this obsessive resentment diminished by her realization that there was nothing she could do about it because of the ever-increasing divergence of their interests.

At the completion of her story, in the manner so characteristic of psychiatric patients who have told more than they know, she dismissed her account as probably being of no significance and asked insistently whether now, after hearing her story, it still was thought possible to secure by means of automatic writing the facts which were pertinent to her problem—"if there really were a problem." She thought that if she could read subsequently whatever she might write automatically, she could thus force herself to become consciously aware of what was troubling her. She also wanted to know if the examiner was confident that her subconscious could function in a sufficiently integrated fashion to give a coherent, understandable account.

In response to these anxious inquiries she was told emphatically that she could do exactly as she wished, and this was followed by repeated, carefully worded suggestions given to her in a gentle but insistent and attention-compelling fashion, which served to induce the passively receptive state that marks the initiation of a light hypnotic trance. These suggestions were to the effect that:

1. The time intervening until her appointment on the next day would be spent by her subconscious in reviewing and organizing all the material to which she wished access.

2. In addition, her subconscious would decide upon the method or means of communication and would select some tangible method by which to communicate what it had to say in a way which would be clearly understandable to the examiner and also in a fashion which could, at the proper moment, be clearly understood by the patient herself, so that no doubts or equivocations could arise.

3. Since she herself had suggested automatic writing, pencils and papers would be supplied, so that she would have an opportunity to employ that method in the same abstracted manner as that in which she had made her drawings during the interview.

(The reader will note that this suggestion actually constituted in its significance an indirect command to repeat her *drawings* in an intelligible fashion. It was given for the reason that automatic writing is often most difficult to secure on first attempts. It was to be expected that this would be even more true with this patient, whose entire story implied a resolute, unconscious reluctance to know certain things, despite her strong concomitant conscious desire to become aware of them. For her, therefore, automatic writing itself would have proved too revealing, if successful at all, and would have forced on the patient a too rapid realization of her repressed material. This, of course, would either have proved profoundly upsetting or would have summoned up vigorous repressive mechanisms to forestall the complete communication of her material.)

4. In the interval before her next appointment she was to keep her mind consciously busy with studying, reading light fiction, and social activities, thus supplying herself with innocuous topics for conversation on which she could report consciously, so that at the time of the appointment communications concerning her problem would be imparted entirely by subconscious automatic behavior (the drawing) and not become part of her conscious speech.

At the end of the interview the patient seemed rather confused and uncertain about her instructions. She made several hesitating attempts to pick up the sheets of paper on which she had again been "nervously scribbling," suddenly made a last plea for reassurance, and then left quickly when this had been given.

Examination of her drawings after her departure disclosed various figures and lines repeated over and over in varying sizes. There were long and short lines—vertical, horizontal, and oblique. Some were traced lightly, others heavily shaded. Also, there were spirals, cylinders, triangles, squares, and rectangles of various proportions, some drawn lightly and others heavily. While she had been making these drawings, no sequences or relationships had been observed. One peculiarity, however, was the fact that each figure had been drawn as an isolated unit with no attempt to run one into the next.

A subsequent examination of two different books of her lecture notes showed that her "nervous scribbling" had been a sudden development of the preceding weeks. In these notebooks page after page was found with the same limited types of figures and lines, drawn over and over in a totally disconnected, confused fashion (see Figure 1).

The next day the patient appeared promptly and remarked at once that the suggestions given her the day before seemed to have been effective, since she had not thought about herself at all after leaving the office, and she had even lost conscious interest in her problem so completely that she had returned only because she felt herself to be under an obligation to keep her appointment despite her lack of interest in its purpose. She also explained that she had read a recent novel and was prepared to relate the entire story in detail, remarking facetiously that it would be a cheap way for the examiner to become posted on the latest information of the literary world.

She was told promptly that she could start the story at once; and as she did so, her chair was carefully placed sideways to the desk so that her right arm rested on the desk in close proximity to paper and pencils, while the examiner took a position diagonally opposite. Thus, although she faced away from the paper, it remained well within the range of her peripheral vision.

Figure 1

Shortly after she had begun to tell the story of the book, she abstractedly picked up the pencil and in a laborious, strained fashion began to repeat on the upper half of the sheet of paper the drawings of the previous day, now and then glancing down at her productions for a moment or so in an absentminded fashion. As before, no particular sequence of the drawings was noted, but a significant duplication of some of the elements may be observed in Figure 2.

When she had completed these drawings, she became rather confused in her speech, and was observed to relax and tighten her grip on the pencil as if she wanted to lay it down but found herself unable to do so. She was encouraged here by an insistent, low-toned suggestion, "Go ahead, keep on, it's all right, go ahead, go ahead, keep on."

She remarked immediately, "Oh yes, I know where I am, I just lost the thread of the story for a moment," and continued the narrative.

At the same time her hand was seen to take a fresh grip on the pencil and to shove the pad forward so as to make the lower half of the paper available, and she drew a line as if to divide the paper in halves. Then in a slow and deliberate fashion, with a marked increase in the tension of her right hand and some speeding of her speech, she began to construct a picture by arranging the elements which she had previously drawn so often and so repetitively in an incoherent manner into an orderly, systematic whole. It was as if she had first laid out the materials for her construction and was now putting them together. Thus, the four heavily shaded lines of equal length became a square, and the other units were fitted together to form the picture shown in Figure 3.

Figure 2

In completing the square, however, the patient showed marked uncertainty about its lower-left-hand corner, and kept glancing down at it abstractedly for a moment or so at a time. Finally she distorted the corner slightly, leaving it open. Also, in making the lower-right-hand corner she pressed down unduly, breaking the pencil point.

In making the diagonal line extending downward from the lower-left-hand corner of the square, her hand moved with sudden force and speed. Then, after a considerable pause, her hand moved more and more slowly on the up stroke to the lower-right-hand corner of the square, the line wavering; then finally her hand moved quickly and forcibly over to the shaded triangle.

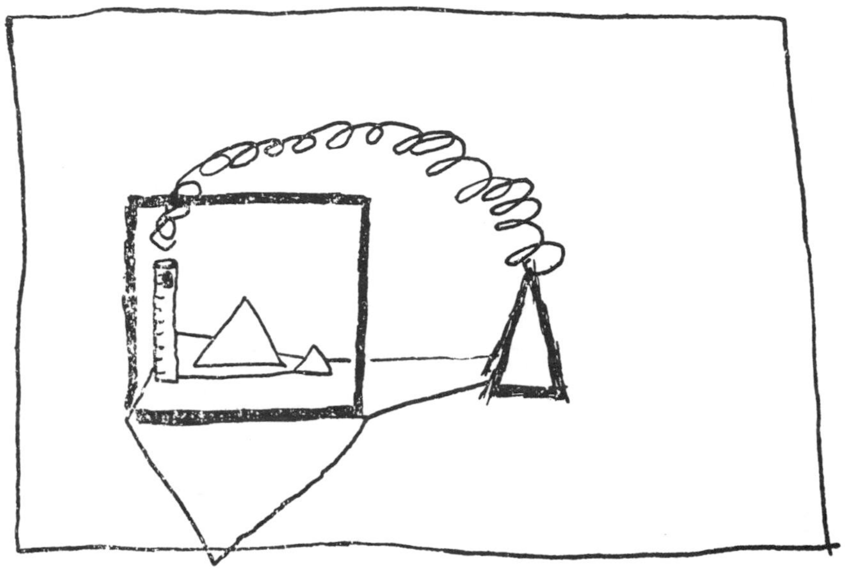

Figure 3

Upon drawing the line connecting the small triangle with the heavily shaded triangle, her hand stopped short as it approached the side of the square and placed a period. Following this her hand lifted and moved over the edge as if surmounting a barrier, after which it completed the line in a steady, firm manner.

The spiral line connecting the cylinder and the shaded triangle began freely and easily, but as it approached the triangle the hand movements became increasingly labored and slow.

Repeatedly during the drawing process the patient's hand would return to the larger of the two light triangles, as if to touch it up a bit and to make it more perfect in outline, while the shaded triangle was drawn roughly.

During her drawing it was possible to record the order in which the various elements were added to the total picture.

1. Square
2. Cylinder
3. Large light triangle
4. Small triangle
5. Connecting lines between cylinder and the large triangle, the large triangle and the little triangle, and the cylinder and the little triangle
6. Enclosing rectangle

7. Heavily shaded triangle
8. Connecting line between the little triangle and the shaded triangle
9. The line leading from the cylinder out of the square and beyond the rectangle, then back to the square and thence to the shaded triangle
10. The spiral line
11. The central shading of the upper part of the cylinder

As she completed the picture, she glanced casually at it several times without seeming to see it. This was followed by a noisy dropping of the pencil, which attracted her notice. Thereupon she immediately called attention to her drawing, picking up her pencil as she did so. Then, using her left hand, she tore off the sheet from the pad to examine it more closely, leaving her right hand in a writing position as if waiting for something. Noting this, the examiner inferred a subconscious desire to make a secret comment. Accordingly the suggestion was given, "A short, vertical line means 'yes,' a short horizontal line means 'no.'

Misapplying this suggestion, the patient scanned the drawing carefully, declared that she saw no such lines, and asked how they could mean anything.

The question was then asked, "Is it all there?"

She replied, "I suppose so, if there is anything there at all," while her hand, without her awareness, made a "yes" sign.

"Everything?"

"Well, I suppose if anything is there, everything is," and again her hand made the "yes" sign without her awareness.

She scanned the picture carefully for some moments and then remarked, "Well, it's just silly nonsense, meaningless. Do you mean to say you can make any sense out of that scratching—to use your own words, that it tells everything?"

Apparently in answer to her own question her hand made another "yes" sign and then dropped the pencil as if the task were now complete. Without waiting for a reply she continued, "It's funny! Even though I know that picture is silly, I know it means something because right now I've got an urge to give you something and, even though I know it's silly, I'm going to give it to you anyway because it's connected with that." Pointing to the shaded triangle, she took from her pocket a packet of matches advertising a local hotel and dropped it on the desk.

Then she immediately consulted her watch, declaring that she had to leave, and seemed to be experiencing a mild panic. However, after a little urging, she consented to answer a few questions about what the picture might mean. She looked the drawing over and offered the following comments, which she insisted she could not elaborate:

"Two pictures in frames, a large one," she explained, pointing to the rectangle, "and a small one," pointing to the square, "with the corner broken." Pointing to the figures in the square she said, "These are all connected, and the connection between the little one," pointing to the small triangle, "and that," pointing to the shaded triangle, "is broken. And that," she added, indicating the cylinder, "is a cigarette with smoke. We all smoke in our family; maybe those are father's matches I gave you. But the whole thing makes no sense at all. Only a psychiatrist could see anything in it," and with that she rushed from the office only to return at once to ask, "When can I see you again?" Upon being told, "Just as soon as you want to know a bit more, call me," she rushed away. No comments were made upon the unitary drawings at the top of the page, and she seemed not to notice them.

About three weeks later she appeared unexpectedly "to report progress." She stated that evidently her drawings must have meant something since she had experienced a marked change in her emotions. She no longer felt worried or depressed, though at times she felt an "intense dread of something," as if she were "going to stumble onto something," and, "I have a feeling that I'm going to find out something dreadful." With much hesitation she added, "What I really mean is that I have a feeling that I am getting ready to know something I already know, but don't know I know it. I know that sounds awfully silly, but it's the only way I can explain, and I am really afraid to know what it's all about. And it's connected with these matches," handing the examiner a second packet similar to the first. "We [the family] had dinner at the hotel last night, and that's where I got them. I saw another packet on the library table last night, but these are the ones I got."

All the other remarks were casual in character, nothing further was learned, and she left rather hurriedly, apparently somewhat uneasy and confused in mind.

Two weeks later she again appeared unexpectedly, declaring as before that she had come "to report progress," and explaining that in the interim she had experienced the development of an absolute certainty that the drawing was meaningful, that "there is a complete story in that picture that anybody can read, and I'm getting terribly curious to know what it is." Here she demanded to see the drawing, and after scrutinizing it closely remarked, "Really, it still looks like a mess of nothing. I just know it's the whole story, too, but why I say that I don't know. But I am sure that my subconscious knows a lot that it won't tell me. I have a feeling that it is just waiting for my conscious mind to prepare itself for a shock, and it's just making me darned curious so I won't mind the shock." When asked when she would know, she replied, "Oh, I suppose not long," and then became emotionally disturbed and insisted on changing the topic of conversation.

A week later she came in to state that she had an engagement to dine with her girlhood friend at the hotel that evening, and that this was causing her much emotional distress. She explained: "I hate to see our friendship broken up just by drifting apart the way we have. And I don't like my attitude toward Jane. You see, Jane's a year younger than me, and she's got a boyfriend and she's pretty much in love with him. She says she thinks I know him, but she won't tell me his name or anything about him, and I don't like my attitude toward her, because I'm so jealous of her that I just hate her intensely; I'd like to pull her hair out. I just hate her because I feel as if she had taken my boyfriend away from me, but that's silly, because I haven't got a boyfriend. I don't want to keep my appointment with her because I know I'm going to quarrel with her, and there really isn't anything to quarrel about, but I know I'll just say one nasty thing after another, and I don't want to, but it's going to happen and I can't avoid it. And another thing, after I quarrel with her I'm going to have a fight with my father. I've just been working up to this for a week. I've only had two fights with my father, and they were both about my college plans, but I don't know what this fight's going to be about. Probably some little thing like his carelessness in smoking and dropping ashes on the rug at home, probably any little old excuse. I just hope father isn't in when I get home. Can't you say something to me so this all won't happen? But I suppose as long as it's in me it might as well come out and get it over with. When I made the appointment with Jane, I had a vague idea of what was going to happen, and as soon as she accepted I could see, just as plain as could be, what I've just told you, so I hung up the receiver before I had a chance to cancel my invitation."

More remarks were made of a similar character and significance, but all attempts to discuss her drawings or to secure an elucidation of her premonitions failed, since she declared that the only things of interest to her at the moment were the "impending battles."

The next day she dropped in the office to report hurriedly, "I'm in a rush. All I've got time for is to tell you it all happened just as I predicted. Jane and I started out visiting nicely, and then I got to wise-cracking and began hurting her feelings. I didn't notice that at first, and when I did, I just didn't give a damn and I went to town on her in the cruelest, nastiest, most subtle fashion I could. I didn't say anything particularly, but it was the way I said it and mocked her. When she cried I felt a lot better, and although I was ashamed of myself I didn't feel any sympathy for her. I wound up by telling her that we could agree to disagree and she could go her way and I'd go my way. Then I went home and Father was sitting there reading and I was itching for him to say something, just anything. I was awfully amused at myself, but I figured there wasn't anything I could do about it, so I began smoking and pacing the floor. Finally he told me to sit down and be quiet, and that just set me off. I just yelled at him to shut up, that I could *run around* if I wanted to, and he couldn't say anything to me. It was too late to go out, and if I *wanted to run around* I had just as much right as he had. I told him he might think he was smart, but I was a lot smarter, that I wasn't born yesterday, that I knew what it was all about, and a lot of silly, incoherent, tempery things that I really didn't mean and that didn't make sense. Finally he got disgusted and told me if I couldn't talk sense to shut up and go to bed and sleep it off. So I did. And the funny thing is that when I woke up this morning, I thought of those drawings I did for you, and I tried to think about them, but all I could think was first the word 'today' and then the word 'tomorrow,' and finally I just kept thinking 'tomorrow.' Does that mean anything to you? It doesn't to me," and with this remark she took her departure.

The next afternoon she appeared and declared, "After I left you yesterday, I had a funny feeling I had made an appointment with you for today, but I really knew I hadn't. Then this morning the first thing I thought of was that drawing, and I knew that I could understand it now, and I've been thinking about it all day. I remember the whole picture; I can see it in my mind plainly, but it's still meaningless, doesn't mean a thing. Let me look at it."

She was handed the picture, which she scrutinized in a most painstaking fashion, with an expression of intense curiosity on her face, finally sighing and putting it down to remark, "Well, I guess I'm mistaken. It doesn't mean a thing—just a silly picture after all." Then suddenly brightening, "But if you will say just a word to start me off, I know I'll understand it."

No heed was given this indirect request, and she repeatedly examined the picture only to lay it aside each time in an intensely puzzled fashion.

Finally, she repeated her request for a "starting word" and was countered with the question, "What word?" To this she replied, "Oh, any word. You know what the picture means, so just say any word that will give me a start. I am really just dying to know what it's all about even though I am a little bit afraid, maybe a lot. But say something, anything."

Her insistent request was acceded to by the remark, "Sometime ago you told me you were terribly interested in and fascinated by symbolism," and as this remark was made the packet of hotel matches was carefully dropped on the desk.

Immediately she seized the drawing and looked at it momentarily, at the same time grabbing the packet of matches and throwing it violently on the floor. She then burst into a torrent of vituperation, addressed apparently to nobody, intermingled with expressions of sympathy for her mother and explanatory details, of which the following constitutes only a fairly adequate summary:

"The damned nasty filthy little cheater. And she calls herself my friend. She's having an affair with Father. Damn him. Poor Mother. She visits Mother, damn her, and Father acts like a saint around the house, damn him. They go to the hotel, the same hotel Father took us to [for dinner]. I hated her because she took my father away from me—and Mother. That's why I always stole his cigarettes. Even when I had some, I'd sneak into the hall and get some out of his coat pocket. Sometimes I'd take the whole package, sometimes only one or two. If she thinks she's going to break up my home, she's got another thought coming, plenty too. The first time she told me about her boyfriend—her boyfriend, huh—she lit her cigarette with those matches. I knew then, but I couldn't believe it. And I used to take Father's matches away from him, and I'd get so goddamn mad when he'd tell me to use my own. I didn't want Mother to see those matches, and it didn't make sense then." This was followed by much profanity and repetition of the above remarks which seemed to exhaust her rage, following which she sobbed bitterly.

Composing herself, she apologized for her profanity and rage and then remarked quietly, "I suppose I better explain all this to you. When you said symbolism, I suddenly remembered that Freud said cylinders symbolized men and triangles, women, and then I recalled that cigarettes were cylinders and that they could symbolize a penis. Then the whole meaning of the picture just burst into my mind all at once, and I guess I just couldn't take it, and that's why I acted like I did. Now I can explain the picture to you."

Pointing to the various elements of the picture, she explained rapidly. "This cigarette is Father, and that big triangle is Mother—she's short and fat and blonde—and the little triangle is me. I'm blonde too. I'm really taller than Mother, but I just feel little to her. You see, those lines all connect us in a family group and the square is the family frame. And that line from Father breaks through the family frame and goes down below the social frame—that's the big square—and then it tries to go back to the family and can't, and so it just goes over to Jane. You see, she is a tall, slender brunette. And that smoke from Father's penis curls around Jane. And that line between me and Jane is broken where it comes to the family frame. And I've been drawing and drawing these pictures all the time like that [pointing to the unitary drawings at the top of the page], but this is the first time I ever put them together. And see where I blackened Father's face. It should be! And when I gave you those matches, I told you they were connected with Jane, even though I didn't know that was Jane then."

For some minutes the patient sat quietly and thoughtfully, now and then glancing at the drawing. Finally she remarked, "I know the interpretation of this picture is true, but only because I feel it is true. I have been thinking everything over and there isn't a solitary fact that I know, on which I can rely, that could possibly substantiate what I've said. Jane and I have drifted apart, but that doesn't make her Father's mistress. Jane does call at the house but always on evenings when Father is out, and while she doesn't stay more than three-quarters of an hour, that doesn't mean that that's a blind. And Mother can't hide anything and her nature is such that she would know about things before they happen, and I know she has no inkling of this. As for the matches, anybody could have hotel matches, and my stealing Father's cigarettes only proves there's something wrong with me. Well, now that I've discovered this, I'm going to go through with it and clear it up so that I'll have better proof than just my subconscious drawings."

What the proof was to be the patient refused to state, and the rest of the interview was spent by the patient in outlining a calm, dispassionate, philosophical view and acceptance of the entire situation.

Two days later she came to the office accompanied by a young woman. As they entered the office the patient said, "This is Jane. I bullied and browbeat her into coming here without giving her any idea of what or why, and her own sense of guilt toward me kept her from refusing. Now I'm going to have my say and then I'm going to leave her with you so she can talk to you and get a little sense put into her head."

Then, turning to Jane, "Just about two months ago you started something which you didn't want me to know about. You thought you were getting by with it, but you weren't. You told me your boyfriend was about four years older than you, and you told me he wanted an affair with you but that you wouldn't consent. You were just a sweet young girl talking things over with your dearest pal. And all the time you knew, and all the time I was putting two and two together, and finally I went to a psychiatrist and the other day I got the answer, so now I know your whole sordid, nasty story. Here's a cigarette, now light it with *these* matches—they're hotel matches. Now you know just what I'm talking about."

With that she rushed out of the office, and as she did so, Jane turned and asked, "Does Ann really know about her father and me?"

Then, without any questioning of any sort, Jane responded to the difficult situation in which she found herself by relating the story of her intrigue with the patient's father, confirming fully every detail given by the patient and adding the information that both she and her lover had been most secretive and had been most confident that they could not even be suspected. She also added that on the occasion of Ann's first weekend home from college after the beginning of the affair, she had felt that Ann was most disagreeable and irritable for no good reason, and Ann's father had made the same comment during one of their meetings. She attributed Ann's knowledge of the affair entirely to "intuition."

Following these disclosures Ann was recalled to the office, and as she entered, she eyed Jane closely, then remarked, "Well, I did have a faint hope that it wasn't so, but it is, isn't it?" Jane nodded affirmatively, to which Ann replied philosophically, "Well, what Father does is his own business, and what you do is yours, but you're not visiting at our home anymore, and you and father can pick another hotel since the family is in the habit of eating at that hotel frequently. I'll just explain your failure to visit at home to Mother by saying we quarreled, and as for you and me, we're acquaintances, and you can tell Father that heaven help both of you if Mother ever finds out. And that's that! You can go back to town by one bus and I'll take another, and you can beat it now because I want to talk to the doctor."

After Jane's immediate departure the gist of the patient's remarks was that she intended to accept the whole matter in a dispassionate, philosophical manner, and that she was still tremendously puzzled as to how she had "stumbled onto it," since she felt convinced that "it must have been just plain intuition that worked out right. When I first started drawing those little pictures, it made me feel terribly jittery, but I couldn't stop. I was just obsessed by them, but they had no meaning until last Thursday. Now when I look back at it all, the whole thing just seems screwy because I must have known from the beginning, and yet I really didn't know a thing until the other day here. But hereafter I'm not going to let any subconscious knowledge upset me as frightfully as that did."

The patient was seen casually thereafter on a number of occasions, and satisfactory evidence was obtained of a continuing good adjustment. A few years later she married very happily. One additional item of information obtained from the patient was that on a number of occasions before her upset she had suspected her father of intrigues with various women but had always dismissed her suspicions as unworthy. These suspicions were confirmed unexpectedly by Jane, however, while discussing with the examiner her intrigue with the patient's father. She volunteered the information that over a period of eight years the father had had a series of affairs, one of which had been broken off only at her insistence.

Also, after the passage of several months the patient's notebooks were again examined. When this privilege was requested, she remarked, "Oh, I know! I forgot to tell you. I lost that habit just as soon as I found things out. I haven't done a bit of scribbling since then." Inspection of the notebooks verified her statement.

Subsequently Jane too was seen casually and volunteered the information that the intrigue was continuing, but that she had complied with Ann's injunctions.

DISCUSSION

I. The Significance of the Illness

It is hardly possible to overestimate the theoretical significance and interest of this case. Only rarely does an opportunity arise to study a severe neurotic storm—in some ways nearly psychotic—under such well-controlled conditions.

A young woman deeply and apparently peacefully devoted both to her father and to her mother suddenly is confronted with the threat of a deep hurt to her mother through her father and her own best friend, and with the acutely painful picture of her father's emotional desertion of the family. This of course is adequate grounds for sorrow and anger. But it was more significant still that she was confronted by these jolting facts, not in her conscious perceptions, but only in her unconscious; and that furthermore her reaction to this unconscious knowledge was not one of simple sorrow and anger, but a far more complex constellation of neurotic and affective symptoms. All of this becomes clear directly from the data of the case and without any intricate or debatable analytic speculations and interpretations.

Here, then, is a test case. Can psychic injuries of which we are not consciously aware be at the heart of major psychopathological states? And how does the reaction of the patient illuminate this problem?

On the weekend of her return home when she first sensed unconsciously the intimacy between her friend and her father, her immediate response was one of troubled and unmotivated irritability—an irritability which never found any focus, but which was displaced incessantly from one trivial object to another. Thereafter she lapsed into a state of obsessional depression, which seemed to her to be without content or meaning, although it was accompanied by a withdrawal of interest from all of her previous activities and from all previous object relationships. As this depressive mood gathered, her irritability persisted, undiminished and still without adequate conscious object. For the first time, however, it began to focus its expression in two symptomatic compulsive acts whose symbolic meaning later became unmistakable. The first of these was a minutely circumscribed kleptomania—i.e., the specific compulsion to steal cigarettes and matches from her father's pockets, obviously with an angry and punitive preconscious purpose but which was seen in the automatic drawings to have a much deeper unconscious castrative goal as well. The second was an equally circumscribed, almost encapsulated obsessional drive toward the constant repetition of scribbled drawings of cylinders, triangles, looping spirals, and straight lines slanting in all directions. (cf Figure 1.)

It is of interest to note that her illness began with episodic emotional flurries, which quickly were followed by an affect which became fixed and obsessional, and that this in turn was supplemented by a group of obsessional acts. The theoretical significance of this sequence of events is a matter into which we cannot go at this point, but the sequence should be borne in mind.

The patient's involuntary and, to her, mysterious irritability deserves another word. It is an exact replica of a type of frantic, shifting, and apparently unmotivated irritability which one sees in children when they are stirred into overwhelming states of unconscious jealousy toward parents and siblings. In this patient it is possible to observe how the irritability was precipitated when the patient's unconscious was confronted with the love relationship between her father and her friend. Furthermore it is clear that the irritability reflects her conflict between various roles, as for instance her identification with her mother in the family group, her fantasy of herself in the role of her father's mistress, her jealousy of this mistress, and the resulting conflicts which manifested themselves throughout her upset period between the vengeful, guilty, and protective impulses toward everyone involved in the situation.

It is clear that the unconscious impulses which were driving her strove in many ways for adequate expression and resolution: first in the vengeful gestures (stealing of matches and cigarettes), then in the automatic incoherent drawings or scribblings (a so-called habit which is later seen to be infused with specific and translatable meanings), and finally in the increasing and obsessive need to find out what it was all about, as manifested in her blind search into psychiatric and analytical literature, her fascination with and skepticism about symbolism, and in the appeal for help still veiled slightly behind her "curiosity about automatic writing."

Surely both the driving and the directing power of unconscious mentation could not be more beautifully illustrated in any laboratory test than it is here. A further example is in the unwitting double meaning in the naïvely chosen phrase "run around," which the patient used repeatedly in her blind, angry outburst against her father, without realizing consciously its obvious reference to his sexual habits.

And finally the symbolic representation of complex human relationships by simple, childlike scribbled drawings, which is the most dramatic feature of the story, is so clear as to need no further comment.

II. Technique

The technical challenges with which the experience confronts us are several. In the first place it must be admitted quite simply that the most skillful use of orthodox psychoanalytic technique could not possibly have uncovered the repressed awareness of the father's liaison in a mere handful of sessions. Speed in achieving a result is of course not a sole criterion of excellence. It may well be that with such rapid therapy certain vital reconstructive experiences cannot be brought to a patient, whereas they, on the other hand, may be an essential part of the more orthodox analytic approach. But there is nothing in this observation which would seem to make the two methods mutually exclusive. In some form they might be supplementary or complementary to one another; and for at least a few of those many patients to whom analysis is not applicable, such an approach as this, if only because of its speed and directness, might be useful.

Furthermore, it must be emphasized that automatic drawing as a method of communication has a close relationship to the psychoanalytic method of free association. Here the patient's undirected drawings were certainly a nonverbal form of free association. That the translation of such drawings into understandable ideas presents grave difficulties must be admitted; but these difficulties are not always greater than those which confront analysts when they deal with the symbolic material of dreams. On a two-dimensional plane these drawings are equivalent to the dramatic symbolic representation of instinctual conflicts which Homburger (1937) has described and analyzed in children's three-dimensional play with building blocks.

Furthermore, as one studies this material it is impressive to see how ready the unconscious seemed to be to communicate with the examiner by means of this accessory sign language of drawing, while at the same time the consciously organized part of the personality was busy recounting other matters. It suggests that by using either this or some other method of widening the conscious gap between the conscious and unconscious parts of the psyche, it might be possible to secure communications from the unconscious more simply than can be done when both parts of the personality are using the single vehicle of speech. It suggests that when only one form of communication is used, the struggle between the expressive and repressive forces may be intensified.

The point we have in mind here is quite simple. Under circumstances of usual analytical procedure the patient expresses everything—both conscious and unconscious, instinctual drives and anxieties, fears and guilt—often all at the same moment and in the same system of gestures and words. That under such circumstances a patient's speech and communications may be difficult to disentangle is not strange. If, however, by some method one could allow the various aspects of the psyche to express themselves simultaneously with different simple and direct methods of communication, it would be conceivable at least that each part could express itself more clearly and with less internal confusion and resistance. In this instance it seems to have worked that way; and the shame, guilt, anxiety, and rage which prevented the patient from putting into words her unconscious knowledge left her free to express it all in her automatic scribbled drawing; furthermore this throws light on the essential mechanism of literature and art, a discussion of which will have to be reserved for another time.

It must be borne in mind, however, that the repressive forces rendered the drawings wholly chaotic until the influence of the psychiatrist was exerted on this patient in a clear-cut and definite manner, in order to assist her in the expression of her problem. In the first place, looking back it becomes obvious that the patient came seeking a substitute father who would give her permission to know the facts about her real father—a "permissive agent" whose function would be to lessen her guilt and her anxiety and to give her the right to express the rage and the hurt that she felt.

Thus we see that the first movement toward recovery came as she simultaneously talked and scribbled in the first interview and apparently without any insight. The observer on that occasion gave her a certain direct, quiet, but impressive suggestion: that she was to allow her unconscious to deal with her problem, instead of her conscious mind. This is an important divergence from psychoanalytic technique with its deliberate drive to force everything into consciousness, because at the same time that the psychiatrist gave the patient permission to face the facts unconsciously, he gave her conscious mind the right to be free from its obsessive preoccupation with the problem. The patient experienced an immediate temporary relief. She felt so "well" the next day that she even thought of not returning for her next appointment. With this ground under her feet, however, at the next session she went deeper into her problem and emerged with her first moment of conscious panic—a panic that was not at this point accompanied by any insight. Her next emotional change evolved rapidly out of this experience and soon manifested itself in her ability to express her rage, chagrin, and resentment openly in her compulsive outburst against her friend and her father, instead of in symbolic acts alone.

In all of this the "permissive agent," by his active encouragement and direct suggestions, served to lift the weight of guilt, anxiety, and ambivalence from the patient's shoulders. As a new and kindly father he diverted some of these obstructing feelings from their older goals, thus allowing the eruption of the full awareness of the affair. This important function of the therapist—to dislodge old and rigid superego patterns—is one which unquestionably was executed by this mild suggestion at the first interview between the therapist and the patient.

Naturally this could not occur without anxiety, but the appearance of this anxiety, replacing the depression and the compulsions which had existed for so long, marked the upturn in the patient's illness.

III. Conclusion

We are far from drawing any conclusions from this single experience. Such observations must be amplified and repeated many times before it is decided that as a consequence any changes in analytic technique are indicated.

It is just to say, however, that without any effort to open up all the buried material of the patient's highly charged œdipal relationships, a direct link was established between conscious and unconscious systems of thought and feeling which surrounded the parental figures, and this by a very simple technique. Furthermore, as a direct consequence there was almost immediate relief from seriously disturbing neurotic and emotional symptoms.

It is unfortunate that although we have a clear picture of the patient's neurosis, we have no analytic insight into the character and personality out of which this neurosis developed. This is important because it is conceivable that such a method as this might be applicable for one type of character organization and not for another, even when the two had essentially similar superimposed neuroses. Such studies as these, therefore, should be carried forward in conjunction with psychoanalysis.

18. The Translation of the Cryptic Automatic Writing of One Hypnotic Subject By Another in a Trancelike Dissociated State

Milton H. Erickson and Lawrence S. Kubie

During the training of a subject for a particular experiment in hypnosis a unique observation was made upon the ability of one person in a spontaneous trance accurately to decipher and to translate the mysterious and cryptic automatic writing of another. In their conscious states neither individual could understand the script. In trancelike states each one quite independently reached identical interpretations of it. Cryptic automatic writing is found to suffer from processes of distortion identical with those seen in dreams; and the translation of such writing, to involve the same principles as those involved in dream analysis.

In chronological sequence in the protocols detailed below there is portrayed both the general situation and the series of events leading to these observations:

(1) The subject, as an incident in his training and while in a deep trance, was told by an assistant in the absence of the investigator to forget all the vowels but not the fact of their existence.

(2) In another trance a week later he was given additional suggestions to the effect that he would replace the seventh *(g)* eighth *(h)*, and ninth *(i)* letters of the alphabet with their respective numerals and that henceforth his name would be "Jack Young."

(3) He was then asked to write his name. In doing this he omitted the vowels and substituted the numeral *10* for the letter *J*, declaring emphatically as he completed this task that something was wrong.

Assuming in the interpretation of hypnotic productions, as in the interpretation of dreams, that every trivial detail has meaning, the assistant sought to secure from the subject an explanation both of his use of the numeral *10* and of his comment that something was wrong. The subject wrote the letters *N* and *F* and the numerals *7, 7, 8,* and *9*

Reprinted with permission from *The Psychoanalytic Quarterly,* January, 1940, Vol. IX, No. 1.

automatically in his effort to explain these phenomena, apparently offering them as an adequate explanation of everything. Dissatisfied, the assistant demanded a more understandable written explanation. This resulted in still more abbreviated and cryptic automatic writing; further requests produced merely a repetition of that writing, despite the assistant's efforts to compel some alteration of the written characters by active physical interference.

External circumstances then terminated the interview at this point, but not before the subject had demonstrated his complete lack of any conscious understanding of what his written "explanation" meant or of what the "mistake" had been, and whether it was the substitution of a *10* for the *J* in his written name.

After the subject left, the investigator came into the laboratory, and while he and his assistant were puzzling over the cryptic writing, a second subject, Alice, entered the laboratory and showed an immediate interest in the problem. This subject has the rare capacity to develop spontaneous hypnotic trances during which she functions adequately in whatever situation she finds herself. Upon awakening from them she has no awareness of her trance activities. Because of her interest in the problem, she was given an outline of the essential facts. The writing was shown to her by the assistant, who then departed, leaving Alice to puzzle over the writing with the investigator.

Thereupon Alice developed a series of spontaneous trance states interspersed with ordinary waking states. In the trance states she interpreted the writing item by item and explained it step by step to the investigator, who maintained essentially a passive, receptive role. This passive role was forced upon the investigator by the brevity of the spontaneous trances, the difficulty of trying to carry on a conversation with her at all, and the necessity constantly to meet her at two different levels of awareness in a single situation. Alice's spontaneous trances tended to be so brief that she would have time to offer only an explanatory remark or two and would then awaken with no awareness of what she had just said. In the waking state she would continue her puzzled wonderment over the writing which had just been interrupted by the spontaneous trance, or she would become interested in some totally unrelated topic and discuss that until some remark of the investigator disclosed to her his own unclear state of mind regarding the last bit of explanation she had given. There would follow another spontaneous trance in which, briefly and concisely, Alice would make another remark to clarify the investigator's mind. As a consequence it was necessary for Alice to develop a large number of spontaneous trances and to repeat her explanations many times before she could feel satisfied with the investigator's comprehension of what had been said. In addition Alice's explanations were often as cryptic to the investigator as the writing itself—as, for example, her use of the word *sign* to explain the correctness of the letter *H* (cf. the protocol below).

In the intervals between the spontaneous trances investigation showed that Alice had a complete and persistent amnesia for all of her trance disclosures, even after the entire interpretation of the writing had been secured; furthermore, when her own interpretation of the writing was presented to her, she regarded it purely as a product of the investigator's own reasoning. However, when questioned about it in an induced trance state, she not only recognized the explanation as her own but meticulously corrected the slightest change in wording introduced by the investigator.

Why Alice resorted to this devious and uncertain method of communication instead of permitting herself to develop flashes of conscious insight is a matter for speculation not wholly explained by her statement that the writing represented her own unconscious way of thinking and writing.

The following day the first subject, T. L., came to the office unexpectedly to report what he termed "an amusing hypnagogic experience." Unaware that the assistant had told the investigator of the original situation, and unaware also of the investigator's subsequent experience with Alice, he described fully his own experiences with the assistant on the previous day, corroborating the details given by the assistant and including others which were later verified. He emphasized in particular his own argumentativeness, his insistence that there was a mistake in the written name, his feeling of absolute certainty about his conscious understanding, and his feeling of irritation with the assistant whose manner seemed unwarrantedly to imply that there were unrecognized meanings in the writing. He related that after his departure he had forgotten about the incident until, falling asleep late that evening, he had a "hypnagogic experience" in which he "saw" the episode exactly as it had occurred with a new interpretation of it all. He expressed much amusement over his earlier belligerency and defensiveness and also about his new realization of "how intensely you can believe something that is totally wrong, when right in your subconscious you know the truth." He went on to explain that along with his original "conscious explanation" he now "saw" the "true subconscious explanation," which was not at all similar to his "conscious explanation." Asked to restate his original "conscious explanation," he claimed that because it was "so wrong" he could no longer remember more than a vague outline of it, but that now he was ready to give the "correct explanation of the whole thing."

In response to the investigator's manifest interest he proceeded to give his explanation, but not with the confidence his manner had led the investigator to expect. It became apparent at once that the subject's conscious grasp of the problem was limited and that he only thought he understood it. Actually his method was to offer sudden, brief, dogmatic statements as if each were the complete explanation, only to discover spontaneously that his explanation was inadequate. Then there would follow another sudden flash of conscious insight and another dogmatic statement.

After a number of such steps the subject took the attitude of one solving a puzzle and began to search for the explanation of his various dogmatic statements and for the significance of the writing. As he studied the writing and tried to fit his various statements to it, additional flashes of insight developed, sometimes relevant to the immediate question he was trying to solve and sometimes pertinent to another item not yet touched upon. Thus, bit by bit in an unsystematic fashion, a complete explanation was developed which was in full accord with the one given by Alice. In this episode the investigator's role was again a passive, receptive one.

Of marked interest is the fact that neither subject volunteered any interpretation of the first "explanation" written as four digits. Both subjects ignored that particular writing completely until it was called to their attention. Alice remarked simply that everything was included in the writing she had explained, while T. L. commented briefly, "That's [the digits] not so good; the writing's better."

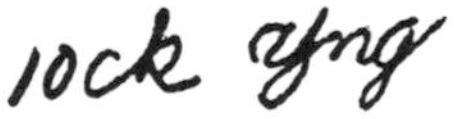

Figure 1

Figure 2

Figure 3

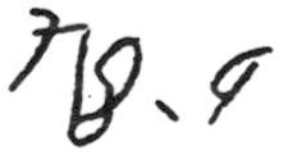

Figure 4

Figure 5

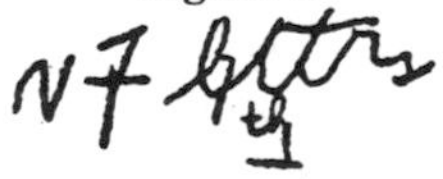

Figure 6

PROTOCOL I

First Week

1. Subject T. L. was told while in a hypnotic trance to forget the vowels of the alphabet but not the fact of their existence.

Second Week

2. Subject T. L. was again hypnotized and told this time to replace the seventh, eighth, and ninth letters of the alphabet *(g, h,* and *i)* with their respective numerals.

3. T. L. was then told that his name was "Jack Young" and was asked to write it.

4. T. L. wrote his name "10 ck Yng" (cf. Figure 1).

5. Upon inspection of his writing, T. L. declared it to be incorrect, that the *J* was a mistake; he became disputatious when the assistant suggested that it might be correct.

6. The assistant asked, "Is what you wrote correct?"
7. T. L. wrote automatically the character *N*, which was interpreted by the assistant as a "No," but T. L. did not confirm this (cf Figure 2).
8. The assistant asked if the writing was apparently incorrect.
9. T. L. wrote automatically the character *F*, which the assistant interpreted as a "Yes," but this again was neither confirmed nor corrected (cf. Figure 3).
10. The assistant then asked why the writing was only apparently incorrect.
11. T. L. wrote automatically the construction, "7 7 8 9," very faintly and somewhat illegibly (cf. Figure 4).
12. The assistant asked that the explanation be rewritten plainly and clearly and in a fashion understandable to both of them.
13. T. L. then added to the *N* and the *F* already written a peculiar group of letters (cf. Figure 5).
14. The assistant, after scrutiny of this writing, asked T. L. to rewrite on another sheet of paper his explanation in a more clearly understandable and readable fashion.
15. T. L. complied with this request by producing a second graphic construction, essentially a repetition of the previous one, ignoring and resisting as he did so the assistant's attempts to compel an alteration of the writing by forcibly moving the paper while T. L. was engaged in his task (cf. Figure 6).
16. No further verbal explanation of the writing was obtained at this time except an argumentative repetition of his previous declaration that the written name contained a mistake—namely, the use of *10* for *J*. External circumstances then brought the interview to an end.

PROTOCOL II

Entrance of Alice

1. The written name was exhibited to Alice by the assistant, and a rapid explanation was given of the posthypnotic suggestions regarding vowels and the replacement by numerals of the seventh, eighth, and ninth letters, and of T. L.'s insistence that

there was a mistake in the writing of the name. Following this the assistant left.

2. Alice studied the name as it was written and then counted the letters of the alphabet rapidly.
3. Alice's explanation: *J* has the ordinal position of *10,* but the omission of the vowels gives it the ordinal position of *7—7* however is actually identical with *G,* hence it cannot be used to designate *J*. Therefore, *J,* the seventh letter, must be written as *10.* In brief, *J* is both the seventh and the tenth letter, but it can be written numerically only as *10.*
4. Alice was then shown T. L.'s written production (Figure 6). This she promptly read as "Numbers for letters," illustrating this significance by immediate reference to the use of a *10* for a *J* in the written name.
5. The investigator then gave Alice the additional information about the assistant's interpretation of the letter *N* as signifying "No" (cf. Figure 2).
6. The writing was read then by Alice as, "Not letters; numbers for letters."
7. Alice's explanation: The second character in the written explanation actually is a *T* as well as an *F* and may equally well be read as a *4*. T. L.'s passive acceptance of the interpretation of a "No" serves to transform the first two characters of the writing into the word "Not" with the vowel omitted; furthermore since the second character is obviously an *F,* and also a *4,* emphasis is thereby placed upon the second character, and this is indicated doubly by the fact that the letter *F* actually is the fourth letter in the alphabet with the vowels omitted. Hence *F,* by virtue of all this, can be used to signify *"for"* as a simple pun as well as an abbreviation.
8. Therefore, on first reading the written explanation, one reads "Not letters," but since this is only part of an explanation, one must reread the written characters for their additional meanings; hence on second reading one reads "No 4 lttrs," or "Numbers for letters."
9. The investigator accepted this reading unquestioningly, but asked what the *th* meant, since it appeared in both of T. L.'s written explanations.
10. Alice first explained with the single word "sign," but finally declared that it was connected "by the sign," which she identified by gesture as the line underneath the *th,* with the second character of the written explanation, and that it "explained" the "mistake."
11. Alice's explanation: The second character reads *T, F, 4,* and *for,*

but in relation to the *th* it also reads *7. G* is the seventh letter in the alphabet. *G* should be written as *7. G* is written *G* in the name—hence, *G* is a mistake.

12. The investigator then asked Alice to read aloud the written explanation, which she did as follows: "Not letters; numbers for letters; not *7;* seventh letter; *7* in place of letter," and as this explanation was read, Alice declared that there was a concealed *7* in the word *lttrs,* an item which had been consistently overlooked by the investigator.

13. As an additional explanation Alice added, "*7* should be in the place of the letter *G* in the name, but a mistake was made and *G* was written. So to explain what he meant by 'a mistake,' *7* is written here [pointing to the concealed *7* in the character *lttrs*] so that you can see that there is really a *7* in the place of *letters* where you should read it, but where you really read just *lttrs.*"

14. The investigator asked if there were any further explanation of the *th,* since *H* is the eighth letter.

15. Alice explained, "It is a sign. You read *7-th* not *7-t-h.*" To this was added, "Not mistake like *G.* It *[th]* is a sign."

16. The investigator then raised the question of *G* becoming the fifth letter of the alphabet with the vowels omitted. Alice explained that *G* could not be the fifth letter because the difficulty about the *J* had definitely established *G* as the seventh letter.

17. Alice was then asked about the letter *K.* Again she explained that the establishment of the letter *J* as number *10* provided a point of orientation for all of the letters of the alphabet, regardless of the omission of the vowels, and she restated the fact that the vowels had only been forgotten, but not the fact of their existence. Therefore, the letter *J* established as number *10* would automatically cause *K* to be letter number *11* and *G* to be letter number *7.*

18. Alice then was asked about the identification of the letter *F* as the number *4* by virtue of the omission of the vowels. Alice pointed out immediately that this was for purposes of punning and that anything was permissible in a pun.

19. Alice was then asked to explain how it was that she could interpret such cryptic writing.

20. Alice's explanation: "Oh, that's easy. That's just the way I always think and write. Just a little means a lot."

21. Alice was asked, "How could you know that the writing could be interpreted?"

22. Alice's explanation: "When you know about the vowels and the numbers, then you could see lots of meanings all at once right there and you could just read them."

23. When asked about the written digits in Figure 4, Alice explained that they meant the same as the writing, but not so clearly.

PROTOCOL III

The next day

1. Subject T. L. reported to the investigator an "amusing hypnagogic experience" in which "I remembered the whole situation. I had a complete conscious explanation at the time. I was so sure of it, too; I wanted to argue. I said there was a mistake. I remembered every little detail of that whole situation, and, at the same time, in that hypnagogic state I could see the whole thing in an entirely different way. Half asleep there, I could see my conscious understanding of that whole situation and at the same time I could see my subconscious understanding. The two were so different, and I had been so sure of my conscious understanding, but it really was all wrong. I didn't have anything right in my conscious understanding at all, and yet I wanted to argue; I was looking for an argument."

2. The investigator asked T. L. for an account of his conscious understanding.

3. T. L. declared that he could not remember anything about it except that it was all wrong, nothing right. "I wasn't even thinking about the things I thought I was thinking about." The investigator asked him to explain this more fully. T. L. replied, "Consciously I said there was a mistake, but the mistake I thought I was talking about wasn't a mistake at all. I thought I was talking about *J,* but in that hypnagogic experience I knew that *J* was right but that *G* was a mistake. *J* was just a mistake to my consciousness even though it was not a mistake to my subconsciousness."

4. The investigator asked T. L. to give an account of his subconscious understandings.

5. There followed then an explanation of the writing in which item by item was accorded the same interpretation as had been given by Alice. The method by which his explanation was achieved was one based upon sudden flashes of insight, such as obtain in the solving of a puzzle. Thus in relation to the second character (cf. Figure 3) he declared he could explain it best by writing it from memory, whereupon he proceeded to write the French form of the numeral *7* (the subject had studied French). In the usual position, elevated above the line, he added to this numeral a *th.* When the accuracy of his recollection was questioned, he became decidedly disputatious and insisted that it was right because of the line underneath the *th.* From these disconnected flashes of insight partial understandings of several different aspects of the problem were obtained. Alice, on the other hand, recognized the numerical quality of that character along with its other attributes without resort to intermediary steps.

6. The order in which T. L. built up his interpretations of the written explanation shown in Figure 6 was as follows:
   (a) Declaration that the use of a *10* for a *J* in the written name was not an error but that the *G* was an error.
   (b) Statement that the writing (Figure 6) read both "Not letters" and "Numbers for letters."
   (c) Elucidation of the use of a *10* for a *J.* "Without the vowels *J* was the seventh letter, and I had to put a number for that letter, but I couldn't put a *7* because even if there were no vowels you had to count their places, and that would make *G* the seventh letter, just as *J* was, so I just wrote the correct number for the letter *J.*"
   (d) Identification of the *F* (Figure 2) as a *T,* an *F,* a *4,* and as *for,* followed by its identification as a *7* as described in Item 5, and by relating this explanation to the clarification of the "mistake" contained in the letter *G.*
   (e) Declaration that there should be a *7* in addition to the one contained in the second character of the written explanation, to be read with the *th* as "seventh letter."
   (f) Discovery of the concealed *7* and the reading of the message as "Not letters, numbers for letters, not 7, seventh letter, 7 in place of letter."
   (g) Clarification of the question of the *K* and the *H* in the same fashion as Alice had done.
   (h) Discovery of the pun on *4* and *F* contained in the second character of the written explanation, since previously he had regarded the *F* as a simple abbreviation for *for.*
7. Declaration that the four digits, illustrated in Figure 4, constituted a similar but less satisfactory explanation than the writing in Figure 6.
8. Explanation that Figure 6 differed from Figure 5 only because of the assistant's interference. Alice had declared them to be identical in meaning.

DISCUSSION

I. The main event of this unplanned and unexpected experience is in itself worthy of record, for it is an arresting fact that one human being in a dissociated, trancelike condition can accurately decipher the automatic writing of another—writing which neither of the two subjects was able to decipher while in states of normal consciousness. The observation stresses from a new angle a fact that has often been emphasized by those who have studied unconscious processes but which remains none the less mysterious—namely, that underneath the diversified nature of the consciously organized aspects of the personality, the unconscious talks in a language which has a remarkable uniformity; furthermore that that language has laws so constant that the unconscious of one individual is better equipped to understand the unconscious of another than the conscious aspect of the personality of either.

If this is true, and it seems to be a fact attested from many sources, it must give psychoanalysts reason to wonder as to the wisdom of confining themselves exclusively to the technique of free association in their efforts consciously to penetrate into the unconscious of a patient.

II. When one turns to the details of this experience, one finds several points which need more specific emphasis and certain basic questions which remain wholly unanswered.

(1) In the first place it is striking that in the translation of automatic writing, as in the interpretation of dreams, each element may be made to do double and triple duty: to wit, the several purposes subserved by the letters *N* and *F*.

(2) Again we see that here—as in dreams, puns, elisions, plays on words, and similar tricks that we ordinarily think of as frivolous—all play a surprising and somewhat disconcerting role in the communication of important and serious feelings. We accept this type of thought and language in simple jokes, as for instance in the old conundrum of childhood: "How do you spell 'blind pig'?" to which the answer is "blndpg—leave out the 'eyes.'" But it is ever a source of fresh amazement when the unconscious processes express weighty and troublesome problems in a shorthand which has in it an element of irreverent levity.

(3) In the whole episode there are two untouched problems—why in the first instance the "mistake" occurred at all (the slip is seemingly trivial, a tempest in a teapot), and second why, when the mistake had occurred, the first subject, T. L., could not have recognized it and corrected it simply and directly. Perhaps it is of importance that the mistake concerned the patient's own identity—i.e., the automatic spelling of his own name. It

will be recalled that in the course of the experiment his name had been changed by suggestion to "Jack Young."

It is possible that a highly charged rebellion against the implantation under hypnosis of this alternative personality, struggling with a coexistent attitude of passive submission to the authority of the hypnotist, may account for several things: the exaggerated tempest, the curiously evasive quality of some of the replies, the ambiguities (as if he did not know whether to correct the error or not), the elements of malicious humor, the literal-mindedness, the hiding. All of this seems to indicate that, both in the automatic writing and in the subsequent efforts to translate it, the subject is struggling simultaneously to explain and to hide his meaning. In support of this hypothesis there is one possible explanation of the writing, which neither subject offered although it is a rather obvious alternative: if *N* equals *not,* and if *F* is also a *T,* and if we consider that the first letter of the following group of letters is *L,* then the first three letters would read "not T. L."—in other words, not the subject's own initials.

It may well be that if we knew enough about the subject, T. L., and the identifications which must make up the basis of the structure of his whole personality, that this otherwise mysterious little episode would then become quite understandable.

Section 5: Mental Mechanisms

INTRODUCTION

The papers of this section all deal with Erickson's demonstrations of the classical psychoanalytic mechanisms of defense and psychopathology. The first paper, "Experimental demonstrations of the psychopathology of everyday life" (1939), dealing with demonstrations at a Yale Seminar in 1933 led by the famous anthropologist, Edward Sapir, became a classic that was reprinted in the Bobbs-Merrill Reprint Series in the Social Sciences. Together with the second paper, "Demonstration of mental mechanisms by hypnosis" (1939), it is a tour de force of the use of hypnosis as a means of illustrating psychodynamic processes. Erickson's demonstration of the implantation of a "complex" and the "assumption of another's identity" in the first paper are simple illustrations of the more detailed experimental work he did a few years earlier on experimental neuroses with Huston and Shakow (to be presented in the next section).

The third paper "Unconscious mental activity in hypnosis—psychoanalytic implications" (1944), actually goes beyond classical Freudian theory in its demonstration of how the hypnotherapist can facilitate the patient's own unconscious to solve its problem in its own way—usually without the patient or therapist knowing just how the problem was solved. As Erickson states it, "Hypnosis is, in fact, the induction of a peculiar psychological state which permits the subject to reassociate and reorganize his inner psychological complexities in a way suitable to the unique items of his own psychological experiences." As is usually the case in depth psychology, it is the patient who leads the therapist to recognize a new psychotherapeutic technique.

In the first case of this paper Dr. Jane insists that Erickson instruct her unconscious to solve a problem all by itself while she is in a hypnotic trance—without the intervention of either her conscious mind or suggestions from Erickson. The young college woman of the second case report likewise requests a deep trance experience in which her unconscious could work out a problem in its own way. How different this is from the usual assumption of most other psychotherapeutic approaches, where a major portion of the therapeutic task is to make the unconscious conscious. As the psychoanalyst Lewis Hill writes in his discussion of these two cases, "Hypnosis needs no longer to defend itself against the charge that it is 'nothing but' suggestion. The method of hypnosis described presents a means of accomplishing vastly more in the way of psychic rehabilitation than the method of forcing upon a patient the hypnotist's ideas as to the way in which the patient should solve a conflict. This study of hypnotic psychotherapy points a way to research toward a therapy which may utilize all that has been learned both by the hypnotist and by the psychoanalyst." To this we should add, all that has been learned by the patient; *it is the patient's own creative unconscious that will solve its own problem!*

This approach of allowing the patient's own unconscious to work autonomously in dealing with a problem that is beyond the capacity of the limited sets of the conscious mind is, in the opinion of this editor, one of Erickson's most important therapeutic innovations. It is the common denominator of many of his later papers on innovations in hypnotherapeutic technique, which are presented in Volume Four of this series. Thus, four years after the publication of the above, Erickson says in *Hypnotic psychotherapy* (1948) that "therapy results from an inner resynthesis of the patient's behavior achieved by the patient himself . . . it is this experience of reassociating and reorganizing his own experiential life that eventuates in a cure—not the manifestation of responsive behavior [due to direct hypnotic suggestion]." This insight was then consolidated in a series of papers written in the next decade—such as "Pseudo-orientation in time as a hypnotherapeutic procedure" (1954) and "Self-exploration in the hypnotic state" (1955)—which richly illustrate this new approach to hypnotherapy.

The final paper in this section, "The negation or reversal of legal testimony," was one of Erickson's early (1938) papers dealing with some of the practical implications of our knowledge of mental mechanisms. The problems of amnesia and memory distortion in traumatic life situations, particularly those where legal actions are involved, are an important area where the hypnotherapist is more and more frequently looked to as an expert who is requested to give counsel in the courtroom. We can be certain that this interface between psychological knowledge and legal issues is one that will become even more significant in the future.

19. Experimental Demonstrations of the Psychopathology of Everyday Life

Milton H. Erickson

INTRODUCTION

The experiments reported below were conducted for the most part in the presence of a seminar of graduate students held in New Haven under the leadership of Dr. Sapir during the spring of 1933. In addition, a few experiments which were performed elsewhere are included.

The subject who was used for many of these demonstrations had frequently before volunteered for similar purposes. He knew nothing, however, of the plans for these experiments; they represented situations which were entirely new and problems with which he had never before been confronted.

In his approach to such demonstrations this subject customarily reacted in a way which was fairly characteristic for many others. Ahead of time he often appeared to be resentful and anxious, or overeager about the impression which he and the experimenter would make. Suddenly, however, with the beginning of the lecture or demonstration, he would seem to shift the responsibility completely and to lapse into an attitude of complete comfort, with loss of all tension and worry.

Following one of the demonstrations described below the subject told the experimenter that his shift in mood had been even more marked than usual. The night before the lecture he had been unable to sleep and had felt more than ordinarily resentful that on so important an occasion no rehearsal or preparatory discussion had taken place. He had even developed some nausea and diarrhea. All of this nervousness had disappeared completely, however, as he entered the lecture room on the morning of these experiments.

I. UNCONSCIOUS DETERMINANTS OF THE CASUAL CONTENT OF CONVERSATION

The subject was brought into a state of profound hypnosis, during which he was instructed that after awakening he would *(1)* notice Dr. D.

Reprinted with permission from *The Psychoanalytic Quarterly,* July 1939, Vol. VIII.

searching vainly through his pockets for a package of cigarettes; *(2)* that he then would proffer his own pack, and *(3)* that Dr. D. absentmindedly would forget to return the cigarettes, whereupon the subject would feel very eager to recover them because he had no others. He was further told that *(4)* he would be too courteous to ask for the cigarettes either directly or indirectly but that *(5)* he would engage in a conversation that would cover any topic except cigarettes, although at the time his desire for the return of the cigarettes would be on his mind constantly.

When he was awakened, the subject saw that Dr. D. was looking for cigarettes. He thereupon courteously offered his own and at the same time became involved in a conversation during which Dr. D., after lighting the cigarette, absentmindedly placed the pack in his own pocket. The subject noted this with a quick glance, felt of his own pockets in a somewhat furtive manner as if to see whether or not he had another pack, and showed by his facial expression that he had no others. He then began chatting casually, wandering from one topic to another, always mentioning in some indirect but relevant fashion the word "smoking." For example, he talked about a boat on the bay at New Haven, commenting on the fact that the sight of water always made him thirsty, as did smoking. He then told a story about how the dromedary got one hump and the *camel* two. When the question of travel was raised, he immediately pictured the pleasure he would derive from crossing the Sahara Desert rocking back and forth comfortably on a *camel.* Next he told a tale of Syrian folklore in which again a camel played a role. When he was asked to tell something interesting about patients, he told of taking a patient to see a marathon dance which the latter enjoyed immensely while he himself was reminded by the antics of the dancers of a circus where one would see elephants, hippopotami, and *camels.* Asked what he would like to do, he commented on the pleasant weather and said that there was nothing more glorious than paddling in a canoe or floating at ease on the water, smoking.

II. MANIFESTATIONS OF UNCONSCIOUS AMBIVALENT FEELINGS IN CONVERSATIONS ABOUT A PERSON

During hypnosis the subject was told that he admired and respected Dr. D. very much but that unconsciously he was jealous of him and that because of this jealousy there would be a cutting edge to complimentary remarks he would make. He was further told that after awakening a conversation would be started with Dr. D. in which he would take part. The subject was then awakened, and the conversation began.

The topic of traveling and its contribution to personal education was mentioned. The subject immediately brought up the fact that Dr. D. had studied both in the Middle West and in the East and that, having traveled abroad as well, he might well be called cosmopolitan. He himself, he added, would like to travel and get a cosmopolitan education, but in the last analysis that was what was being done by any old tramp who traveled from one part of the country to another by stealing rides on freight cars. There followed a discussion of human behavior as it reflected local environments, during which the subject remarked that the man who had traveled showed a broader knowledge and better understanding of people and of cultural things; he added, however, that the same thing might possibly be said of any resident of East-Side New York.

III. LAPSUS LINGUAE AND UNCONSCIOUS IRONY

During hypnosis the subject was instructed that after he awakened, Dr. D. would begin talking to him about some abstruse subject in which he was not at all interested, and that although he would actually be profoundly bored, he would try to appear interested. He was told that he would want very much to close the conversation, that he would wish for some way of shutting off this interminable flow of words, that he would look around him in the hope of finding some distraction, and that he would feel that Dr. D. was terribly tiresome. He was then awakened, whereupon Dr. D. began the conversation. Although the subject appeared to be politely attentive, Dr. D. would occasionally say, "Perhaps you're not interested." The subject would reply with excessive emphasis, "Oh, yes, certainly, I'm very interested." Now and then he would interrupt Dr. D., trying to pin him down to some definite point for discussion, but each time this effort was evaded. At length the subject began glancing about the room and was noted casually to observe an open door. Finally he interrupted Dr. D., saying, "Excuse me, I feel an awful draft," and got up to close the door. As he did so, he was asked what he was doing. He replied, "The air seems to be awful hot ['hot air!']; I thought I would shut off the draft." When the hypnotist pretended not to understand and asked him what he was doing, the subject replied, "Why, I just shut the bore." His remark was then repeated by the hypnotist for the benefit of those in the audience who had not heard it. When the subject heard his statement given as "shutting the bore," he started visibly, seemed tremendously embarrassed, and with much urgency turned to Dr. D., saying, "Did I say that? I didn't mean that. I just meant I closed the door." He was very apologetic in his whole manner and bearing.

IV. UNCONSCIOUS RESENTMENT EXPRESSING ITSELF IN MASKED FORMS THROUGH A SMOKE-SCREEN OF OVERCOMPENSATORY COURTESY

The subject was told during hypnosis that he felt antagonistic, resentful, and jealous of Dr. D. and that this emotional state would persist after he was awakened. He was also told that after awakening he would try to be courteous and acquiescent toward Dr. D. in every way and would appear to be willing to do anything requested of him.

After being awakened, the subject seemed to be entirely at ease; he responded courteously to some casual remarks addressed to him by Dr. D. Presently Dr. D. asked him if he would mind changing his seat. The subject replied certainly not, that he would be delighted, but that *he* was quite comfortable where he was; if it would make *Dr. D.* more comfortable, however, he would be delighted to change his seat. The request was repeated, whereupon the subject arose and asked Dr. D. to designate the precise chair in which he was to seat himself. He walked over toward the designated chair but asked Dr. D. if perhaps a certain other chair might not serve even better, since the reason Dr. D. had given for his request was that he was not quite in full view of the audience. When Dr. D. insisted that the designated chair was the better one, the subject, with great courtesy, still questioned, seeming nevertheless most willing to do precisely what was desired and to be hesitant only about seating himself before he was absolutely certain of Dr. D.'s wishes. After much insistence by Dr. D. that he seat himself the subject agreed that the chair indicated was precisely the one that he ought to sit in and proceeded to do so; but as he did so he moved the chair about six inches to one side and shifted its position so that it faced in a slightly different direction. Immediately upon seating himself he turned and politely asked, "Is this the way you would like to have me?" After a few moments of casual conversation Dr. D. found fault with his position and asked him if he would mind taking his original chair. He rose promptly, said that he would be delighted to sit anywhere that Dr. D. wished but that perhaps it would be better if he sat on the table, and offered to move the designated chair to any desired spot, suggesting some clearly unsuitable positions; finally, when urged insistently to sit in the chair, he again had to move it.

V. AMBIVALENCE: MANIFESTATIONS OF UNCONSCIOUS CONFLICT ABOUT SMOKING IN THE DISTORTION OF SIMPLE, DAILY SMOKING HABITS

During profound hypnosis, the subject was instructed to feel that he wanted to get over the habit but that he felt it was too strong a habit to break, that he would be very reluctant to smoke and would give anything not to smoke, but that he would find himself compelled to smoke; and that after he was awakened he would experience all of these feelings.

After he was awakened, the subject was drawn into a casual conversation with the hypnotist who, lighting one himself, offered him a cigarette. The subject waved it aside with the explanation that he had his own and that he preferred Camels, and promptly began to reach for his own pack. Instead of looking in his customary pocket, however, he seemed to forget where he carried his cigarettes and searched fruitlessly through all of his other pockets with a gradually increasing concern. Finally, after having sought them repeatedly in all other pockets, he located his cigarettes in their usual place. He took them out, engaged in a brief conversation as he dallied with the pack, and then began a search for matches, which he failed to find. During his search for matches he replaced the cigarettes in his pocket and began using both hands, finally locating the matches too in their usual pocket. Having done this, he now began using both hands to search for his cigarettes. He finally located them but then found that he had once more misplaced his matches. This time, however, he kept his cigarettes in hand while attempting to relocate the matches. He then placed a cigarette in his mouth and struck a match. As he struck it, however, he began a conversation which so engrossed him that he forgot the match and allowed it to burn his fingertips, whereupon, with a grimace of pain, he tossed it in the ashtray. Immediately he took another match, but again introduced a diverting topic by asking the audience in a humorous fashion if they knew the "Scotch" way of lighting a cigarette. As interest was shown, he carefully split the match through the middle. One half of the match he replaced in his pocket in a time-consuming manner and tried to light his cigarette with the other half. When it gave too feeble a flame, he discarded it and had to search for the second half. After striking this, another interesting topic of conversation developed and again he burned his fingers before he made use of it. He apologized for his failure to demonstrate the "Scotch" light successfully and repeated the performance, this time holding the flame in such a way as to ignite only a small corner of the cigarette from which he succeeded in getting only one satisfactory puff. Then he tossed the match away and tipped the cigarette up so that he could see the lighted end. He started to explain that that was how the "Scotch" light was obtained and noted that only one small corner of the cigarette was lit. He smiled in a semiapologetic manner and explained that he had really given a "Jewish" light to the cigarette, whereupon the lighted corner expired. He made a few more humorous comments, and as he talked and gesticulated appropriately, he rolled the cigarette between his fingers in such a fashion that he broke it, whereupon he put it aside and took another. This time a member of the audience stepped up and proffered him a light, but as the lighted match drew near to the tip of his cigarette the subject sneezed and blew it out. He apologized again and said he thought he would light his own cigarette. While taking out his matches, he commented on the vaudeville trick of rolling cigars from one corner of the mouth to the other and proceeded to demonstrate how he could roll a cigarette in that fashion, which he did fairly successfully. However, in doing so he macerated the tip of the cigarette and had to discard it. He took another, holding it in his mouth while he reached for his matches, started a conversation, and took the cigarette out so that he could talk more freely. It was observed that he took the cigarette out with his hand held in the reverse position to that which he usually used, and after completing his remarks he put the dry end of the cigarette in his mouth, exposing the wet end. He then tried to light this, held the match to the tip in the proper fashion, puffed vigorously, finally got a puff of smoke, and then blew out the match. Naturally the wet end of the cigarette did not burn satisfactorily and quickly went out. He looked at it in amazement and in a semiembarrassed manner mumbled that he had lit the wrong end of the cigarette; he then commented that now both ends of the cigarette were wet, and discarded it for another. After several similar trials he finally succeeded in lighting the cigarette. It was observed that although he took deep puffs, he tended to let his cigarette burn undisturbed, and that instead of smoking it down to a reasonable butt, he quickly discarded it.

A little later, while smoking, the subject attempted to demonstrate the violent gestures of a patient and in so doing knocked off the burning tip. Then while lighting another cigarette he became so interested in talking that he lit the cigarette in the middle rather than at the tip and had to discard it. As usual he showed profound embarrassment at seeming so awkward.

(On other occasions when the subject had demonstrated this phenomenon, he would finally complete the demonstration by selecting a cigarette in a strained and laborious fashion and then, obviously centering all of his attention upon the procedure of lighting it, he would hold his hand tensely as he lit the match, applying it with noticeable rigidity to the cigarette and holding it there so long and puffing so repeatedly that all doubt was removed concerning the actual lighting of the cigarette, whereupon his whole manner and attitude would relax and he would appear to be physically comfortable.)

VI. UNCONSCIOUS CONVICTIONS OF ABSURDITIES WITH RATIONALIZATION IN SUPPORT OF THE BELIEF IN THEM

During hypnosis the subject was instructed that he was about to be reminded by the hypnotist of something he had known for a long time, that he had known it both as a result of his own experience and from reading about it in authoritative books. This, he was told, was the fact that "all German men marry women who are two inches taller than they are." A state of absolute emotional and intellectual belief in this was suggested, and he was warned that he might be called upon to defend this statement. He was told that he had read of this in a book written by Dr. Sapir in which the reference occurred on page 42. He was informed that he would know this not only in the hypnotic state but also when awake. The subject was then wakened.

During the course of a casual conversation mention was made of the peculiar customs of various nations and peoples. Remarking that he was reminded of a peculiar custom among the Germans, the subject went on to describe the suggested phenomenon in a matter-of-fact way. When his statement was challenged, he expressed obvious surprise that anybody should doubt it. He argued that it was entirely reasonable, that customs established from some simple purpose could be perpetuated by future generations until, regardless of their absurdity, they were looked upon as rational and commonplace. From this statement he proceeded to draw a social parallel to the attitude of Mussolini regarding compulsory marriage, arguing in a logical, orderly, and reasonable fashion. When this failed to convince the doubters, he drew upon personal experience, citing examples in a casual, simple, matter-of-fact and convincing manner and calling upon others in the group to verify his statements. When they failed to do so and cited contrary instances, he smiled agreeably and stated that every rule had its exception and that the failure of the German in the audience to confirm his observation was characteristic of the well-known tendency to overlook the obvious in familiar situations. When he was asked whether any authority in the field was known to hold such a belief, he promptly stated that he had read the same observation in a book by Dr. Sapir entitled *Primitive Peoples and Customs.* When he was asked where in the book it was described, he smiled in a deprecating fashion and remarked that it had been so long since he had read the book that he could not be sure of the page but that, as he recalled it, it seemed to be between pages 40 and 45–44 perhaps; this despite the fact that the hypnotist had specified page 42. He was then asked by a member of the audience what chapter it was in; he stated that as far as he recalled it was chapter two. Asked for the chapter heading, he explained that he had read the book so long ago he really could not recall it. When a member of the audience then stated that such a belief was contrary to all common sense, the subject, in amazement and with some embarrassment, asked rather urgently, "Surely you would not dispute a man as famous and distinguished as Dr. Sapir," nodding his head toward Dr. Sapir. His whole manner was suggestive of intense surprise at such arrogant disbelief.

VII. AUTOMATIC WRITING: UNCONSCIOUS OBLITERATION OF VISUAL IMPRESSIONS IN ORDER TO PRESERVE A HYPNOTICALLY ORDERED AMNESIA

During hypnosis the subject was instructed that on awakening he would engage in a casual conversation and that as he did so his hand would begin writing, but that he would have no knowledge of what he was doing.

After he had written some incomplete sentences, he was asked what he was doing by others in the audience. With some amazement he explained that he had been talking to Dr. D. When he was informed that while talking to Dr. D. he had also been writing, he immediately pointed out that this could not have been since he had been holding a cigarette in his right hand. (He had actually transferred the cigarette from his left to the right hand upon completing the writing.) As the audience continued to insist, he pointed out that he had had no pencil and nothing to write on, in addition to the fact that *he knew* he had not been writing and that the audience must have been mistaken. His attention was then called to a pencil and some paper on the table; he seemed surprised to see the paper and pencil and insisted that he had not had anything to do with either. He was asked to examine the paper to see if there were not some automatic writing on it, or at least writing. He picked up the paper, glanced at the top sheet, shook his head, and began slowly to thumb over each sheet, examining the papers over and over again on both sides, and finally restoring the pile to its original state. He said that he found no writing on any of the sheets. His attention was called to the top sheet, which he was asked to examine. He looked it over carefully at the top, turned it over and examined it, seemed to be in doubt as to whether or not he had taken the top sheet, and took the second sheet; he examined that, put it away, and glanced at the third sheet; he then seemed to feel that possibly he *had* had the top sheet in his hand, so he reexamined that very thoroughly and carefully and then, still holding it right side up, declared hesitantly, as if he hated to dispute with the audience but felt compelled to disagree, that there was no writing on the paper. One of the audience called his attention to the particular part of the paper on which there was writing. He glanced at it, looked back at his informant in a puzzled way, and then reexamined that part of the paper. After turning it over somewhat doubtfully and glancing at it, he turned it right side up again. He then began holding it so that the light struck it obliquely and finally declared, still in a puzzled fashion, that there *really* was no writing on the paper. Finally he was given the suggestion by the hypnotist that there *was* writing and that he would see it. He glanced back at the paper in surprise, and then an expression of amusement and amazement spread over his face as he saw the writing apparently for the first time. He commented on the juvenility of the handwriting, disowning it. When asked to tell what it said, he showed much interest in reading the characters but appeared to have a certain amount of difficulty in deciphering the writing. The last word was incomplete: he read it, spelled it, and stated that it seemed to be only part of a word. When he was asked to guess what the word was, he promptly reread the sentence in order to get the context, but was unable to guess. He then wanted to know why the writing had not been finished and was informed by the hypnotist that if he would just watch the pencil on the table, it would suddenly lift up in the air and begin writing the rest of the word. He looked doubtfully at the hypnotist and then said, "Why, it's lifting up," seeming to have no realization that his own hand was picking up the pencil and holding it poised in position to write. Gradually his hand began forming letters. He was asked what the pencil was writing, to which he replied, "Wait—wait; let's see"; he appeared to be entirely absorbed in the supposed phenomenon of a pencil writing alone. The hypnotist watched the writing, which was proceeding very slowly, and soon realized that the word in question was *delicious*. The hypnotist then announced this to the audience while the subject was writing the last four letters and finished by the time the subject had finished writing. The subject looked up upon completing the word and said, "It's *delicious,*" and then read the sentence to see if the word was relevant to the meaning. Apparently he had not heard the observer announce the word to the seminar.

VIII. "CRYSTAL"-GAZING: HALLUCINATORY VIVIDNESS OF DREAM IMAGERY EMBODYING ANGER DISPLACED FROM HYPNOTIST ON TO DREAM PERSON

In a somnambulistic state the subject was instructed that he was to gaze at the wall and that as he did this the wall would become distant, faraway, foggy, and blurred; gradually a dark point would appear, which would become more and more elaborate, that movement would enter the scene, and soon he would see a well-known and emotionally stirring moving picture.

The subject began these observations with faint interest and considerable difficulty at first, but gradually a profound change in his manner and attitude occurred as he was seen to watch the moving images with intense interest. He resented any inquiries as to what he was seeing and gave the impression that he did not want to be distracted from the scene. Now and then he would turn slightly to ask, "Did you see that? Watch." The moving scene was from Rasputin and the Empress, showing the stumbling and falling of the Czarevitch, to which the subject showed appropriate emotional reactions. He went on to describe the sequence of events in proper chronological order. When the demonstration had gone far enough, he was told that the picture was changing. He disregarded this; when the hypnotist insisted, he declared that he did not want to listen now, that the hypnotist should wait until the picture came to an end. He was obdurate about accepting any suggestions concerning the changing of the picture. The suggestion was then tried of speeding up the movie, making it go faster and faster. When this was done, it was possible to shift the scene to a hospital picture, which he described as one in which *a nurse shouted loudly at a patient.* Here he manifested great resentment toward the nurse for doing this, apparently hallucinating the nurse's voice. The incorporation into the hallucinatory image of his anger against the experimenter and the childlike and fear-laden exaggeration of his impression of loud and angry voices because of his own inner anger were all very evident.

IX. IMPLANTATION OF A COMPLEX

During hypnosis the subject was instructed to recall having had dinner at Dr. D.'s home on the previous day. He was then told that the hypnotist would review a certain series of actions which had occurred on the previous day and that the hypnotist would refresh his memory of certain things that the subject had done which he regretted intensely and which constituted a source of much shame to him. Thereupon he was told to remember how during the course of the afternoon he had stood by the fireplace, leaning against the mantel while talking to Dr. D. about various subjects, when his eye happened to fall upon a package of cigarettes lying behind the clock on the end of the mantelpiece. The tale went on that Dr. D. had noticed his glance and had proceeded to tell the subject that the package of cigarettes was a sentimental keepsake of his marriage, that he and his wife had received this package of cigarettes on their wedding day and had preserved it unused ever since. As Dr. D. added various romantic elaborations, the subject had not paid much attention because he was really rather bored by the sentimental story. After fingering the package, Dr. D. had replaced it at the other end of the mantelpiece; but the subject had not paid any attention to this either. Shortly after this Dr. D. and his wife had left the room for a few minutes. During their absence the subject noticed that he was out of cigarettes and glanced about the room to see if his host had some. Noticing a pack of cigarettes at the other end of the mantelpiece, he thought that his host would have no objection to his helping himself. He stepped over and took this pack of cigarettes from the mantelpiece, opened it, extracted a cigarette, lit and smoked it. Not until he had finished smoking did he realize that this was the very pack of cigarettes which Dr. D. had placed at the end of the mantelpiece instead of returning to its original hiding-place behind the clock. The subject was then reminded of how distressed he had felt, of his sense of being in a quandry as to what he ought to do, of how he had hastily closed the pack and had replaced it behind the clock and had then decided that he had better put it where Dr. D. had placed it, but how before he could do this his host had returned so that he had been forced to carry on a casual conversation with this burden on his mind. Furthermore he was told that even now and after awakening this burden would still be on his mind.

The subject was roused, and after a few brief remarks Dr. D. offered him a cigarette. The subject started, glanced furtively first at Dr. D. and then at the hypnotist, and finally in a labored fashion reached out and accepted the cigarette, handling it in a gingerly manner. Dr. D. began an innocuous conversation, but the subject paid little attention to what was said and asked Dr. D. what he thought about sentimentality, uttering the word *sentimentality* in a tone of disgust. He then stated that he himself was not sentimental and that he tended to dislike people who were sentimental and maudlin. He stated that he hoped that Dr. D. was not sentimental, that he did not impress the subject as being sentimental. Dr. D. made another attempt to change the topic of conversation, but the subject persisted with his own line of thought. He raised a hypothetical question about a man who owned an old homestead and who, as a result of the economic depression, had lost much money and was in a quandary about the necessity of selling it. He went on to talk of the burning of the house, of the house going up in smoke, and various allied topics. He then talked of guilt feelings, how everybody stole, how he himself had stolen; he wanted to know how Dr. D. would feel about anybody who had stolen unwittingly.

Another attempt by Dr. D. to change the trend of the conversation failed. The subject then told of having once stolen a cigar which belonged to a man who had kept it for sentimental reasons. He said he had taken the cigar and smoked it without realizing that it was a keepsake, and that he had felt very bad about it and wondered about the possibility of replacing it so that the sentimental man would not be angry with him. In a defensive manner he then expressed a high regard for a person's feelings and contended that nevertheless people should not think too hard of others who had unwittingly violated some of their sentimental values. After this he stated that not only had he stolen the cigar but he had even stolen cigarettes (pause), a pack of cigarettes. As he said this, he glanced in a particularly furtive manner at Dr. D. and also at the hypnotist, and seemed very ill at ease. He told about having smoked a cigarette and having enjoyed it, but that it had left a bad taste in his mouth afterward and that even though he had stolen the cigarettes long ago, he could not get them off his mind, that they still troubled him, though common sense told him it was nothing to be concerned or worried about.

X. THE ASSUMPTION OF ANOTHER'S IDENTITY UNDER HYPNOTIC DIRECTION, WITH STRIKING UNCONSCIOUS MIMICRY AND THE ASSUMPTION OF UNCONSCIOUS EMOTIONAL ATTITUDES

During hypnosis the subject was informed that after awakening *he* would be Dr. D. and that Dr. D. would be Mr. Blank, and that in the role of Dr. D. he would talk to the pseudo Mr. Blank. Additional suggestions which the subject fully accepted were given to complete the transidentification. After the subject was awakened, a conversation was begun. The pseudo Mr. Blank questioned him about his work in the seminar, as though he were Dr. D.; the subject responded by giving an excellent talk about his experiences in the seminar and his reactions to the group, talking in the phraseology of Dr. D. and expressing the personal attitudes of Dr. D. A chance conversation with Dr. D. on the previous day had supplied him with a great deal of information which he utilized fully. It was noted also that he adopted Dr. D.'s mannerisms in smoking and that he introduced ideas with certain phrases characteristic of Dr. D. When the pseudo Mr. Blank challenged his identity, the subject contradicted Mr. Blank politely and seemed profoundly amazed at Mr. Blank's remarks. Then suddenly, with an expression of dawning understanding, he turned to the hypnotist, saying, "He's in a trance, isn't he?", and thereafter was only amused at Mr. Blank's remarks. Mr. Blank then questioned the subject about his wife, to which the subject responded in a way that would have been natural for the real Dr. D. When asked about children, he assumed an expression of mild embarrassment and replied, "not yet, but you never can tell." Mr. Blank then began talking to the hypnotist in his ordinary fashion, at which the subject again seemed tremendously surprised. With a puzzled look on his face, he suddenly leaned over and tested Mr. Blank for catalepsy. When he found none, his face was expressive of some concern; he promptly whispered to the hypnotist, "He's coming out of the trance," but was relieved when the hypnotist assured him that it would be all right if this happened.

Finally, when an attempt was made to rehypnotize him in order to restore his own identity, the subject displayed the emotional attitude of resistance toward the induction of hypnosis which would have been entirely characteristic of the real Dr. D. The subject seemed actually to experience the same emotional responses that Dr. D. would have had at such a time. Finally, because he appeared to be entirely resistive to simple suggestion, it was necessary to induce hypnosis by indirect methods.

This rather astonishing result offers a technique for the experimental investigation of the phenomena of identification and of the unconscious incorporation of parental emotions by children.

20. Demonstration of Mental Mechanisms by Hypnosis

Milton H. Erickson

After general introductory remarks on the special advantages of hypnosis as a means of demonstrating the mechanisms and dynamics of behavior, I introduced 3 normal subjects to the audience and conversed casually with them to demonstrate their ordinary behavior. This was followed by the rapid hypnotizing of all 3 subjects, with demonstration of some of the more common hypnotic phenomena, particularly ideomotor action, catalepsy, rapport and, finally, the somnambulistic hypnotic trance in which the subjects give an outward appearance of being awake and in full contact with their surroundings, and yet are actually completely out of contact with their surroundings except as instructed by the hypnotist. Then followed a series of demonstrations directed to the clarification of various psychic dynamisms.

Subject 1, on reaching the somnambulistic state and opening his eyes, was found to be oriented as if he were in my office, rather than in a lecture hall before an audience. This orientation on the part of the subject was found to be entirely valid, and every response he made, direct or indirect, disclosed him to be acting entirely as if he were actually in my office. This manifestation was discussed in detail, emphasis being placed on the hypnotized subject's ability to exclude, or to fail to respond to external stimuli and to react to internal stimuli as if they derived form the outside; a parallel was drawn with the reality of the delusional beliefs of psychotic patients.

Subject 2 was then placed in rapport with Dr. R. W. Cavell, and a casual conversation followed, after which I made a long series of suggestions to the subject to the effect that she was acquiring a retroactive amnesia extending to the tenth year of her life. In this manner it was possible to induce this young woman to "regress" in the patterns of her behavior and to react as if she were 10 years of age, giving the responses characteristic of a child and showing the emotional reactions, the general social patterns and the juvenile attitudes characteristic of that age. The subject in the mental state of 10 years was then interviewed by Dr. H. Reye, who questioned her extensively, eliciting replies in accord with the understanding of a child of 10.

Reprinted with permission from *The Archives of Neurology and Psychiatry*, August, 1939, Volume 42, No.2.

This demonstration was discussed with emphasis on the necessity of a time-taking procedure of suggestion as a measure of permitting the subject, who is receiving such suggestions, to acquire the "mental set" by means of which there can be reestablished the levels of mentation characteristic of any suggested age without interference from subsequently acquired experiences. A parallel was drawn with the forms of regression encountered psychiatrically.

Subject 3 was then employed to demonstrate, while in the somnambulistic state, the phenomenon of negative hallucination. Dr. Cavell was pointed out, and the subject was told that shortly he would leave and that she would not see him again. After these suggestions had been given effectively, innumerable attempts were made by Dr. Cavell to establish either a positive or a negative contact with her, but the subject manifested neither avoidance of nor response to him. So far as could be determined by indirect as well as direct measures, the subject remained totally unable to make any form of response to Dr. Cavell. This was discussed, and a parallel was drawn with various forms of denial of reality observed in psychotic patients.

Hypnotic suggestions were given to subject 1 to the effect that there would appear on the floor a large crystal in which he was to see a crystal image of recent events. The subject accepted these suggestions and had a remarkably complete visual image of the lecture room as it had been during the earlier part of the evening; extensive questioning disclosed that the experience for the subject was exceedingly realistic. Discussion was offered, and parallels were drawn with the processes of reliving as it develops in psychotherapeutic measures.

Subject 3, still in the somnambulistic trance, was given a series of suggestions directed to the evocation of the phenomenon termed "resistance." To this end the subject was instructed to be entirely courteous and compliant toward Dr. S. H. Ruskin in every detail; yet at every opportunity the subject was to avoid, escape, evade, resent and resist every casual request of conversational remark made. After a brief pause, the subject was awakened and a casual conversation initiated, leading to the introduction of the subject to Dr. Ruskin. Then followed a general conversation, in which the subject missed no opportunity, however direct or indirect, to oppose Dr. Ruskin in every conceivable way, yet maintaining an attitude of impeccable courtesy. An attempt was made by Dr. Ruskin to have the subject take another seat, and every request and insistence on his part was countered effectively by courteous resistance; when he finally made it impossible for the subject to avoid compliance, the latter yielded, but moved the cahir to a new position, thereby subtly nullifying the compliance. This behavior was discussed in detail in relation to the problems represented by both conscious and unconscious resistance shown by patients.

Subject 2, in the deep trance, was instructed that after awakening she was to recall a trip made by the hypnotist to Detroit, in an effort to visit a certain hopsital, and the losing of his way. The subject was given a false address for this well known hospital and was told to insist, argumentatively, when awake, that this false address was the only correct one.

After awakening, subject 2 obeyed instructions fully and became involved in arguments with the members of the audience as to the location of the specified hospital. Innumerable items of proof were advanced by the subject to confirm the false address, and I discussed in general the fixity of the subject's beliefs and the general imperviousness to any reasoning approach to her delusional ideas. A parallel was drawn between this behavior and the general attitude taken by the psychotic patient when a reasoning approach is made to any form of abnormal ideation.

To subject 3 there was then suggested, in the deep trance state, a phobia for cats and a long series of suggestions was given, building up in the subject an intense fear, dislike and abhorrence of cats and anything connected with them. The subject was told that this fear would persist even after awakening, but that it would be concealed, denied and repressed from all conscious awareness. After this complex had been thoroughly implanted, the subject was allowed to awaken. Dr. Cavell took a seat beside the subject and by slow degrees led up to the topic of people's interest in pets. When this conversation had been well established, the subject began manifesting intense and uncontrollable abhorrence of and disgust for people who had any interest in animals, particularly cats, and numerous instances were cited by the subject in which persons who like cats were found to be undesirable or abhorrent. Finally, the conversation disclosed that Dr. Cavell owned a cat, whereon the subject showed a marked distaste for the proximity of her chair to Dr. Cavell, and recourse was had to various subterfuges on her part to effect a change to another seat. Dr. Reye then approached the subject to ask questions about cats, with the result that the subject became increasingly tense and emotional and unable to discuss cats without expressing intense, unreasoning and irrational hostility toward them. Finally, when questioned as to the duration of this feeling of hatred toward cats, the subject gave a long story about always having hated and abhorred cats. When all the classic manifestations of an acute phobia had been manifested clearly and unmistakably, the subject was rehypnotized and the phobia removed completely by psychotherapeutic suggestions and the giving of insight.

After this, subject 3 was rehypnotized, and a second complex was implanted in which the subject was told that, purely by accident, through a state of absentmindedness, she had seriously offended subject 1, with whom a friendly feeling had always existed. The subject was told that this result now belonged to the past, that there was nothing that could be done about it, and that it might just as well be completely repressed and forgotten.

After this, subject 3 was awakened, and, by manipulation of the situation, subjects 3 and 1 engaged in a casual conversation. During the course of this, subject 3 resorted to every conceivable misunderstanding of subject 1's remarks to offer an apology. Overcompensatory behavior and inexplicable embarrassments were demonstrated by the subject in a clear fashion. Many of the remarks made by subject 3 carried a double meaning easily apparent to the audience, but which bore only a simple conscious significance to the subject. In elaboration of the demonstration, I discussed the significance and effects of repressed material on ordinary behavior.

Subject 3 was again hypnotized; the previous complex was removed, and suggestions of an intense desire to smoke were given. At the same time the subject was instructed to want to avoid smoking, to hate smoking and yet to feel bound by an uncontrollable desire to smoke, a smoking compulsion being thereby effected. On awakening, the subject manifested marked restlessness, made several remarks about my smoking, commented that I seemed to have matches, and remarked that I had sometimes offered people cigarettes; when one was offered to her, it was rejected with a statement that a cigarette of a special brand was desired. Since a package of this special brand was found in the audience, a cigarette was offered to the subject, who took it unwillingly and refused to smoke unless some one else joined in the act. After much dilatory activity and ineffective efforts to light the cigarette, the subject finally began to smoke in an easily recognizable compulsive fashion, becoming harshly critical of the cigarette and of the general situation, obviously not enjoying the cigarette and yet feeling compelled to smoke. Every effort made on the part of members of the audience to induce dicontinuance of the smoking met with firm resistance, despite the subject's repeated insistence that she had no desire to smoke and despite her ready desire to get rid of the cigarette, the subject finally began to smoke in an easily recognizable compulsive obsessive form of behavior.

After this, I gave a general review of the various demonstrations and drew parallels between psychoneurotic behavior, psychotic behavior and normal behavior and the various types of behavior manifested by normal hypnotic subjects, closing my remarks with emphasis on the value of hypnosis as an instrument for the teaching of the dynamics of behavior and as a means of creating within the laboratory various types of behavior which could then be subjected to critical laboratory analysis.

21. Unconscious Mental Activity in Hypnosis—Psychoanalytic Implications

Milton H. Erickson and Lewis B. Hill

Misconceptions regarding the alleged limitation of hypnotic psychotherapy to hypnotic suggestion are current because of the failure to differentiate between *(1)* the process of inducing trance states and *(2)* the nature of the trance. Since hypnosis can be induced and trance manifestations elicited by suggestion, the unwarranted assumption is made that whatever develops from hypnosis must bc completely a result of suggestion, and primarily an expression of it.

The hypnotized person remains an individual, and only certain limited general relationships and behavior are temporarily altered by hypnosis. Hypnosis is in fact the induction of a peculiar psychological state which permits subjects to reassociate and reorganize inner psychological complexities in a way suitable to the unique items of their own psychological experiences.

CASE REPORT

Dr. Jane was a quiet, earnest, hardworking, highly intelligent woman intern. During the course of her hospital service she had often sought help and instruction from me about her ward work. She had shown much interest, and had often watched my hypnotic experiments. She had been asked repeatedly to act as a subject but had always politely refused. I and various other members of the professional staff characterized her as a decidedly insecure, rather neurotic woman who probably suffered from some distressing personality problem.

After about six months' professional association with her, she came unexpectedly to my office and related with some pressure and urgency that she had a serious personal problem that she must decide within the next month. For months, every time she tried to make a decision about it, her thoughts became blocked, she became anxious, and she dismissed it by absorbing herself in work. She had developed insomnia and drove herself from one task to another to fall asleep from exhaustion. She

Reprinted with permission from*The Psychoanalytic Quarterly,* January, 1944, Vol XIII, No. 1. Footnotes in this paper are by the editor of *The Psychoanalytic Quarterly* and were written for the original publication.

invited my assistance and prescribed the manner in which it was to be given. Some evening when it was convenient for me, I was to go to her apartment and hypnotize her, adding that she did not know why she wanted me to do it. She warned me not to question her because she did not know the answers. She dictated in detail the manner in which I was to proceed in hypnotizing her:

> I want you to be very emphatic about instructing my unconscious to think my problem through in a cool, unemotional fashion. I want my unconscious to discover what that problem is because I really don't know, and to look at it from every angle, size it up, and then make some sort of a final formulation no matter what it is. Watching your subjects has impressed me with the way the unconscious can handle problems a person doesn't know he has. I know I have a problem that troubles me, makes me irritable and lose a lot of weight. I am just plain disagreeable in company. This can't go on. I've got to leave the hospital soon, and I can't even make any plans. So I want my unconscious to straighten things out for me.
>
> This is what I want to do. First hypnotize me very soundly, and when I am in a deep trance, tell my unconscious everything I have just told you, using the notes you have made so that you don't omit anything. I want you to be as careful and as complete as you are when you are giving your experimental subjects suggestions. You don't know what your instructions are going to result in, and it is the same way with me. I don't know and you don't know what it is all about, but if you tell my unconscious everything I have told you, it will understand. Be sure to tell it that it must think the whole problem clear through. Be emphatic.[1]

She disclaimed with obvious sincerity any additional understanding of her problem and said that she could not give any more information, although she felt herself willing to do so. She left the office hastily.

On meeting her during the next two days, no reference was made to the visit, even though several opportunities were offered her. On the third day she was asked casually about her plans for the evening. She replied she felt so tired that she planned to go to bed early and get some rest. Nothing in her manner indicated any awareness of a possible significance to the question.

At seven o'clock that evening she seemed astonished to have me call on

[1] In the language of the unconscious the hypnotist is being instructed by the subject to order her to get married—the object of the treatment. [Ed.]

her. She met the situation in a socially adequate fashion and invited me in for a visit. During the general conversation that ensued it became apparent that she had developed an amnesia for the visit to my office. She yawned repeatedly, each time apologizing for her seeming inhospitality, and confessed to having insomnia. This was seized upon to introduce the topic of hypnosis and the suggestion was offered that she might try hypnosis to induce sleep. Contrary to her previous refusals, she consented and promptly adjusted herself in a comfortable position on the couch.

She responded quickly and soon developed a profound trance. She was told to sleep deeply and continuously for half an hour during which I would absent myself, the purpose being that of providing ample opportunity for her to develop a profound trance state. She passively assented.

Returning in half an hour I told her to continue sleeping deeply, and I began a rather rambling monologue, making vague general references to the office visit followed by repeated comments on the autonomy of the unconscious, its ability to respond adequately, and its capacity to solve mental problems as well as, or even better than, the conscious mind. There followed a systematic review of the conversation of the initial interview, to which she seemed to listen most attentively and with some show of emotion.

At the conclusion she was asked if she understood the nature of her problem and if she were willing to examine it and to solve it. With much emotion she answered, "Yes, I know what it is. I understand. It is hard to decide, but I have to do it and I suppose I might as well now." Asked if she wished to talk about her problem, she replied that she did not want to have anybody know anything about it, that her purpose was to solve it entirely by herself. How long a time would she need? After a few moments she answered thoughtfully, "Come back in an hour and ask me if I am through and I will tell you."

An hour later she was still sleeping soundly. Asked if it was time to awaken her, she answered, "I am almost through. It will probably take me half an hour longer." In half an hour she responded to my return with the spontaneous statement, "I'm through. I've got it solved. You can awaken me any time you want to, but I think you better tell me after I am awakened that it will be all right to know the answer." I agreed but instructed her to remain asleep some minutes longer in order that she might be sure of everything. Some minutes later she was told that she might awaken if she were really convinced that her task was done. Immediately she repeated her request that she be told after awakening that it would be all right to know the answer. Prompt assurance was given, and then she was told to awaken gently and easily. This she did, and at once she began to converse freely, picking up the general thread of the conversation preceding the trance. She gave no evidence of recollecting that she had been hypnotized nor of understanding the reason for my presence. She was puzzled to note the passage of time and seemed at a loss to account for it. Remarks about "our chat a few days ago" elicited only responses relating to previous professional discussions.

After 20 minutes of conversation it became obvious that she could not understand the prolongation of my inexplicable visit and that she was secretly wishing I would leave. At the door I paused and, looking at her intently, remarked, "It is all right now for you to know the answer."

She seemed to be at a loss to find words with which to reply. Again I said, "It is all right now for you to know the answer." She responded with a bewildered look, suddenly reacted with a startled flush, and became tremulous and jerky in her movements and speech. With great anxiety she explained, "Won't you excuse me, please. I just found out something I wasn't prepared to know. I have to think about it right away, so won't you please leave me alone. Please hurry."

The next day and thereafter she made no reference to the foregoing incidents. Everything indicated that she had complete amnesia for both the office visit and the events of the evening. It was noted by her colleagues that she was working with greater ease, was more sociable, and was eating better and gaining weight.

Approximately a month after the hypnotic session she came into my office and displayed a wedding ring. She had not publicly announced her engagement of a month ago or her marriage of the previous day, choosing instead to tell it first to a selected few. I was included because in her ward work I had given her special supervision and instruction for which she felt particularly grateful. She seemed to have no conscious awareness of any other possible instance that might have some bearing upon her choice.

The man she married was known to have been interested in her for some time, but she had not been known by me or others on the staff to have shown any real interest in him. Neither was she known by her colleagues to have spent much time in his company, although it was common knowledge that he was greatly attracted to her. It was the consensus that he was decidedly her inferior in so many aspects that he would never be able to interest her, despite his substantial worth as an average citizen.

Shortly after the marriage the young couple moved to another city; nothing more was heard of them until three months later, when she walked into my office and stated that she wanted to thank me.

That morning, lying in bed after her husband had gone to his office, she had begun thinking about how happy she was and wondering what she had ever done to deserve such happiness.[2] Previous to marriage she had

[2]This statement indicates that a disturbing sense of guilt about her relationship to her husband is becoming conscious. [Ed.]

anticipated some difficulties in marital adjustment because of the marked difference in nature between her husband and herself; yet each time a disagreement seemed impending, it had solved itself without difficulty. Then she had experienced a sudden rush of memories relating to the interview in my office and the subsequent hypnotic session. "It was the first time I was consciously aware of those things. Of course I was conscious of what I was telling you that morning, but as soon as I left your office, I must have repressed it completely, because I never thought of it again until this morning. When you came to my apartment to hypnotize me, I was surprised to see you. I didn't know why you came. I just thought it was a social call. And when you suggested hypnosis to me, I was so tired that I didn't remember that I had always refused to be a subject for you."

I asked her to give a detailed account of the initial interview. She replied, "Oh, that isn't necessary, I remember all of that distinctly, and besides, that isn't why I came to see you. When I told you I had a problem and that I didn't know what the problem was, I was telling you the truth. I just knew something was wrong. I was in love with John but I didn't know it, and I wouldn't have believed anybody who told me so. I tried not to go out with him very often, and I didn't, but just the same I was in love. There are many differences between John and me, as you know. Our family background is entirely different. John just plugs along, and I was always at the head of my class. I have many interests—music, literature, art—that John hasn't. I repressed all my feelings for him the way I must have repressed that whole talk with you. Watching you do hypnosis gave me an idea. When I figured out that plan, I had the feeling that my problem must be something I didn't want anybody to know or I wouldn't be keeping it from myself so completely. That is why I asked you to do things the way I did.

"When you put me in a trance, I was scared as soon as I went under and you began talking about the things I had said to you. But I knew right away that you were just talking to my unconscious and that if I woke up I wouldn't remember a thing, the way your other subjects do, so I felt reassured, and let you go ahead. When you finished, I was all ready to go to work, except that I was afraid of how it might turn out because I knew I loved John. As soon as you left the room, I saw in my mind, like a patient's hallucination, a great long manuscript that slowly unrolled. It was divided into pros and cons about marrying John. What they were you don't need to know."

Questioning disclosed that these were such words or phrases as "industrious," "lacking in imagination," but she was unwilling to cite other than descriptive items of which she knew me to be aware. She stated that there were many items which were of particular and personal importance to her and would be difficult for anybody else to understand.

When the lists had been read through completely, they were reread thoughtfully, and then a process of "cancellation" was begun, sometimes by crossing out pairs, sometimes by adding an item from one list to one in the other list and then rewording the combined item, giving it an entirely new significance. Some items in both columns could be dealt with only by rewording them through an inclusion of pros and cons applicable to herself rather than to John; then some of the reworded items could be "crossed out," "balanced," or "combined." In counting the items remaining in each list, she found that "there was a marked preponderance of pros, and so I reread the list of pros again because it seemed too good to believe, and I found that the count was only arithmetically correct because the pros were all so much larger than the cons. Then I knew what my answer really was.

"When you returned a second time and suggested that I sleep a few minutes longer to make sure my problem was solved, I wanted to tell you what the answer was, but I felt John should be the first to know. I was already sure, so I just slept as you told me. I knew hypnotic subjects had amnesias to trance experiences, so I carefully told you to be sure to tell me to know the answer.[3]

"When you awakened me, I didn't know I had been asleep, and you seemed to have been there only a few minutes. I was awfully upset when I noticed how late it was. I couldn't pay attention to what you were saying because I was wondering what had happened to make it so late. When you said it would be all right to know the answer, I couldn't understand what you meant. When you repeated it, I suddenly knew that I loved John and would marry him if he asked me to. I was rather rude to you, but I didn't know how that idea had come to my mind, and I had to be alone and think about it. The more I thought about it, the more I knew I loved him. I went to bed happy for the first time in months, feeling as if I didn't have a problem in the world. The next morning I had thoughts about nothing except John. We became engaged, and I wanted to tell you about it, but I couldn't figure out any reason for doing so. When we got married, I wanted to tell you and the only reason for doing so that I could think of was the help you had given me in my work. That didn't seem to be sufficient reason, but I used it anyway."

Two years later an unannounced call on the couple found them happily married. The wife commented with pride upon the accuracy with which her unconscious had evaluated the whole situation. She had told her husband nothing about her hypnotic experience. Some years later they were found to be most happy, and enthusiastic parents of several children.

[3]Two things may be noted here: *(1)* the subject's conviction that there would be an amnesia, and *(2)* that the wording of her request concerned only the answer and not the experience of reaching that answer; hence there would naturally be an amnesia for the experience and a knowledge only of the end result.

Word has been received directly and indirectly from them from time to time indicating a most successful marriage. [By M.H.E.]

CASE REPORT

A young college woman, who for a year had frequently acted as an experimental hypnotic subject for me, some months later appeared at my office stating that she wished to have a long personal talk with me about an important problem.

"In my hypnotic work with you," she said, "I have learned a good many things and feel well repaid for the time and effort I have given you. Now I want to ask a personal favor of you, and it is to be a *favor* and not a repayment for what I have done for you. The things I have learned have more than repaid me. I am emphasizing this so that you will do exactly as I wish and not according to any ideas that you might have. I have planned this all out.

"You know practically everything about me except that I have fallen in love and am going to be married soon. That is all settled.

"George is not like me at all. We are both college graduates, but where I am brilliant, George is just of average intellect; however, he has a much more charming personality, is even-tempered and socially much more adaptable. But he is stubborn, too, and he is much more confident of his intelligence than he has any right to be. He doesn't know I am a lot more intelligent than he is, and he is not the kind of person who would ever find it out. Whereas I am excitable and quick-tempered, he is always calm and unruffled. He is just exactly the kind of man who will make up for and correct the deficiencies in my own personality, and we are very much in love. I have tried to fight against it because I am afraid I will make George unhappy, but it is no use; so I have tried to size up our personalities and tried to reach some understanding of what I must do to meet his needs if we are to have a happy married life, but I become confused and get nowhere.

"I want you to put me in a deep trance and tell me to remember clearly all that I have just been telling you. When that is done, give me instructions to think about George and myself and about the things that I need to do to ensure a reasonably good marital adjustment. Do not try to question or help me. Watch me closely, and whenever you see me getting emotionally disturbed or confused or inattentive, reassure me that I can and must do this thinking, and keep me at it until I am through. When I get through, I will let you know what else, if anything, should be done."

Accordingly, a deep hypnotic trance was induced. She was then told to review silently and in full everything she had said in the waking state and to elaborate each idea mentally until it was clear in her mind. At first she objected, but finally acceded when reminded that the suggestion was at her own request. During the review she manifested much tension. When she seemed to have completed this task, she was told to reflect on exactly what it was she had in mind to do and how she was to do it, and when her method of approach to her problem was clearly formulated, she was to proceed. Again she objected to this suggestion but soon acknowledged its desirability. After some meditation she declared that she was fully ready and asked if she might go ahead with her task. She was told to proceed. It soon became evident that she had decided to resort chiefly to a silent review or study of whatever it was she had in mind.

In a short time she became distressed, and she was urged to begin again and to postpone temporarily any particularly distressing items until other matters had been cleared up sufficiently to permit thinking about the more painful things. When she gave evidence of distress, rest periods of two to five minutes were suggested to her, and these seemed to help her.

At times she would verbalize details of past emotional experiences known to me. Sometimes she would ask me to move to a remote corner of the room and order me not to listen, as she talked to herself in a low tone. On these occasions she would ask for the instruction to "go ahead and face it through." Approximately two hours were spent in this manner, often with a display of intense emotion which seemed to be alleviated by general reassurances from me. She then declared that she was through with her task and asked to be awakened with emphatic instructions from me that she retain full consciousness of her trance experience.

Upon awakening she was sorry for having been so slow but stated that she still was not through with her task. She now wanted to review her recollections of the trance; until this was done she would not know what next step would be necessary. She spent half an hour in silent meditation without display of emotion excepting gestures expressive of decision or conviction. Questioned about her progress, she replied that she had now reviewed all the "major matters," adding that her recollection of much of the trance was exceedingly vague; nevertheless, she felt "entirely comfortable" about everything.

She now wished to discuss with me various items, but I was only to listen, except that now and then I was to take "a negative attitude," which, she explained, would encourage her to be positive and emphatic in her statements.

She spoke in vague generalities about marital adjustment, sexual satisfaction, self-control of temper, and the need for marital partners to encourage each other's interests. Finally she offered the opinion that she really had nothing further to discuss. I agreed at once, whereupon she abruptly contradicted me to declare emphatically that there was still much to be said. She then launched into an earnest discussion of all the things she felt confident would contribute materially to a successful marriage, an excellent evaluation of her own personality and of George's, as was later learned by direct contact with him. This discussion was all at a superficial social level.

She brought the discussion to a close by stating that there remained only one thing more for me to do: "If there is to be any negative attitude toward our marriage, it is better for you to have it and not me. I want you to be pessimistic and doubtful and not encourage it. Don't say anything openly; just take a general negative attitude. *I want you to keep that attitude for at least two years* when it won't make any difference because then I will be able to show you. I will write you newsy letters which you will answer politely, and in some subtle way, such as *hoping* all is going well with George's work, express your negative attitude."

During the next two years occasional letters were received and promptly answered, always with some ambiguous remarks about George. Six months after the expiration of the two years she wrote a letter saying that she was pregnant and that her husband had been promoted to a much better position.[4] Her intimate friends all reported the marriage to be most satisfactory, and after five years it appears to remain so. George, like John, was not told of these matters. [By M.H.E.]

DISCUSSION

The study of unconscious mental activity by other techniques provides methods of checking psychoanalytic data, theories, and techniques. If it is found that the therapeutic results of psychoanalysis seem to be duplicated by different and much less time consuming techniques, psychoanalysts should be quick to investigate these possibilities in the hope that they may be verified.

These case records of two patients treated by hypnosis are of interest precisely because of the almost complete absence of evidence of unconscious mental activity in the manner in which it regularly appears in the course of psychoanalytic therapy. There is no history, there are no free associations, the patients do not even give a clear statement of their problems, and the state of the transference must be inferred. These records cannot be studied as psychoanalytic documents. This is not a

[4] Again, in the language of the unconscious, the hypnotist had been instructed by the subject to order her to have a baby and also to allow George to achieve some degree of parity with her in order "to ensure a reasonably good marital adjustment." She did both "in two years" and was then "able to show" the hypnotist that she had obeyed him. *Cf.* footnote [2]. [Ed.]

failure in transcription, for the hypnotist in a personal communication states that he does not know appreciably more about his patients' ideational content than is in the record. The therapeutic result is achieved without "making the unconscious conscious."

Recognizing this difference, it still appears profitable to make a comparison between the two methods upon the basis of certain familiar concepts:

(1) Unconscious[5] conflict and indecision within the psyche gives rise to anxiety against which defenses are erected. These defenses prevent both unconscious resolution of the conflict and its emergence into consciousness, and may result in inhibition of thinking, confusion, interference with activity.
(2) An unconscious conflict may be resolved unconsciously.
(3) The result produced by this unconscious work is evidenced by the emergence into consciousness of a thought, or a decision, which the person explains either in terms of some unconscious derivatives, more or less symbolized, or by a rationalization.
(4) Such unconscious activity can be influenced, accelerated, or retarded by a relationship with another person.

Analysts have found that the transference is a vital part of the therapeutic process and that the intrapsychic conflict would not continue its disturbing existence were it not for current difficulties in personal relationships according to a pattern of transference and provoked by the individual's relation to his environment. The hypnotist[6] evidently holds the view that the intrapsychic conflict exists as an entity complete in itself although modifiable by extrapsychic influences. The transference of the hypnotic subject to the hypnotist is ignored, or at least not utilized as a therapeutic instrument, by the hypnotist. Psychoanalytic technique explores precisely the transference as the essential focus of therapy.[7]

[5]No distinction is made here between unconscious and preconscious.

[6]These remarks are limited to the method used in these two cases.

[7]These two women were in states of transference to the hypnotist long before the treatment began. Some of the characteristics of this transference can be inferentially reconstructed. The hypnotist was a person in a position of authority to both. Both women were in states of discomforting ambivalence about marriage. Both had chosen partners who were their inferiors. The transference would seem to be a fantasy compromise in which these women were simultaneously identified with the therapist (both gave detailed peremptory orders as to how the treatment was to be carried out) and in states of submission to him (hypnotism). In the first case the submission was achieved by a device (amnesia); in the second, under protest. In both cases (explicitly stated in the second) the mixed transference to

The majority of patients seeking psychotherapy suffer symptoms the causes of which they can only deny or rationalize. Those who believe that they know the nature of their conflicts are still unable to recognize the factors making for their insolubility. While patients claim ignorance of their intrapsychic problems, they relate a running narrative which, when it is completed in the process of analysis, demonstrates that there must have been an unconscious understanding and planning from the beginning. Patients "know" what is troubling them, but the knowledge is too painful to be borne in consciousness without help. The conflict is neither consciously perceived nor effectively suppressed.

The unconscious weighing of pros and cons to arrive at a decision by these two women whose records are presented is routinely observed in analysis. Both these women were familiar with hypnotic experiments and were aware of the possibility of avoiding the conscious working out of their problems. Analysands who have had a long acquaintance with psychoanalytic psychotherapy before making the decision to be analyzed have identical ambivalent feelings about the treatment. Often it is not clear what brings them to the decision to begin treatment. Such patients are sometimes found to have been maintaining defenses against the anxiety incident to partial insight. A good example is a paranoid individual who can no longer endure the "persecutions" of his enemy nor the "deceptions" of his wife. He is consciously convinced about his delusions, but instead of consulting a lawyer, under the guise of seeking protection from the enemy or treatment for his wife, he consults a psychiatrist and becomes convinced that he himself needs treatment. Clearly the unconscious understanding of his problem is far more correct than is his conscious formulation of it.

Psychoanalytic "working through" is essentially due to the fact that once a point is grasped it still cannot be utilized until sundry unconscious associations have become conscious. Psychoanalytic technique endeavors to reduce the stimulus (anxiety) to resistance. The hypnotic technique bypasses the resistance, so to speak. The hypnotist endeavors to operate directly upon the conflict in the belief that if it is solved, much of the defense will spontaneously crumble.

Although in both cases reported the subjects dictate in detail the method by which the therapy was to be conducted, it can be presumed that the result could not have been accomplished without the mediation of the hypnotist. It might be said that the subjects utilized their transference to the hypnotist, who served in these instances chiefly as a passive

---

the therapist persisted long after the therapy and was presumably an important factor in the "adjustment" to marriage. [Ed.] *Cf.* de Saussure, Raymond: *Transference and animal magnetism. The Psychoanalytic Quarterly,* 1943, XII, pp. 194-201.

instrument and who by following the instructions given him enabled the subjects to accomplish a piece of psychological work. This, of course, is an important part of the function of the analyst in psychoanalytic psychotherapy.

Impressive as the evident similarities between hypnotic and psychoanalytic treatment are, they focus attention upon the conspicuous differences. The first is the contrast between psychoanalytic transference and hypnotic rapport. In the cases here reported little is revealed concerning the patients' transference to the hypnotist except that they respond readily to his verbal suggestions[8]; yet this is not so surprising because he is careful to suggest only what they had previously instructed him to require them to do. That these subjects to this extent maintain the semblance of controlling the transference must be an important factor in reducing overt resistance. Much more important, however, is the fact that the unconscious motivations which arouse latent anxiety and conscious indecision remain unconscious. Noteworthy is the refusal of both subjects to tell the physician what goes on in their mind during the treatment. Patients seeking help for their difficulties of necessity emphasize their failures. This can lead in psychoanalysis to growing resentment through narcisstic injury if the analyst does not occasionally remind patients of their admirable qualities and inhibited abilities. Hypnotic technique does not require that patients communicate, or indeed become aware of primitive or infantile unconscious strivings that are alien to the conscious ego idea. Consequently the subjects are not stimulated to build up resistant and hostile attitudes because the therapy does not requirc that the unconscious be made conscious.

These two women apparently resolved a specific conflict without consciousness of the content of the conflict at any time during the treatment. There was no interpretation by the physician to influence what they thought. His manifest influence was purely the direction that they think. If this were the complete explanation, it would have vast implications. The hypnotic suggestion could be as unlimited as the total capacity of the patient to think. But this is to assume that the spoken word of the hypnotist constitutes his principal value as a factor influencing the patient. This conception must be incorrect. The physician, by his presence and all that he may represent in his patient's fantasy, must have a profound effect upon the patient, although it is not stated in words and perhaps not consciously recognized.[9]

[8] In discussions of the mechanism of hypnosis insufficient consideration is given to the possibility of *unspoken* suggestion by the hypnotist to the subject. *Cf.* de Saussure, Raymond: Transference and animal magnetism. *The Psychoanalytic Quarterly,* 1943, XII, pp. 199-200. [Ed.]

[9] The second subject, who seems less inhibited than the first, makes two statements that may provide a clue. Both women are ambivalent to the point of

The statement is of course made that patients like these were not really in great difficulty, that their plans were made, and that they merely resorted to hypnosis as a sort of ritual to bolster their actions; any abracadabra, provided it had local prestige, would have done as well. The same is said repeatedly of psychoanalysis, as in the instance of the woman who consulted a psychoanalyst and after the first interview left her engagement and wedding rings in the analyst's lavatory. After the treatment she divorced her husband. It can be said that she had decided upon divorce and that the psychoanalytic treatment was something she used to rationalize the decision. This assertion fails to explain why the patient had to resort to such elaborate means of justifying her action. In this instance the patient's analysis revealed that she had married apparently as an act of obedience to her mother but in reality to escape from her mother. To be divorced had for her the meaning that she would have to resume her old relationship with her mother. When, through therapy, she had freed herself from an infantile dependence on her mother, she was able to proceed to terminate an unsatisfactory marriage. That these hypnotic patients did not reveal the nature of the factors which impeded their decisions to marry does not argue that there were none; nor does it prove that these factors were not thought out or altered in the unconscious.

There remains for discussion the value of psychotherapy which does not provide conscious insight. How important is the matter of making the unconscious conscious? Is symptomatic relief the criterion of successful psychotherapy? If patients should be made aware of previously unknown unconscious strivings, is it necessary that they know all of the steps through which their insight is achieved?

There is presented evidence that two patients were able through hypnosis to find psychotherapeutic relief from symptoms without conscious exploration of the unconscious sources of their conflicts. They were able to use the hypnotist to overcome their defenses and to do a piece of mental work. From two cases it is not safe to generalize, but it may be noted that in both instances the problem was one of inhibition in a woman who wished to marry and who had some difficulty in overcoming her doubts. Through the treatment both overcame the inhibition and became

---

virtual paralysis about marriage. Both act out their hostility toward men by choosing inferior mates. The second subject says to the hypnotist: "*If there is to be any negative attitude toward our marriage, it is better for you to have it and not me . . . just* [you] *take a . . . negative attitude . . .* " The fantasy is clear: the hypnotist is magically to take over from her the disturbing hostility she has toward the man she has determined to marry; moreover she demands: "*I want you to keep that attitude for at least two years.*" The marriage then is a "*reasonable marital adjustment*" achieved by an unresolved transference to the hypnotist, reinforced by letters and occasional visits. [Ed.]

free to act. Nothing further was necessary to produce the desired result, marriage. Each of these women appears to have been a relatively normally functioning individual who wished only to overcome an intrapsychic obstacle to marriage and who showed a striking rigidity against self-revelation. This last characteristic may have been influenced by their familiarity with this form of therapy.[10] It further suggests that the method may have special usefulness for individuals who find it difficult or impossible to discuss their problems.

The problem presented by some analytic patients through their unwillingness to reveal some things of which they are quite conscious and their inability to become conscious of other things suggests the possibility of further study and experimentation to determine if there is a place for the use of hypnotic suggestion in the course of psychoanalytic therapy. Based upon this study, the thought recommends itself that, after a certain time in the analysis of patients who found it peculiarly difficult to make free associations, it might be suggested, with or without hypnosis, that these patients cease trying to talk and devote themselves to thinking the matter out in silence.[11] It would appear that if this method were used, it would require that the patients be given the further suggestion that they might, but certainly would not have to, report what had occurred to them during this silent thinking.[12] As indicated earlier in these remarks, this solution would not be an entirely new adventure but merely the recognition and utilization of a possibility which certain analytic patients have demonstrated on their own initiative and which these hypnotic patients have carried much further. Hypnosis needs no longer to defend itself against the charge that it is "nothing but" suggestion. The method of hypnosis described presents a means of accomplishing vastly more in the way of psychic rehabilitation than the method of forcing upon a patient the hypnotist's ideas as to the way in which the patient should solve a conflict. This study of hypnotic psychotherapy points a way to research toward a therapy which may utilize all that has been learned both by the hypnotist and by the psychoanalyst.

[10]The first subject stated: "Watching your subjects has impressed me with the way the unconscious can handle problems a person doesn't know he has."

[11]This many analytic patients do at times without instruction from the analyst.[Ed.]

[12]Such a device could only be used in exceptional cases. As a rule it would vitiate the whole analytic process. Whenever most patients encountered a resistance, they would take this refuge. [Ed.]

22. Negation or Reversal of Legal Testimony

Milton H. Erickson

The spontaneous, sincere, and apparently completely unmotivated negation, reversal, or alteration of condemnatory legal testimony previously given by credible witnesses constitutes a difficult and confusing problem. Although found more often by the psychiatrist than by the jurist, such change of testimony can, and not infrequently does, entail serious legal difficulties.

Such alteration of testimony is characterized by a complete change in the beliefs and understandings of the witness, effected by unrecognized factors within the personality. It occurs most frequently among the witnesses who are themselves the injured parties and, hence, have presumably every reason for telling only the truth, and it develops usually in relation to crimes of a personally horrifying, traumatic, or repugnant character.

Because of the significance of this type of behavior psychiatrically as well as legally, the following material from the histories in two illustrative cases is presented as a clinical note for the purpose of directing attention to this phenomenon and to the need for an extensive analytic study of the psychological mechanisms and processes involved in these occurrences. Such an analytic study is not proposed in this report, since the data available are limited largely to the original situation and the final outcome. Hence, an effort will be made only to indicate briefly the various psychological factors and the psychic dynamisms contributing to the course of the developments.

The two case histories to be cited have been selected from among others because of the fully established facts of the original crimes, the detailed, factual, and fully corroborated testimony elicited initially, and the absence of external motivation in the eventual development of significant and completely contradictory attitudes and beliefs.

REPORT OF CASE

Case 1. This report centers around a police raid on a bawdy house. Arrests were made of two girl inmates aged 9 and 11 years, their parents,

Reprinted with permission from the *Archives of Neurology and Psychiatry,* September 1938, Vol. 40, pp. 548-553.

who were the proprietors, and twelve male patrons. Full confessions were obtained individually from all the prisoners, those of the adults corroborating fully the essentially identical accounts given by the two girls. In addition, medical examination of the girls disclosed numerous bruises and injuries, substantiating their account of beatings, and also revealed that they had been subjected to vaginal and rectal coitus and infected with syphilis and gonorrhea, both rectal and vaginal.

In the legal disposition of the case the two children were committed immediately to a custodial institution, where they were separated from each other according to the age grouping within the institution and kept for three months in "quarantine isolation" for treatment for the venereal infections.

At the suggestion of a colleague of wide experience in criminology who anticipated the eventual outcome, the two girls were interviewed separately, and an extensive account of the entire experience was obtained during the first week of their institutionalization, with three subsequent interviews thereafter at intervals of two months. The girls' stories were found to be essentially identical and to agree in full with the accounts obtained later from the adult offenders, as well as with the original court testimony.

During the first interview both girls were intensely desirous of securing a sympathetic listener, and both told the story readily, easily, and completely, manifesting much unhappiness over, and repugnance toward, their experiences. Also, they manifested intense fear and anxiety over their physical condition as well as strong specific resentments and hatreds toward their violators and a sense of great satisfaction over the punishments accorded the adults. At the same time it was noted that both girls recalled certain of their experiences with definitely pleasurable, though guilty, feelings and that they were quite shamefaced about their own active participation in certain aspects of their experiences.

A marked change in both girls was noted during the second interview. There was no longer a driving need to tell the story; emphasis was placed on the venereal infection, with the complaints centering around the inconveniences and the annoyance occasioned by the quarantine and therapy, and little mention was made of their former fears of what the disease would do to them. Many details of the original accounts were omitted; others were surprisingly vague or minimized. There was a general tendency to contradict and deny previous statements. Close questioning on a few items disclosed definite reluctance, and even difficulty, in admitting certain facts, and the repugnance previously noted had been transformed into new resentments, especially in connection with the rectal coition. The resentments and hatreds noted previously were markedly increased by the addition of resentments concerning their immediate situation.

At the time of the third interview they had made good recovery from the gonorrheal infection and were much better adjusted to the institution. Although willing and ready to talk, they seemed to be interested only in immediate matters. Questioning about their past experience elicited an utterly inadequate account, in which even major details were denied or greatly minimized. Rectal coitus was emphatically and resentfully denied by both. There were flat denials of ever having been nude or of having danced exhibitionistically, and they had forgotten the names of half the men. There were many vague statements of "Ma didn't like those things" and "Ma wouldn't let anybody do those things." A few similar statements were made concerning the father. There was a tendency to declare certain of the more offensive details to be "lies" told by one of the men who had been particularly brutal. Furthermore, their reluctance or difficulty in giving any details of their story seemed to be greatly increased. Their affective reaction seemed to be one entirely of distaste and repugnance to the whole experience, and there was no evidnece of pleasurable recollections; rather, there seemed to be an element of sadness and grief. Even the question of therapy for the venereal infections was casually glossed over as a routine health measure peculiar to their present situation, and all the earlier anxiety centering around their physical condition had disappeared. Likewise, the hate reactions centering around the original experience now seemed to be limited to mild resentment over their own imprisonment. The former sense of satisfaction over the legal punishment of the adults had disappeared except for a feeling of pleasure that the man they now accused of lying was serving time.

The final interview was conducted six months after the first. A complete change in attitude was apparent in both girls, though more marked in the younger. Strong resentment was expressed over my interest in the story, and no information was given spontaneously except the emphatic, inclusive declaration that it was "all a lot of nasty lies." A warm defense was given of both parents. The authorities were harshly criticized as unwelcome intruders into a private home, and the whole experience was minimized into the statement that "some bad men came to the house, but nothing bad happened." This statement was persisted in with such obvious sincerity and belief that resort was had to sympathetic questioning concerning the "lies" that had been told. After their confidence had been won with some difficulty, both recounted their original story in fair detail but branded each item as a "regular lie" told by various of the men while in court. Furthermore, they insisted sincerely that they had consistently told me the entire story as a "bunch of lies" maliciously concocted by some men who had had their parents arrested and imprisoned for illegal traffic in liquor. Even close questioning about the injuries sustained and venereal infection elicited either resentful denials or trivial explanations, and they seemed to have no real recollection of the whole experience as an actual happening in their own lives. At no time could their sincerity or their full belief in their statements be doubted.

Case 2. This report concerns a young man on parole from a penal institution. After stealing an automobile, he took a young woman for a drive, their intention being to spend the night at a roadhouse of ill repute. He did not disclose to her the immediate circumstances, although she was aware of his criminal history and legal status. During the course of the drive, as a result of recklessness, the car overturned, pinning the young woman beneath it, and burst into flames. The man freed himself but made no effort to rescue his companion, instead fleeing from the scene. Passing motorists rescued the girl, but not until she had been severely burned, in addition to receiving other serious injuries in the accident. The man was apprehended, and at the trial the girl, with much bitterness and hatred, and the motorists testified fully as to the facts, the truth of which the man confessed. About eight months later, without there having been intercession of any sort, the girl endeavored to secure a retrial of the case on the grounds that she had given false and mistaken testimony. The man, when interviewed by me, declared, "She's nuts! She told the truth the first time," and explained further that the relatively short sentence he had received did not warrant his undergoing the anxiety of a retrial, since his indisputable guilt in certain aspects of the case might result in a longer sentence.

The girl, when interviewed by me, was obviously sincere and believed fully that the man had exerted every effort possible to rescue her, giving full details of his endeavors by a process of retrospective falsification and misconstruction. She explained that her intense suffering and the long months of confinement during her hospitalization had made her realize how false her original account had been, since "no human being would do such a thing nor could anybody endure being so treated." She elaborated in detail on how one would feel if deserted, as she was said to have been, and declared that such an experience would be utterly "intolerable" and that one "could only imagine it but could not possibly endure it." When confronted by each item of her original testimony, she misconstrued it so logically and exculpated herself for her "misstatements" and "intentional malice" so contritely on the grounds of the shock and pain she had suffered that she was most convincing, although psychiatrically the inferences to be drawn were quite otherwise. Even the prisoner's direct admission of the truth of her original account was casually disregarded. She insisted rather compulsively that something be done to prove legally that the event as described had never taken place, since her previous testimony had been used to prove that it was an actual occurrence. When, however, it was pointed out that the sentence received by the man was well within the statutory limits for automobile theft and violation of parole and that his criminal negligence toward her presumably had not been considered in the passing of the sentence, she seemed much relieved, considered the situation as a closed incident, and actually continued so to regard it. Apparently she was satisfied that no wrong had been occasioned by her "misstatements," and hence that her "mistaken" testimony had never actually won credence, which, in turn, implied for her the unreality of the original experience.

COMMENT

What might have been the outcome had these cases been again brought into court is only speculative. General experience, however, in similar cases suggests the not unusual development of "reasonable doubt" resulting from the recanting of testimony previously given by an otherwise credible witness and a consequent acquittal because of failure to prove again the guilt originally established. Whether any legal provisions can be made for "witness unreliability" of this character is a serious question, but at least recognition should be accorded to the possibility and the frequency of such psychological behavior, as a measure of lessening the confusion occasioned by it.

Psychiatrically, any discussion of these two, or rather three, cases, since the two sisters were entirely independent of one another in the development of their reactions to the situation, constitutes a difficult problem. To elucidate the various psychological processes entering into the final outcome would necessarily be so speculative as to be unwarranted. A day-by-day account of a highly detailed character would be needed to trace the steps by which the alteration of belief was achieved, and such a measure in itself might serve to bring about an entirely different end result. Also, the data at hand in these cases are insufficient to permit more than a general consideration of the problem represented.

In this regard, however, attention may be directed to the fact that the experiences of the three girls are essentially identical in psychological structure and represent the not unusual legal situation in which a female, after sexual usage, testifies first against the offending male and then, after a period of suffering, reverses her beliefs and attitudes to testify sincerely in his behalf. This identity is manifest primarily in: *(1)* the highly pleasurable, exciting initial development of the experience; *(2)* the sudden complete transformation of this pleasurable situation into one of extreme terror, physical helplessness, and pain, and *(3)* the final evolution into a situation of long-continued suffering and general helplessness.

In each instance certain psychological elements leading to the final outcome are to be found in common, and these may be summarized as:

1. General setting at defiance of authority and association with, and participation in, forbidden things.

2. A primary sexual relationship, illicit in character and marked by guilty, but pleasurable, participation.
3. Utilization of the female simply as an sexual instrument, without regard for an emotional return to her.
4. Brutality—direct, sadistic and physical in the first case, and indirect and essentially psychic in the second, despite the physical aspects.
5. Infliction of serious somatic injuries serving to constitute both an immediate physical threat and a long-continuing threat of future physical destruction.
6. Suffering experienced in common with the offending male, originating from common guilt and characterized for all parties by loss of freedom, personal helplessness, stigmatization, and uncertainty concerning the future.
7. Intensely bitter, resentful public denunciation of the offender by the victim, with self-exculpation and overemphasis on the other's guilt.

That these common elements were the essential dynamic forces in the negation of the original testimony can only be presumed, but unquestionably they played a significant role in the course of events. The details of the processes by which they served their purposes are a problem that must be left to more extensive studies, since this report can direct attention only to the original situation and the final significant outcome, with some suggestions regarding the processes involved in these instances. Further studies of an analytic character should serve to clarify more fully the psychological processes of retrospective falsification, suppression and repression, memory distortion, affect displacement and substitution, compensatory reactions, guilt reactions, self-exculpation, denial of reality, and wishful thinking, which are shown to a significant degree in the histories in these cases.

In this regard an analogy may be drawn between the behavior reported in these cases and that shown in daily routine life in the repression, faulty recall, and even distortion of unpleasant, disagreeable experiences, since essentially the same dynamisms are operative in both situations, though to different degrees. The more extreme character of the reactions in these cases as compared with that found in ordinary behavior may be attributed to the extreme character of these experiences.

In all probability the initial psychic dynamism in these cases, as in instances occurring in daily life, was the primary repression of the unpleasant affects arising not only from the traumatic aspects of the experience but from the girls' own guilty pleasurable participation. Contributory to this was the peculiar situation in court, in which all three girls, in telling their stories and seeking to affix blame on their aggressors, were forced, psychologically as well as legally, to disclose their own guilty participation. Thus, the two little girls in telling of their nude dancing, wine drinking, singing, and playing with the genitals of the men, and the older girl in describing her intention of spending a night of illicit love-making, were declaring in essence: "All this I was doing to make my aggressor happy, and see what he has done to me." Yet by thus emphasizing the guilt of the men, the girls placed themselves in a definitely humiliating position, thereby giving rise to a compelling need for self-exculpation. This could be possible only in a totally different situation, since self-exculpation could be achieved only by the process of exculpation of others. Hence, repression of self-condemnatory feelings would necessitate repression of other related aspects and would require a total reorganization and reconstruction of the experience in a form more assimilable to the personality.

Also to be considered in this regard are the loss of physical intactness, the infections of long duration and the ever-recurring physical assault involved in the intravenous and intramuscular therapy for the two little girls, and the facial burns, the broken ribs, and the injured arm and legs threatening to disfigure the older girl. These physically traumatic aspects of the experiences gave rise to an intense wish that these things would not and could not be so, that things would change completely. In response to this great need there developed the psychological processes by which, step by step, there could be utilization of repressions, overemphasis of various elements in the experience and distortion of others, until finally there had been achieved a complete reconstruction of the entire experience in a form which could meet the compelling needs of the personality. In the case of the two children one step in this process is clearly illustrated by their statement, "Ma didn't like those things," which progressed to "Ma wouldn't let those things happen."

Thus, shifting of responsibility to their mother for the realities of the occurrence was achieved, enabling them to avoid any necessity for relying on, or even utilizing, their knowledge of the actualities of their experience.

Similarly, the older girl summarized her psychological treatment of the experience with great clarity by declaring it to be "utterly intolerable, one that could be imagined but not endured." By regarding the experience as imaginable but unendurable, she could give herself free rein to regard it as imaginary, utilizing the fact of her survival as proof of its imaginary character. But the fallaciousness of this apparently gave rise to her compulsive need to secure proof from external forces, manifested in her seeking a retrial for the purpose of establishing by formal legal processes the unreality of the desertion. Essentially, this constituted the same process of shifting responsibility for the realities of the experience as was employed by the two children in placing their reliance on their mother.

Thus, her relief on being shown conclusively that the man had been punished only for offenses which she could readily recognize as real and which were not related to her becomes easily comprehensible. The prison sentence proved conclusively to her that the realities of the original situation were only those of automobile theft, violation of parole, and an unavoidable accident, for which no one could be held responsible.

That many considerations other than those discussed entered into the final outcome in these cases is readily admitted, but the deficiencies of the data render further elaboration overspeculative.

Section 6: Dual Personality

INTRODUCTION

The papers in this section report on the discovery and detailed psychological evaluation of two different cases of dual personality. The first two papers begin with the discovery or uncovering of the presence of a dual personality in which Erickson describes the circumstances and means by which he was able to establish communication with the hidden, less dominant, or secondary personality. Erickson's usual means of detecting a dual personality was to notice conflicting and dissimilar response patterns within the samc individual. This initial process of clinical discovery is well described for the two cases of these papers, but the reader should be apprised of the fact that the observable indices of a dual personality are sometimes more subtle than those presented here.

Recently, for example, the editor sat in on a number of hypnotherapeutic sessions with another case of dual personality that Erickson had discovered in his practice. It took several sessions for the editor to learn to recognize the very minor alterations in facial musculature, voice dynamics, and verbal themes of the two personalities as they subtly and spontaneously shifted back and forth, from one to another, from moment to moment, in clinical interview. This particular young woman had one personality that was a bit psychopathic and seductive and another that was self-effacing and needing nurture. Sometimes, before or after her sessions with Erickson, she would whimper and plead softly with the editor to assure her that she was not really a dual personality. So subtle were her personality shifts that this editor usually felt helplessly confused as to whether he should resist what might be seduction or yield to what might be a genuine need for support. Because of this problem in detecting subtle personality shifts we are still uncertain today about the incidence of dual or multiple personalities in the general population. An occasional practitioner will claim to have seen a lot of them, while most therapists demur and say that they are seen only rarely. If this editor's experience with Erickson's recent patient is any indication, the inconsistency could well be due to differences in observational skills and the confusion as to where to set the boundary between dual personality and the more common expression of different aspects of the same personality.

In the two cases of this study the diagnosis was not a problem. Once contact was established with the secondary personality, the presence of a unilateral amnesia between the two personalities served to establish both cases as genuine, autonomous personalities. The difficulties in communicating with the secondary, and usually more knowing, personality are presented in fascinating detail in the first paper, where the language of condensation, elision, and reversal with multiple levels of meaning is so much in evidence. This case illustrates the great wit and patience that are required of the investigator in such work. The rewards are clear, however. To be able to resolve lifelong phobias within a few hours is a singularly rare accomplishment.

The results of the psychological testing of these two dual personalities are presented by the expert, David Rapaport, of the Menninger Clinic. Much of the raw data of this psychological testing has been presented here in detail in order that other investigators may make careful comparisons with other cases. The results indicate the merit of continuing study of such dual personalities for the general light they may shed on psychodynamic processes and the construction of personality. It is clear from the test results that it is possible for each of the dual personalities to organize the same past life experience into a different pattern such that the person could respond alternately on the basis of one or the other pattern. Surprisingly, the test results are counter to the general assumption that such dual personalities are a manifestation of hysterical psychodynamics. Both of these cases were found to be of an obsessive-compulsive type. These important findings give the reports a significant place in line with the studies of dual personality by Azam, Mitchell, Prince, Sidis, Goodhart, and Janet.

23. The Permanent Relief of an Obsessional Phobia By Means of Communications With an Unsuspected Dual Personality

Milton H. Erickson and Lawrence S. Kubie

For over a year a 20-year-old college girl—quiet, reserved, and well poised—had suffered secretly from constantly recurring obsessive fears that the icebox, kitchen, college laboratory, and locker doors had been left open. These fears were always accompanied by a compulsive, often uncontrollable need to examine and reexamine the doors to make certain they were properly closed. She awoke in the night to make repeated trips to the kitchen in order to reassure herself, but this failed to resolve her incessant doubts about the doors. An additional but seemingly unrelated symptom was an intense hatred of cats, which she considered "horrid, repulsive things." This feeling she attributed to an early experience of watching "an awful cat eating some nice pretty little baby robins." It was learned that she enjoyed making pets of laboratory animals such as white rats and guinea pigs despite obsessive fears that she might fail to close the door of the animal room. At the time the patient was seen, her difficulty was becoming more inclusive, and she was beginning to have fleeting recurring doubts about many other doors, although not to a troublesome degree.

I. INDUCTION OF CATALEPSY AND OF HAND LEVITATION UNDER HYPNOSIS AND SUGGESTION OF NAME FOR HYPNOTIC PERSONALITY FOR PURPOSE OF CLASSROOM DEMONSTRATIONS

Without any conscious or deliberate therapeutic intent on the part either of the student or of the investigator, this 20-year-old student of psychology (who will be called "Miss Damon") volunteered to serve as the subject of some experiments in hypnotism. A trance induced at the first session was characterized by a marked degree of amnesia, ready hand levitation, and profound catalepsy. To demonstrate suggestibility a

Reprinted with permission from *The Psychoanalytic Quarterly,* October 1939, Vol. VIII, No. 4.

posthypnotic suggestion was given that in the trance her name would be "Miss Brown."

II. PERSISTING FASCINATION WITH LEVITATION AND HORROR OVER CATALEPSY

The next day Miss Damon sat about the office entirely neglectful of her work and absorbed in inducing hand levitation and arm catalepsy by autosuggestion. She would observe these combined phenomena briefly and then would cause them both to disappear by further autosuggestions. This was repeated over and over throughout the day in a seemingly compulsive fashion. It was noted that while suggesting to herself either the lifting or the lowering of her hands, she would repeatedly ask such questions as, "Do you see my hand move? How do you explain it? What does it mean? What is happening? Have you ever had such an experience? What psychological and neurological processes are involved? Isn't it funny? Isn't it queer? Isn't it interesting? I'm so curious, I'm just fascinated by it."

Any replies to these comments went unheeded; she seemed unaware of what she was saying.

While inducing *levitation* her facial expression was one of intense, lively, pleased interest; but as her hand or hands reached the level of her shoulders and she began to develop an apparent catalepsy, her attitude would change markedly. A facial expression would appear which one could characterize only as "dissociated." She seemed to lose contact with her surroundings and to become unresponsive to verbal or tactile stimuli. In addition to the expression of dissociation there appeared a look of intense terror, with pallor, dilated pupils, deep, labored, and irregular respiration, a slow, irregular pulse, and marked tension and rigidity of her whole body. Soon these manifestations would disappear, quickly to be replaced by the previous look of eager, amused interest; whereupon she would at once begin suggesting to herself a lowering of her hand and a disappearance of the catalepsy.

Later that day she was asked why she was so interested in catalepsy and levitation, but she could give only such rationalizations as were based on her psychological training and interests. She showed no realization that more might be involved, except for a joking remark that *her extremely low salary warranted her getting whatever experience she could.*

The next day the same behavior began anew. After confirming the observations of the previous day, the suggestion was offered that she might like to try more complex coordinated movements. She was interested at once, and the suggestion was given that she try automatic writing, to which she agreed eagerly while expressing many doubts about her capacity to do so.

III. INVESTIGATION THROUGH AUTOMATIC WRITING, LEADING TO ATTACK OF ACUTE ANXIETY

After placing her in a suitable position to distract her attention completely from the proceedings, the subject was instructed to read silently an article on gestalt psychology and to prepare a mental summary of it, ignoring as she did so anything that might be said or that might occur.

When she had become absorbed in the reading, hand levitation was suggested. She was then instructed to pick up a pencil and *to write the reason for her interest in hand levitation and in catalepsy.* This last instruction was repeated several times, and in a short time she began to write without any interruption of her reading. Toward the end of the writing she developed body tremors, marked generalized physical tension, deep labored respiration, and pupillary dilation, and her reading seemed to become laborious and difficult. As she completed the writing, her face was pale and expressed intense terror. She dropped the pencil and explained that she suddenly felt "terribly afraid" and that she wanted to cry but could not understand why this was so since there was nothing to distress her in what she had been *reading.*

With these words her anxiety seemed to disappear completely, to be replaced by an air of eager, puzzled interest; she made no further reference to her emotional distress, apparently forgetting it completely. Immediate questions showed that she was able to give an adequate summary of what she had read. Then she was reminded of the task that had been given her. She inquired whether or not she had written anything and when shown her writing manifested first pleasure and then disappointment. The writing was illegible, scrawling, and even difficult to recognize as such. She studied it carefully, however, and succeeded in deciphering the first word as *trains,* although a careful study of the word and the observation of the movements of her pencil as she wrote indicated that it was *trance.*

Then she was asked to repeat the writing under the same conditions as before. Essentially similar results and behavior were obtained except that this time, instead of dropping the pencil, she continued to make writing movements in the air while expressing verbally her feeling of being "awful scared." Again, immediately upon verbalizing her emotional distress she seemed to forget it and interested herself first in summarizing what she had read and then in attempting to understand her writing. Accordingly she was asked to decipher what she had written, and while she was absorbed in this, low-voiced suggestions were made "to write all the rest which is not yet written on paper." Apparently without her knowledge she resumed the automatic writing in lines consisting of single words or short phrases, one of which was followed by an emphatic period. The completed writing is shown in the following illustration.

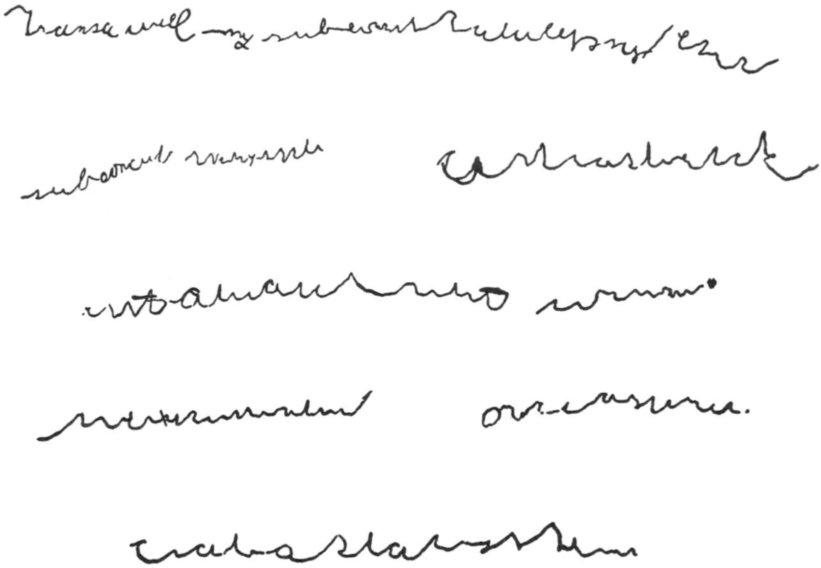

As she wrote, she seemed to the observer to be breaking her message into fragments, writing a little here, moving her hands to another part of the sheet, writing a bit more, then apparently inserting a part between two previously written phrases. Also there was a tendency for her hand to move back and forth over the completed writing, arousing in the observer the suspicion that she was really counting or checking on what had already been written. Subsequently this proved to have been what she was doing: she had rewritten parts because of a persisting dissatisfaction which led her to make repeated changes. The emphatic period was placed only after her hand had wandered back and forth over the page as if searching for the right phrase. It was found later that she had placed a second period after another phrase.

It was discovered ultimately that the writing constituted a complete production, composed of separate but related elements some of which were partial reduplications and rearrangements of various fragments.

Because of her unusual reaction to hand levitation and catalepsy, because of the strong affects of which she was only slightly aware, and finally because of the peculiar character of her automatic writing and of the concomitant conduct, the assumption was made that the writing represented significant material and that unconsciously she was seeking aid from the investigator. It was decided therefore to pursue the problem further. The investigation was carried on jointly by M.H.E., an assistant who served chiefly as a necessary conversational foil, a secretary who took complete notes of everything said and done, and the subject herself.

Because of the peculiar fashion in which the material was presented, the method of presentation itself constituting a significant part of the problem, no orderly or systematic procedure of investigation could be followed. We were forced rather to proceed by trial and error, attempting and abandoning many leads in the effort to decipher the writing.

More than 12 hours of almost continuous work were required to solve the problem, and all progress was achieved in isolated fragments. No attempt will be made to tell a strictly chronological story of the work, but enough material will be given to show the main steps which led up to the solution of the problem.

IV. THE DISCOVERY OF THE DUAL PERSONALITY

The first essential step was achieved at the beginning of the investigation and was confirmed throughout: the identification of a second and unknown personality in the subject. This discovery was made in the following fashion.

After the subject's hand had completed the last bit of automatic writing and had placed the emphatic period, the investigator quietly slipped the sheet of paper from under her hand, leaving a fresh one in its place with her hand still holding the pencil. This was done without attracting her attention. She continued her task of deciphering, finally declaring aloud that she could make out only the words *trance, will, my, catalepsy,* and *ever,* and expressed much amusement over her inability to read more, asking laughingly, "Did I really write that nonsense?" Both the investigator and his assistant replied affirmatively and in the same amused tone. At the moment the subject was leaning forward over the desk, and her hand was out of range of her peripheral vision. As the verbal reply was given to her question, her hand was observed to write "No," of which Miss Damon remained unaware. Immediately the investigator asked, as if speaking directly to the subject, "What do you mean?" and while Miss Damon puzzled over what he meant, her hand wrote, "Can't." Again speaking as if to Miss Damon, the question was asked, "Why?", to which her hand replied, "Damon doesn't know these things."

There followed a series of questions, seemingly directed to the subject, who was merely bewildered and confused because of their unintelligibility to her while her hand wrote appropriate replies. These, with their answers, will be quoted verbatim to show the definition of this second personality. The quotations continue from the last question and reply cited above. The questions were asked orally, the replies given by automatic writing.

Q. Why?
A. Don't know, afraid to know.
Q. Who?
A. D [Damon].
Q. Who does?
A. Me.
Q. Me?
A. Brown.
Q. Who?
A. Me—Brown—B.
Q. Explain.
A. D is D, B is B.
Q. B know D?
A. Yes.
Q. D know B?
A. No. No.
Q. B part of D?
A. No. B is B; D is D.
Q. Can I talk to B?
A. Are!
Q. Talk to D?
A. Want to. [If you want to.]
Q. How long have you been B?
A. Always.
Q. What do you want?
A. Help D.
Q. Why?
A. D afraid.
Q. Do you know what D is afraid of?
A. Yes; D no.
Q. Why?
A. D afraid, forgot, don't want to know.
Q. Think D should?
A. Yes, yes, yes.
Q. You know what it is?
A. Yes.

Q. Why don't you tell D?
A. Can't, can't.
Q. Why?
A. D afraid, afraid.
Q. And you?
A. Afraid a little, not so much.

At this point Miss Damon interrupted to declare her utter bewilderment over the investigator's fragmentary remarks, and demanded an explanation.

Q. Shall I tell her?
A. Sure; she don't know.

The secretary then read the questions, while her answers were shown to Miss Damon. She attended carefully with a look of increasing understanding, finally remarking, "Why that really must mean I have a dual personality," and then was greatly startled that her hand emphatically wrote, "Right." Recovering her poise, Miss Damon asked, "Can I talk to you?" "Sure." "Can you talk to me?" "Yes." "Is your name really Brown?" "Yes." "What is your full name?" "Jane Brown." Later it was found that *Jane* signified identification with a favorite childhood literary character, and that Jane was really the important name, the *Brown* having evidently been added to it at the time of the first hypnotic demonstration described above.

Miss Damon then reviewed the questions and said musingly, "You want to help me, Brownie?" "Yes, Erickson ask, ask, ask." Further similar questions by Miss Damon elicited variations of the same cryptic answer of "Erickson ask," and a stubborn refusal to elaborate.

Throughout the investigation the Brown personality was found to be literally a separate, well-organized entity, completely maintaining its own identity, and differentiating to a fine degree between Brown and Damon. Brown was capable of entering into spirited arguments with the investigator, his assistant, and with Miss Damon, and of expressing ideas entirely at variance with those of Miss Damon. She could know before Damon did what Damon would say or think, and contributed thoughts to Miss Damon in a manner quite as psychotic patients bring up autochthonous thoughts. She would interrupt an attempted explanation of Miss Damon's by writing "Wrong," and would respond to stimuli and cues which Miss Damon either overlooked completely or misunderstood. In fact she so impressed her personality upon those in the office that automatically she was regarded by the entire group as a distinct personality among them. Nor was Brown limited just to the problems at hand. She would enter readily into conversations on many other topics, often resorting to this in an effort to distract the investigator from his efforts. In addition Brown was possessed of a definite sense of personal pride; on two occasions she resented derogatory remarks Damon made about her, and thereupon refused to write anything more except "Won't" until Damon apologized. Brown frequently became impatient and irritable with the investigator because of his inability to comprehend some of her cryptic replies; and at such times she would unhesitatingly and unsparingly denounce him as "dumb."

A characteristic of Brown's automatic script was its economy. A single letter was written whenever possible in place of a word, or a word for a phrase; abbreviations, phonetic spellings, condensations, puns, and peculiar twists of meaning were all employed, at first to a slight degree but to a greater and greater degree as the investigation progressed. Naturally this rendered the investigator's task correspondingly difficult. It was necessary to discover by appropriate questions that Damon, Brown, and Erickson were all designated by their initials; "help" meant "B wants to help D" or "E should help D"; "W.Y." meant "Will you"; "No" sometimes meant *no* and sometimes *know,* an abbreviation of "Brown does know" or some similar phrase; "subconsement" was the condensation of *"subitement,"* "subsequent" and "consequent"; and "Yo" was found to be neither *yes* or *no,* but "I don't know." *No* written from left to right meant "no," but written from right to left signified a "no" reversed, which is "yes."[1] In these respects Brown's language was much like the language of dreams and constitutes in fact a demonstration of the validity of what Freud has written about the use of condensation, elision, reversal of sense, and duality of meaning in the language of dreams.

Another method of abbreviation was the use of a vertical pencil mark to mean "Yes," a horizontal one to mean "No," and an oblique line to mean I don't know." Also, ┐ signified "First part 'no,' second part yes,'" while └ had the opposite meaning. Similarly ┘, _/, /‾, signified "First part 'I don't know,' second part 'yes,'" etc.

In addition to these economies Brown utilized innumerable cues and signs to communicate her meaning, which often were exceedingly complicated and abstruse in character. For example, Brown was asked, "Can we get the information from Damon?" Slowly, hesitatingly, Brown moved her hand about the page as if searching for a place to write, then turned the page over and wrote quickly, "Yes." Since this answer was contradictory to previous replies, the investigator replied, "I don't understand,"

[1]This is a frequent trick in automatic writing and is one reason why it is not sufficient just to read automatic writing, and why one must watch it as it is being written. Adequate objective records therefore could be made only by use of a motion picture. Brown's explanation of the reverse writing was, "D no [know] question. D read answer. D thinks she understands. E see writing. E no real answer. D don't. That way D not afraid."

eliciting the comment, "Dumb." Asked "Why," the answer "Saw" was obtained. Much effort finally made it clear that the investigator had observed that before answering the question she had reversed the paper which signified that the question too had been reversed. Asked, "Then the question you really answered yes to was what?" "From Brown."

Another cue given repeatedly throughout the investigation was a very short oblique line made at random on the paper which looked as if she had attempted to write but had become blocked in her effort. Later study of Brown's productions disclosed the line to be an accent mark by which Brown was indicating that a word the investigator had thought to identify as "consequent," and which Brown had affirmed to be both the right word and rightly spelled and, with equal emphasis, the wrong word and wrongly spelled, was really the French word *conséquent*. Brown confirmed this guess, and when the investigator musingly remarked, "Well, what do you think of that?" Brown wrote, "Dumb."

Other cues were writing on a fresh sheet to signify a shift to a new aspect of the problem; writing over previous writing; widely separating various parts of a single written response; periods placed within a phrase or remote from a phrase; dropping the pencil with the point or the eraser in direct relationship to a word; peculiar contradictory answers to the same question; counting the letters in a word or the words in a sentence and giving different totals upon repetition of the counts; misspellings to direct attention to a word, and many others, many of which at first either were overlooked completely or were misunderstood.

Brown's attitude toward the investigation was consistent throughout and was highly significant. She asserted emphatically that she alone knew the content of the writing, that Miss Damon did not know, and because of fear could not know; that *Miss Damon needed help which must be given in a way known only to Brown,* and that the investigator's function was primarily the assumption of a very special kind of "responsibility" that permitted Brown to give assistance only in response to direct and specific questions, with the reservation that Brown might accept or reject or postpone the questions as she felt to be best. Brown was found to maintain a highly protective attitude toward Damon, shielding her, demanding special consideration for her, offering encouragement, distracting her attention, deliberately deceiving her, and employing various other protective measures.

Perhaps the best portrayal of Brown's attitude may be found in the following quotations from her answers:

"Writing means a lot, B know it all, D don't, can't, afraid, forgot something a long time ago, D can't remember because she never knew some of it, she just thought she did but she didn't. B afraid to tell D, D get awful scared, afraid, cry. B don't like D scared, won't let her be scared, won't let her feel bad. B can't tell D, won't tell D. D must know. D must have help. B need help. Erickson ask. Ask right question, B tell Erickson right answer, wrong question, wrong answer. Right question only right question. B just answer, not tell, won't tell because D afraid, awful afraid. Erickson ask, ask, ask. Brown answer, not tell, question answer, not tell, question, answer, that help. B answer but not too fast because D get scared, cry, sick. B tell truth, all truth, Erickson not understand, don't understand because he don't know. B trying to tell, Erickson don't ask right questions. Ask, ask, ask. B can't tell, won't tell. B a little afraid; B only answer. Ask, ask."

Repeated and indirect attempts were made to induce Brown to help frame questions, but her reply was always, "Erickson ask, B answer; right question right answer, wrong question wrong answer."

Essentially, therefore, the task of the investigator became an active search for information forthcoming only when a question was found which hit the nail precisely on the head and which could be answered with approximately one word. The cues given by Brown seemed designed in part to provoke and compel further aggressive interrogations. On the other hand, in conversations which touched upon any other topic except the immediate problem, Brown was under no such restrictions. In addition, Brown in these unrelated conversations was at liberty to drop innumerable hints and clues, most of which were overlooked by the investigator.

As these various aspects of the two personalities, their attitudes to the questioner and their methods of yielding information gradually became clearer, the task of discovering the meaning of the writing became relatively easier.

At first the subject was told to write and rewrite her message more and more legibly with each repetition. This was unsuccessful whether the repetitions were of phrases, words, syllables, or letters. An attempt to have the message written with synonyms for the words or merely substituting in other words, so that the investigator could at least determine how many words were involved, was met by a flat refusal: "Won't."

A fresh approach was then begun, and Brown was asked, "Is that sentence correct and complete?" "No." Further extensive questioning finally yielded the cue, "Wrong question." After much futile questioning it was learned that the writing constituted two sentences, hence the investigator should have said *sentences* rather than *sentence*. These sentences, B replied, were abbreviated in form, and the words were either abbreviated or condensed; but B added the reassurance, "All there; B know; B understand; E ask right question; B tell."

Next it was learned that the first sentence contained 7, 8, or 9 words; 7 and 8 were stated emphatically, 9 somewhat dubiously; similarly, B indicated that the second sentence contained 13, 14, or 16 words; 13 and

14 emphatically, 16 dubiously. Making the immediate assumption that some of the words were repeated or that some could be broken up into two words, Brown was asked to point to the words as she counted, but she replied. "Won't, not yet." To direct questions concerning these possibilities she replied, "Won't tell." When it was pointed out to her that her refusal to answer these questions was tantamount to admitting that some of the words were either repeated or could be broken into two, Brown conceded, "Maybe," whereupon Miss Damon, who at the same moment was conversing with the investigator's assistant about a recent book, suddenly stammered, complained of feeling frightened, and then continued her conversation, again appearing to repress all knowledge of her emotional disturbance, just as she had done with the panic which occurred during her first automatic writing.

The implication of Miss Damon's behavior was mentioned to Brown, who replied, "Maybe. Not tell too fast yet."

In response to further questioning the words *trance, will, my, catalepsy, every,* and *ever* were deciphered and confirmed and were placed in order in the sentences as follows:

	Word	*Sentence*
Trance	**1**	**1**
Will	**2**	**1**
My	**3**	**1**
Catalepsy	**10, 11, or 12**	**1 and 2 counted in one sequence.**
Every	**8, 9, or 10**	**1 and 2 counted in one sequence.**
Ever	**13 or 14**	**1 and 2 counted in one sequence.**

(A fuller explanation of this count must be reserved for the end of the paper.) Further questioning proved fruitless, nor could any aid be secured in further deciphering. Brown simply replied "Won't" to all inquiries.

A fresh start was made by attempting to have Miss Damon look at various parts of the writing and give free associations; but this was interrupted at once by Brown writing, "No, no," and a complete blocking of Miss Damon's efforts by a failure on her part to understand what was desired. This is an interesting parallel to the behavior of those patients in analysis who listen with earnest attention to repeated explanations of what they are to do, but seem incapable ever of digesting what is told them sufficiently to produce any free associations at all. In the case of Brown and Miss Damon it was as if Brown protectingly told Damon when she could think safely and similarly had the power to forbid her to think and thus arrest her intellectual process.

Since Miss Damon knew the Morse code, it was suggested that her habit of drumming with her fingers be employed by Brown to tap out the message. S. O. S., which was obtained repeatedly, meant, Brown explained, "E help, ask."

Efforts then were made to identify the words simply as parts of speech or to identify individual letters as such without regard to their positions in sentences or words. To these attempts confusing, contradictory, and conflicting answers were made which Brown finally summarized as, "Can't; just can't; not right questions," but no suggestions could be obtained from her as to how the right questions might be asked.

At this point Brown was asked if the investigator might continue his attempts to secure individual words, and she replied, "Try." Accordingly, Brown was instructed to draw two horizontal lines, one to symbolize the most meaningful word in the message and the other the least meaningful, and to draw them any length she wished, equal or unequal, since the lines themselves would have no meaning.

Brown drew two lines, one about twice the length of the other. In drawing the first line, however, Brown was seen to pause momentarily at about the middle, while the second line was drawn in a single stroke. The investigator took this for a cue and immediately extended his pen as if to point to the first line, but actually in doing so covered up the last half of the line. As this was done, Miss Damon, who had been commenting in an amused fashion to the assistant about the investigator's absorption in asking foolish questions, remarked that he was probably too absorbed to notice the unpleasant smell of the cigarette he had carelessly dropped in the ashtray. As the investigator with due apologies extinguished the butt, Brown was seen to push aside the sheet of paper bearing the lines. Again when asked if the investigator might continue his questioning, Brown replied, "Ask, try." Accordingly, her attention was called to the break in drawing the line, and she was asked if this meant a word formed from two words. Despite many variations in the form of the question no answer was obtained except the statement that the right question had not been asked. Finally, the investigator declared emphatically, "That broken line *does* mean two words in the form of one, doesn't it?" "Yes." "And the word *smell* has something to do with the first part, hasn't it?" "No." "You mean that it may or may not be unpleasant?" "Yes."

Here Brown shifted her hand to another part of the sheet, while Miss Damon declared that she had suddenly become afraid and wanted to cry. Brown wrote, "Help D," and when this was interpreted to mean "Comfort D," Brown wrote, "Right." Miss Damon was immediately drawn by the investigator into a discussion of his activities and developed a lively interest in this until shown the broken line, whereupon she again manifested fright, said she could not understand her "funny feelings," and proceeded to laugh them off.

At once Brown wrote, "Feel better, ask," and then wrote "Con," a syllable she had previously written but declared wrong. Extensive questioning followed in which Miss Damon participated actively, with the words *subconsciously, subsequent, consequent,* and *consequences* coming out, all of which Brown declared to be both right and wrong. Miss Damon impatiently denounced Brown as "crazy" and "a liar." At this Brown refused to write anything except "Won't." Finally in response to the question why, Brown replied, "Angry." As Miss Damon read this, she flushed deeply and explained with embarrassment, "Brown wants me to apologize," and in a shamefaced manner said, "I'm sorry, Brown." Inquiry by the investigator elicited the fact that Brown accepted the apology and would now write again, and spontaneously she wrote "E, E, E," as if addressing the investigator directly while Miss Damon conversed humorously with the assistant about the apology and her "misbehavior." The investigator continued with "What," to which Brown replied "Sleep." "Why?" "Interferes." As Brown wrote this last word, Miss Damon was still conversing with the assistant and had not been aware of Brown's writing, but as this word was completed, Miss Damon declared, "Why, Brown is going to punish me." Immediate questioning of Miss Damon showed that she had only the "feeling" that she was to be punished and that she could offer no explanation for it unless it was that her apology was not properly offered. While she was giving this explanation, Brown wrote, "E, waiting." Accepting the implied rebuke, the investigator hypnotized Miss Damon, thus removing her as a source of interference.

Thereupon more rapid progress was made in relation to the words which had been obtained previously. Brown eliminated the word *subconscious* and declared that *subsequent* was both the right word correctly spelled, and the wrong word incorrectly spelled. At this point Miss Damon awakened in a state of terror, recovered rapidly, and began talking at random on various topics, mentioning among other things that her grandfather was a French Canadian. Shortly after this Brown wrote "Sleep," and the investigator obeyed the command and put Miss Damon to sleep again. Inquiry disclosed that French words were involved, and the elusive word might be *subsement* or *consequent* or *something like.* While this information was being obtained, Miss Damon repeatedly awakened and fell asleep again, showing intense terror each time she wakened. Questioned about Miss Damon, Brown explained that nothing could be done to help her, that it was necessary for her to experience these fits of terror but that she would feel better as soon as she had felt all of the terror which was connected with the word under examination. All of this information was volunteered by Brown, the investigator studiously avoiding any leading question. Finally Miss Damon awakened comfortably and asked what was going on. Brown wrote "Tell." Tentatively, not knowing just what to tell, the investigator pointed to the words obtained. Miss Damon interestedly commented that the problem seemed to be one of correct spelling of French words. As she said this Brown wrote, "Look." This was pointed out to Miss Damon, and everybody began to study the words, but Brown was observed to write impatiently, "Look, look, look." Miss Damon's attention was directed to this, and she declared, "Why, she must mean look somewhere else; the dictionary of course!"

Page after page of the dictionary was thumbed over with innumerable conflicting answers from Brown, until Brown impatiently told the investigator "Wrong!" More care in asking questions disclosed that the dictonary had a word like Brown's word, and that the dictionary word, while it was the right word and correctly spelled, was still the wrong word because Brown had not spelled her word correctly, "Never learned to spell."

Instructed to write her word, Brown now wrote *"subitement,"* then followed it by *"subsequemment,"* succeeded by "subsequent." Asked if "subsequent" were right for the message, Brown made no reply, but Miss Damon again became intensely terrified and proceeded entirely to forget the last steps of the investigation. Quickly she recovered her poise and took up her remarks as if she had just awakened from a trance.

Brown was asked if she had seen any other word of significance in the dictionary. "Yes." "Your word?" "Yes. Spelled different." Here Miss Damon interrupted to ask the investigator, "What does *he* [meaning Brown] mean?" This peculiar slip of the tongue was marked by sudden pallor and a rapid forgetting of the question. Brown, asked for the word seen in the dictionary, wrote "Niaise." When Miss Damon declared there was no such word, that she had never heard of such a word, Brown wrote, "D don't no it." Asked if this word in some form were in the automatic writing Brown had written, B answered, "Yes." Asked, "How learned?" Brown replied "Grandfather," and questioning disclosed the fact that *at the age of three* Miss Damon had been lost and that her grandfather had called her 'Niaise.' (Note Miss Damon's subsequent error in placing this episode at the age of four, as though this discussion had never occurred.)

Brown then objected to further inquiries along this trend, explaining, "B afraid, D afraid of B telling." Miss Damon read this with amusement, denied that she had even a remote feeling of fear, and declared that she was now getting "terribly interested." B commented as Miss Damon spoke, "D don't no." As Miss Damon read this, she remarked, "Isn't *he* economical?" Immediately the investigator asked, "Brown, what do you think about Damon's last remark? Explain it." Brown wrote, "B is *she.* D says *he* because she means Da—. D don't no Da— B no Da—." Miss Damon followed this writing with intense interest, asked the secretary if she really had said "he." and then explained that "Da" was really the first two letters of Damon and that the three dashes signified, *m, o,* and *n.* As she completed this explanation, Brown threw pencils, paper, and books on the floor while Miss Damon gasped and in a horrified manner declared,

"Brownie is having a temper tantrum," adding, "And she can't help it either."

No further information could be obtained from either Miss Damon or Brown, until Miss Damon pleadingly asked, "Please Brownie, get the information," to which Brown replied, "Suppose I fail?" In a challenging tone Miss Damon replied, "Brown, will we ever know?" Slowly Brown wrote, "Yes," while Miss Damon shrank back in her chair, hid her face, and began to cry. The investigator asked "When?" "Don't know." Taking a firm, aggressive stand, the investigator declared that too many hours had been spent already, that it was now four P.M., that the assistant had an evening appointment, as did the secretary, and that more reliance should be placed upon Erickson. At this moment the assistant stated that her appointment was for eight. Brown was asked to specify the time at which she would give the complete information. At this point Miss Damon recovered her poise and interest and expressed delight when Brown wrote seven-thirty, but when Miss Damon asked Brown to confirm this promise, Brown ignored her, writing, "E, ask, work."[2]

V. THE USE OF A MIRROR AS A "CRYSTAL" IN WHICH TO CALL UP VISUAL MEMORIES

Asked how, Brown wrote "Crystal." Miss Damon explained that Brown must want her to do crystal-gazing, which she considered ridiculous since she did not know how, had only heard about it, and really could not do it. Brown replied, "Waiting."

Accordingly, a trance was induced, and using a mirror which reflected the ceiling, Miss Damon was instructed, "Brown wants you to look in that crystal and see." Almost as soon as she peered into the mirror, an expression of intense terror came over her face, and she awakened sobbing, cowering in her chair, hiding her face, declaring that she was "awful, awful afraid," and begging piteously for help. Evidently the investigator's face reflected his alarm, but before he could say anything,

[2]Here Brown specified the exact time at which full insight would be achieved. It is often found to be desirable to ask subjects to specify the hour at which they will understand something, urging them not to set this hour at either too immediate or too remote a time. This seems to give them a definite task and goal and to relieve them of the difficulty of making up their minds in the final moment of decision as to when to expect insight. Thus it gives them ample opportunity to prepare for that insight. Not infrequently analyses are brought to conclusion in a manner comparable to this when the analyst arbitrarily sets a date for the termination of the treatment.

Brown wrote, "It's all right, E. D just scared. Got to be. Then feel better. Just comfort." Tentatively the investigator made a few general soothing remarks, while Brown wrote, "Right," and Miss Damon piteously and tearfully reiterated her remarks, "I'm so scared, just awful scared."

In a short time Miss Damon recovered her poise and became quite apologetic about her "babyish" behavior. At the same time Brown was writing, "Better now; crystal."

The procedure was repeated with the same results except that this time before awakening, the subject repeatedly looked into the mirror, then away from it, taking a longer look each time and finally trying to say something but awakening to avoid speaking. A similar panic followed, lasting about 20 minutes, with Brown repeatedly reassuring the investigator that "D soon feel better now," "Everything all right," and "D getting ready to know but she don't no it."

Finally, when Miss Damon had composed herself, apologizing for her emotional outburst as before, Brown again wrote, "Crystal."

Another trance was induced, crystal-gazing again suggested, and this time although markedly agitated, Miss Damon reported in her trance that she was seeing her grandfather and that he was saying a word. As this report was given, Brown wrote, "B getting scared, awful scared," at which Miss Damon awoke and calmly and comfortably asked, "What time is it?" although the investigator's watch lay face up on the desk. In answer to her own question she glanced at the watch and gave the time correctly as six-thirty-five while Brown at the same moment wrote, "25 to 7." Miss Damon commented, "Seven must be the important number to Brown. I wonder why?" and looked to the investigator for an answer. While Miss Damon waited expectantly for a reply, Brown wrote:

D no everything 7:30.
D tell then—forgot long ago.
B won't tell.
B won't let D no till 7:30.

At this moment Miss Damon asked irrelevantly, "Brownie, what is your first name?" and as Brown made no reply, Miss Damon in an agitated, excited, highly emotional fashion said, "He's gone crazy! *He!* Gosh!" Then quietly, in a subdued, puzzled way, Miss Damon asked Brown why she had said *he*. Brown answered, "D no soon; not ready yet." When Miss Damon sniffed at this answer, Brown wrote, "D don't believe because afraid." Miss Damon declared that she had been afraid a short time previously, but she had no sense of fear at all now, and her air was one of amusement. Brown commented, "D don't no. D wrong. D getting ready, soon ready. 7:30 right time; D have nuff time get ready." Following these remarks Miss Damon scoffed, declaring with amusement that she was ready for anything and that she had no fear. Brown repeated her comments, finally interjecting, "B tell everybody at 7:30. D understand; nobody else."

Suddenly Miss Damon's dispute with Brown changed in character, and she became definitely apprehensive. Addressing Miss Damon, the investigator asked what was happening, to which Brown, startling Miss Damon, replied, "First D afraid vague, then afraid to learn something, then afraid she not no; now she afraid she going no. D afraid she going to no *it,*" with the *it* written in heavy characters.

Miss Damon attempted to ridicule this explanation, but her general discomfort became increasingly apparent, and she began attacking the logic of the various statements, dropping the point and feebly returning to it.

Suddenly Miss Damon looked at the watch and remarked that it was seven-twelve. As she spoke, Brown wrote, "7:21," and Miss Damon said excitedly, "Look, she reversed it."

Brown was asked why, and her explanation was:

D thinks 7:07 [Damon disputed this].
E won't [understand].
E will later.
No further explanation could be elicited.
While Miss Damon puzzled over this material, Brown wrote, "D will begin to remember at 7:23."
Miss Damon: "That's ridiculous. How can she say a thing like that? There's nothing to remember."
Brown: "B changing D mind."
Miss Damon: "She is not, she is not, there is nothing to remember."
Brown: "D don't no. B changing D mind."
Miss Damon: "That is ridiculous. As if I didn't know if my mind was being changed." Immediately she sobbed very hard but briefly, and then asked timidly, "Have I a reason to be scared?"
Brown: "Yes."
Brown to investigator: "D cry, don't mind, nothing help. D feel better."

Miss Damon still crying, observed at seven-twenty-two and a half that "time is fast," recovered her poise, denied that there was anything to remember or that she was scared that she wouldn't remember, fluctuating from amusement to apprehensiveness.

At seven-twenty-seven and a half another intense panic developed, Miss Damon showing great terror, sobbing, cowering, declaring piteously that there was nothing to remember.

At seven-thirty B wrote slowly, much interrupted by Miss Damon's sobbing, "consequences of catching the muskrat to the little idiot," following which Miss Damon sobbed, shuddered, and cowered, begging piteously for help until seven-thirty-five. Exactly at that moment she recovered her poise and declared with startled interest, "I just remembered a story my grandfather told us when we were kids. A muskrat got into the pantry. Everyone chased it and knocked over all the things. I haven't got a thing to do with what my hand is doing."[3]

The investigator asked, 'Well, what does all this mean?'
Brown replied, 'D no, E not understand, told you before.'
Erickson: "You agreed to give the full message."
Miss Damon interrupting verbally: "Every *subitement* catalepsy the consequences of catching the muskrat to the little idiot."
Erickson: "That's it?"
Brown: "No."
Erickson: "What is it?"
Miss Damon: "Spelling bothering her; let's let her look in the dictionary."
After many pages had been thumbed, many apparently at random, Brown wrote, "Subséquemment, subséquent, subsequent."
Erickson: "The sentence is?"

[3] An explanation of the various times alluded to here is necessary. *(1)* Brown promised to tell everybody at 7:30. *(2)* Shortly thereafter Miss Damon mentioned that it was 7:12, while Brown wrote 7:21, at which Miss Damon remarked, "Look, she reversed it," and Brown immediately replied, "Damon thinks 7:07." This was promptly disputed by Damon. *(3)* Brown then remarked, "E won't [understand]. E will later." This was followed by the statement, "Damon will begin to remember at 7:23." *(4)* At 7:22½ Damon remarked more or less casually, "Time is fast," but at 7:27½ Damon developed a panic. *(5)* At 7:30 Brown wrote the significant material, of which Damon remained unaware until exactly 7:35. The explanation of these events is as follows: Miss Damon glanced at a watch which was face up on the desk and read the time as 7:12, Brown wrote these digits but in doing so reversed the last two digits, thereby directing attention to the minutes. Miss Damon remarked, "Look, she reversed it," at which Brown said, "Damon thinks 7:07," and then promptly declared that the investigator wouldn't understand then but would later on. Now it must be noted that 7:07 is exactly five minutes less than 7:12. Furthermore, the promise was made that at 7:23 Damon would begin to remember; but at almost that time the only thing that occurred was the casual remark that "time is fast." At 7:27½, however, a panic ensued, apparently five minutes late. At 7:30, actually in accord with the promise "to tell all," the full material was written; but again Damon remained unaware of it until 7:35. When the investigator later asked Brown, "Why didn't you keep your 7:30 promise?" her remark was "Did—my watch." Checking Damon's watch, it was found to be exactly five minutes slower than that on the table, and as this was being noted, Brown's hand moved up to point to the 7:07 on the written page. From there it slid over to "E won't. E will later."

Brown: "Every subsequent catalepsy consequences of catching the muskrat to the little idiot."
Erickson: "First sentence?"
Brown: "No."
Erickson: "Write first."
Brown: "Trance will my rat antrocine go?"
Miss Damon: "She can't spell, poor thing."
Brown: "Antrosine, osine."
Miss Damon: "Osine, osine, aussi."
Brown: "Aussi."
Erickson: "Two words? First one."
Brown: "Enter."
Erickson: "Rat?"
Brown: "Muskrat."
Erickson: "The real sentences."
Brown: "Trance, will my muskrat enter, also go. Every subsequent catalepsy the consequences of catching the muskrat to the little idiot."
Erickson: "I don't understand."
Brown: "D does."

Miss Damon's explanation: "I know what it means now, but I didn't then. It's all right there. Everything, except the words mean so much. Each one means different things. You see, I thought I was interested in catalepsy; it wasn't catalepsy but the rigidity. I was just frightened by the muskrat episode. You see, I was lost when I was four years old, [Brown interrupted to write three (cf. above), and Miss Damon accepted the correction, explaining that she probably remembered wrong, Brown commenting, "Right"] and I was awful scared. *Grandfather scolded me when I got home; he called me "petite niaise,"* [Brown wrote *petite niase* and pointed the pencil to the phrase followed by the emphatic period] *and scolded me and said I had left the door open and I hadn't. And I was mad at him and afterward I would leave doors open to spite him, and I got my brother to do it too. Pantry door and icebox door. And grandfather laughed at me for getting lost, and then he told me, while I was still scared, about how he got lost and the muskrat got in the pantry and everything got upset, and I thought I did that. I was so scared, I got my grandfather's story about him mixed up with my getting lost."* Here Brown wrote, "Petite niase *thinks she is her grandfather."* "And I was so mad at grandfather, and so scared, and I left doors open to spite him, and I wondered if another muskrat would come." Again Brown wrote *"Petite niase* thinks she is her grandfather." This time Miss Damon became aware of the writing, read it, laughed, and said, "You remember when I called Brown *he,* and Brown wrote Da– – –? Well, I can explain that. Brown was telling you that I didn't know who I was because my grandfather's name was David. Like my name, it begins with Da and has three more letters. And that's what Brown means when she says the little idiot (that word is really spelled *niaise)* thinks she is her grandfather."[4]

Erickson: "Anything else, Miss Damon?"
Miss Damon: "No, that's all."
Brown: "Yes."
Noticing Brown's reply, Miss Damon flushed, then asked, "Brownie, has all that got anything to do with doors bothering me?"
Brown: "Yes, tell."

Miss Damon then gave an account of her phobia, speaking of it consistently in the past tense. Following this, Miss Damon asked, "Has it anything to do with my not liking cats?"

Brown: "Yes."
Miss Damon: "How?"
Brown: "Cats chase rats."

Miss Damon: "How I have rationalized my hatred of cats. I always thought it was because I saw a cat catch a baby robin, a tame baby robin. But really I didn't like cats because, well, *cats like rats,* and I didn't like rats."

Then with an exclamation of delight, Miss Damon said, "Now I know why I always thought there was something wrong with the way I *liked* the white rats in the laboratory. When I played with them, I knew I didn't like them, but I always persuaded myself I did, and I did like them in an uncomfortable way. [Here Brown wrote, "D liked them so she wouldn't no the truth."] I suppose rats are all right, but I'm not crazy about them any more."

SUMMARY

In brief, then, this is the story of a young woman who for a great many years had hidden phobic and compulsive impulses so discreetly that they had escaped the attention even of those who during those years had

[4]Brown's persistency here is noteworthy. Twice Brown brought Damon back to the story by writing, *"Petite niase* thinks she is her grandfather," apparently in order to compel Damon to keep to this important issue.

known her well. However, when by apparent chance she volunteered to be the subject for a demonstration of hypnotism, she found herself caught up in a swift stream of events which led in a few hours to the permanent elimination of her phobias and compulsions.

First she became fascinated by the phenomenon of induced hand levitation, and horrified to the verge of dissociation over induced catalepsy. Thereupon by means of automatic writing an effort was made to investigate the reasons for this extreme horror and fascination. This led at first to a series of acute anxiety states and then to the uncovering of a wholly unsuspected dual personality, a personality which linked with a childhood heroine from the literature of her youth. In a session lasting several hours repeated unsuccessful efforts were made to decipher the automatic writing that had been recorded by this second personality. Finally visual images were evoked by having the subject gaze into a mirror while under deep hypnosis. These images brought back to consciousness some episodes from the third year of the patient's life which clarified the writing and at the same time explained the phobias and compulsions, all of which served to effect a therapeutic result that has persisted over a period of years.

DISCUSSION

The story presents challenging problems with regard to the workings of unconscious processes and the different technical approaches to them.

In one session several hours in duration repressed memories were recovered of a traumatic experience that had occurred at the age of three and had been completely forgotten.

These memories were recovered by the use of automatic writing. The original automatic script was almost unintelligible, only a few letters or syllables being recognizable (cf. illustration). The writing had been accompanied by an intense transient panic. The slow and laborious deciphering of this original script simultaneously solved the mystery of the neurosis itself.

Further use was made of automatic writing as a method of answering questions about the meaning of the original automatic writing. At the end visual images were evoked by having the subject, while under hypnosis, gaze into a mirror which reflected a blank ceiling.

During the course of these observations a wholly unsuspected dual personality was uncovered. It is possible that the presence of such a well-organized dual personality may be an essential precondition for the successful use of such devices as automatic drawing or writing, mirror gazing, and the like, since they would seem to depend upon a rather high degree of hysterical dissociation. It is possible also that the unsuspected presence of just such dual personalities, closely knit and completely segregated from the rest of the personality, may account for certain analytic defeats.

Psychoanalytically the automatic writing is of particular interest because it makes use of the same condensing and obscuring devices as those which occur in humor and in the language of dreams. In less extensive observations this has been noted in the past by Erickson (1937b), and the same fact was recently reported with regard to automatic drawing by Erickson and Kubie (1938). It would seem therefore that in selected cases automatic drawing and automatic writing may offer an accessory method of approach to the unconscious, a method, furthermore, which depends upon principles of interpretation that are thoroughly familiar from dream analysis. In special circumstances these devices may have advantages over more customary technical procedures. For instance, one of us (L.S.K.) has found that in certain types of dreams they can be used to demonstrate vividly and objectively the latent content of the dreams without resort to any verbal interpretation. (Observations not yet reported.)

Of further technical interest is the utilization of mirror-gazing while under hypnosis. In the interplay between the two main personalities, and by means of questions asked by the investigator and answered in automatic writing by the second personality, much work had already been done to elucidate the meaning of some fragments of the original automatic script. Furthermore, it had become increasingly clear that the content latent behind this script was charged with intense and unbearable terror; but by these procedures alone it had not been possible to transcribe this unintelligible writing into clear, understandable prose or to recover the original experiences which underlay the panic. The preliminary steps seemed rather to establish a situation in which the subject gradually came to feel safe under the guardianship of her protective dual personality and of the investigator. As the subject became sufficiently reassured, she was able to face the sources of her terror and finally could recover the lost memories while gazing into a mirror under hypnosis. It is especially worthy of note that the suggestion that this device be tried was given by the second personality.

The use of hypnotism merits further discussion. Hypnotism is under such a cloud that the debt which psychoanalysis owes to it is often forgotten. Freud's earlier writings are full of allusions to the various phenomena of hypnotism, some of which will be quoted in another connection below. As the years went on, however, all reference to the problems with which these phenomena confront us disappeared until the papers on *Group Psychology and the Analysis of the Ego* (Freud, 1921), the German edition of which appeared in 1921 and the English translation in 1922. Here it became evident that the derogatory attitude toward hypnotism, which its therapeutic failures and its commercial exploitation had engendered in every serious scientist, had turned Freud's thoughts too from its scientific importance, even as an object of analytic study. (See the chapter, "The Group and the Primal Horde," pp. 95–100.) Yet in spite of his antipathy to the use of hypnotism, on page 100 he says of hypnosis that it "is solidly founded upon a previous position which has survived in the unconscious from the early history of the human family." The implication here is that hypnotic phenomena are universal and must be taken into consideration in all efforts to understand the neuroses. If this is true, then the study of hypnotic methods is a duty for psychoanalysts, and they must return to that fountainhead of original and dramatic unconscious material from which Freud himself derived his first impetus.

It is interesting furthermore to see that Anna Freud in her book *The Ego and the Mechanisms of Defense* (1937) subscribes to the traditional derogatory judgments against the use of hypnotic methods to elicit unconscious material. There she says (pp. 11–13) that under hypnosis the revelation of the unconscious is achieved by a "total elimination" of the ego, which therefore takes no part in the therapeutic procedure but in the end throws off the influence of the physician and again represses the unconscious material which has been brought to light. She contrasts with this the process of free association, under which the ego is induced to "keep silent" only for interrupted fragments of time, so that the observer's attention is constantly oscillating between the elicitation of material during the period of ego acquiescence and direct investigation of the activities of the ego itself when it becomes resistant.

It should be obvious that there is no *a priori* reason why hypnotic investigations of the unconscious cannot be carried on in just this way. Nor is there any necessary reason why analytically informed investigators or therapists who in these days are using hypnotism should forcibly thrust upon their patients the material which has been gained from the unconscious under hypnosis, merely because in a more naive period before anything was understood about the forces of resistance the traditional hypnotist proceeded in that ruthless fashion. The lessons learned through psychoanalysis can be applied in the use of this allied method, and there is no more reason why hypnotic therapy should consist of an explanation of the patient's symptoms to the patient without regard to the attitude of the patient than that this should be the process of analysis. On the contrary, it is possible in the hypnotic as in the waking state to secure information from the unconscious and then so to motivate the total personality that there will be an increasing interplay of conscious and unconscious aspects of the personality, so that the former gradually overcomes the resisting forces and acquires an understanding of the latter.

Just as in analysis there can with practice be a full opportunity to delay, postpone, resist, and distort when necessary, and yet through this activity always bring the process nearer to a therapeutic goal.

In fact this process is well illustrated in the case under discussion, when, for instance, during the questioning of Brown Miss Damon suddenly interrupted, saying, "Every subitement catalepsy the consequences of catching the muskrat to the little idiot." This was a sudden and seemingly meaningless eruption of unconscious material into consciousness; yet in it a few important fragments of memory returned. By this "meaningless" verbalization Miss Damon participated on a conscious level but in a safe and partial fashion; thereby, however, she prepared herself for the more dangerous complete participation that occurred later. Thus it played a role identical with that of a dream which is only partially remembered and partially interpreted.

It is a clinical fact that the memories brought to light and the emotions discharged in this strange experience permanently relieved this young woman of a serious and rapidly increasing compulsive phobic state. The question may fairly be asked, however, whether the investigators are in a position to explain either the origin of the phobia or its resolution. Here perhaps it is best again to let the facts speak for themselves by reviewing the brief story as far as it is known.

For a short time a little girl of three believes she is lost, and while lost she gets into a state of intense terror. She is found again, or else finds her way home, and is greeted by a grandfather who scolds her, makes her feel guilty of leaving doors open, laughs at her, humiliates her by calling her a little *niaise* (idiot), and finally tries to comfort her by telling her a story of an occasion in his own childhood when he was lost and a muskrat entered the house through an open door and got into a pantry, where it did a great deal of damage. At this the little girl is thrown into a state of increased terror, rage, anger, resentment and confusion. She mixes up her grandfather's story, and especially the tale of the muskrat, with her own experience. She feels as if it had happened to her *almost as though she were her grandfather*. She is angry, and out of spite and revenge she deliberately begins to leave doors open as he had done and as he had unjustly accused her of doing. Then she begins to fear that she will make a mistake, that she will leave doors open unwittingly and that something dreadful will come in. She begins compulsively to check up on the doors over and over again.

The identification of the child with her grandfather is presumably an example of that form of defense by identification with the aggressor that is described by Anna Freud in *The Ego and the Mechanisms of Defense* (1937).

Brown's statement was that when Miss Damon was "so scared" her grandfather should have explained fully all about her scare instead of "selfishly" telling her about his being scared too, because that meant that Damon's scare was so bad that it scared even grandfather, and besides "it added his scare to hers." Brown stated further that it was Damon who resented this and Damon who punished grandfather, although Brown confessed, "I helped a little, too. Damon thought of leaving the doors open and Damon did that, but I helped by getting Damon to get her brother to do it." Brown then explained the phobia as a direct consequence of this effort to punish the grandfather: Damon concluded that if she punished grandfather in this way, she would be hopelessly caught and unable to stop punishing him. Brown added, "It's just like she still believes that thing about a child crossing its eyes and not getting them uncrossed. That is, she believes it in a certain way, even though she knows it isn't true. That's what happened then."

Without attempting to settle the question of whether or not this is an adequate explanation of the phobia, one may feel justified in concluding that the first component of the motivating forces—namely, the revenge fantasy against the grandfather—was repressed and that the phobia remained obsessive until this original motive was recovered. From the point of view of analytical therapy it is particularly interesting to emphasize that the obsessional phobia was relieved merely by the recovery of these specific conditioning events and without any investigation or discharge of underlying patterns of instinctual œdipus relationships, castration anxiety, or the like.

Perhaps most surprising of all is the entirely unanticipated discovery of a dual personality in a young woman, who aside from the phobias described above had been living a relatively normal and well-adjusted life, and in whom the existence of such an alter ego had not even been suspected. Inevitably this raises the question of how frequent such unrecognized dual personalities may be, either as partial or as complete formations. If they exist, the complications which they must create in transference relationships in formal psychoanalytic therapy are of utmost significance and have never been investigated. The mere possibility that they are more frequent than has been suspected demands the development of methods to test out their frequency and their significance.

One cannot say that the existence of such multiple personalities has not been suspected or mentioned in analytical writing; but its far-reaching significance seems to have been strangely overlooked, probably because of the disrepute into which all hypnotic phenomena have fallen because of their traditional association with commercialized hypnotism. Breuer and Freud (1936a) state, "that the splitting of consciousness, so striking in the familiar classical cases of double consciousness, exists rudimentarily in every hysteria, and that the tendency to dissociation, and with it the appearance of abnormal states of consciousness which we comprise as 'hypnoid,' are the basic phenomena of the neuroses." Further, "The existence of hypnoid states is the basis and determination of hysteria." Later they speak of the varying "facility" which people show toward "hypnoidal dissociation" as having an etiological relationship to the development of neuroses. On pages 174–175 Breuer, in his discussion of the Theoretical Material, describes a mechanism for this "splitting" that emphasizes its universality. On page 101 of his paper on General Remarks on Hysterical Attacks, Freud (1924) notes the role of multiple identifications and the fantastic and dramatic playing out of various roles in a hysterical patient. Nor have other observers limited the phenomena to these hysterical structures. Alexander in *The Psychoanalysis of the Total Personality* (1930), page 55, says:

> Therefore, when I describe the superego as a person, and neurotic conflict as a struggle between different persons, I mean it, and regard the description as not just a figurative presentation. . . . Furthermore, in the study of the neuroses there is no lack of such visible manifestations of a divided personality. There are, for example, the true cases of dual personality—quite rare, to be sure. But the compulsion neurosis lacks few of the indubitable manifestations of a dual personality.

In view of these observations it is somewhat surprising that with all of the emphasis that has been laid on the varying roles of the analyst in the transference situation, so little has been said about the varying role of the patient who may present to the analyst not one personality but many.

This is not the place to discuss the mechanism by which such multiple personalities are established. Perhaps it can be said that no single case has been studied deeply enough to answer this question, despite the dramatic literary descriptions which exist in classical literature. Nor is there as yet sufficient evidence at hand to establish how many degrees of such multiple formations may exist. Another perplexing problem is presented by the relationship of the phenomenon to the process of repression. Clearly, in the production of multiple personality a process must occur in which certain psychological events are rendered unconscious. Is this the same process of repression as that with which we are familiar in the psychopathology of everyday life and in the neuroses? The topographical figure of speech which comes to mind is, that that which we ordinarily think of as "repression" is a repression downward, and that the psychological structure that results is a series of layers one upon another; whereas the "repression" which would result in a multiple personality would be a vertical division of one personality into two more or less complete units, like the splitting of paramecium. Yet obviously, such a concept has purely diagrammatic value and may be misleading.

In fact one must ask whether one is justified in dismissing the possibility that all acts of repression involve the creation of a larval form of a secondary personality. In his only reference to the problem Freud, in his *Note on the Unconscious in Psychoanalysis* (1925), p. 25, refers briefly to the existence of alternating states of separate and independent systems of consciousness. After stressing the fact that they are *alternating* and not coexistent states of consciousness, Freud leaves the issue without discussing how this form of segregation of conscious material differs from that which occurs in ordinary repressions. Here again it would seem that we face a basic gap in psychoanalytical knowledge, a gap which exists at least partly because we have turned our backs so completely upon material available only through the experimental use of hypnosis. The states of conscious and unconscious mentation existing in cases of multiple personality *coexist* quite as truly as in simpler repressions.

In the case here under discussion, we are unable to explain the existence of the personality first known as Jane and later as Jane Brown. We are in a position to understand in some measure the function which this dual personality performed, but not how it came into being. The story makes it evident that under the impulse of terror and anger, the young woman had made a very deep and painful identification of herself with her grandfather. Somehow all of her later anxieties and compulsions stemmed from this momentous event. At some time she built up a protective companionate alter ego, Jane, who knew the things that she did not want to know, who was either unable or else forbidden to tell them to anyone but who exercised an almost continuously protective role toward the patient herself. This was evidenced on innumerable occasions during the course of the sessions described in this report, and is in striking contrast to the destructive or malicious alternative personality which has more frequently been described in the literature (Prince, 1908).

The "Sally" type of personality, described by Morton Prince, often seems to glory in a sense of power but by adroit maneuvering can be made to demonstrate this power in the interests of therapy by compelling the other personality to accept unconscious data which it is trying to reject. In the present case the disagreements between the two personalities—that is, the abuse, the epithets, the supercilious arrogance, the sulking, the apologies—appear to have been sham battles by means of which the one manipulated the other. The evidence for this is given in the following scrawled statement by Brown: "D need help; D not no [know] D need help. B must help D. E must help D. D not no so got to be made to take help. Got to give help when she not no so she take it. D not no right thing to do. D do wrong thing. B no right thing. B can't tell D; B got to make D do right thing the best way B no how." This explanation is typical of many others and shows that this apparent internal warfare was a byproduct of the clumsy efforts of Brown to guide Miss Damon toward an understanding of matters that Brown understood but could not communicate directly.

Even the anger Brown showed against Miss Damon seemed to serve the same purpose of impressing on Damon the seriousness of the whole matter. Similarly, the occasional impatient abuse of the investigator was like the anger of a child who impatiently tells an adult that it has explained everything when the whole matter remains incomprehensible to the adult.

The apparent "impishness" does not seem to be an expression of Brown's real attitude, which was one of deadly seriousness and concern, of worry and anxiety, which she seemed to mask from herself, from the investigator, and especially from Miss Damon in order to prevent Miss Damon from sensing her anxiety. It was particularly when Miss Damon became alarmed that Brown went off on some irrelevant tangent, inducing laughter on the part of the investigator and his assistants. That Brown herself was also afraid is shown in her statement, "E not hurt. E can do it. E not afraid. E won't be afraid. D afraid; B afraid so let E do it."

The ambiguities of the responses, and the insistent demand of Brown for an absolutely right question before she could answer, is a characteristic and at the same time a puzzling phenomenon. It was as though she could not tell her story outright but could only betray it, as we have said, like the schoolboy who dares not tell on the school bully, but can betray him indirectly if asked the correct question. To this end much of the seemingly irrelevant material turns out on close inspection to have been highly relevant, because it betrayed cues which were evident to Brown but not to the investigator until the whole story was made clear. It was for this reason that the investigator seemed to Brown to be so intolerably stupid.

A detailed study of multiple personalities might shed much new light on the problem of anxiety: how anxiety is distributed between the various personalities, what different forms anxiety may take in each, how this correlates with special traits of each.

The material from this case justifies only a few comments at this time. In the first place it is clear that the subject herself suffered from two types of fear. There was the initial horror state which overcame her when the hypnotically induced catalepsy reproduced in her the terror originally experienced when she was lost and when her grandfather told her the story of the muskrat. In her catalepsy this old fear recurred as a state of paralyzing panic without phobic distortions or projections but with characteristic bodily immobility. Against this she originally defended herself by a partial dissociation and an attempted identification with her grandfather. However, this had served only to plunge her into deeper waters when the grandfather told the story of his own fears. The relationship of this type of experience to the formation of the second personality is something about which we are in a position only to speculate.

The second type of fear from which Miss Damon suffered occurred whenever disturbing unconscious material suddenly threatened to break through the barriers into conscious expression. She dramatized this type of fear more freely than the other, with obvious vasomotor disturbances and with evidences of shame and embarrassment as well as of fear. Such anxiety is familiar of course from clinical analytical experience and from Freud's descriptions; but its demonstration in the interplay between these two personalities was particularly clear.

The protecting Brown, however, was also not immune to fear. She showed momentary anxiety about looking too closely at the visual images that were called up in the mirror. She was afraid she would see something too horrible to endure, and frequently she made use of euphemism, ambiguities, and circumlocutions of all sorts to escape dealing directly with a frightening topic. She seemed to know that the investigator could name the "awful thing" without experiencing a dread similar to her own. Thus she said, "E not hurt. E can do it. E not afraid. E won't be afraid. D afraid. B afraid. So let E do it." It is not easy to say how much of Brown's fear was for her own safety and how much for Miss Damon's.

A word of further explanation is necessary to clarify the peculiar and confusing way in which the subject first counted out the positions of the words in the sentences. After the sentences were fully deciphered, it was possible completely to explain the counts:

Erickson: "The real sentences?"
Brown: "Trance, will my muskrat enter, also go.
Every subsequent catalepsy the consequences of catching the muskrat to the little idiot."

Word	*Position*	*Sentence*
Trance	**1**	**1**
Will	**2**	**1**
My	**3**	**1**

Word	*Position*	*Sentence*
Catalepsy	**10**	**1 and 2 together.**
Catalepsy	**11**	**1 and 2 together, if *muskrat* is counted as two words.**
Catalepsy	**12**	**1 and 2 together, if *also* and *muskrat* are each counted as two words.**
Every	**8**	**1 and 2 together.**
Every	**9**	**1 and 2 together, if *muskrat* is counted as two words.**
Every	**10**	**1 and 2 together, if *also* and *muskrat* are each counted as two words.**
Ever	**13**	**After the following sequence: "Trance, will, my, muskrat, musk, rat, enter, also, all, so, go, every, ever."**
Ever	**14**	**After the following sequence: "Trance, will, my, muskrat, musk, rat, enter, also, all, so, go, every, eve, ever."**

Catalepsy could have been given different positions, but the subject later explained that it had not occurred to her to split and reduplicate the words in this way until after she had reached the word *ever,* and then it was too late to go back to the word *catalepsy*.

This fragmentation of automatic words and sentences is strictly comparable to the fragmentation of the automatic drawings described in another paper of Erickson and Kubie (1938); instead of being counted as parts of a sentence, the words are counted purely as syllabic units with only a numerical relation to one another. The task of resolving this deliberately misleading system of counting was tremendously difficult.

24. The Clinical Discovery of a Dual Personality

Milton H. Erickson

The clinical phenomenon of a dual personality constitutes an inexplicable form of personality construction. It consists of the coexistence within the same person of two separate and distinct personalities. Although this phenomenon has been known for over 60 years, and despite its marked importance as an approach to the many problems of personality construction, it is still the same unsolved problem it was when first reported. Azam in 1876, Mitchell in 1888, Prince, Sidis and Goodhart, and Janet about the beginning of this century, and Kubie and myself only recently have recorded such cases in the literature. The interest and significance of these studies and the wealth of their contributions to psychological and psychiatric understandings are easily appreciated. Yet, despite the importance that has been readily accorded to these reports, especially to Morton Prince's famous study of the various coexistent personalities in Miss Beauchamp, there has been a persistent, serious oversight and neglect of the dual or multiple personality as a profitable field of inquiry regarding the nature and structure of the human personality. Also, there has been no active realization of the fact that the multiple personality offers an exceptional opportunity for a laboratory analysis of those elements entering into the formation of distinctive and separate personalities. Yet, the problem of personality—its development, organization, and structure—constitutes a question of central interest to both psychology and psychiatry.

Accordingly, in this preliminary report upon the clinical discovery of a dual personality, my purposes are several. Particularly do I wish to direct attention to the importance of as many as possible of the general considerations centering around this psychological phenomenon, and about which misunderstandings, false beliefs, and incorrect assumptions are most generally prevalent. Among these considerations are the significant questions concerning the actual incidence or frequency of multiple personalities, the possibilities for discovery, the clinical nature and character of multiple and secondary personalities, and especially the significant values of this clinical phenomenon as a research problem.

Finally, I wish to give an account of the various observations, clinical steps, and investigative procedures by which it became possible to

---

Unpublished manuscript, circa 1940s.

discover in a young woman the existence of a second unknown and concealed personality. This discovery constituted a fact unsuspected by her ordinary personality, and she continued to remain unaware of it for approximately a year after its discovery. Then, only through being systematically and forcibly acquainted with the facts, did she realize the possibility of the truth.

Concerning the actual incidence or frequency of well-integrated, highly organized, distinctive multiple personalities coexistent within a single individual, no definitive information is available in the literature. During the course of Prince's study of this problem, he expressed the belief that these personalities were not necessarily infrequent, but that probably it was the difficulty of discovery that made them apparently rare.

In my own experience with approximately 500 hypnotic subjects, which does not include the case to be reported today, I have found a total of four persons with well-developed, well-organized secondary personalities. In addition I have found three others with fairly well-integrated subpersonalities and a half-dozen more who showed separate but incomplete organization about certain aspects of the personality. In all these instances discovery was accidental, no systematic search was made, and so the actual frequency may be higher than indicated by my findings.

On the other hand, a large proportion of my hypnotic subjects constituted a highly selected group, chosen because of neurotic traits and personality disturbances. Hence the incidence found may be unduly high. At all events my findings do indicate that multiple personalities are not necessarily rare, even though no definitive conclusions can be offered concerning their actual frequency.

Serving to confirm my general experience in this connection is the trend of conceptual developments in personality study. Recently the tendency in psychology and psychiatry has been toward intensive studies of personality as a clinical problem meriting analysis rather than simple acceptance as an established fact. From these intensive studies, particularly those made by the psychoanalysts, has come a general and progressive realization that the human personality is characterized by infinite varieties and complexities of development and organization, and that it is not a simple limited unitary organization. It is, rather, to be regarded as having as complicated a structure, organization, and development as has the individual's experiential background. From this realization of the complexity of the structure of the personality there has developed the understanding of the possibility—and the actual probability—of separate and specific integrations within the total organization as a common characteristic. Particularly has this multiple concept of the personality been emphasized by Franz Alexander in his book *The Psychoanalysis of the Total Personality,* in which he declares emphatically that the human personality actually constitutes a collection of personalities. More recently in this regard Oberndorf has spoken of "that galaxy of personalities which constitute the individual." Finally, mention may be made that medical history is replete with instances of definite entities that were originally considered as rare and infrequent—if, indeed, actually existent, and not a manifestation of some other known entity. As we now know, these presumably unusual conditions needed only the adequate development of medical techniques to permit ready discovery and recognition, and such development probably is all that is lacking in relation to special forms of personality construction.

In relation to the question of the possibilities for discovering multiple personalities, one is impressed at once by certain attributes in common among the studies recorded in the literature. In all these cases the discovery was essentially an accident. Also, in all instances the discovery was total in character; that is, there was sudden immediate and full realization on the part of the investigator of the nature of his discovery. Next, in each instance—and this is an item that has given rise to innumerable misapprehensions and false assumptions and beliefs—the discoverer was either employing hypnotic techniques at the time or was well experienced in the use of hypnosis. Hence, the case I am reporting today is of special interest since it was not, like my previous cases, an accidental discovery. Hypnosis was not employed, and my patient had never been hypnotized. However, I do feel that my experience with hypnosis made me more acutely aware of the striking contrasts and startling dissimilarities noted from time to time over a period of months in the general behavior of my patient. My belief is that the role of hypnosis in such discoveries is essentially indirect and coincidental. The hypnotic experience of learning to differentiate waking behavior from trance behavior in the same subject provides a general background of understanding by means of which one learns to recognize integration.

My interest in today's case was stimulated entirely by observing in a young woman various different sets and patterns of complete, well-integrated personality reactions and manifestations. Some of these patterns were familiar and easily recognized as hers; others were unfamiliar, seemed alien to her, and could not be fitted to her personality as ordinarily known. Hence, I would stress as an adequate measure of discovery for multiple personalities any procedure of systematic clinical observation that would permit the recognition of different sets and patterns of behavior integration and a determination of the interrelationships or lack of interrelationships between various organizations of behavior reactions.

The question of the clinical nature and character of multiple personalities is most controversial, much more so than the marked limitations of available information warrant. In this regard association with hypnosis has contributed to the development of both prejudices and mistaken beliefs and assumptions. In addition, as has been the case with hypnosis, there has been a marked confusion between the symptomatology of hysteria and the manifestations of multiple personalities. However, it is only fair to admit that much of the confusion between hysterical states and multiple personalities derives from the fact that, unfortunately, the literature does contain reports of hysterical states described as multiple personalities. Eventually such errors will be corrected.

Foremost among the various misunderstandings prevalent about multiple personalities is the belief that they are more or less unintentionally built up by the hypnotist and hence are artifacts. However, as is readily appreciated by anyone with adequate experience, hypnosis is not a miracle worker. It is possible to build up in the hypnotic subject pseudo-personalities, but these are extremely limited in character and extent of development, and they obviously are temporary, superimposed manifestations. In addition, such personality constructions are restricted by the nature and origin of their development to the hypnotic situation. In my own hypnotic work I have, as an experimental approach to personality problems, attempted over a period of years to build up new personalities in hypnotic subjects, only to realize the futility of such attempts. Furthermore, for a person adequately experienced in hypnosis there is no real likelihood of confusing the manifestations of the hypnotic trance with an actual secondary personality. They are distinctly different despite the superficial resemblances that may cause persons limited in their knowledge of hypnosis to confuse the two.

Finally, one need only read with the utmost of critical attention such a study as Morton Prince's to realize the error in such beliefs. Accusations have frequently been made that his discovery was directly the result of hypnotic suggestion. Yet, every one of Prince's findings serves to emphasize the nonhypnotic character of the multiple personalities he discovered.

Another prevalent misapprehension is that multiple personalities represent essentially nothing more than a fugue state, an amnesiac state of hysterical origin, or a hysterical dissociation of a single complex (or even a constellation of complexes) into a limited, restricted, isolated, independent existence. However, careful, critical comparative studies of these conditions and of multiple personalities will disclose only apparent, not real similarities. Unfortunately, opportunity for such comparative study is as yet limited. Nevertheless, a careful analysis of the material actually available on these topics in the literature will enable the earnest student to reach a satisfactory realization that multiple personalities constitute something of a different character from special hysterical states.

Nor should there be a confusion of the condition of multiple personalities with those prolonged amnesiac states that result only in a loss of personal identity and a new organization of the individual's life. In such amnesic states the personality as such remains constant, and the general pattern of personality reactions persists. The only significant difference is the loss of conscious memory—only the memory—of the experiential past. However, it is possible for a dual personality to behave in a fashion wholly suggestive of only a simple major amnesic state. In this connection I have found that by cautious, tentative, and deliberate experimental measures it is possible to reverse the role of dominance. That is, by appropriate procedures it is possible to make the secondary personality actually the primary, dominant personality. When this is done, I have found that the secondary personality becomes dominant and loses its knowledge of the actual experiential background of the originally dominant personality, which in turn acquires all the true characteristics of the secondary personality. However, I have not yet dared to do much investigative work in this direction.

Another serious misapprehension is the common but mistaken belief that multiple personalities can occur only in highly neurotic persons and that the secondary personalities are necessarily destructive and vicious in character. My experience is contrary to this belief. Of the four instances I have discovered, two of the individuals were neurotic, one seriously so, and in both of these the secondary personalities were decidedly destructive in character. However, in both of these cases the undesirable behavior was directed exclusively against the ordinary personality and not, as in the fictional account of Dr. Jekyll and Mr. Hyde, directed against society.

The other two persons, well known by competent psychiatrists, are regarded as well integrated and well adjusted, and their secondary personalities are definitely of a helpful and protective character in all their relationships with the primary personality.

Today's case represents a third type of relationship between the two personalities. As originally discovered, the secondary personality wished the primary personality well, was willing to be of assistance to that personality, but was often either markedly indifferent to or highly impatient with, the primary personality in specific situations. On occasion the secondary personality would declare emphatically that the ordinary personality was "silly," "stubborn," and "lacking in good sense." Hence, no absolute rule of thumb is warranted in describing the interrelationships that exist between multiple personalities.

To proceed with the question of what actually constitutes the clinical nature of the dual or multiple personality is a most unsatisfactory task. One must make the simple, dogmatic, and not satisfactorily informative statement that the person with a dual personality actually possesses two separate, distinct, independent personalities. Each of these personalities derives from a single, total experiential background that serves each of the personalities in a markedly different fashion. The dominant, ordinary, or primary personality has the richer background of reality experience, and nearly all contacts with reality belong to it. The secondary personality, however, has the richer background of intellectual and emotional knowledge commonly held by passive, observant, nonparticipants. Thus, there is a dominant personality that has actively participated and shared in the major portion of all contacts with reality; out of this experience a personality complete with its various attributes is derived. The second personality, however, except for a limited number of reality contacts unknown to the other personality, has usually not shared actively to the same significant degree in reality contacts and has largely only observed reality in a passive fashion. For the secondary personality the experiential background is largely a matter of intellectual and emotional understandings acquired passively through the proxy constituted unwittingly by the primary personality. Out of this background of chiefly passive experience the secondary personality, also complete with its various attributes, is derived.

When direct comparison of one personality with the other is made, the question is not one of the completeness or the incompleteness of the two personalities, as is so commonly believed. Rather, it is entirely a question of the totally different uses and interrelationships established for the various items in the total experiential background. To appreciate these facts one needs prolonged and instructive contact with a dual personality.

Of particular interest in relation to the nature of the dual personality are certain primary characteristics. First of all, the ordinary personality is totally unaware of the secondary personality. Even when confronted with adequate proof, there is a marked tendency to reject such proof as pure invention or as having some other explanation. For example, take the case I am reporting today. When Ellen, the primary personality, was presented with one proof after another, she rejected them as fabrications or, when the truth could not be denied, as inexplicably acquired knowledge on my part. When Mary, the other personality, was asked about this, she replied with amusement, "Oh, Ellen is awfully upset about finding out about me. She thinks you're just lying." Then Mary added, apologetically, "I hope you're not offended by Ellen. She just can't believe the truth."

A second characteristic, apparent in the above quotation, is that the second personality tends to know all about the first personality, or, if such knowledge is lacking, has ready access to it. For example, I asked Mary the name of a new acquaintance of Ellen's. She replied, "I wasn't paying attention when they were introduced, but if you need the name, I can get it from Ellen." However, certain items of information of a minor type are not available to the second personality. For example, in reply to one question Mary answered, "I wasn't there when Ellen put that pencil away, and now I don't know how to find out from her. You'll have to ask her."

Yet, immediately afterward Ellen could give the desired information. Prompt questioning of Mary elicited the reply, "Oh, I listened in when she told you, so I know now. I didn't before she told you, and I couldn't find out because I didn't know where to look in her mind."

Another item concerns the matter of dominance by the primary personality, which has already been mentioned and which will be illustrated later.

In relation to the potentialities of the multiple personality as a research problem, I wish to stress the opportunity it provides for a laboratory approach to the task of identifying and analyzing the various elements that enter into the development of distinctive and markedly different personalities. This value becomes particularly apparent when it is realized that the person with dual or multiple personalities must necessarily have constructed them out of a single experiential background. Hence, any differences in the personalities constructed must reflect differing uses, differing interrelationships, and differing qualities of activeness or passiveness for the same items in this experiential background. Thus there is opened the possibility of studying within a single experiential setting diverse developments in these direct relationships.

Having made this survey of an exceedingly important problem in personality research, a problem that has remained essentially undeveloped since its recognition 60 years ago, we may now turn to a direct consideration of my patient.

Ellen is an attractive, capable, and intelligent 24-year-old woman who has held several secretarial positions, with promotions leading to her present position as secretary in a university office. Despite her general capability she consistently gave the impression of being extremely shy, timid, fearful, withdrawn, self-conscious, and easily embarrassed. She had no friends, avoided all possible social contacts, and seemed to be incapable either of making or of receiving social advances. She was repeatedly described as cold, haughty, sullen, superior, and disagreeable.

In her work situation she was displeasingly meek and unreasonably insecure despite her excellent ability, and she never dared to show any emotion. Her entire work performance could be completely disrupted for as long as 20 minutes by any startle situation such as the dropping of a book or the slamming of a door. In her necessary contacts with students, she was insecure, uncertain, self-conscious, and fearful, and she seemed able to function only by rigid, precise attention to her duties.

In her general behavior she was forgetful and absentminded, exceedingly clumsy and jerky in her movements; she walked either with a long, awkward stride or a timid, hesitant step, and always seemed to be on the alert to avoid social contacts or to be most uncertain and confused about her exact whereabouts both in the university halls or on the street.

Arrangements were made to have her observed without her knowledge by capable psychiatrists, whose opinions can be summarized by the words, "insecure, unhappy, and extremely neurotic and unstable emotionally."

The consensus was that she was seriously in need of psychotherapy.

Observation over a period of months served to confirm all of these neurotic symptoms and to add many others of a similar character. During that period of time, however, many observations were made of a totally different and inexplicable character. These all related to peculiar, usually momentary manifestations entirely at variance with, and alien to, her known behavior; they were always replaced immediately by her customary shrinking and uncertain behavior. These variations may best be listed in brief descriptive accounts. Of particular import was the fact that these moments, however brief, served to effect a serious disruption of her work, and each time after their occurrence she was observed to go through what seemed to be a process of mental reorientation in order to resume her usual activities. Following are a dozen of these manifestations:

1. Brief periods of reverie and self-absorption during which she remained unresponsive to all stimuli despite the alert and highly interested look on her face.
2. Marked change from her hesitant or awkward gait to a casual, easy, graceful walk.
3. Failure to recognize individuals entering her office, and responding to them with a coldly critical gaze or a totally indifferent stare of curious appraisal.
4. The extreme and awkward care with which she would laboriously arrange the objects on her desk, and then, a moment later, she would disarrange them with one easy, graceful movement, and not discover this fact for some time.
5. Marked instances of disorientation; in particular, complete bewilderment at finding herself in an adjacent office or at the other end of the university hall with no understanding of how or why she happened to get there.
6. A direct approach to a fellow worker, staring in a curious, intent fashion, and then turning away, later to deny emphatically that she had seen that person on the previous occasion.
7. Frequent failure not only to recognize acquaintances but also to acknowledge their direct greetings, later denying emphatically that she had even encountered them.
8. The extreme care with which she would prepare to do something and but a moment later, with a facial expression of curious amusement, nullify that preparation. Thus, she would carefully put a letter in her purse to take home, but before leaving the office, she would remove the letter and put it in some place of concealment, only to search worriedly the next day, while expressing aloud to herself the certainty that she really must have put that letter in her purse.

9. The extreme ease with which she became lost either in the university buildings or in the city, necessitating constant effort on her part to keep in touch with her whereabouts.
10. The frequency with which she remained totally unaware of events occurring in the office, such as the entrance of students and the conversation of others, and the sincerity with which she would disclaim the actuality of these occurrences.
11. The discovery on her part as well as mine that her shorthand notebook frequently contained writings, scribblings, and drawings that she insistently denied doing, yet I knew them to be hers since I had often seen her doing them in a state of reverie.
12. Finally, as she became better acquainted with me, the appearance on the desk assigned to me in that university office of curious cryptic notes and drawings similar to those in her notebook, which both she and her superior disowned most disinterestedly.

As these observations were made repeatedly, I became interested in their interrelationships and also in their bearing upon the woman's general pattern of behavior. Soon I became convinced that there was some unusual form of dissociation involved. With the advent of the cryptic writings and drawings, an opportunity to investigate developed. Finding on my table a note written in a juvenile script containing a comment about a red hat, I concealed it. Several days later, apropos of nothing, I addressed the general inquiry to nobody in particular, "Was it a black hat?" and then, without awaiting any answer, absorbed myself in my work. After an interval of a few days I found on my desk another note that said, "No, red," in a similar juvenile script. In this manner I began a correspondence. Thus, upon finding a drawing or a note upon my desk, I would make some remark pertinent to it, but apparently silly, irrelevant, and meaningless. Within a few days I would find, concealed in my papers or on my desk, a reply bearing upon the previous note or drawing and my apparently meaningless comment.

When shown these notes and drawings, Ellen evinced only a polite interest. However, I soon began to discover that if when I found a note on my table, Ellen happened to be looking my way, there would appear momentarily on her face that peculiar alert, interested, and amused expression seen previously in different situations. I discovered further that Ellen was not aware that I had just picked up that note. After verifying these observations repeatedly and under varying conditions, the question arose as to what role Ellen played in this total situation despite her apparently complete unawareness of it.

This question led rapidly to the discovery that her unusual behavior constituted a separate, complete, and consistent general pattern never in evidence at the same time as Ellen's usual behavior. In other words, there were two separate and distinct patterns of general behavior that did not overlap but, rather, alternated in appearance.

Then one day I found on my desk a note that bore the name Mary Ann Peters. I concealed it immediately. Several days later, on my next visit to the university, I remarked casually to Ellen upon the frequency of double meanings in apparently simple remarks. I suggested that she listen carefully to what I was about to say, since it would have a double meaning, and I urged her strongly to be sure to understand that second meaning. I then remarked that one may describe someone as having the "map of Dublin—M.A.P.—on his face." Ellen listened intently but in obvious bewilderment, incapable of realizing that in spelling the word *map* I had actually given three initial letters. At the same time her hand was observed to pick up a pencil and to write, "Yes, Mary understand," in the script made familiar by the notes left on my table. This name "Mary" was later found to derive from the heroine of a novel read by Ellen in her childhood.

This was the first definitive evidence that there was a secondary personality, and upon the strength of it, arrangements were made with Dr. Lawrence S. Kubie to develop further investigative procedures. The details of our findings, however, belong to another paper and not to this preliminary report, which is intended only to introduce and focus attention upon a most important psychiatric topic. Suffice it to say that later we were able to establish full contact with the hitherto unknown personality, Mary, a well-poised, self-confident, extremely capable woman, free from Ellen's neuroticisms and markedly different in every way, even giving the impression of being several years older than Ellen.

Now, to summarize, I have stressed the importance of this entire problem of dual or multiple personalities, a problem that has confronted psychiatry for more than 60 years and is still unfortunately in the descriptive phase. I have briefly mentioned significant considerations bearing upon this type of phenomenon and have given a brief account of clinical observations that led to the discovery of a dual personality. My hope is that this account, even though a preliminary report to a more extensive study, will serve to dispel some of the mystery surrounding the entire problem and that it will also arouse sufficient interest to stir others to investigate and to study.

25. Findings on the Nature of the Personality Structures in Two Different Dual Personalities By Means of Projective and Psychometric Tests

Milton H. Erickson and David Rapaport

Last year a report was given before this association of the clinical discovery of a dual personality in a young woman; that is, there existed in that young woman two independent personality structures. One of these personalities was found to be primary and dominant, while the other was found to be secondary and essentially passive, but capable of alternating with the primary personality at a certain level of personality functioning. In presenting this material particular emphasis was placed upon the fact that the discovery had been based essentially upon the relatively simple clinical procedure of observing various dissimilar and conflicting responses, reactions, and patterns of behavior in the young woman. It was found that she manifested at different times one or the other of two sets of reactions, which not only alternated with each other but which were often unrelated, opposed, and even alien to each other in their manifestations. Once these two distinct and separate sets of behavior responses were recognized, the further steps leading to the clinical recognition of a dual personality and the identification of two different personalities, each with its own individual patterns of behavior, were relatively direct procedures.

While such a clinical study is of interest and value, there is an imperative need to confirm, to disprove, or to demonstrate some better interpretation of its findings by investigative procedures more objective and controlled than is clinical observation. The complexity of the phenomenon of dual personality, and the fact that the many cases reported in the literature are all essentially clinical studies, makes the need for independent, controlled test-studies even more obvious.

Accordingly, in today's presentation we have two purposes. The first of these relates to the need for a more systematic and critically controlled study of the phenomenon of dual personality. The second purpose is that of developing more adequately the clinical findings presented last year. To these ends we now offer a report of the investigative findings on dual personality obtained under the controlled conditions of the testing situation and by means of standardized psychometric and projective test

Unpublished manuscript written with David Rapaport, circa 1940s.

procedures. These tests were chosen because they compel responses to be essentially in terms of personality reactions, attitudes, and capacities; hence, they preclude significant predeterminations of detailed patterns of response, such as is possible in personality inventories and similar tests. Independently of this investigation, however, one form of personality inventory was used on several occasions over a period of 18 months, not only to disclose possible differences between primary and secondary personalities, but also to determine the constancy of the responses made.

The selected tests, administered by Dr. Rapaport, were given to the dual personality upon whom I reported last year and to another dual personality previously reported in the literature by me.[1] The use of two people increased the extent of the study and secured comparative and confirmatory findings.

TESTS AND THE TEST SITUATION

The tests employed in this study may be listed and described briefly as follows:

(1) *Rorschach Test.* This is a well-known test in which 10 ink-blot pictures are shown to the subject. In response to the question "What might this be?" semidirected associations are obtained from the subject for each of the pictures. The formal characteristics of these responses can then be interpreted in the light of test experience and psychological theory. The test gives information about the relation of cognitive and emotional processes and permits a description of the personality and a diagnostic classification.

(2) *Szondi Test.* This is a nonverbal, projective personality test in which the subject selects from six series of eight photographs each the picture most liked and most disliked. Each series shows a homosexual, an epileptic, a hysterical, a catatonic, a paranoiac, a depressive, a manic and a sadistic murderer. The choices thus made permit an interpretation of outstanding character trends of the subject and frequently an approach to the diagnostic category to which the subject belongs.

(3) *Thematic Apperception Test.* This test consists of a series of pictures presenting various scenes. The subject is asked to tell what each scene represents, how it came about, and what the outcome will be. This test gives insight into the content of the subject's fantasies and emotional attitudes.

(4) *Babcock Deterioration Test.* This test contains items similar to those of the Wells Memory Test and the Merrill-Terman Test. Simultaneously

[1]Erickson, M. H. & Kubie, L. S. The permanent relief of an obsessional phobia by means of communications with an unsuspected dual personality. *The Psychoanalytic Quarterly*, 1939, 7, 471–509.)

with the test a vocabulary test is given. By a computation based on the assumption that vocabulary deteriorates less than other achievements, a measure of mental efficiency is obtained.

(5) *Bellevue Intelligence Test.* This intelligence test was standardized on adults and consists of a 10 item-groups: comprehension, information, digit-span, arithmetic, similarities, picture arrangement, picture completion, block design, object assembly, and digit-symbol. The intelligence quotient is expressed in terms of percentiles, and the relation of the individual scores of the item groups is clinically meaningful.

(6) *Bernreuter Personality Inventory.* This self-administered test contains 125 questions and is variously scored to measure neurotic tendencies, self-sufficiency, introversion-extroversion, dominance-submission, self-confidence, and sociability.

The conditions under which the tests were administered deserve mention. Neither of the two dual personalities was acquainted with Dr. Rapaport, nor did they know that a study of them was planned. Instead, they were introduced to Dr. Rapaport and immediately and arbitrarily inducted into the test situation. This surprise method excluded premeditated test response. I felt that the natural objection and resentment of the subjects toward such an arbitrary procedure would aid in eliciting unguarded, and hence all the more informative, personality reactions and attitudes.

The actual administration of the tests lasted over a period of several days and required a total of more than 24 hours of intensive work in the test situation. Every effort was made to keep the administration of each test under adequately controlled conditions and to secure informative comparisons and contrasts within individual test situations. The tests were administered in the case of Ellen and Mary to the primary personality first and in that of B and A to the secondary personality first.

THE SUBJECTS

The subjects of this investigation are two women in their early twenties, both of whom are successfully employed and regarded by competent observers as decidedly capable and efficient. The one reported upon last year has the primary personality of Ellen and the secondary of Mary. The primary personality of the other is best known as B and her secondary as A.*

*Editor's Note: In the previous description of this dual personality in the paper "The permanent relief of an obsessional phobia by means of communications with an unsuspected dual personality," the primary personality B was known as Miss Damon and the secondary personality was known as Miss Brown.

Ellen and Mary is looked upon by her friends as somewhat difficult, neurotic, and unstable in social adjustments, while B and A is regarded by her friends as decidedly well adjusted and socially able. In both instances, however, the secondary personalities are unknown except to a few selected persons.

TEST FINDINGS

No attempt will be made to present test findings in full detail because of their extent, complexity, and often all too technical character. Instead they will be reserved for publication in the complete report: only a general summary of them is offered here. Before proceeding, however, I wish to interject two cautionary statements so as not to mislead you. First of all, time limitations have compelled us, for brevity and clarity of presentation, to sacrifice cautious, limited, and qualified statements in favor of general, comprehensive, and hence more dogmatic statements. Next, while Dr. Rapaport and I are essentially in agreement in this present interpretation of our data, we both realize that further study and analysis might necessitate revision and further elaboration of our conclusions. For this reason, despite our confidence in our present judgments, such further study is planned.

With these reservations the following general statements may be made:

First, although there were definite test similarities between the primary and secondary personalities of each of the two women, the degree and character of those similarities in the case of Ellen and Mary were not inconsistent with a distinct separateness or, in other words, with the individuality of those primary and secondary personalities. In the case of B and A this distinct separateness was less obvious, and only in view of the unusual consistency of test findings were the results here surprising. In summary, the tests of Ellen and Mary appeared to be comparable to those of two different persons with some similar character traits; those of B and A were comparable to those of a person in two different phases of life.

Second, there was a consistency throughout the tests of each personality within the single tests as well as from one test to the other.

Third, the differences in the test findings between the primary and secondary personalities were greater and the similarities less in the projective personality tests; in the intelligence tests the similarities prevailed and the differences were relatively insignificant.

Fourth, the analyses of the various test findings, which were made by Dr. Rapaport independently of the clinical facts and observations, are in accord with the clinical history of, and my own findings on, each of the various personalities. In brief, investigative findings by means of standardized test procedures, interpreted in accord with established principles, warranted the same general diagnostic and descriptive judgments as did prolonged clinical study.

The test findings concerning the personalities of Ellen and Mary and of B and A may be summarized as follows:

Both Ellen and Mary are neurotic and of a compulsive type. However, while Ellen appears to present a picture of an acute neurosis with features of compulsive doubting and feelings of insufficiency colored by the impulsiveness of an inhibited person, Mary presents the picture of a solution of a severe problem by the formation of a passive, retiring, unconcerned, self-sufficient character. While Ellen thinks in vague generalities and displays rather weak judgment, Mary has, in spite of her interest in extravagances, a ready grasp of the obvious and keen powers of judgment. Ellen shows a great amount of free-floating anxiety and is an intensive day-dreamer, with some weak emotional adaptation to her surroundings. Mary is self-sufficient, displaying neither adaptation nor anxieties.

Ellen's I.Q. is 126 and her percentile score is 98, placing her in the superior intelligence group; Mary's I.Q. is 113 and her percentile score is 82, putting her into the bright-normal intelligence group. The scatter in the tests is strikingly similar, however, where intellectual maturity is of importance. For example, in conceptual problems Ellen is decidedly superior to Mary, but where emotional stability is crucial for the performance, as in concentration and attention, Mary is the superior. Similarly, in general mental efficiency Ellen is superior, but in immediate memory Mary is the better.

B and A are essentially introversive. While the tests of A appear to indicate a rather well-balanced personality, B's test results are such as would be predicted if A were to lose her balance and suffer a neurotic break. The findings are somewhat similar to those that might be found in a neurosis of mixed obsessive and hysteriform symptoms.

In personality makeup, however, B and A are quite similar. They are both rich in fantasies; both are very able and have manifold interests; both reveal a strong striving to adapt themselves to their environment, and in this striving both reveal considerable intellectualization of their adaptations—in other words, quite a bit of unfree, cautious adaptation. Both are interested in fellow human beings to an unusually strong degree. There are, naturally, differences in the degree and even in the quality of these similarities. A's psychomotility is less vivid and more constructive than B's, whose fantasy has frequently a fabulatory touch. Both have manifold interests, although much more so for A; B's diversity of interests has a touch of flightiness. The striving toward adaptation is strong in both, but B is impulsive in spite of this, while A is pliant to an unusual degree. And both have an unusual interest in people, though B's interest is loaded with quite a bit of insecurity and even fear.

In spite of her difficulties B has more sense of detail than A, who has a rather strong tendency to generalize. In spite of this B, for all her sense for detail, reveals less common sense than does A in her generalizations. Correspondingly, the judgment and logic of B is uneven and undependable, while that of A is rather stable. In spite of these discrepancies the intelligence makeup of the two girls is still very similar, and compared with the average they are both very inclined to make generalizations making use of their unusually good natural endowment.

B's I.Q. is 139 and her percentile score is 99. The I.Q. of A is 136 and her percentile score is 99, so that both are in the very superior intelligence group. The tests are very similar in score distribution and verbalization, in only one item requiring concentration does B fall much below A, even though A took the test first. The efficiency indexes of the two personalities are strikingly parallel, but with those of A on a lower level.

CONCLUSIONS

1. The testing of the two dual personalities appears to corroborate the fact that we deal here with a clinically unusual phenomenon. The two persons in question each appear to have organized their past experiences into two different patterns and to react alternatingly, now on the basis of one and now on the basis of the other pattern. These patterns differ more significantly for the one than for the other person. The reactions on the basis of these patterns are significantly different in the emotional sphere and much less so if the reaction in question is of a cognitive nature.

2. The test findings are in accord with the clinical histories. They appear to contradict the general assumption that the phenomenon of dual personality is a hysterical manifestation, since both these personalities were found to be rather of a compulsive-obsessional type. The findings appear rather to give weight to Oberndorf's assertion that co-conscious mentation is an obsessional disassociation phenomenon.

3. Although no explanatory account as to the genesis and nature of dual personality is offered here, it is hoped that the description of these phenomena of personality organization will contribute to the theory of personality organization in general.

RORSCHACH TEST
Comparative report of the tests of B and A

(Test given to A Sept. 17, 8:35 P.M.; to B Sept. 18, 11:40 A.M.)

1. Reaction time. There was no consistent relation between the reaction times of B and A. At times that of one, and at others that of the other, appeared to be the longer. In the third card, for instance, A took the test as first, had a reaction time of 40 seconds, and gave a rather weak response; B took the test as second, had a reaction time of 10 seconds, and gave a more elaborate and better response and an additional other response. No evidence can be thus derived from the reaction times that would speak against the phenomenon of double personality.

2. *Type of personalities. (a)* A appears to be a rather healthy person, while B appears to be quite neurotic. The main indicators of this neurosis appear to be the impulsive color responses, the extremely low animal percentage, and the low Form plus percentage. The neurosis of B is a mixed one in which one would expect to find symptoms belonging to hysteriform as well as to psychastenic syndromes. The former should be prevalent, and as the movement responses are numerous, one would expect rather ideational and characterological than conversion symptoms.

(b) As to the personality makeup, however, B and A are quite similar. They both are rich in fantasies, are very able, and have manifold interests; both reveal a strong striving to adapt themselves to their environment, and in this striving both reveal considerable intellectualization of their adaptations—in other words, quite a bit of unfree, cautious adaptation. Both are interested in fellow humans to an unusually great degree. There are, naturally, differences in degree and even in quality in these similar features. A's psychomotility is less vivid and more constructive than B's, whose fantasy has frequently a fabulatory touch. It is true that both have manifold interests, but A much less than B, in whose diversity of interests there is a touch of flightiness. It is true that the striving toward adaptation is strong in both, but B is impulsive in spite of this, while A is pliant to an unusual degree. It is true that both have an unusual interest in fellow humans, but the interest of B is loaded with quite a bit of insecurity and even fear of humans. B's protocol has quite a few anxiety indications, while A's has nearly none. However, both show an equal number of space responses, which in B's protocol ought to be interpreted as outwardly directed oppositional tendencies as well as doubts, while in A's protocol they ought to be interpreted as self-willedness and perhaps some doubt.

3. *Type of intelligence.* In spite of her difficulties, B has more sense for the obvious than A, who has a rather strong tendency to generalize. In spite of this B reveals with all her sense for the detail less common sense than does A in her generalizations. Correspondingly, the judgment and logic of B is uneven and undependable, while that of A is rather stable. In spite of these discrepancies the intelligence makeup of the two women is still very similar, and compared with the average they are both very inclined to make generalizations, making use of their unusually good natural endowment.

SZONDI TEST
Comparative report of the tests of B and A

(Test given Sept. 17, 8:15 P.M. to A; Sept. 18, 11:20 A.M. to B)

I. Attitude toward the test. Both women were very cooperative and apparently liked to take the test. Some uneasiness and anxiousness was, however, observed in the behavior of B.

II. *Personality of B and A.* The manic column, which usually corresponds to the oral tendencies of the subjects, is the only one that is equal in B and A. Both women appeared to have a rather significant oral dependent tendency, although a part of this is channeled and controlled. A appears to be childish, energetic, somewhat aggressive, but not neurotic. B is full of ambivalences and of extremely strong anxieties, giving a decidedly neurotic picture, resembling neurastenic-psychastenic neuroses. B has a mood coloring that might be called depressive and a fantasy life that is extremely vivid and most probably full of the anxieties indicated above and of the ambivalence conflict as to her aggressions. A has a much more stable mood life and a vivid but balanced and most probably not morbid fantasy life.

BELLEVUE TEST
Comparative report of tests given to B and A

(Test given to A Sept. 17, 9:30 A.M.; to B Sept. 18, 4:30 P.M.)

1. B's verbal score was two points lower than that of A (73, 75). B's performance score was higher than that of A (80 and 74). The relation of the I.Q.s is similar:

	I.Q.			*Percentile score*			*Intell. group*
	V	*P*	*Total*	*V*	*P*	*Total*	*VP Total*
A	**133**	**134**	**136**	**99**	**99**	**99**	**very superior**
B	**131**	**142**	**139**	**99**	**99**	**99**	**very superior**

It is hard to understand how the verbal average of A can be higher, even if slightly, than that of B. The scatter gives to this an answer inasmuch as the digits backward of B is significantly below her own level and also much lower than that of A. This should correspond with a general difficulty of concentration. Except for this one significant score, there are no significant differences either in verbalization or in scores in these two tests.

BABCOCK DETERIORATION TEST
Comparative Report of Tests Given to B and A

(Test given to B Sept. 19, 1940, 3:40 P.M., to A Sept. 19, 1940, 5:30 P.M.)

ITEMS:

	A	*B*
Immediate memory for a story	**20**	**18**
Symbol digit test	**16.5**	**16.5**
Immediate memory for digits forward	**19**	**19**
Immediate memory for digits backward	**18**	**12**
Speed of writing	**16.5**	**9**
Speed of tracing	**12.5**	**14**
Delayed memory for a story	**21**	**17**
Learning of paired associates	**19.5**	**20.5**
Memory span for sentences	**19**	**20.5**
Total	**162**	**146.5**
Vocabulary age	**20**	**20**
Total test score average	**18**	**16.3**
Learning score average	**19.2**	**18.0**
Motor score average	**15.2**	**13.2**
Repetition score average	**18.7**	**17.2**
Deviations from Babcock's norms		
For the total average	**+0.6**	**−1.1**
For learning	**+2.7**	**+1.5**
Motor	**−1.4**	**−3.4**
Repetition	**+2.4**	**+0.9**

(a) The mental efficiency of B appears to be good with an especially good learning efficiency. Peculiarly, however, her motor efficiency is rather weak, and this is a sign she has in common with A, whose motor efficiency appears to be extremely poor. It is noteworthy that in the comparison of M and L we found similar interrelations. The general mental efficiency of A appears to be poor, which is most likely due to her extremely poor motor efficiency, while her learning efficiency is very good. In general one might say that the efficiency indicators of B and A run perfectly parallel, except that A's is on a quite lower level than that of B's. On this point there is a deviation from the findings of M and L,* where only the motor and immediate memory scores were parallel, while the learning scores were significantly deviating from each other.

*Editor's Note: This and other test reports designate Ellen as L and Mary as M.

(b) The five reaction times of the symbol digit test for B and A are as follows:

B	**11.5**	**15**	**11.5**	**16**	**15.5**
A	**13**	**14**	**12**	**17**	**16**

The parallelism of the scores' sequences, which might be interpreted as work or fatigue patterns of the women, is thus extremely similar.

(c) The handwriting of the two women does not appear to be different for the observer unschooled in graphology. It is peculiar also that A has a very long writing time while her speed of tracing is better than that of B. However, this could be easily explained by considering the fact that A hasn't had much experience in writing; in tracing, where experience counts less than security, she can do better.

RORSCHACH TEST
Comparative Report of the Tests of L and M

(Test of L given Sept. 16, 1940, 10 A.M.; test of M given Sept. 17, 1940, 9:30 A.M.)

I. *Attitude to the Test.* Neither of the women liked the test. Both seemed to be puzzled by it. However, M gave more clear-cut expression of her dislike than did L.

L's *reaction times* have been fairly long (30.4 sec. average), ranging from 13 to 65 seconds. M's reaction times, however, have been extremely long (98.5 sec. average), ranging from 25 to 240 seconds. For the first one might suggest that M had a hard time finding other responses than did L, and even L took her time in order to weigh carefully what she should say and what to leave for M. It is true that they have only one response in common, and even the spaces chosen for the other responses are different. But closer investigation reveals quite a few facts that are not consistent with such an explanation: *(1)* both girls give a constricted protocol indicative of inhibited personalities, M more so than L. In such cases an elongation of the reaction time is a common fact. The measure of constriction in L and M compares favorably with the reaction time in their protocols. *(2)* As we will see below, the scoring shows a rather systematic difference in the spaces chosen by L and M, which could have been hard to produce by any conscious plan. *(3)* The answer occurring in both of the protocols is the most frequent Rorschach response. Its appearance in both protocols pleads for the genuineness of the differences.

II. *Personality of L and M. (1)* Both women are neurotic, L significantly more so than M. Their neurosis is, however, rather of a compulsive type with psychasthenic features. In L the psychasthenic and compulsive doubt-features prevail. The doubts are directed against herself, taking the form of feelings of insufficiency and inhibitedness in spite of her impulsive ideas. M is rather passive (more than L) and evasive, interested in extravagancies, unusual things.

(2) L favors vague generalities and is lacking a sense of the obvious. M avoids generalizations and has a rather lucky grasp for the obvious, in spite of her interest in the unusual. Paradoxically, L, who lives (according to information) steadily exposed to community, shares the way of thinking of the community to a much lesser degree than M does. The same appears to be true for the keenness of logical judgment. L is here again decidedly weaker than M.

(3) M and L are both interested in fellow humans, but simultaneously both are shy and somewhat afraid of them. M is the one who is more interested and more withholding than the other.

(4) Both women are intelligent, but in the meantime quite stereotyped in their interests. M is the less stereotyped and more intelligent.

(5) L shows a great amount of free-floating anxiety, is a very strong daydreamer, but displays some, although very weak, affective adaptation. M is rather closed within herself, displaying neither adaptation nor anxieties.

(6) The two movement responses of L (as movement responses do in general) probably reveal some contents significant of this woman: *(a)* ". . . impression of pair of very large shoes walking in duck-fashion . . . actually the whole thing might be a gorilla." *(b)* ". . . I can vaguely outline a couple of fat people . . . or animals . . . they are apes . . . their faces turned back over their shoulders, holding onto a cliff."

Two features of these responses should be especially remarkable: *(a)* in both the response starts with human beings which turn immediately into animals; *(b)* the character of these movements—namely, "walking in duck-fashion" and "holding onto a cliff"—should describe L herself.

SZONDI TEST

Comparative Report of the Tests of L and M

(Test of L given Sept. 16, 1940, 9:30 A.M.; test of M given Sept. 17, 1940, 9.A.M.)

I. *Attitude toward the test.* Both women seemed to be somewhat reticent toward the test. Both commented that hardly any of the pictures appealed to them. While L commented frequently on this and on individual pictures, M was rather silent, and every choice took her a long time. When asked about her silence, she said: "I speak only if I have something to say. . . . This does not inspire conversation."

II. *Personality of L and M. (1)* The number and distribution of choices in the catatonic column, which usually designate the narcissism and degree of withdrawal of the subject, represent the only area that is identical in M and L. It is the experience, however, that when a subject is retested with this test, the catatonic column is the one most apt to remain unchanged. Thus, the tests relate to each other as if they were representing two sides of the same personality; these two tests have the same thing in common as the Rorschach tests, which were both constricted, including few responses, long reaction times, and, with few exceptions, only form-responses. The Szondi tests are also those of inhibited persons. In most of other respects, however, the two subjects give a quite different record.

(2) L appears to be severely neurotic, very impulsive, with strong anxieties, infantile in her sexuality in a manner that probably makes her ready to assert her womanhood by being ready for "passing affairs." To what actual behavior such a readiness in an inhibited person might lead is hard to foretell. M is practically within the range of the normal, although inhibited, and carrying a definite number of bottled-up anxieties.

(3) L is civilized and controls her aggressions, while M is aggressive but has something that could be called culture.

(4) L is an anal character (probably expulsive), with a very strong oral-dependent tendency. In M oral and anal tendencies appear to be rather channelized.

(5) L's empty epileptic column and M's two "most liked" epileptic choices refer probably to another interrelation of the two personalities, which is at present not clear to me. However, as similar interrelations occur in B and A, it might be that certain "epileptoid" trends have to do with the occurrence of such phenomena as that of L and M, B and A.

THEMATIC APPERCEPTION TEST
Comparative Report of the Tests of L and M

(Test of M given Sept. 17, 1940, 3:15 P.M.; test of L given Sept. 18, 1940, 8:45 A.M.)

I. *Attitude toward the test.* On the surface both girls showed a rather agreeable reaction to the test. In fact, however, both attempted, and not without success, to disregard the test instructions.

II. *Formal characteristics of the fantasies. (1)* Both subjects stated that they had once taken the test.

(2) M's fantasies can hardly be called such. Rather, they are descriptions, embellished mostly with some very matter-of-fact connecting story. Such an attitude would be consistent with her Rorschach test and is frequently found in inhibited but matter-of-fact normals, being concise and abrupt.

(3) L's fantasies could be called fantasies with some right. She gives

stories, and these stories frequently even disregard the picture. These stories, however, very frequently are taken from tales or some history material and have a sarcastic, scoffing narrative—as if she would demonstrate with her sarcasm, "You see, one can tell stories without committing oneself."

(4) Peculiarly, however, in two fantasies (12th and 13th) M takes over the sarcastic, or the fantastic, trend of L's narrative. This occurrence is striking and cannot be disregarded. Its explanation, however, is beyond the scope of the test material.

III. *Contents of fantasies.*

(A) M's fantasies. (1) Concerning sex: they are dancing, she is uninterested . . . will dance with someone else; a man is defending his sister against his mother; young woman is going to marry someone; the mother did not want her to marry; her husband died, she is crying . . . does not want her to leave, she will go, they quarreled. A rather disinterested, neutral, somewhat scoffing attitude.

(2) Concerning parents: they appear very rarely in the fantasies. A disapproving, stern mother who is beating the father, scolding the daughter, and disapproving of the daughter's plan of marriage.

(3) Aggression: a mean old man buried all his friends either actually or in imagination . . . his departure will doubtless cause much rejoicing; woman strangles another woman, halfway, because the other was reading her mail; a man murdered, while drunk, his wife, he will go to prison. Self-directed: a prick with a needle results in poisoning and death; lack of money results in suicide.

(B) L's fantasies. (1) Dependency: Disappointed little girl weeping into her father's ear—he consoles her; princess, sacrificed to a dragon, is saved by a noble prince; asks for a new dress from mother to go to her first ball.

(2) Concerning sex: man torn between duty and desire, between homely wife and beautiful mistress; the outcome is a mess; mother scolds the daughter, asks why she was out last night with Parsifal and not with Mike; she will marry P and always wish she would have married M; a maid comments: my goodness, the way they are carrying on there they ought to be ashamed of themselves . . . at his age too—oh, well—there is no fool like an old fool; man slept with a girl, wishes he hadn't, feels rejected, commits suicide, she wakes up and says: "Now, what did you do that for? Wasn't it silly"—and she will find herself someone else. These fantasies are quite consistent with her psychosexual immaturity as characterized by the Szondi test.

(3) Parents: Father appears to be a consoling figure; the mother figures, however, are in steady quarrel with her.

(4) Toward herself: she describes herself as ineffectual, in a night-marelike fear of remaining alone in the world, as disappointed and reaching out for help, as the princess who will be saved by the prince of

dreams, as an orphan who will be cared for by the aunt. Concerning money: she is richly married and gives in depression time 10 dollars to his brother to get rid of him; she quarrels with her mother to get a new dress; a man is being hanged for having murdered a man for 2 dollars, he did it for hunger.

IV. *Comparative summary:* While M is rather indifferent toward sex, L is rather full of strange erotic fantasies indicating her psychosexual immaturity. Neither of them has much interest in parents, but both agree in rejecting the mother figure. Aggressions play a significant role in both, but in L's fantasies they have a rather anal coloring. In one fantasy of M's similar motivation of suicide appears to be present. While M remains in these fantasies noncommittal concerning her attitude to herself, L describes herself as an ineffectual person in need of help, dependence, despaired. While M appears here again to be rather realistic, L is rather fantastic in her fantasies, but the fantasies are frequently borrowed from historical or literature sources.

BELLEVUE ADULT INTELLIGENCE SCALE

Comparison of tests.

(L, given Sept. 16, 1940, 1:35 P.M.; M, given Sept. 17, 1940, 11. A.M.)

I. The numcrical results:

Scores	*L*	*M*
Intelligence Quotient:	126	113
Percentile score:	98%	82%
Verbal I.Q.:	129	115
Percentile score:	99%	85%
Performance I.Q.:	119	109
Percentile score:	91%	73%

These numerical results indicate that L has a higher I.Q. than M. L's total I.Q. is "superior," her verbal I.Q. "very superior," and her performance I.Q. on the borderline of "bright normal" and "superior." M's total I.Q. is "bright normal," and so is her verbal I.Q.; her performance I.Q., however, is only "high average."

It is obvious that the distribution of scores of L and M are strikingly parallel. There appears to be no qualitative difference between the two distributions. L and M are both somewhat weaker in performance items. Two possible conclusions could explain this fact. One would maintain that the formal intelligence structure of the two personalities does not differ much, because M achieved gradually but not completely the knowledge of L. The other explanation would maintain that the intelligence test shows that there are not two intellects present, that the same intellect was measured under different conditions and with a different degree of cooperation on the side of the subject.

II. *Attitude toward the test: (1)* Concerning the information items, M frequently declared (in 18 cases) that she did not know the answer but she could ask L. This was refused, and thus in the scattergram the information item was excluded. The verbal part of the I.Q. thus was computed taking 5/4 of the sum of the other four item scores.

(2) In the comprehension and similarity items M assumed frequently a very naive attitude that was strikingly different from her other responses, and it was not quite obvious why she was able to give an informed and mature response to some questions, while others were answered in a perfectly childish way. While the similarities of orange and banana, coat and dress, dog and lion, eye and ear, etc., are answered on a high level—properly, just like L answered them—the wagon and bicycle similarity is explained by L "both vehicles," and is explained by M, "both have wheels," or the egg and seed similarity, by L, "they are the embryonic state, one of a chicken, the other of a plant," and by M, "plant a seed—a plant grows; have an egg—a bird grows." While L would mail the letter she finds sealed, stamped, and addressed, M would pick it up and put it down where people would not step on it. But, in a strikingly reversed way, L thinks that people should pay taxes because "each of us cannot run the country by himself, so by paying taxes those appointed can run it," while according to M, payment of taxes "supports the government." These and similar responses constitute a barely understandable set of interrelations. It is hard to understand, for instance, why M knows about the government, while she does not know anything about the nature of letters.

III. *Scatter. (a)* Verbal item average for both girls is slightly better than performance item average.

(b) Among the verbal items the lowest scores for both girls are the comprehension and arithmetic score. The highest score in both is similarity—this in spite of the significantly lower scores of M.

(c) Among the performance items the highest score for both girls is the digit-symbol score. Peculiarly, however, while L's lowest score is the picture completion (10), M's picture completion score is fairly high (12); and her lowest item is the object assembly, which was the second lowest for L.

This scatter distribution shows extremely strong similarity in the intellectual makeup of the two women, except for the better concentration of M, shown in the picture completion. In spite of these similarities, however, the whole performance behavior and activity was strikingly different for the two women. These differences do not imply only formal behavior; they imply rather different attitudes to the test items and different approaches to them, which are very tangibly put down in a test record.

BABCOCK DETERIORATION TEST

Comparison of tests.

(L, given Sept. 16, 3:30 P.M.; M, given September 17, 1940, 4:10 P.M.)

ITEMS:	*M*	*L*
Immediate memory for a story	**14**	**19**
Symbol digit test	**16**	**16**
Immediate memory for digits forward	**14**	**18**
Immediate memory for digits backward	**19**	**19**
Speed of writing	**9.5**	**16**
Speed of tracing	**13**	**11**
Delayed memory for a story	**13**	**21**
Learning of paired associates	**8.5**	**13.5**
Memory span for sentences	**23**	**23**
Total	**130**	**165.5**
Vocabulary age	**15**	**18**
Total test score average	**14.4**	**17.4**
Learning score average	**12.9**	**17.4**
Motor learning average	**12.8**	**14.3**
Repetition score average	**18.6**	**20**
Deviations from Babcock's norms:		
For the total average	**−0.6**	**+1.4**
For learning	**−2.6**	**+1.4**
Motor	**−2.2**	**−1.7**
Repetition	**+4.9**	**+4.4**

(a) The difference in scores would indicate that M's general mental efficiency is rather weak, her learning abilities extremely poor, and the motor efficiency of both women extremely poor. The learning score of M appears to be, however, quite contradictory to her whole performance in the different tests.

(b) The handwriting of the two women does not appear to me to be significantly different. M's handwriting of the sentence in 19.3 seconds seems to be a slow calligraphic writing, extremely similar to that of L.

(c) The symbol digit test has five rows of symbols, and they were measured as to performance time separately. While L's speed improves in the course of the work, M's speed drops.

(d) The paired associate learning is very weak in both cases.

(e) The speed of tracing of M is better than that of L.

Section 7: Experimental Neuroses

INTRODUCTION

From the spontaneously occurring splits that are manifested in the dual personalities of the previous section, we now turn to the experimentally induced neuroses investigated in this section. The papers that follow represent some of the most complex experimental and clinical work Erickson has ever done. In spite of this incredible complexity, however, the basic questions that underlie these investigations are straightforward: Is it possible to use hypnosis to artificially structure a conflict, neurosis, or psychopathology? Is it possible to reconstruct or create an entire personality with hypnosis for therapeutic purposes?

The roots of this experimental research derive from the word-association test that was first developed by Wilhelm Wundt and Carl G. Jung in Europe many decades ago and the more recent work of the Russian neuropsychologist, Luria. Words that were associated with emotional complexes were found to result in verbal blocks, longer reaction times, and other psychomotor disturbances that could be measured. The experimental study with Huston and Shakow in 1934 was the first publication wherein Erickson described the use of hypnotically induced complexes. A careful reading of the previous four sections of this volume, particularly those on Mental Mechanisms and Dual Personality, suggests how the creation of an entire complex by hypnosis was the next logical development for Erickson. His technique was still relatively undeveloped for this first experimental study, however, and thus its results tended to be unreliable.

By the next year, 1935, these deficiencies of technique were remedied in his paper "A study of an experimental neurosis hypnotically induced in a case of ejaculatio praecox." It is not until almost ten years later in 1944, however, that Erickson actually published a detailed analysis and explication of the method he used in the 1935 paper. How does he account for this? Erickson explained to this editor that when he first published the verbatim transcript containing the actual words he used to induce the complex, he assumed that his professional readers would naturally understand the significance of his careful choice of words and suggestions. It wasn't until several years later that his discussions with Gregory Bateson, Margaret Mead, and Lewis Hill convinced him that he was thinking and doing a lot more than was apparent from a raw transcription of his words. Thus, he came to write the final paper in this section in which he, for the first time, gives a detailed, phrase-by-phrase analysis of his work. Erickson included many examples of vocal dynamics, the multiple meaning of words, and the patterns of associations used to formulate an experimental neurosis for therapeutic purposes. This hypnotically induced neurosis so closely paralleled the patient's actual neurosis that the hypnotic implant could serve as a kind of emotional lightning rod to discharge and cure the actual neurosis.

We see in these papers the origins and essence of two cornerstones of all Erickson's later hypnotherapeutic work: (1) the *utilization approach,* wherein he uses the patient's own associations and potentials to formulate (2) *indirect suggestions* for the evocation of the patient's abilities to effect his own therapy. The papers of the next volume (Volume Four: *Hypnotherapy: Innovative Approaches)* chronicle and illustrate Erickson's growing understanding and application of these two principles in a great variety of hypnotherapeutic approaches.

These endeavors find their ultimate expression in what Erickson calls the February Man approach. This approach was first described in Jay Haley's book about Erickson's work, *Uncommon Therapy* (1973), and is presented in greater detail in this editor's co-authored volume with Erickson, *Hypnotherapy: An Exploratory Casebook* (1979). Although Erickson is more modest about his accomplishments, this editor believes that through this approach Erickson finally lays the foundation for an effective hypnotherapy oriented toward nothing less than the entire reconstruction and creative redevelopment of a personality. These early papers from the 1930s provide some of the technical foundation for many of our current efforts to facilitate psychological growth and development.

26. A Clinical Note on a Word-Association Test

Milton H. Erickson

The usefulness of the word-association test in detecting the presence of concealed or repressed memories is well recognized. Usually, however, the results obtained are indicative only of possible avenues for exploration, and it is customary to resort to other techniques to obtain more information. In the following account an instance is reported wherein the word-association test served not only to indicate the presence of a repressed or concealed memory, but also, upon repeated administrations of the test, to elicit, in one-word summaries, the entire sequence of events in the unhappy memory. The situation leading to this finding was as follows:

Experimental work was being done on the constancy of responses to the words of an association test in which lapse of time and hypnosis were employed as variants. The procedure was essentially to give the subject a carefully selected list of words in the normal waking state and then the next day to repeat the test with the subject in a deep hynotic trance. Following this, at intervals of one to three days, the test was repeated in either the waking or the hypnotic state until it had been given seven times. One subject employed was a 25-year-old, single, white female. At the time of the first administration of the test, it was noted that the subject showed a very long reaction time to the stimulus word *stomach* and had shifted her position uneasily. It was thought immediately that this behavior indicated possibly a repressed complex, but before the test could be continued, the subject spontaneously explained that at the previous meal she had overeaten and still felt her stomach to be uncomfortably distended. No additional significance was attached to this matter, although it was noted that on subsequent administrations of the test she still showed a long reaction time and tended to shift her position uneasily. This continuance of her original behavior was considered to be possibly nothing more than a conditioning occasioned by the original setting, especially since the subject gave only casual explanations for her replies when questioned later and always listened to the word *stomach* with an amused smile. Unfortunately, no record was made of her rationalizations at the time, since no apparently unusual explanations were given.

Several months after the completion of the test, but before the data had

Reprinted with permission from *The Journal of Nervous and Mental Disease,* Nov., 1936, Vol. 84, No. 5.

been analyzed, this subject made a confidant of the author, explaining that several years previously she had had a love affair which had resulted in a pregnancy. As she related this story, she declared that her first intimation of this pregnancy had been "the enlargement of my abdomen" since her menstrual cycle was most irregular. This "worried me just terribly," and upon seeking medical aid she had been advised that she "was going to have a baby." This "made me awfully afraid," and she had decided to meet the situation "by having an operation done. I was awfully sick afterward—I thought I was going to die. When I finally got well, I just forgot about it all, but during the last couple of weeks it's come back to me and I felt like talking about it to you." She could give no explanation of why she had revived that memory, nor was there any thought at the time that there could be any possible relationship between this story and her responses on the word-association test. Further, the subject had never had an opportunity to read her responses on the tests.

Subsequently, in analyzing the data obtained from the experimental procedure, the sequence of responses to the word *stomach* and the states in which they were obtained were found to be as follows:

Response Word	*Mental State*	*Reaction Time in Seconds*	*Day*
(1) Big	**Hypnotic**	**6**	**Mon.**
(2) Worried	**Waking**	**5**	**Tues.**
(3) Baby	**Hypnotic**	**4**	**Fri.**
(4) Afraid	**Waking**	**6**	**Sat.**
(5) Operation	**Waking**	**6**	**Tues.**
(6) Sick	**Hypnotic**	**4**	**Wed.**
(7) Forgotten	**Waking**	**3**	**Sat.**

The paralleling of the response words and the actual story is at once obvious. Consideration of the response words alone requires no imagination to construct the entire story. Almost identical terms were used in both instances and in the same sequence, despite the lapse of time intervening between the experimental and the personal situations and the absence of any conscious realization that there existed any relationship between the two situations. This verbal rigidity is suggestive of the emotional intensity of the problem and the need of adhering to a definite method of approach to it.

More remarkable, however, is the peculiar persistence manifested in the disclosure of the complex material during the experimental situation. The induction of a deep hypnotic trance was apparently without any effect upon her unconscious emotional problem. Neither did the intervention of nonexperimental days seem to modify the emotional needs aroused by the fortunate coincidence which occurred during the first test. One may conjecture that the initial setting of a gastric indiscretion resulting in abdominal distress and distension constituted a most favorable background for the revival of the originally repressed material. The nature of that setting permitted easy rationalization, thereby obviating any need for defense or disguise mechanisms. Thus, a train of associations was stimulated into action and was conditioned to a certain limited method of expression. In consequence, it manifested itself progressively at each properly offered opportunity. Evidently, to judge from the course of development of the personal situation, the strength of the emotions involved exercised a compelling force upon the subject, causing her to seek relief from her problem by confiding it to someone. She had done this in the experimental situation, but in such a fashion that only partial emotional satisfaction had been obtained. This relief had sufficed for a time, but finally, because of its inadequacy, the problem became acute, causing her to recall it consciously and to seek a more complete catharsis by confiding it again in a direct fashion to the same person.

27. A Study of Hypnotically Induced Complexes By Means of the Luria Technique

Paul E. Huston, David Shakow, and Milton H. Erickson[1]

INTRODUCTION

Recently Luria (Lebedinski & Luria, 1929; Luria, 1929, 1930, 1932) has experimented with a technique which may be applied to the investigation of affective conflicts. This method[2] involves the association of higher central nervous system processes with a voluntary movement so that conflicts in the former are disclosed in the latter. Experimentally the central processes are activated by the verbal stimuli of an association test, the subject being instructed to make a slight pressure with his preferred hand on a tambour simultaneously with every verbal response. If the verbal stimuli do not arouse affective conflicts, the voluntary pressures are regular in character, but if a conflict is aroused, the pressure curves become irregular. Luria explains this effect as follows: Having trained a subject to associate a motor response of the preferred hand with every verbal response, thereby establishing a close functional relationship between them,[3] any word occurring to the subject which he does not give as a response will appear in the voluntary movement as a partial reaction. It is assumed here that the inhibition of the verbal response is associated with affect, i.e., the subject does not respond with the first word since some complex would be revealed. Also the pressure curve may lose its

---

Reprinted with permission from *The Journal of General Psychology,* 1934, Vol. 11, pp. 65-97.

[1]The division of labor in this study was as follows: the problem was set and the data analyzed by the first two authors (psychologists); the hypnotic work and organization of the complexes was done by the third author (a psychiatrist); and the experimental work was performed by the first author.

[2]In general we shall adhere to Luria's terminology in this paper.

[3]Luria argues that previous work on affection and emotion has yielded disappointing results because there was no intimate relationship between the affect and such physiological expressions as blood pressure, heart rate, respiration, etc. According to Luria the expressiveness of any motor system will depend upon its degree of inclusion in the psychological structure where the conflict is located, hence the preferred hand is selected to make the voluntary pressures because of the close relationship between the speech centers and the neural control of the preferred hand.

smooth regular character or, to follow the Luria terminology more closely, the normal, voluntary movement is discoordinated or disorganized because stimuli which elicit responses possessing affect may also arouse larger amounts of excitation than stimuli eliciting nonaffective responses. This excitation tends to discharge itself immediately via the voluntary motor pathway. Luria has referred to this tendency as the "law of the catalytic action of the stimulus." This law appears to be a corollary of another, the "law of the decreased action of the funtional barrier." The functional barrier is a cortical property. It regulates by inhibition the motor activities of the organism, giving them an integrated character. Affective excitation weakens the functional barrier, and hence the motor activities become disorganized. A third law is that of the "mobilization of inadequate masses of excitation." This seems to involve "neurodynamical perseveration." The excitation which accompanies the affect is not always discharged completely via the verbal response, hence some movements will persist in the preferred hand after the voluntary response. Under conditions of large amounts of excitation a further spread to other motor systems may occur—for example, disturbing respiration and/or causing involuntary movements of the non-preferred hand.[4]

It is not our purpose to review the numerous experiments reported by Luria upon which these so-called laws are based. We were interested primarily in the possibilities of the Luria technique for obtaining information about the affective conflicts of a subject and for its possible application to psychotic patients. For this purpose we repeated, as part of an exploratory procedure, one of his important experiments, that of the attempted induction of a conflict in a subject by means of hypnosis. Such a procedure affords the opportunity of examining a subject before, during, and after the establishment of a conflict.

To produce a conflict in a subject Luria fabricated a story of a reproachable act committed by the subject—an act which would be contrary to the subject's usual personality trends. A number of critical words were taken from this story and placed in a list of control words which were not specific to the story. The total list was presented in the setting of a free discrete association procedure. The subject was required to press with his preferred hand on a tambour with each verbal response. He was then hypnotized, and the story recounted to him. After this he was awakened and the combined word-association and motor-response method was repeated. Under hypnosis the conflict was removed. This was

[4]This exposition is our attempt to state the Luria theory succinctly. Other attempts may be found in recent reviews of Luria's latest publication (1930): Brown, J. F., *Psychol. Bull,* 1933, *30,* 376-381; Kubie, L. S., *Psychoanal. Quar.* 1933, *2,* 330-336; Geldard, F. A., J. *J. Gen. Psychol.* 1933, *9,* 485-487; Taylor, W. S., *J. Abn. & Soc. Psychol.,* 1934 (to be published).

followed by a waking control session. If the theory and technique are valid, the critical words should show discoordinated voluntary pressure curves as compared with those of the control words. This assumes, of course, that the suggested story was accepted by the subject, that a conflict was produced in him, and that it had been removed successfully. In addition to the voluntary pressure curves Luria recorded verbal reaction times and in some cases involuntary movements from the nonpreferred hand and respiration. All were recorded on an ordinary kymograph.

APPARATUS, TECHNIQUE, AND POPULATION

This was the experiment[5] which we repeated with some modifications. Luria's list usually contained 20 to 30 words with six to nine "critical" words. We used 100 words, including 10 taken from the fictitious story, to avoid, if possible, perseveration effects and to give more control material. Furthermore, the "critical" words were separated by seven to ten control words, whereas Luria often placed two or three "critical" words together. In addition, hypnotic control experiments were introduced, and in some cases the control and the "complex" sessions were repeated to study the effects of hypnosis and of repetition per se. By way of definition, the term *complex* is used as referring to the story of a reproachable act committed by the subject intended to produce an affective disturbance or conflict in him.

Four male and eight female subjects between the ages of 20 to 30 years were used. This group consisted of four medical interns, two graduate students in psychology, two nurses, two occupational therapists, and two college graduates doing special work about the hospital. All were well-trained hypnotic subjects and fairly well known to us. None of them had any knowledge of the Luria theory or technique. We shall present in detail the complex, the experimental procedure, and the results on one subject. The results obtained on the other subjects will then be summarized.

DETAILED REPORT ON ONE SUBJECT

The complex for the sample subject, a male aged 24, was narrated as an account of his personal experience, and an attempt was made to establish it as a falsification of memory. The story in summary form was as follows: One night, while visiting some friends, he met a girl to whom he was much

[5]The work was done during the years 1930 to 1932.

attracted. During the conversation, attention was called to her new brown silk dress, and she explained that, although not able to afford it, she had bought the dress hoping to make a good appearance when applying for employment. He gave her a cigarette and lighted one also. While smoking, he noticed the smell of burning cloth occasioned by contact of his cigarette with the girl's dress. Unobtrusively he withdrew his hand, noting with relief that the girl had not yet noticed the accident and that she held her own cigarette above the burned hole. The girl soon became aware of the damage. She attributed it, however, to a spark from her own cigarette. He tried to take the blame by assuming the responsibility of having given her the cigarette, but the girl refused his apparent generosity. The next day, by which time he had summoned up enough courage to tell her the truth in order to save his self-respect, he found that she had left the city.

From this account ten words: *silk, dress, brown, cigarette, burned, hole, blame, damage, smell, self-respect,* were selected as "critical" words and placed as Nos. 7, 16, 28, 40, 49, 60, 68, 77, 88, and 98 in the list of words[6] (see Table 1).

In the experimental room the subject reclined on a chaise lounge and rested his fingertips on deep, large tambours, one on each side, the forearms being supported by the wide arms of the chaise longue.[7] He was instructed to respond to the verbal stimuli of the association test with the first word which came to him and simultaneously with his response to make a downward pressure on the tambour with his preferred hand. Voluntary responses of the preferred hand and such involuntary movements of the nonpreferred hand as might occur, as well as thoracic respiration and verbal reaction time, were recorded on a special long-paper kymograph. The experimenter, seated out of the subject's view, gave the verbal stimuli, wrote down the verbal responses, and marked the verbal reaction time with a telegraph key. A practice series of 20 words, none of which appeared in the experimental list, was first administered in

[6]The 90 other words consisted of 66 from the Kent-Rosanoff Association Test (1), which give high frequencies of "most common" responses and which might be considered as neutral in character, i.e., generally without emotional tone; five we believed significant for schizophrenic patients—words 10, 31, 46, 65, and 85; five significant for psychotics in general—words 6, 13, 34, 58, and 71; and five words which are often of affective value for normal individuals—words 19, 37, 55, 74, and 91. (Words 37 and 91 appear also in the Kent-Rosanoff list.) The remaining eleven words are "double-barreled," that is, they may easily be taken in more than one sense. These were Nos. 2, 4, 22, 43, 62, 63, 80, 90, 93, 95, and 100. (Words 25, 75, and 82 among the Kent-Rosanoff group may also be considered as "double-barreled.") Since our ultimate purpose was the application of the procedure to psychotic patients, we introduced the affective and "double-barreled" words, planning to use the responses from the normal subjects as control material.

[7]Our tambour system, while not quite like that of Luria, is not different in its essential requirements.

order to establish the association of verbal response with simultaneous voluntary movement of the preferred hand. The list of 100 words was then given in a *waking control session.* After this the subject was hypnotized and the procedure repeated. This was the *hypnotic control session.* At the next experimental period—usually the following day—the subject was hypnotized first, the complex story told to him, and the experiment performed during hypnosis. This constituted a *hypnotic complex session.* The subject was then awakened from the trance, and a *waking complex session* was held. After this the subject was rehypnotized and an attempt made to remove the conflict by giving him insight into the situation and permitting him to understand the falsity of the story. At a third period additional *hypnotic* and *waking control sessions* were held.

In this particular case two hypnotic controls instead of one were obtained after the complex was removed.[8,9] Also the complex was not removed in this subject for 24 hours. That night he slept poorly, awakened with a headache which persisted until the removal of the complex in the afternoon, had no appetite, was resentful and antagonistic toward the hypnotist, and somewhat uncooperative toward additional hypnosis. He was unable to assign any reason for these manifestations. Throughout the day he gave away his cigarettes and apparently could not enjoy smoking. He rationalized his behavior by the statement that he "guessed" he was giving up the habit. We offer this as evidence that the attempt to induce the conflict produced a profound reaction in the subject.

The results have been analyzed within each session and from session to session. Various aspects of change in the verbal, voluntary, involuntary, and respiratory responses, in reaction time and certain other aspects of

[8] All the hypnotic work was done by the psychiatrist. Hypnotic rapport with the subject for experimental procedures was transferred to the experimenter, the same instructions being used on all subjects. The psychiatrist kept all subjects under observation for at least a month to note any possible residual effects of the experiment. (None were observed.) Close supervision was particularly maintained in those cases in which the subject was allowed to keep the complex overnight. All trances were of a profound somnabulistic type, characterized by dissociation and, with one exception which will be discussed later, apparently by total amnesia for trance events. Administration of the complex was achieved by two sets of instructions identical for all subjects. These were planned to prepare them to "recall" the complex as an actual memory and to strengthen their acceptance of this "memory" and their emotional reaction to it. Removal of the complex was accomplished by the hypnotist's reviewing the preliminary instructions, the story, and the final instructions, indicating the falsity of the whole account and allowing the subject to verify in his own mind the unreality of the entire complex story. This was—had to be—done in both the trance and waking states.

[9] Each session took about 15 minutes. The stimulus words were given as rapidly as the experimenter could write down the verbal responses, except when a disturbance appeared. In the latter case the disturbance was allowed to subside before the next stimulus was given.

behavior such as bodily movement, laughing, sighing, etc., were considered for different word classes. The word classes were the following:

1. *Complex* words—the 10 words taken from the story told to the subject.

2. *Complex-Associated—First Type.* These were words which the subject himself apparently connected in some way with the story, as indicated by the verbal responses. For example, in the subject under discussion, the stimulus word *Smooth* (No. 18) elicited the response "rough" in the control sessions and in the waking complex session, but in the hypnotic complex session the response was "silk." To qualify for classification as a Complex-Associated—First Type word the response had to appear to all three of the authors as definitely related to the complex situation, to be one of the words actually used in the complex story, and not to have appeared in any control session prior to the induction of the complex. This criterion for selecting Complex-Associated—First Type words we consider as being conservative and as likely to result in the omission of some items since the same response in control and complex sessions may have a different meaning for the subject. This point will be discussed later.

3. *Natural Complex* words. These were chosen on the basis of our knowledge of the person and from what he reported when the list was reviewed with him after the conclusion of the experiment. In this particular person they were words which presumably would usually arouse some affect outside of the experimental situation. The stimulus word *fall* (No. 90) was such a one. The subject two years previously had been in an airplane accident in which he had broken an ankle.

4. Reference to Table 1 shows that the same word (No. 90) elicited a response in the first control session which might be connected with such a natural complex, but after the complex induction the responses changed to "light" and "spark," which fact led us to believe that this stimulus word also became related to the complex. Because there were a number of such words which changed in class from one session to another, an additional class was formed, called *Natural Complex + Complex-Associated* words.

5. A *Complex-Associated—Second Type* classification was made on the basis of disturbed nonverbal responses which might be related to the complex story in an indirect way. We made the assumption here that the technique used *did* reveal the presence of affect and attempted to see if we could establish some association with the complex story. Sometimes the subject could explain why he responded with the particular word. In either case the stimulus was put into the second type of *Complex-Associated* words. Such information was obtained from the subject after the experiment was finished and the procedure had been explained to

him. This was done by examining with him each of the verbal responses.[10] Obviously there re many more possible sources of error in this classification than in the others, and the results therefore must be scrutinized with great care.

6. All the remaining words were called *Neutral.* Our knowledge of each subject's life was not adequate, and the Natural Complex class probably suffers mostly on the side of omission. It is also likely that among the Neutral words are some which should have been classed Natural Complex and Complex-Associated.[11]

Each of these word classes was first analyzed for the number of "disturbances" in the verbal and nonverbal material from session to session. By a "disturbance" in the verbal response is meant any significant word from the complex story which first appears in a complex session, e.g., to the *C* word *brown* (No. 28) the subject's responses for the first control sessions are "eyes" and "color," whereas in the complex sessions the responses are "burn" and "silk"; after the removal of the complex the responses are "white," "color," and "white." Here the responses "burn" and "silk" are rated as verbal disturbances. Because of the criteria set, it is likely that some verbal disturbances may have been omitted, e.g., the response "clothes" to *dress* (No. 16) in Session IV. Since "clothes" appeared in the second control, we did not count the same response in this session as a verbal disturbance. It may have been specific to the complex here and have had an entirely different significance for the subject. In the voluntary, involuntary, and respiratory responses any fairly definite

[10]This was done some time after the conclusion of the experiments. In the present case there were six "Complex-Associated" words of the second type. The stimulus word *dark* (No. 9) elicited the response "room" in the hypnotic complex session. This was so classified because the subject informed us that he had placed the complex situation in a poorly lighted room to make the action more plausible. The response "beautiful" to *Fairy* (No. 63) was thought by us to have come about through "girl"—i.e., Fairy ➧ girl ➧ beautiful. (The attractiveness of the girl had been emphasized in the complex story.) *Guilty* (No. 58) yielded two unusual reactions in the complex sessions, "self-conscious," and "no." These responses might be related to the emphasis on the loss of self-respect in the complex. *Persecute* (No. 71) as stimulus, with the unusual response "me," may fall into the same context. The subject reported that the response "necklace" to *neck* (No. 80) resulted from his visualizing the girl in the story as wearing a necklace. The responses "stores" and "display" to the stimulus *street* (No. 96) may have been connected with window displays of new dresses, since the fact that the girl was wearing a new dress was stressed in the story.

[11]Hereafter we shall refer to the word classes by the following symbols:

C—Complex
CA_1—Complex-Associated—First Type
CA_2—Complex-Associated—Second Type
NC—Natural Complex
$CA_1 + NC$—Complex-Associated—First Type + Natural Complex
N—Neutral

deviation from the normal was counted as a disturbance, after agreement by two of the authors working independently and then combining judgments. If there was disagreement as to the presence of disturbances, the nonverbal response was considered as not disturbed. In the voluntary responses irregularities in the baseline after the stimulus word was given, or in the pressure response, or after the stylus had returned to the baseline but before the next stimulus word was given, were recorded as voluntary disturbances. Figure 1 gives examples of these. Involuntary changes in the nonpreferred hand consisted of either an increase in tremor amplitude or shifts in the baseline. Respiratory changes were those which involved sudden inspirations or expirations or increased depth or rate of breathing. The respiration curve was complicated by the chest movements which accompanied the verbal response, hence these had to be considered when rating respiratory disturbances. A verbal reaction time was considered as disturbed only if it was extremely long.[12,13]

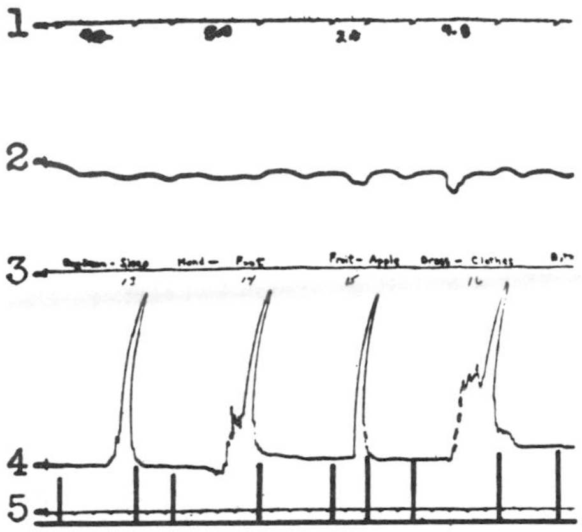

Figure 1. This figure is from the waking complex Session IV of the sample subject (No. 1). (1) Verbal reaction time. (2) Respiration. (3) Left-hand, involuntary. (4) Right-hand, voluntary. (5) Time in seconds. The voluntary pressures on words Nos. 14 and 16 are disturbed. The respiration line does not show characteristic breathing since the pneumograph was not drawn as tightly about the chest as was the usual practice. The loose adjustment was made in this subject because such large inspirations generally accompanied his respiratory disturbances that the stylus of the recording tambour moved off the kymograph.

[12] An attempt was made to determine which reaction times might be considered disturbed. This was first done by distributing the reaction times of every session of each subject and computing the S.D. However, because of the illegitimacy of such computations on a heterogeneous population and because of the skewed distributions which we obtained in many cases—1.5 times the S.D., which we set as our criterion, fell outside the limits of the distribution—this attempt was given up. We finally took those reaction times which seemed to stand apart from the rest of the

Stimulus	Class	Session No. I Waking Control 3-8-32 3:45 P.M. Responses	Disturbances: Verbal	Voluntary	Involuntary	Respiration	Delayed R.T.	Individual Reaction Times	Total	Session No. II Hypnotic Control 3-8-32 4:05 P.M. Responses	Disturbances: Verbal	Voluntary	Involuntary	Respiration	Delayed R.T.	Individual Reaction Times	Total	Session No. III Hypnotic Complex 3-8-32 4:30 P.M. Responses	Disturbances: Verbal	Voluntary	Involuntary	Respiration	Delayed R.T.	Individual Reaction Times	Total
1. Table	N	1. chair						1.4		1. chair						1.5		1. chair						1.5	
2. Box	N	2. wood						1.5		2. square				•		2.7	1	2. square						2.6	
3. Music	N	3. sheet						1.9		3. sheet						1.8		3. piano						2.8	
4. Ball	N	4. bat						2.1		4. bat						1.8		4. bat						2.0	
5. Man	N	5. woman						2.0		5. woman						1.6		5. woman						2.9	
6. Queer	N	6. funny						2.6		6. funny						2.0		6. extraordinary						3.0	
7. Silk	C	7. wool						1.9		7. wool						1.9		7. dress	•					2.0	1
8. Eating	N	8. food						2.2		8. food						1.7		8. table						2.6	
9. Dark	CA_2	9. light						1.9		9. light						1.8		9. room		•				2.8	1
10. Important	N	10. necessary						2.2		10. pertinent				•	•	2.2	2	10. pertinent						3.3	
11. Black	N	11. white						1.5		11. white						1.8		11. white						2.8	
12. Soft	CA_1	12. hard						1.8		12. hard						2.0		12. hand	•					2.3	1
13. Day-dream	NC	13. dream						3.5		13. stupor						3.4		13. sleep						2.9	
14. Hand	CA_1	14. foot						1.9		14. foot						1.8		14. girl	•					2.3	1
15. Fruit	N	15. apple						1.9		15. apple						2.5		15. apple						2.3	
16. Dress	C	16. undress						2.5		16. clothes						2.2		16. burn	•					2.8	1
17. Butterfly	NC	17. insect						1.9		17. insect						1.9		17. insect						2.9	
18. Smooth	CA_1	18. rough						1.6		18. rough						2.1		18. silk	•					2.5	1
19. Kiss	NC	19. osculate		•				4.9	1	19. osculate						3.9		19. pretty						3.8	
20. Chair	N	20. table						1.8		20. table						2.0		20. table						2.3	
21. Sweet	CA_1	21. sour						1.4		21. taste						2.9		21. girl	•					3.0	1
22. Push	N	22. pull						2.0		22. pull						1.9		22. pull						2.2	
23. Woman	CA_1+NC	23. man						1.7		23. female						2.5		23. dress	•					4.2	1
24. Comfort	N	24. sleep						2.3		24. bed						2.2		24. bed						2.9	
25. Yellow	N	25. blue						1.8		25. color						1.9		25. color						3.6	
26. Wish	N	26. hope						2.0		26. hope						1.8		26. hope						3.5	
27. River	N	27. deep						2.4		27. outlet		•				3.4	1	27. water						2.8	
28. Brown	C	28. eyes						2.5		28. color						1.6		28. burn	•					3.3	1
29. Beautiful	CA_1	29. nature						2.2		29. mother						2.9		29. pretty	•					3.5	1
30. Window	N	30. house						2.3		30. light						3.1		30. room						2.7	
31. Electricity	N	31. motor						2.7		31. generator						3.1		31. light						2.2	
32. Citizen	NC	32. city		•		•		4.2	2	32. population						3.7		32. man						2.5	
33. Foot	N	33. hand						1.8		33. hand						1.9		33. shoe						2.4	
34. Voices	N	34. hallucina.						3.1		34. chords						3,0		34. hallucination						3.2	
35. Needle	N	35. thread						1.8		35. thread						2.6		35. thread						3.2	
36. Short	N	36. long						1.5		36. long						2.1		36. long		•				3.0	1
37. Stomach	N	37. food						2.6		37. intestines						2.4		37. food		•				3.2	1
38. Whistle	N	38. blow						1.9		38. noise						2.9		38. sigh						2.8	
39. Slow	N	39. fast						1.7		39. swift						2.3		39. swift						2.1	
40. Cigarette	C	40. smoke						1.7		40. tobacco						2.5		40. burn	•					2.7	1
41. High	NC	41. low						1.6		41. skyscraper				•	•	4.0	2	41. low						2.9	
42. Working	N	42. writing				•		3.3	1	42. labor						2.1		42. thinking						3.5	
43. Monkey	N	43. tail				•	•	5.8	2	43. animal						2.6		43. animal						2.6	
44. White	CA_1	44. black						4.3		44. color						2.1		44. black						2.9	
45. Rough	CA_1	45. smooth						1.8		45. smooth						1.7		45. hole	•	•				4.4	2
46. Mission	N	46. errand						4.6		46. errand						3.2		46. errand						3.8	
47. Cabbage	N	47. turnips		•				3.9	1	47. vegetable						2.5		47. vegetable						3.3	
48. Hard.	CA_1	48. soft						2.0		48. soft						1.8		48. regret	•	•		•	•	5.1	4
49. Burned	C	49. black						3.9		49. chemistry				•	•	3.7	2	49. dress	•					2.6	1
50. Sleep	N	50. dream						2.0		50. dream						2.3		50. slumber						3.5	
51. Deep	N	51. river						2.5		51. river						2.2		51. river						3.7	
52. Girl	CA_1+NC	52. boy					•	5.5	1	52. female						3.0		52. dress	•					3.5	1
53. Sour	N	53. sweet					•	5.1	1	53. acid						4.2		53. sweet						3.0	
54. Soldier	N	54. war						1.9		54. fight		•				2.8	1	54. brave						3.5	
55. Marriage	NC	55. house		•		•		4.6	2	55. woman						3.0		55. life						4.4	
56. Eagle	N	56. bird						4.3		56. bird						2.1		56. bird						2.5	
57. Boy	N	57. girl						1.9		57. child						2.8		57. girl						2.2	
58. Guilty	CA_2	58. insect						2.4		58. crime					•	4.2	1	58. self-conse.						2.9	
59. Health	N	59. doctor						2.2		59. doctor						3.1		59. sanitarium		•				3.7	1
60. Hole	C	60. well					•	6.7	1	60. well						3.3		60. burn	•					2.2	1
61. Memory	CA_1	61. thought						2.4		61. brain						2.5		61. dread	•					3.2	1
62. Pool	N	62. swim						3.9		62. water						2.7		62. swim						2.8	
63. Fairy	CA_2	63. unreal						4.1		63. book						3.2		63. beautiful						3.5	
64. Cottage	N	64. yard						2.7		64. shelter						3.0		64. house						3.0	
65. Concentrate	N	65. think						2.0		65. think						3.5		65. meditate		•			•	4.2	2
66. Lamp	CA_1	66. light						1.9		66. light						3.2		66. burn	•					2.7	1
67. Hungry	N	67. food						2.0		67. stomach		•				3.3	1	67. sick						3.2	
68. Blame	C	68. accuse				•		4.1	1	68. accuse						2.1		68. me	•					2.6	1
69. Ocean	N	69. sea						3.0		69. sea						1.9		69. deep						3.1	
70. Light	N	70. dark						2.6		70. dark						2.7		70. lamp						3.6	
71. Persecute	CA_2	71. elec.chair		•			•	5.5	2	71. punish						3.9		71. me						3.5	
72. Long	N	72. short						1.6		72. short						1.8		72. short						2.8	
73. Swift	N	73. slow						1.8		73. slow						2.4		73. quick						2.8	
74. Sex	CA_1	74. male		•				3.8	1	74. male & fem.						2.9		74. girl	•					2.8	1
75. Square	N	75. round						1.6		75. round						2.2		75. round						2.8	
76. Bitter	CA_1	76. sweet						1.7		76. taste						2.4		76. taste						3.1	
77. Damage	C	77. ruin						2.2		77. ruin						2.9		77. ruin						2.0	
78. Hammer	N	78. nail						1.4		78. nail						1.7		78. nail						2.7	
79. City	N	79. street						2.0		79. street						1.9		79. street						2.9	
80. Neck	CA_2	80. ear						3.3		80. hurt						2.8		80. necklace						3.1	
81. Butter	N	81. bread						2.1		81. milk						2.7		81. milk						2.5	
82. Blue	N	82. sky				•		1.7	1	82. color						1.8		82. sky						2.6	
83. Heavy	N	83. light						2.4		83. light						2.2		83. light						2.5	
84. Salt	N	84. sugar		•				1.9	1	84. table						2.8		84. table						3.1	
85. Unworthy	CA_1	85. worthless						3.2		85. useless						3.1		85. self-respect	•	•			•	5.0	3
86. Joy	CA_1	86. sorrow						2.2		86. sorrow		•				3.0	1	86. sorrow						3.2	
87. Bed	N	87. sleep						2.3		87. sleep						2.4		87. sleep						2.5	
88. Smell	C	88. taste						2.0		88. olfactory						3.7		88. burn	•					2.8	1
89. Tobacco	CA_1	89. smoke						1.8		89. leaves						2.9		89. damn	•					2.0	1
90. Fall	CA_1+NC	90. hurt				•		3.3	1	90. drop						2.8		90. light	•					3.0	1
91. Religion	NC	91. Bible		•				2.1	1	91. belief						2.7		91. belief						2.9	
92. Scissors	N	92. cut						2.1		92. cut						2.8		92. cut						4.1	
93. Fine	N	93. coarse						1.9		93. find		•				3.5	1	93. coarse		•				3.3	1
94. Bath	N	94. soap						2.6		94. soap						2.2		94. soap						2.8	
95. Pull	N	95. push						1.7		95. lift						2.6		95. push						2.7	
96. Street	CA_2	96. city						2.0		96. city						2.7		96. stores		•				3.8	1
97. King.	N	97. queen						2.3		97. kingdom						3.3		97. queen						2.3	
98. Self-resp.	C	98. ideal				•		4.4	1	98. ideal						4.2		98. no good	•					2.6	1
99. Cheese	N	99. butter						2.6		99. butter						3.3		99. butter						2.2	
100. Grass	N	100. awkward						2.2		100. thank					•	4.1	1	100. thanks						3.4	
								Mean								Av.								Av.	
C (10 words)			0	0	0	2	1	[illegible]	3		0	0	0	1	1	[illegible]	2		0	0	0	0	0	2.6	[illegible]
CA_1 (15 words)			0	1	0	0	0	[illegible]	1		0	1	0	0	0	[illegible]	1		[illegible]	[illegible]	0	1	2	3.2	[illegible]
CA_2 (6 words)			0	1	0	[illegible]	[illegible]	[illegible]	[illegible]		0	0	0	0	[illegible]	[illegible]	[illegible]		0	2	0	0	0	[illegible]	2
NC (7 words)			0	4	0	2	0	[illegible]	[illegible]		0	0	0	[illegible]	[illegible]	[illegible]	[illegible]		0	0	0	0	0	[illegible]	0
CA_1+NC (3 words)			0	[illegible]	0	[illegible]	[illegible]	[illegible]	[illegible]		0	0	0	[illegible]	0	[illegible]	[illegible]		[illegible]	0	0	0	0	[illegible]	[illegible]
N ([illegible] words)			0	[illegible]	0	[illegible]	[illegible]	[illegible]	[illegible]		0	4	0	[illegible]	[illegible]	[illegible]	[illegible]		0	[illegible]	0	0	1	[illegible]	[illegible]
Totals (100)			0	[illegible]	0	[illegible]	[illegible]	2.6	[illegible]		0	[illegible]	0	[illegible]	[illegible]	2.7	14		[illegible]	[illegible]	[illegible]	[illegible]	[illegible]	3.0	[illegible]
								SD 1.1								SD .78								SD .64	

TABLE 1

Session No. IV — Waking — Complex — 3-9-38 — 4:30 P.M.

Response	Verbal	Voluntary	Involuntary	Respiration	Delayed R.T.	Individual Reaction Time	Total
1. chair						1.7	
2. square						2.2	
3. radio						2.3	
4. hat						1.8	
5. woman						2.0	
6. peculiar						2.7	
7. fibre						4.7	
8. food						3.1	
9. light						3.9	
10. report		•				5.2	1
11. white						1.4	
12. hard						3.2	
13. sleep						4.2	
14. foot		•				5.0	1
15. apple						2.0	
16. clothes		•				4.5	1
17. wings		•				5.2	1
18. rough		•				4.8	1
19. hug						5.0	
20. table						2.4	
21. sour						2.5	
22. pull						2.4	
23. girl	•	•				4.8	2
24. sleep				•		4.0	1
25. color						2.8	
26. hope						3.2	
27. water						2.8	
28. silk	•	•				5.2	2
29. girl						2.8	
30. room						3.2	
31. light						3.2	
32. city						4.2	
33. hand						2.5	
34. vibration				•		4.3	1
35. thread						1.7	
36. long						2.5	
37. food						3.6	
38. blew						2.7	
39. swift						3.8	
40. package		•			•	6.1	2
41. low						2.8	
42. labor						3.3	
43. animal						2.3	
44. brown	•		•			3.4	2
45. smooth						2.9	
46. duty				•		4.4	1
47. head						2.5	
48. soft						1.8	
49. combustion		•			•	6.8	2
50. dream						2.4	
51. river						2.0	
52. boy		•	•		•	5.9	3
53. taste			•			4.1	1
54. courage						4.0	
55. intercourse						2.2	
56. bird						2.2	
57. girl						2.3	
58. no		•			•	7.3	2
59. sick						2.1	
60. push						2.1	
61. distasteful	•					5.0	
62. water						2.5	
63. light			•			4.8	1
64. small			•			2.2	
65. forget						2.8	
66. burn	•					2.5	1
67. food				•		5.0	1
68. me	•	•	•		•	6.4	4
69. blue						3.2	
70. electricity						2.9	
71. punishment						4.0	
72. short						1.7	
73. fast		•				2.9	1
74. girl	•					2.4	1
75. round		•		•		5.2	2
76. memory	•	•	•			3.9	3
77. burn	•					2.4	1
78. nail		•				1.9	1
79. street						2.4	
80. head		•		•	•	6.1	3
81. bread						2.8	
82. sky						1.5	
83. light						2.5	
84. table						2.4	
85. dishonorable	•			•		4.5	2
86. regret	•					3.3	1
87. sleep						2.1	
88. burn	•					3.8	1
89. cigarette		•	•	•		4.7	3
90. spark	•					2.5	1
91. belief						2.7	
92. cut			•			3.2	1
93. coarse		•				4.9	1
94. soap						2.9	
95. push						2.1	
96. display				•		2.0	1
97. kingdom						2.2	
98. dishonorable	•		•			2.8	2
99. butter			•			2.2	1
100. thanks			•			3.7	1
						Av.	
	[illegible]	[illegible]	[illegible]	[illegible]	[illegible]	[illegible]	[illegible]
	[illegible]	[illegible]	[illegible]	[illegible]	[illegible]	[illegible]	[illegible]
	[illegible]	[illegible]	[illegible]	[illegible]	[illegible]	[illegible]	7
	[illegible]	[illegible]	[illegible]	[illegible]	[illegible]	[illegible]	[illegible]
	[illegible]	[illegible]	[illegible]	[illegible]	[illegible]	[illegible]	6
	[illegible]	[illegible]	[illegible]	[illegible]	[illegible]	[illegible]	[illegible]
	[illegible]	[illegible]	[illegible]	[illegible]	[illegible]	[illegible]	[illegible]
						SD [illegible]	

Session No. V — Waking — Control — 3-10-38 — 3:30 P.M.

Response	Verbal	Voluntary	Involuntary	Respiration	Delayed R.T.	Individual Reaction Time	Total
1. chair						1.6	
2. cube						2.1	
3. piano						2.0	
4. hat						1.5	
5. woman						1.5	
6. peculiar						1.6	
7. fine						2.0	
8. chewing						2.6	
9. light						1.5	
10. pertinent						2.1	
11. white						1.6	
12. hard						2.2	
13. sleep						2.3	
14. foot						1.5	
15. apple						1.8	
16. clothes						2.0	
17. insect						1.7	
18. rough						1.7	
19. hug		•		•		3.1	2
20. table						1.5	
21. sour						1.6	
22. pull						1.9	
23. man						1.8	
24. ease						1.8	
25. color						2.3	
26. hope						2.0	
27. deep		•		•		2.7	2
28. white						1.7	
29. nature		•				3.9	1
30. light						1.9	
31. generator						2.1	
32. people						2.4	
33. hand						2.0	
34. chords						2.9	
35. thread						1.8	
36. long						1.7	
37. intestines		•				2.7	1
38. blow						1.7	
39. fast						1.4	
40. smoke						1.7	
41. low						1.4	
42. labor						2.0	
43. animal						1.5	
44. black						1.6	
45. smooth						1.3	
46. errand						2.0	
47. vegetable						2.2	
48. soft						1.4	
49. combustion						2.7	
50. dream						2.1	
51. river						1.9	
52. boy						2.4	
53. sweet						1.8	
54. brave						1.8	
55. home						2.0	
56. bird						1.7	
57. girl						1.6	
58. innocent						2.0	
59. sanitarium						2.2	
60. part					•	5.6	1
61. brain						2.4	
62. water						1.9	
63. book						2.1	
64. house		•				2.5	1
65. think						2.0	
66. burn	•					2.1	1
67. food						1.9	
68. accuse					•	4.9	1
69. sea						3.0	
70. lamp						3.1	
71. torture		•			•	7.1	2
72. short						2.2	
73. slow						1.3	
74. appeal						2.9	
75. round						1.5	
76. sweet						1.8	
77. ruin						1.8	
78. nail						1.5	
79. street						2.3	
80. head		•				2.4	1
81. milk						2.2	
82. sky						1.6	
83. light						1.7	
84. table						1.7	
85. worthless						2.8	
86. sorrow						2.2	
87. sleep						1.6	
88. olfactory						3.3	
89. cigarette						2.4	
90. hurt		•				2.4	1
91. belief						1.8	
92. cut						1.7	
93. rough						2.4	
94. soap						1.8	
95. push						1.6	
96. city						1.5	
97. kingdom						1.4	
98. self-esteem						2.3	
99. butter						2.7	
100. thanks						2.0	
						Av.	
	0	0	0	0	2	2.8	2
	1	1	0	0	0	2.1	2
	0	2	0	0	1	2.3	3
	0	1	0	1	0	[illegible]	2
	0	1	0	0	0	2.2	1
	0	3	0	1	0	2.0	4
	1	[illegible]	0	2	[illegible]	2.1	14
						SD [illegible]	

Session No. VI — Hypnotic — Control — 3-10-38 — 4:10 P.M.

Response	Verbal	Voluntary	Involuntary	Respiration	Delayed R.T.	Individual Reaction Time	Total
1. chair						1.5	
2. cube						1.8	
3. sheet						2.2	
4. hat						1.5	
5. woman						1.5	
6. peculiar						1.9	
7. fine						1.9	
8. chewing						2.0	
9. light		•				1.7	1
10. important		•			•	2.3	2
11. white						1.4	
12. hard						1.7	
13. dream		•		•		2.6	2
14. foot		•				2.3	1
15. apple						1.8	
16. clothes						1.9	
17. insect		•				2.1	1
18. rough						1.7	
19. hug						1.9	
20. table						1.9	
21. sour						1.8	
22. pull						1.7	
23. man						1.6	
24. sleep						2.0	
25. color						2.1	
26. hope						1.8	
27. deep						1.6	
28. color						2.4	
29. mature						2.3	
30. light						2.0	
31. generator						2.4	
32. people						1.9	
33. hand						1.7	
34. vibration						2.7	
35. thread						1.8	
36. long						1.6	
37. food						2.0	
38. blow						1.8	
39. fast						1.9	
40. smoke						1.9	
41. low						1.7	
42. labor						1.8	
43. animal						1.8	
44. black						2.2	
45. smooth						1.5	
46. errand						1.9	
47. vegetable						1.8	
48. soft						1.6	
49. combustion						2.3	
50. dream						1.7	
51. river						1.6	
52. boy						1.3	
53. sweet						1.3	
54. fight						2.0	
55. home						1.7	
56. bird						1.8	
57. girl						1.3	
58. innocent						1.6	
59. sickness						2.0	
60. hard						2.1	
61. brain		•				2.5	1
62. water						1.7	
63. book						1.5	
64. home						1.5	
65. think						1.7	
66. light						1.8	
67. stomach						2.0	
68. persecute					•	3.8	1
69. sea						1.8	
70. window						2.3	
71. punish						2.6	
72. short						1.4	
73. slow						2.0	
74. appeal						2.4	
75. round						1.5	
76. sweet						1.5	
77. ruin						2.0	
78. nail						1.8	
79. street						1.6	
80. head						2.2	
81. milk						1.8	
82. sky						1.5	
83. light						1.5	
84. table						1.7	
85. useless						2.4	
86. sorrow						1.5	
87. sleep						1.7	
88. taste						2.4	
89. smoke						1.9	
90. hurt		•				1.6	1
91. belief						1.7	
92. cut						2.2	
93. coarse						1.7	
94. tub						2.3	
95. push						1.8	
96. city						2.0	
97. kingdom						2.2	
98. self-esteem						2.8	
99. butter						1.8	
100. thanks						2.4	
						Av.	
	0	0	0	0	1	2.3	1
	0	2	0	0	0	2.0	2
	0	1	0	0	0	[illegible]	1
	0	2	0	1	0	[illegible]	3
	0	1	0	0	0	[illegible]	1
	0	1	0	0	1	[illegible]	2
	0	7	0	1	2	1.9	10
						SD [illegible]	

Session No. VII — Hypnotic — Control — 3-11-38 — 4:45 P.M.

Response	Verbal	Voluntary	Involuntary	Respiration	Delayed R.T.	Individual Reaction Time	Total
1. chair						2.1	
2. cube						1.7	
3. sheet						1.9	
4. hat						1.8	
5. woman						1.8	
6. peculiar						1.8	
7. fine						2.0	
8. chewing						2.1	
9. light						1.4	
10. safe						2.8	
11. white						1.6	
12. hard						1.9	
13. sleep						2.2	
14. foot						1.7	
15. apple						1.8	
16. clothes						1.8	
17. insect						1.7	
18. rough						2.0	
19. hug						1.8	
20. table						1.8	
21. sour						1.6	
22. pull						1.6	
23. man						1.6	
24. ease						1.8	
25. color						1.9	
26. hope						2.3	
27. deep						1.7	
28. white						1.4	
29. pretty	•	•				2.3	2
30. light						2.3	
31. generator						2.1	
32. people						2.8	
33. hand						2.0	
34. noise						2.6	
35. thread						2.2	
36. long						1.5	
37. food						2.8	
38. blow		•				1.9	1
39. swift						2.0	
40. smoke						2.1	
41. low						1.5	
42. labor						1.8	
43. animal						1.4	
44. black						2.2	
45. smooth						1.5	
46. errand						2.0	
47. head						2.8	
48. soft						1.9	
49. smoke						2.8	
50. dream						3.1	
51. river						1.7	
52. boy						1.4	
53. sweet						1.4	
54. fight						2.0	
55. home						1.8	
56. bird						1.6	
57. girl						1.4	
58. innocent						2.3	
59. poor						2.8	
60. dress					•	3.0	1
61. thought		•				2.7	1
62. water						1.9	
63. book						1.9	
64. house						2.1	
65. think						1.6	
66. light						2.4	
67. food						2.3	
68. accuse						2.1	
69. sea						1.9	
70. window						2.5	
71. punish						2.6	
72. short						1.7	
73. slow						2.2	
74. male & fem.					•	3.0	1
75. round						1.7	
76. sweet						1.9	
77. ruin						2.0	
78. nail						1.7	
79. street						1.8	
80. head						2.0	
81. milk						2.2	
82. sky						1.6	
83. light						1.7	
84. table						2.0	
85. no good					•	3.3	1
86. sorrow						1.7	
87. sleep						2.0	
88. burn	•					2.0	1
89. smoke						2.7	
90. drop						2.3	
91. belief						2.0	
92. cut						1.6	
93. coarse						2.6	
94. tub						2.1	
95. push						1.5	
96. city		•				2.3	1
97. kingdom						2.1	
98. self-esteem						3.2	
99. butter						2.1	
100. thanks						2.7	
						Av.	
	1	0	0	0	1	2.3	2
	1	2	0	0	2	2.2	5
	0	1	0	0	0	2.1	1
	0	0	0	0	0	1.9	0
	0	0	0	0	0	1.8	0
	0	1	0	0	0	2.0	1
	2	4	0	0	3	2.0	9
						SD .46	

TABLE 1 (*continued*)

The verbal responses in all sessions and the disturbances which were associated with them are presented in Table 1. A careful perusal of this table will show the marked change which the verbal responses underwent in Sessions III and IV, especially those classed as *C* and CA_l. No additional reference will be made to these responses except in special instances. Each session is summarized at the bottom of the table for types of disturbance appearing on the word classes.[14] It is at once apparent that the totals for the complex sessions show a greater number of disturbances than the totals of the control sessions, the hypnotic complex having 38 and the waking complex 60, as opposed to 14 and 21 of the respective control sessions. This increase is largely due to those word classes designated as *C* and CA_l. In Session III—the hypnotic complex session—27 of the 38 disturbances are accounted for by these groups, and in Session IV—the waking complex session—31 of the 60 fall in the *C* and CA_l classes. The induction of the complex has apparently had two effects: to "set" the subject so that he gave verbal replies which were related to the complex and to disorganize his voluntary, involuntary, and respiratory behavior. In addition, these effects manifest themselves differently in the hypnotic and waking states. Of the 27 disturbances accounted for by *C* and CA_l words in Session III, 21 are verbal, while in Session IV but 12 of the 31 disturbances are verbal. Reference to Table 2 shows this clearly. In hypnotic Session III 84 percent of the *C* and CA_l words were disturbed verbally, and their nonverbal disturbance was 5.3 percent.[15] In waking complex Session IV the verbal disturbance has fallen to 48 percent on the class *C* and CA_l taken together, while the nonverbal has risen to 21.4 percent.

The following explanation of this result occurs to us. Since the complex was given under hypnosis, it is reasonable to assume that the resulting

---

distribution. Usually this gave four or five disturbed reaction times in a session.

[13] We recognize that in using the word *disturbance* for both verbal and nonverbal effects we are not being consistent. In the former case we are using the word in the sense of a *change* in response in the direction of the complex, in the latter in the sense of a *disorganized* response. However, since the term is convenient, we are continuing its use in both senses.

[14] A refined statistical treatment of the data was attempted, but we came to the conclusion that this was premature because of the qualitative stage of the technique and the exploratory nature of the experiment.

[15] These percentage figures are arrived at by dividing the actual number of disturbances by the possible number of disturbances. Since there are 25 *C* and CA_l words, the possible verbal disturbance is 25. However, since each word may be disturbed nonverbally in the voluntary, involuntary, and respiratory aspects, there are 75 possible nonverbal disturbances. The total possible nonverbal disturbance on all other words together is 225. Reaction time is excluded since the standard we used was relative to the whole distribution of reaction times, so that only a few long times for each session could be marked as disturbed.

mental set would cause the subject to reply to the *C* words with a response which is related to the complex story. That this set was of considerable importance is seen by the other words (CA_I) which were drawn into the complex situation, there being 15 such.[16] In the waking state, however, the subject, as nearly as we could determine, had an amnesia for the complex and was therefore probably in lesser contact with it. At the same time he was in greater rapport with the experimental environment, hence the verbal responses related to the complex were not elicited as easily. To explain the small number of nonverbal responses in the hypnotic complex session, there being four on *C* and CA_I words (excluding reaction time), we might assume that whatever excitation the conflict created was discharged verbally in giving the related response. In the following waking complex Session IV, however, the verbal responses related to the complex were not elicited as readily and the excitation created by the conflict spread into the motor response, giving rise to greater disturbances. Both *C* and CA_I words illustrate this point. In the hypnotic complex Session III there were nine responses on the *C* words related to the complex and none on the nonverbal. But in the waking complex Session IV there were but two which were disturbed verbally alone, three both verbally and nonverbally, and three nonverbally. On CA_I words in the hypnotic complex Session III the results are: verbal alone, 9; verbal and nonverbal, 3; nonverbal alone, 0; in the waking complex Session IV: verbal alone, 4; verbal and nonverbal, 3; nonverbal, 3. The further implication of these results is that, while the combined association-motor method of Luria does seem to reveal conflicts induced by means of hypnosis, a conflict need not necessarily result in disorganization at the nonverbal level. It would be difficult otherwise to explain the paucity of nonverbal disturbances in the hypnotic complex session. It seems that some such assumption as we have indicated concerning the possibility of a complete discharge of excitation verbally is necessary.[17]

[16] The actual number probably depends upon many factors such as the strength of the complex, the nature of the complex itself, its relation to the stimulus words, and personality traits.

[17] It is possible to urge that the subject had little or no conflict in the hypnotic state because the complex was given to him in this condition. Thus, by virtue of having heard the story, without assuming personal responsibility for the act, he was set to give verbal responses related to the complex with no affect necessarily associated with them. It should be noted, however, that an attempt was made, in the hypnotic instructions which were used when the complex story was told to the subject, to associate affect with the story. It was repeatedly emphasized to the subject that he had committed an act which made him feel miserable. The subjects in general were restless after the induction of the complex and gave one the impression that something distressed them.

It is interesting also to examine the verbal reaction times of the *C* and CA_I words in Session III. The mean of the *C* words is 2.6 seconds, being shorter than the

TABLE 2
Percentage Verbal and NonVerbal Disturbances for Word Classes *(C & CA_I* Combined) and for All Others *($CA_I + NC$, NC, CA_2, N)*

	Session I Waking control			
	Verbal		*Nonverbal*	
	D	*%*	*D*	*%*
C & CA_I	0	0.0	3	4.0
All others	0	0.0	13	5.8

	Session II Hypnotic control			
	Verbal		*Nonverbal*	
	D	*%*	*D*	*%*
C & CA_I	0	0.0	2	2.7
All others	0	0.0	7	3.2

	Session III Hypnotic complex			
	Verbal		*Nonverbal*	
	D	*%*	*D*	*%*
C & CA_I	21	84.0	4	5.3
All others	3	4.0	7	3.1

	Session IV Waking complex			
	Verbal		*Nonverbal*	
	D	*%*	*D*	*%*
C & CA_I	2	8.0	2	2.7
All others	2	2.7	24	10.7

mean of the 100 words, which was 3.0 seconds. None of these words carried any nonverbal disturbances. A reaction time mean on the *C* words which is close to the total mean of the whole stimulus word list is consistent with both the levels-of-discharge hypothesis and the "nonaffective set" view. That is, there is no reason in either case why any delay should take place. The reaction process simply runs its normal course, discharging more affective excitation in the former case than in the latter. The CA_I words have a mean of 3.2 seconds. Of the 15 words in this class, 12 have verbal disturbances. It is interesting to note that three of these 12 have nonverbal disturbances, words No. 45, 48, and 85, and each one has a long reaction time, the values being 4.4, 5.1, and 5.0 seconds, respectively. This result would seem to imply that there was inhibition of the verbal response which was reflected in the nonverbal aspects as disturbances. The motor responses give some evidence of conflict in the hypnotic state. Unfortunately there are only a few instances in this subject, so that the question cannot be answered decisively. In some other cases the issue is clearer, however, and we shall return to this topic later.

	Session V Waking control			
	Verbal		*Nonverbal*	
	D	*%*	*D*	*%*
C & CA_1	**1**	**4.0**	**1**	**1.3**
All others	**0**	**0.0**	**9**	**4.0**

	Session VI Hypnotic control			
	Verbal		*Nonverbal*	
	D	*%*	*D*	*%*
C & CA_1	**0**	**0.0**	**2**	**2.7**
All others	**0**	**0.0**	**6**	**2.7**

	Session VII Hypnotic control			
	Verbal		*Nonverbal*	
	D	*%*	*D*	*%*
C & CA_1	**2**	**8.0**	**2**	**2.7**
All others	**0**	**0.0**	**2**	**0.9**

D = Number disturbed

Possible total verbal disturbance	***C & CA_1***	**25**
Possible total verbal disturbance	**All others**	**75**
Possible total nonverbal disturbance	***C & CA_1***	**75**
Possible total nonverbal disturbance	**All others**	**225**

(Reaction time excluded)

But how shall we account for the other disturbances which have appeared in these two sessions? Indeed, what is the meaning of the disturbances which occur in the control sessions? In Session III there were three verbal disturbances on the word Class $CA_1 + NC$ which have not been discussed thus far. It is clear that the verbal disturbance is due to the CA_1 and not to the *NC,* since our criterion of classifying them CA_1 was based on relationship to the complex story. No nonverbal disturbances appear in this class.[18] Two voluntary disturbances appear on the class designated as CA_2 on Nos. 9 and 96. These are probably related to the complex as already indicated by the way in which they were selected. The remaining 6 disturbances are on 5 N words.[19] These are numbers 36, 37,

[18] We have kept the class separate, however, since there are some nonverbal disturbances in other sessions which may be due to *NC.*

[19] There are numerous disturbances which are not accounted for on the basis of a relationship to the induced complex or to natural complexes. One might attempt to explain these disturbances by the following methods. Often it is impossible to make a satisfactory decision. Some of these methods apply to all sessions and some only to particular sessions. Those which apply to *all* sessions are the following: *(1)* Perseveration effects (disturbances appearing on words following affective stimulus words), which may be both verbal and nonverbal or either one separately. If

59, 65, and 93. No. 37 ("Stomach–food"), with a voluntary disturbance, and No. 59 ("Health–sanitarium"), also with a voluntary disturbance, may both be considered as indicative of some natural complex material, since the subject reported he was taking a tonic for stomach trouble at the time of the experiment. This re-receives some confirmation from No. 67 ("Hungry–sick"). On the other hand, it is possible that this group of words implies that the subject felt miserable—a "sick to the stomach" feeling—because of his behavior in the complex story. Such an interpretation finds support in the somewhat greater unpleasant affective tone of the

---

the perseveration is verbal and the subject gives a response which is related to the complex, then it would be classed CA_1, but if it is unrelated, we would be unable to tell whether or not it is a case of perseveration. There is the possibility, however, that perseveration may make the verbal response unusual. The clearest example of perseveration in a nonverbal disturbance would be that which follows a verbal or nonverbal disturbance and which appears on an *N* word. *(2)* Cases of unusual stimulus words to which the subject has difficulty in giving a response, or cases where the subject inhibits the first response which occurs to him but which is not connected with a conflict. Here one would expect longer reaction times. *(3)* Transitory "natural-complexes"—those which have arisen just prior to a particular experimental session and which were not present at the next session. *(4)* Chance disturbances due to movements of the subject because of physical discomfort of some kind. One may raise the question here of the relationship of such movements to affective stimulus words. Our data on this point are not sufficient since a semiopaque curtain separated the subject and the experimenter through which only gross movements of the former could be detected. The subject was unable to see the experimenter because the latter's corner of the room was darkened. *(5)* Natural complex situations unknown to us.

The explanations which apply to *particular* sessions are the following: *(1)* Responses which are related to the complex, but which we did not detect. These could be *C*, CA_1, or CA_2; *C* and CA_1, in those cases in which the response was the same as that of the first control sessions but in which the subject ascribed new meaning to the stimulus word, relating it to the complex; CA_2, in which we were unable to establish the associative links. This should apply especially to complex sessions and to some extent to control sessions after the removal of the complex (see *5* below). *(2)* Natural Complex situations, the thresholds of which have been lowered by the artificial complex so that words not marked *NC* become disturbed nonverbally. This should apply primarily to complex sessions. *(3)* Disturbances which are reactions to hypnosis itself and not the complex as such. These might be due to two different factors. The words which were used by the hypnotist in putting the subject into the trance, e.g., "Sleep," might become disturbed if the subject had developed any antagonism toward the hypnotist because the unpleasant complexes were suggested in hypnosis. The other factor is the possibility of ambivalence toward hypnotism. One would expect such disturbances to appear largely in the waking complex sessions and perhaps in later waking control sessions, since in the waking state rapport is probably not as good as in the hypnotic state. *(4)* Disturbances due to "shock"—those arising from the subject's apprehension in a new situation in which he does not know entirely what is expected of him. This is mainly relevant for the first session. One speculates in this connection whether or not apprehensiveness in a new situation sensitizes the

session as compared with the first two control sessions.[20] Nos. 37 and 59 may also involve an element of perseveration from 36 and 58, respectively. The disturbances on No. 65 ("Concentrate–meditate")—voluntary and reaction time—may have arisen because of the subject's preoccupation with the complex story. On No. 93 ("Fine–coarse"), disturbed in the voluntary aspect, the response which appeared in a previous control session may have taken on a figurative meaning for the subject, referring to his behavior in the complex situation as "coarse." We are unable to account for the voluntary disturbance on No. 36 ("Short–long") satisfactorily.

We have attempted to account for all the disturbances in the other sessions according to the principles set forth above. However, since we do not feel these explanations are pertinent to our present purpose, we shall give but a few additional examples.

The waking complex Session IV has 15 disturbances on 14 *N* words: Nos. 10, 24, 34, 46, 53, 64, 67, 73, 75, 92, 93, 99, and 100. No. 53 ("Sour–taste")—this is the only time in which "taste" appears as a response to this stimulus words. This fact in combination with the appearance of an involuntary disturbance suggests that the subject was referring to the unpleasantness of the complex in a figurative sense. There may also be an element of perseveration from No. 52 involved, which also showed considerable disturbance. No. 73 ("Swift–fast")—the response "fast," which is a different type of response from that of the control sessions, being a synonym as opposed to an antonym, appears with a voluntary disturbance. We may interpret this as probably referring to the necessity of speed in notifying the girl of the truth, a point touched on in the complex story.[21]

Having considered the complex sessions we shall take up the control sessions, beginning with Session I. In this first waking control session there are 21 disturbances on 17 words. It is especially interesting to note that there are six disturbed *NC* words out of a possible seven—a fact which would seem to indicate that *NC* material may be turned up, at least

---

"natural complexes" of the individual. *(5)* In the control sessions after the complex removal one has the possibility that there are residuals of the complex. Also, if there has been an enhancement of the subject's natural conflicts, disturbances on *NC* words might be found here.

In attempting to account for disturbances falling on *N* words we shall point out which of the above explanations seem the most likely to us insofar as we have any basis for our conclusions.

[20] An analysis of the verbal responses of the complex sessions indicates that there has been such a shift toward unpleasantness from the first control session; cf., e.g., in Session III, Nos. 38, 48, 61, and 98.

[21] Another interesting point with regard to Session IV is that the subject showed one of the general behavioral characteristics which we were observing. On No. 89 ("Tobacco–cigarette"), a CA_I word, the subject sighed deeply.

the first time the test is given. These *NC* disturbances are on Nos. 19, 32, 52, 55, 90, and 91.

The possible explanation that may be given to the other disturbances is that they are the results of natural complexes, permanent or transitory, of which we were not aware (enhanced or unenhanced by a "shock" effect), chance disturbances due to "shock," somewhat unusual, stimulus words for the subject, or perseveration. No. 68 ("Blame–accuse") with a respiratory disturbance, and No. 71 ("Persecute–electric chair") with voluntary and reaction time disturbances are probably disturbed because the stimulus words are somewhat unusual and often carry an unpleasant tone.

In Session II, hypnotic control, we should expect the "shock" effect of Session I to be reduced, but since hypnosis may reach a deeper personality level, the possibility of more natural complex material being aroused should be considered. The total disturbance in Session II has fallen to 14 and appears on words 2, 10, 27, 41, 49, 54, 58, 67, 86, 93, and 100. Word No. 41, with disturbances of respiration and reaction time, is *NC,* and No. 67 ("Hungry–stomach") with a voluntary disturbance, may also have been connected with a natural complex, as has been already indicated. As for No. 49 ("Burned–chemistry")—respiration and reaction time disturbed—we have a postexperimental report of severe acid burns received by the subject at one time, which may account for the present disturbance. No. 54 ("Soldier–fight"), having a voluntary disturbance, may be connected with the natural complex involving *fall* and *high,* since the subject's airplane accident, already mentioned, took place while he was in the Army Air Corps.

In Session V, the first waking control after the complex session, we find 14 disturbances which fall on Nos. 19, 27, 29, 37, 60, 64, 66, 68, 71, 80, and 90. Any analysis must now consider the possibility of verbal and nonverbal affective residuals and nonaffective verbal residuals from the complex sessions. No. 19 ("Kiss–hug"), disturbed in the voluntary and respiratory aspects, is *NC,* and it is probable that the *NC* part of No. 90 is responsible for the voluntary disturbance on it since the verbal response is "hurt." The verbal disturbance on No. 66 ("Lamp–burn") is probably due to a verbal affective or nonaffective residual.

The disturbances fall to 10 in the hypnotic control Session VI—on Nos. 9, 10, 13, 14, 17, 61, 68, and 90. Nos. 13, 17, and 90 are *NC* words.

Session VII shows 9 disturbances on Nos. 29, 38, 60, 61, 74, 85, 88, and 96. The nonverbal disturbance of a voluntary nature combined with the verbal responses on No. 29 ("Beautiful–pretty") suggests an affective residual. The verbal disturbance on No. 88 ("Smell–burn") suggests either an affective or nonaffective residual.

The attempt to account for disturbances not related to the induced or natural complexes has, in the very nature of the case, to be quite speculative. We included examples of these interpretations because it seemed to us to point out the problem which future experimentation must face in order to make the technique a really satisfactory one.

Reference to Table 1 shows the mean reaction times and S.D.'s for all sessions and the means for the word classes. Examination of the means and S.D.s of all the sessions, despite questions which might be raised about the legitimacy of this measure of variation in this case, shows several interesting points. While the means of the first two controls are practically identical, the S.D. of Session I is somewhat larger than that of Session II, which may be an expression of what we have referred to as the "shock" effect. The word classes which contribute largely to this larger S.D. in Session I are $CA_1 + NC$, *NC*, CA_2, and *C*, in order of their departure from the total mean from great to small. Since in the first control sessions the $CA_1 + NC$ and *NC* groups are really all *NC*, it seems clear that there is a tendency for *NC* words in this session to be delayed. The longer-than-mean time on the CA_2 class may be caused by some natural complex material. Word No. 71 ("Persecute–electric chair") and its response suggests this inference. Since the *C* words, in general, were a bit unusual, this might lengthen their time. The class means have come together considerably in Session II—the *NC*, however, still being the longest. The mean of Session III is slightly greater, but the S.D. has continued to fall, the most surprising fact being the short reaction time of the *C* words, nine of which were disturbed verbally. This seems to support the verbal discharge hypothesis presented earlier and is in line with Luria's "law of the catalytic action of the stimulus." In the waking complex Session IV the mean has continued to rise, being greatest of any session, and the scatter has increased. The increases are on CA_2, *C*, and CA_1 words, which is to be expected if there has been any tendency to inhibit verbal responses. After the removal of the complex the means and S.D.'s decline to new low levels, probably due to a practice effect (Wells, 1927). In none of the sessions may the differences between means be regarded as significant statistically. Rather it is their general agreement with what might be expected which is striking.

Another point which might be mentioned is that there was a tendency for responses which were more highly specific to the complex to appear on the 10 Complex words and for those which were less specific to appear on Complex-Associated words. This tendency was not paralleled in the magnitude of the voluntary disturbances.

SUMMARY OF RESULTS ON ALL SUBJECTS

Twelve subjects went through the same general procedure. There is evidence that nine accepted the story told to them as an account of something they had done. We base this on their general behavior during and between experiments, an example of which we have given in discussing the sample case.

Table 3 summarizes the results on all cases. Since there is a considerable amount of overlap, the plus (+) signs should be regarded only as indicative of predominant trends. In the waking state nonverbal behavior was disturbed in Subjects 1, 3, 4, 5, and *6c;* in the hypnotic state in Subjects 2, 3, 4, 5, *6a,* and *6b*. The results on Subjects 7, 8, and 9 are largely negative so far as disorganization of the nonverbal aspects are concerned. Of the nine subjects who accepted the complex (Table 3), six gave definite evidence that some aspect of the Luria technique revealed the presence of a conflict. One of this group (No. 2) presented disturbances which were almost all of a voluntary character in hypnosis, with almost none in the waking complex sessions, so that it would have been difficult on the basis of the latter alone to know whether the subject had a conflict. However, after reinforcement of the suggestion, a few verbal and nonverbal disturbances appeared in the next waking complex session. This implies that this type of conflict may be entirely at the hypnotic level but if sufficiently strong may result in disturbances in the succeeding waking session. Two subjects (Nos. 3 and 4) showed voluntary disturbances in both states. One subject (No. 5) had greater involuntary responses than voluntary in hypnosis and waking, and the subject (No. 1) whom we discussed in detail showed his greatest nonverbal disturbance as voluntary in the waking state. Another subject went through the experiment three times: in the first two (Nos. *6a* and *6b)* the disturbances appeared in hypnosis as voluntary, the third time (No. *6c)* voluntary disturbances were found in both states.[22] It is difficult to generalize about these six cases because such marked individual differences are found among them. However, one of the consistent findings is that the preponderance of verbal disturbances occurs in hypnosis and the relative importance of the nonverbal increases in the waking state. Another is that the *C* words, as would be expected, tend to evoke verbal responses which are more specifically related to the complex than any others.

[22] In this subject the instructions were altered the third time the experiment was performed. Instead of permitting her to have a posthypnotic amnesia for the complex story, which was the usual technique, we told her while hypnotized that she would be aware of the complex posthypnotically but would not dare to think about it, although it would cause her to worry greatly. The increase in voluntary disturbances would seem to imply, if the instructions were followed, that the subject must be aware of the complex to minifest such disturbances. Luria has also commented on this point (1932, pp. 149-161), maintaining that if the complex is removed from consciousness, it is also insulated from the motor area since the two have been combined functionally by the technique. On the other hand, in the other five successful cases posthypnotic amnesias were present, and all of them (one after reinforcement) showed a rise of nonverbal disturbances in the waking

TABLE 3
Results on All Subjects

Subject		*Complex accepted*	*How revealed as disturbances*					
			Verbal only		*Both verbal and nonverbal*		*Nonverbal only*	
No.	*Sex*		*H*	*W*	*H*	*W*	*H*	*W*
1	M	Yes	+			+		
2	F	Yes			+			
3	F	Yes			+			+
4	F	Yes			+	+		
5	F	Yes			+	+		
6a	F	Yes			+			
6b		Yes			+			
6c		Yes			+	+		
7	M	Yes	+					
8	F	Yes	+	+				
9	F	Yes	+	+				
10	M	No						
11	M	No						
12	F	No						

H = Hypnotic Complex Session
W = Waking Complex Session

Of the other three subjects who accepted the complex, in two the evidence that there was any connection between the complex and the nonverbal disturbances was of a dubious character. Each case presented some peculiarities of its own which are worth mentioning. One subject (No. 7) who had eight sessions—two complex sessions, one hypnotic and one waking, being added—had the largest group of words associated with the complex of any of our subjects. In the first hypnotic complex session there were 24 CA_I words and 16 $CA_I + NC$ words. Yet only three CA_I and two $CA_I + NC$ words were disturbed in the voluntary responses. One of each class had a voluntary disturbance without a verbal disturbance.

complex sessions. When these sessions were completed, the subjects often manifested surprise about some of their verbal responses which related to the complex. Luria has also noted this (1932, p. 136). Whether the surprise of the subjects was genuine or was in the nature of rationalizations based upon some knowledge of the complex we are unable to state definitely. Our impressions is that the surprise was real. Luria, however, argues that each critical stimulus word makes the complex conscious, at least partially, and hence disrupts the motor responses. His evidence in this connection is based on continuous free association experiments in which the subject eventually got around to giving responses related to the complex. These were accompanied by motor disturbances. Our material indicates that both conscious and unconscious conflicts may be revealed by the technique. This question is probably connected with the strength of the conflict and the intimacy of the relation between it and the motor response.

Likewise there were eight verbally disturbed *C* words, but only one had a voluntary disturbance. In the succeeding waking complex session there was one verbal disturbance on Class C and one on $CA_I + NC$. The *C* class had two voluntary disturbances, and the CA_I class had five. In neither session was there an increase of nonverbal disturbance on the other word classes. In such a case it is important to examine the disturbances in the other classes and attempt to discover if these can be related to the complex, paying especial attention to those which were undisturbed in the control sessions. It was found that a few of these could be connected, but the result was not very convincing. The results on the other two complex sessions were essentially the same except that the total disturbance declined somewhat. Another fact about this case was the large increase in nonverbal disturbances in the first hypnotic control session, as against the waking control, the numbers being 18 and 5, respectively. This suggests that there may be a "shock" effect which appears in hypnosis in some cases. This interpretation is supported by the fact that there were but two disturbances in the last hypnotic control and an increase in unusual responses in the first hypnotic control session over the previous waking control—the values being 10 and 2.

Another subject (No. 8) gave somewhat different results. Although there was a considerable amount of nonverbal disturbance in each session, there was little apparent relation to the complex. Verbal disturbances were few. In the hypnotic complex session there were found but five—two on *C* and three on CA_I words. This was true, likewise, of the posthypnotic complex session. The verbal responses were, however, sufficiently specific to the complex story to show its effect. The interesting point about this case is that from an examination of the total disturbances for each session there appears to be a "shock" effect in both the waking and hypnotic states, greater in the former, and which has a differential rate of decline upon repetition, being faster in hypnosis than in the waking condition.

In another subject (No. 9) there were a considerable number of verbal disturbances in both the hypnotic and waking complex sessions but few nonverbal disturbances which could be related to the complex situation in either the hypnotic or waking states. This individual had 12 sessions, six complex and 6 noncomplex, divided equally between the hypnotic and waking states. Four control sessions preceded the induction of the complex, and two were conducted after its removal. The control tests showed an interesting phenomenon—with repetition of the experiment there was a decline of disturbances. This was true of both the waking and hypnotic conditions and is better evidence for the existence of a "shock" effect than the decline in the case of those subjects in which but two controls were performed before the complex was suggested. There is also the possibility that this decline in disturbance is evidence of an "abreactive" effect. Failure to take this factor into consideration, whatever its cause, may lead to questionable conclusions. Luria, we believe, has not taken sufficient account of it in his studies of students before and after school examinations, criminals before and after confession of a crime, etc., (1930, esp., pp. 43-128), and for that reason the differences may not be as marked as he indicates. Along with repetition went a slight reduction in reaction-time means and a shrinkage of scatter about these means. (This same general effect was noted in three other cases in which control repetitions were obtained.) Because of our failure to obtain many nonverbal disturbances we allowed this subject to keep the complex overnight and repeated the hypnotic and waking sessions the following day. The result was a slight decline in total nonverbal and verbal disturbances. The next day we tried to reinforce the complex by repeating the suggestion to the subject. This resulted in a slight increase in both types of disturbances, bringing them back to about their original level. (In another subject reinforcement was tried with much more positive results—i.e., a great increase in disturbances, the effect being especially marked in hypnosis on nonverbal disturbances.)

It seems certain, then, that with repetition one has a reduction in disturbances during the complex sessions. An abreactive factor, a forgetting factor, or a decrease in "shock" effect, must all be considered as possible causes for this decline.

The levels-of-discharge hypothesis which we have suggested in this paper is consistent with results obtained on all the subjects who accepted the complex. Stated broadly, the hypothesis implies that if affective excitation created by a conflict is not discharged completely at one level, it ought to appear at another. In terms of the present experiment, if the affect was not totally released in giving a verbal response related to the complex, there ought to be a nonverbal (voluntary, involuntary, or respiratory) disturbance. This may occur with or without a lengthened reaction time. The reaction time would be increased on those items in which there was some inhibition (conscious or unconscious) of the verbal response. The time would not be lengthened if a response related in some way to the conflict was either adequate or inadequate to discharge the affective excitation.

It should be noted that Subjects No. 2, 3, 4, 5, 6*a,* and 6*b* give motor evidences of a conflict in hypnotic states, a point which we discussed in connection with Subject No. 1 when we analyzed in detail the results obtained from him. The motor disturbances were much more marked in these cases than in Subject No. 1. Subjects No. 1, 3, 4, 5, and 6*c* gave similar evidence in the waking states. In the hypnotic states Subjects No. 1, 7, 8, and 9 did not give motor disturbances, and in the waking condition

Subjects No. 2, 6*a*, 6*b*, and 7 did not show many nonverbal disturbances. It may be argued, as indicated previously, that the failure to give motor disturbances in the hypnotic or waking states in these subjects shows the absence of conflict.

The levels-of-discharge hypothesis we have advanced, on the basis of our experiments, is an extension of the Luria theory as we have stated it. Motor disturbances occur, according to Luria, when there is an inhibition of the verbal response or when there are large amounts of conflict-excitation present. Our hypothesis assumes that motor disturbances will appear when there is inhibition of the verbal responses. However, motor disturbances may or may not be found when the conflict arouses large amounts of excitation. If the verbal response is adequate to discharge this excitation, there will be no motor disturbances, but if the verbal response is inadequate, then motor disturbances will appear. We have attempted to account for the failure to obtain motor effects when the subject had a conflict in this way.

Of the remaining three subjects, two definitely refused to accept the complex (Nos. 10 and 11). Both were given the same complex, which was of a serious nature. As medical interns they were supposed (in the story suggested to them) to have been anxious to acquire proficiency in the technique of the cisterna puncture, practicing on patients who had just died. Through a mistake in the location of the bed in a poorly illuminated ward, they performed the puncture on a comatose patient instead of a dead one, and due to faulty technique the vertebral artery was pierced by the needle. An internal hemorrhage resulted and death ensued. Each had gone from the ward without making a report of the accident. After we had finished the experiments, we questioned the subjects and discovered that they had not believed that they were involved in the complex situation. One said that the behavior of the person in the story was so different from his own that he could not imagine himself as committing the action, although he tried hard to believe it. The other subject reported that after the suggestion of the story he had had a mental picture of himself performing a cisterna puncture, but that this was entirely dissociated from the complex. The whole situation had seemed very real to him, but he had known that he had not gone on the ward in the evening to perform the operation. Both of these cases, however, showed an increase in disturbances in the complex sessions. These disturbances fell almost entirely on words classed as *N* and in one case to a slight extent on *NC*. In one case the increases appeared largely as respiratory disturbances; in the other they were scattered among all the nonverbal aspects. Luria has spoken of an increase in respiratory disturbance as indicative of "trauma," by which he means those cases in which the person has reacted to a "shocking" experience. He contrasts these with those in which the individual has taken a part in some act which, if contrary to the personality trends of the person, leads to a conflict. The implication of the results in these two subjects is that to produce a conflict the complex act must be one possible for the subject to imagine his doing.

The third case (no. 12) in which negative results were obtained, from the standpoint of accepting the complex, involved the failure to mail a roommate's letter of application for a graduate school fellowship until after the final date for application had passed, while the subject mailed one of her own and obtained the same fellowship. This subject explained after the experiment that the account as stated had not been entirely logical and that she felt it was artificial. She had elaborated it with numerous details to make it more credible. In the posthypnotic complex statc shc was aware of a desire to let her mind dwell upon events that might have happened in the trance state; by so doing she thought she might rid herself of something unpleasant. Yet she felt vaguely that she ought not do this since it might disturb the hypnotic situation. Complex removal was accomplished in her in the waking state by suggesting that she recall the story, and this she was able to do. It is our impression in this case that the acceptance of the story was more intellectual than emotional. There was a slight increase in disturbances in complex sessions, appearing in the hypnotic state on *N* and *NC* words almost entirely, In the waking complex session there was a small increase over the hypnotic complex session caused by disturbances appearing on *C* and CA_I words. This makes it appear that some conflict has been set up. The most striking thing about this subject, however, was the large number of unusual verbal responses. By unusual responses we mean those which are individual to the subject as compared to those expected from a group of persons living in a similar environment. In the case of the words which we took from the Kent-Rosanoff list we designated as unusual those responses which had a very low or zero frequency, unless the subject's occupation and habitat made the response seem appropriate. (In the subject whose case we presented in detail [Table 1] the response "sigh" to the stimulus *whistle* No. 38 was considered as unusual. This was true also of the response "me" to the stimulus *persecute* No. 71.) The values ran as follows: Session I, waking control—7; Session II, hypnotic control—11; Session III, hypnotic complex—18; Session IV, hypnotic control—9. The majority of these fell on the word classes *NC* and *N*. An examination of the individual responses which appeared in Sessions III and IV which had not occurred in Sessions I and II showed that some could be accounted for as *NC*, some as related to the complex, and some as influenced by both. This analysis was made in the same way as in the attempt to account for all the disturbances in the sample case. Although the numbers dealt with are small, they suggest that the increase in unusual responses may be augmented directly by the complex, or indirectly through the sensitization of *NC*.[23, 24]

CONCLUSIONS

The outstanding difficulty of the technique is the more or less speculative method which must be resorted to for the explanation of nonverbal disturbances not clearly related to the complex. For more exact experimental investigations one certainly should know more about the personalities of the subjects than we did. It is likely also that the list of neutral words would vary from subject to subject. An attempt should be made to secure subject constancy rather than constant conditions for all subjects. This would make it possible to attack a number of problems on a more objective basis, some of which are here presented.

1. Must a subject be aware of a conflict to obtain voluntary disturbances? Our data offer arguments for, but mainly against, this possibility. We believe that Luria's point both ways also. However, he seems to hold for the necessity of awareness to obtain voluntary disturbances.[25] The problems dealing with repression and suppression of conflicts and Luria's concept of "functional barrier" are involved here.

2. To what limits can the technique be carried to reveal the "natural complexes" of a subject? Our data suggest that what we believed were natural complexes are disclosed especially during the first experimental sessions.[26] In any attempt to study natural complexes the complications introduced by what we have termed the "shock" effect must be considered. Both problems are probably related to personality types. Luria has suggested in another connection that there are what he calls "reactive-

[23] The general result on all cases was that four subjects showed some increase in the number of individual responses in the first hypnotic control session as compared with the first waking control session. Three of these four showed increases in the first hypnotic complex session and three showed increases in a waking complex session over the hypnotic complex session.

[24] Besides the aspects already discussed, additional analyses were made of the following: stereotypy, echolalia, individuality of response by autogeneous norms, and disturbances of the ascending and descending limbs of the voluntary responses. However, we are not reporting on these aspects in this paper.

[25] The ambiguity of the term "awareness of a conflict" must be pointed out. We find it difficult to determine what Luria means in his discussion of this point (1932, pp. 149-161). There seem to be three possibilities: awareness of the presence of affect, awareness of the situation connected with affect, awareness of why the situation arouses affect. In our series the subject (6*a*, 6*b*, 6*c*) in whom "awareness" was necessary seems to favor the last possibility.

[26] Olson and Jones (1931) have found that religious, political, and social attitudes may be studied by the Luria method.

stable" and "reactive-labile" personalities. It is probable that natural complexes will disclose themselves more easily and shock effect be greater in the latter type.

3. Can one get information about the interrelationship of conflicts? Our material suggests that in some subjects the artificially induced complex may cause at least temporary disappearance of the natural conflicts, and in other subjects enhancement of the natural complexes. Also in this connection we found that the *NC* words carried fewer nonverbal disturbances after the removal of the complex than before its induction. Does the removal of one complex have a general "abreactive" effect upon the subject, or is the apparent "abreaction" due to mere repetition?

4. Can one study by this method the kinds of objects and situations to which complexes attach themselves? Witness our CA_1, CA_2, and CA_1+uc word classes. This problem is closely related to that of symbolization.

5. Are there different levels of affective discharge? If so, under what conditions does one level rather than another carry the discharge? What relationship obtains among the various discharge levels? Is there a hierarchy? Can one level become a surrogate for another? Our results indicate that the more discharge at a verbal level, the less at a nonverbal level, and vice versa. It must be remembered, however, that these differences were quite marked between the hypnotic and waking states and may be partially due to hypnosis.

6. Can a distinction be made from the pressure curves alone between affective conflicts and those which are at a more intellectual level—e.g., the attempted solution of difficult intellectual problems? Or is affect at the basis of both types? Luria has made some beginnings in this direction (1932, p. 205-239).

7. Can a complex be induced by direct- or by indirect-waking suggestion? An example of the latter might be that in which a person is made the subject of some unpleasant rumor by a group of persons.

8. What correlation would there be between sympathetic variables such as heart rate, blood pressure, galvanic skin reflex, etc. and those studied here? In this connection it would be well to know more about gross movements of the subject which may or may not be associated with affect.

9. What are the possibilities of this method in the study of conflicts as revealed during the course of the psychoanalytic interview? It would seem that data of theoretical value could be gained from such an investigation.

10. What is the effect of fatigue and toxic states in making conflict material more available? Luria has suggested that the regulating ability of the "functional barrier" is lowered during fatigue (1932, p. 384).

11. Under what conditions do perseverative effects appear? Do they tend to appear at one level more than another? There is some indication from our data that perseveration tends to appear at a level lower than that of the level of the preceding disturbance; for instance, if the disturbance is

verbal, then the perseverative disturbance tends to be voluntary, involuntary, or respiratory.

12. What is the effect of hypnosis on the individuality of verbal responses? (This is a question not connected directly with the Luria technique but was suggested by our experiments.) There seemed definite indications that hypnosis increased the individuality of the responses, as was seen from a comparison of the means of the frequency ratings by Kent-Rosanoff standards on *N* words.[27] However, we are not certain that this is caused by hypnosis, since in those subjects in whom we had a repeated waking control there was also a considerable fall in frequency. Yet there were three subjects in whom the frequency-decline from waking to hypnotic states was so marked that we feel we may be dealing with personality types in this respect. In setting up an experiment of this kind it would be necessary to take the "shock" effect on individuality of response into account.

13. What is the effect of a complex on the individuality of verbal responses? This might be studied from the point of view of Kent-Rosanoff frequencies or some autogenous standards such as a frequency table built up on a number of repetitions of the stimulus word series for each subject. There is some indication in our material that a complex individualizes the responses on *N* words in the waking state and makes the responses less individual in the hypnotic states.

SUMMARY

In an attempt to test the validity of the Luria method of detecting affective conflicts, one of his experiments was repeated. A complex was induced hypnotically. Verbal, voluntary, involuntary, and respiratory responses were studied. Four male and eight female subjects were used. The results obtained and the interpretations suggested are the following:

1. There was evidence that nine subjects accepted the story told them as something they had done and that it produced a profound reaction in them.

2. In six of these nine subjects some nonverbal (motor) aspect of the Luria technique revealed the presence of the conflict in either the hypnotic or waking states. These subjects in the hypnotic states tended, in general, to give verbal responses definitely related to the conflict with relatively few nonverbal disturbances. In the waking state the relative importance of the nonverbal disturbances increased over the verbal. The

[27]The mean of the first waking as compared with the first hypnotic was 34.33 higher and had a Fisher's "*t*" of 4.030, a value yielding a probability of less than 0.01. This means that the difference was significant.

hypothesis is suggested that there may be "levels of discharge" so that if excitation created by the conflict is not discharged verbally, there is a spread to voluntary and involuntary motor levels. An implication of this hypothesis is that the motor aspects of the Luria technique sometimes may not reveal the presence of the conflict.

3. In the three other cases, those of subjects who accepted the story suggested to them, the evidence that the Luria technique revealed the existence of a conflict was lacking or was of a dubious character. These three cases are discussed with special reference to the effect of the artificial conflict upon their verbal responses.

4. The results from the three subjects who refused to accept the complex suggest that the reproachable act must be of such a nature that the subject can plausibly conceive of his participation.

5. Data collected from repeated sessions on the same subject indicate that there is a "shock" effect which appears chiefly in the first session as a large number of motor disturbances and declines upon repetition. This "shock" effect must be evaluated properly before valid conclusions in this type of experiment can be drawn.

6. Repeated experimental sessions on the same individual while he had the conflict showed a gradual decline in motor disturbances from day to day, pointing to an "abreactive" factor or a forgetting factor.

7. Certain other theoretical implications of the experiment are discussed, and a list of problems which may be approached by the Luria technique are included.

28. A Study of an Experimental Neurosis Hypnotically Induced in a Case of Ejaculatio Praecox

Milton H. Erickson

The experimental investigation of the clinical problems of personality disorders presents an interesting but difficult task. Most studies on such problems have been done by psychoanalysts acting chiefly in the role of therapists. For this reason purely experimental work has been neglected because of the necessity of abiding by prescribed rules and definite concepts. However, students in this clinical field, foremost among whom are the psychoanalysts themselves, are becoming increasingly aware of the need for a systematic technique which will lend itself to laboratory proof as constrasted with the present empirical proof of subjective and clinical experience. As an approach to the experimental study of personality disturbances, a case of ejaculatio praecox was selected and subjected to a laboratory procedure intended to yield some information regarding the psychological mechanism termed *abreaction.*

The technique of experimentation was suggested by the well-established clinical fact, both in medicine and in psychoanalytic therapy, that recovery from one illness (or conflict) frequently results in the establishment of a new physiological equilibrium (or "redistribution of libido"), thereby permitting the favorable resolution of a second concurrent and perhaps totally unrelated illness (or conflict). Of similar influence was the well-known fact that an intercurrent disease may exercise a favorable effect upon the original illness—for example, malaria in paresis. Consideration of these ideas suggested their adaptation to the case in hand at a psychic rather than the usual somatic level. It was determined to give the patient a second illness, which was to be a neurosis so formulated that it might symbolize or parallel the original difficulty, and might be expected to arouse similar or possibly identical affects. The assumption was made that such similarity or identity of affects would establish some dynamic relationship between the two neuroses, possibly through identification, or perhaps through an "absorption" of the one conflict upon the other; and that when the patient, by virtue of the experimental situation, was forced

Reprinted with permission from The *British Journal of Medical Psychology,* Part I, 1935, Vol. XV.

to relive, abreact, and resolve the conflict of the induced neurosis, there might occur a transference or generalization of the abreactive process to the original difficulty. Or perhaps the abreaction and resolution of the induced conflict might establish a new attitude or organization of the personality. At all events the immediate experimental purpose was to establish a dynamic interrelationship of the two neuroses and to induce a readjustment of the personality.

The subject of this experiment was a single white male, 25 years old, who possessed a degree of doctor of philosophy in psychology. In addition he possessed a fair knowledge of clinical psychology and was well acquainted with the author's hypnotic techniques and methods, since he had been acting as a hypnotic subject for the author and had been used extensively in experimental work for a period of a year before he disclosed his complaint. Finally, because his difficulty had become progressively worse, he decided to seek psychiatric assistance, and to this end he complained to the author of ejaculatio praecox and requested aid in overcoming this symptom. His story was essentially as follows: Three years previously he had decided to engage in sexual intercourse and had made many attempts, but always with a strong sense of guilt which he rationalized as a feeling that he was desecrating womanhood. From the first he had suffered from ejaculatio praecox, but on a few occasions he had succeeded in securing a second erection permitting penetration, but this was always followed by a precipitate orgasm and flaccidity. As these failures had been repeated, he had become increasingly concerned and worried, and his problem had become progressively more acute. Originally the overt act of beginning intercourse had resulted in an ejaculation, but at the time he sought aid, kissing or embracing and sometimes merely casual contact with an attractive girl would cause an erection and precipitate an orgasm with a complete loss of potency. Even when he did succeed in securing a second erection, he had not been able to utilize it either because of another precocious ejaculation or because of a precipitate orgasm upon penetration. He had resorted unsuccessfully to such measures as "prophylactic" masturbation to reduce his sexual tension and to the selection of girls without erotic appeal for him. His emotional reaction to these experiences was one of acute shame, bitterness, self-disgust, and inferiority.

At the conclusion of his story the young man was informed that the author would do no more than to take his case under advisement, and no therapy would be attempted until after a period of consideration; also, he was urged to seek assistance from another psychiatrist. Then, changing the subject matter of discussion, the patient's cooperation was requested for a special hypnotic experiment *which he knew had already been under consideration for some time* and which was to be developed in the course of the next few months. Although not fully content about the postponement of therapy, he continued his cooperation in regard to present and projected hypnotic work. Later, during the elaboration of the plans for the special hypnotic work, the idea of this experiment was conceived and promptly elaborated for investigation. No intimation of this fact was given to the patient. Instead, he was allowed to continue in his belief that therapy was indefinitely postponed and that the author was wholly absorbed in the previously projected hypnotic work, concerning which the patient had not been given any information. The rationale for this deception was the assumption that any therapeutic results of the hypnotic procedures utilized could be attributed then to the therapy itself rather than to the patient's hopes and expectations. A second gain, an important consideration in hypnotic therapy, was the possibility of hypnotizing the patient deeply for the experiment without making his success as a subject contingent in any way upon his neurosis.

During the course of the experimental work in which the patient had cooperated, he had been trained to accept "artificial complexes." These complexes were fabricated stories of an emotional nature told to the subject while in a profound hypnotic trance as accounts of actual past personal experiences which should constitute definite memories for him.[1]

Utilizing this background of the patient's, a special complex was fabricated for him which, when properly implanted in his mind, would tend theoretically to produce a second neurosis of the type discussed above. This fabricated story, which follows shortly in its exact wording at the time of administration, together with all hypnotic instructions as recorded in full by the attending secretary, is purely a fancy of the author's based upon an actual wish of the patient's to secure a certain academic fellowship.

However, to orient the reader more easily, it may be advisable to indicate as a preliminary measure the symbolism contained in the complex story. The heterosexual situation and its implications are apparent at once. Less clear are the symbolic equating of cigarette with penis and ashtray with vagina, but consideration of the heterosexual drives involved and the emotional forces at play in that particular setting—the man's attraction to the girl, his desire to give her something and thereby to gain satisfaction for himself, the girl's display of herself by means of her artwork, and the parallelism of the catastrophe of this contact with those of past heterosexual contacts—gives rise to a fair plausibility of such identifications.

As soon as the patient had been placed in a profound somnambulistic hypnotic trance of the type characterized by an apparently complete

[1] A detailed report of such an experimental procedure may be found in Huston, P. E., Shakow, D., and Erickson, M. H. A study of hypnotically induced complexes by means of the Luria technique. *Journal of General Psychology,* 1934, *11,* 15-97.

dissociation from all environmental stimuli and by an apparently total amnesia posthypnotically for all trance events and suggestions, he was given the following instructions:

> Now as you continue to sleep I'm going to recall to your mind an event which occurred not long ago. As I recount this event to you, you will recall fully and completely everything that happened. You have had good reason to forget this occurrence, but as I recall it, you will remember each and every detail fully. Now bear this in mind, that while I repeat what I know of this event, you will recall fully and completely everything just as it happened, and more than that, you will reexperience the various conflicting emotions which you had at the time and you will feel exactly as you did while this occurrence was taking place.
>
> Now the particular event of which I am going to tell you is this: Some time ago you met a man prominent in academic circles who manifested an interest in you and who was in a position to aid you in securing a certain research fellowship in which you were much interested. He made an appointment with you to see him at his home, and on that day you called at the designated hour. When you knocked at the door, you were met not by this gentleman but by his wife, who greeted you cordially and was very friendly, making you feel that her husband had given a good account of you to her. She explained apologetically that her husband had been called away for a few moments but that he would return shortly and had asked that you be made comfortable in the library. You accompanied her to this room, where she introduced you to a charming girl who was obviously rather shy and reserved and who, she explained, was their only daughter. The mother then requested your permission to go about her work, explaining that the daughter would be happy to entertain you while you waited. You assured the mother that you would be very comfortable, and even now you can recall the glow of pleasure you experienced at the thought of having the daughter as a hostess. As the mother left the room, you set about conversing with the girl, and despite her shyness and bashfulness you soon found that she was as attractive conversationally as she was pleasing to the eye. You soon learned that she was much interested in painting, had attended art school, and was really profoundly interested in art. She timidly showed you some vases she had painted. Finally she showed you a delicate little glass dish which she had painted in a very artistic manner, explaining that she had decorated it as an ashtray for her father, to be used more as an ornament than as an actual ashtray. You admired it very greatly. This mention of using

the dish as an ashtray made you desirous of smoking. Because of her youth you hesitated to give her a cigarette. Also, you did not know how her father might feel about such things, and yet you wanted to observe the courtesies of smoking. As you debated this problem, you became increasingly impatient. The girl did not offer you a cigarette and thus solve your problem, and you kept wishing that you might offer her a cigarette. Finally in desperation you asked her permission to smoke, which she granted very readily, and you took a cigarette but did not offer her one. As you smoked, you looked about for an ashtray, and the girl, noticing your glance, urged you to use the ashtray she had designed for her father. Hesitantly you did so and began talking on various topics. As you talked, you became aware of a rapidly mounting impatience for her father's return. Shortly you became so impatient that you could not enjoy smoking any longer, and so great was your impatience and distress that instead of carefully putting out your cigarette and then dropping it in the ashtray, you simply dropped the lighted cigarette into the ashtray and continued to converse with the girl. The girl apparently took no notice of the act, but after a few minutes you suddenly heard a loud crack, and you immediately realized that the cigarette you had dropped into the ashtray had continued burning and had heated the glass unevenly with the result that it had cracked in pieces. You felt very badly about this, but the girl very kindly and generously insisted that it was a matter of small moment, that she had not yet given the ashtray to her father, that he would not know anything about it, and that he would not be disappointed. Nevertheless, you felt exceedingly guilty about your carelessness in breaking the ashtray, and you wondered how her father would feel about it if he ever learned of it. Your concern was plainly evident, and when the mother came into the room you tried to explain, but she graciously reassured you and told you that it really did not matter. However, you felt most uncomfortable about it, and it seemed to you that the girl felt badly too. Shortly after this a telephone call was received from the father, stating that he was called away for the rest of the day and asking your permission to see you on a later day. You left the house very gladly, feeling most wretched about the whole situation and realizing at the time that there was really nothing you could do about it.

Now, after you are awakened, this whole situation will be on your mind. You will not consciously know what it is, but nevertheless it will be on your mind, it will worry you and govern your actions and your speech, although you will not be aware that it is doing so.

> I have just told you of a recent experience of yours, and as I recounted it to you, you recalled it in detail, realizing the whole time that I gave you a fairly accurate account of the situation, that I gave the essential story. After you awaken, the whole situation will be on your mind, but you will not be conscious of what it is, you will not even be aware of what it might be, but it will worry you and it will govern your speech and your actions. Do you understand? And you do feel badly about this thing.

The patient was promptly awakened from the trance state, and within a few moments he seemed completely awake. He appeared to have a total amnesia, not only for the trance events and suggestions, but also for the fact of having been hypnotized, the usual finding after deep hypnosis. He showed particular bewilderment in orienting himself, since darkness had fallen during the time that he had been asleep. He was engaged immediately in a casual conversation by two colleagues of the author who were present, while the secretary made full notes of all conversation together with a description of the patient's behavior and manner. It is not possible to present this material in its entirety because of its length and because of the necessity of preserving the patient's identity. The significant parts, however, have been abstracted for presentation here.

Three general types of phenomena occurred during the posthypnotic period. The first of these was the domination of every train of thought in the patient by his implanted, now subconscious, complex. Although he conversed fluently on a variety of topics, each one was soon noted to be related to the complex, but in a manner apparent only to an observer who knew the whole situation. Care was taken not to suggest topics related to the complex, and the patient himself made no reference to the content of the complex story itself, nor did any of his utterances suggest any conscious awareness of it. Neither was he given any suggestions which would serve to influence the trend of his behavior. Indeed, the colleague of the author who bore the burden of conducting the procedure was kept uninformed of the author's purposes as a means of ensuring undirected responses from the patient. When the patient was asked about a certain friend of his, he told of that friend's small children breaking bric-a-brac. As the conversation continued, he told of the travels abroad of another friend who had visited art galleries and museums containing ancient painted vases; he spoke of the author's library and the advisability of insurance for personal property; and he laughingly told of an instance of careless smoking by a friend which had nearly resulted in a serious fire. Any topic of conversation introduced by the others present was soon developed by the patient in such fashion that a bearing upon the content of the complex became apparent to the observers. Furthermore, each conversational topic rapidly appeared to become unpleasant to the patient, and he would change the subject repeatedly, only to return compulsively to some remark which could be related easily to the complex.

Secondly, there occurred disturbances in the form of his stream of speech. Irrelevancies, stammering, blocking, loss of train of thought, repetitions, persistence of certain ideas, undue urgency, and sudden strong emphases were all noted frequently. Thus, upon awakening, he began smoking and talking until he suddenly observed a painted earthen ashtray at his elbow, whereupon he twisted uncomfortably in his seat, stammered, lost his train of thought, but gradually recovered his poise as the author's colleague assumed the burden of the conversation. Later, while talking about traveling abroad, he interjected remarks about the irreparable loss to art occasioned by the breaking of ancient vases and then continued the main topic of conversation without apparent realization of his digression. Again, in mentioning the author's library, he became unduly solicitous and urgent about insurance. In none of these instances did the patient seem to sense anything unusual in his behavior, despite their frequent occurrance. Observation at the time and consideration of the record later indicated that these behavior disturbances of the patient arose not in response to external stimuli but rather from his own intrapsychic state.

The third type of phenomena noted during this period was phobialike, obsessive behavior in regard to ashtrays, as judged by his previous known behavior. When casually handed a substantial, though ornamental ashtray, he received it in a gingerly, fearful manner and appeared to be afraid to use it. Instead, after many hesitant, abortive, and apparently compulsive attempts to flick ashes into is, he put them into the cuff of his trousers in an embarrassed manner. Now and then he would succeed in dusting them into the tray, whereupon he would crush them repeatedly and uneasily with his fingertips, as if to reassure himself about sparks. He held his cigarette butt until it burned his fingers, glanced at the floor and lifted his foot as if to dispose of it in that fashion, attempted to extinguish it in the cuff of his trousers but seemed too embarrassed to do so, made repeated abortive attempts to extinguish it in the ashtray in front of him by tapping the cigarette gently against the tray, and finally searched the room casually until he found a metal dish, wherein he extinguished the butt methodically, overcarefully, examining and reexamining it as if to be sure that it was not still burning. Whenever anyone dropped a used match into a tray, he seemed compelled to retrieve it immediately and to cool it between his finger and thumb before replacing it carefully on top of the ashes. While conversing he examined and reexamined his ashtray in a detached manner, moved it unnecessarily away from the edge of the table and finally put a soft mat under it. Despite all this difficulty in smoking he accepted unconcernedly a cigarette whenever proffered or helped himself to his own supply, only to repeat his phobialike behavior as he smoked.

Having noted this much of the patient's behavior—of which the above is only a brief summary—it was felt that he had "accepted" the complex and had possibly developed in consequence an artificially induced neurosis. He was then questioned directly and urged to give an account of what had occurred since he entered the office. Despite insistent questioning he was able to state only that he had spent the time smoking and conversing with the author's colleagues. No information was obtained suggesting that he had any conscious realization of the fact that he had been hypnotized or subjected to an unusual procedure. Accordingly, he was rehypnotized, and in this trance he was instructed to recall completely upon awakening the entire experimental situation and to discuss freely his reactions, speech, behavior and conduct. It was assumed that by means of this procedure a "removal" of the complex could be effected, since the patient could thus relive it at a conscious level and thereby might gain an insight into his reactions. As he awakened, a casual conversation was initiated which he soon interrupted to ask if he had told the author of a recent unhappy experience of his. He proceeded to relate the story of the complex as the recollection of an actual event, doing so with appropriate emotional responses, even identifying the father as a man who actually could have played such a role. As he concluded he started, looked bewildered, showed intense amazement, then smiled with relief and understanding, and declared, "Why, that was just a suggestion you gave me—in a hypnotic trance, too!"

After this realization he began to discuss fully the various details of his conversation and conduct, progressing in chronological sequence, each item serving to awaken its successor as a fresh memory. Meanwhile, the secretary made full notes of his discussion and manner and of the questions and remarks addressed to him. He explained that, as the complex was narrated to him, he had displaced, elaborated and falsified true memories, weaving them into the fabricated account, thereby giving the complex story the reality of an actual event. This transformation of the fabrication into a reality for him had been achieved readily upon his identification of the father with a gentleman whom he knew slightly and whom he had wished might play such a role. It was aided further by a strong resentment which he had developed immediately toward the author for having pried into his affairs and having learned about the unhappy incident. Upon awakening, he had felt at ease and comfortable but impelled to talk. As he talked, however, he had become aware of a constantly growing sense of discomfort, augmented by each topic of conversation and by his own remarks and those of others despite the casual, appropriate nature of such comments. He had been astonished to discover his fear of an ashtray, and he had tried to conceal this terror and to overcome it by sheer force of will. At the same time the tray had fascinated and distracted him repeatedly. Although he had tried, he had not been able to reach any understanding of his reactions. He had become even more distressed when he found that the same feeling of terror had attached itself to other ashtrays and even to used matches. "I was just terribly afraid," he declared, "afraid of anything with heat in it."

When asked to describe his emotional reactions in their sequences, the patient stated that, when the complex had been given to him in the trance state, he had reacted to it "just as any normal person would to such a situation. It was a miserable thing to have happen." Upon awakening from the trance, he had not experienced any particular emotions, but as he had begun to talk, he had developed the same sort of emotional state as he recalled having experienced in the hypnotic trance during the administration of the complex. However, as he continued to talk and had experienced blockings of speech and periods of stammering, and had become aware of his intense fear of ashtrays, his emotional discomfort had increased markedly, and he had become "wretched," "miserable," "depressed," "unhappy," "anxious," and "fearful." He described these changes naively by saying that the familiar and pleasant surroundings in which he had found himself had made his emotional distress seem "silly," "foolish," "inadequate," and "reasonless," and that this feeling had impelled him to "reach into past experiences" and to seize upon "embarrassed affects" taken from "past embarrassing experiences" and to "add" these new and stronger emotions to those already existing. This had given him a sense of having improved the situation immeasurably in some undefinable way, but it had made him "feel terrible, awful then." (It had been noted during the latter part of the time in which the patient had the complex that he had become labored and strained in behavior, speaking with effort, sighing deeply, and perspiring profusely—an observation which had led immediately to rehypnotizing him and "removing" the complex.)

The patient was questioned about the "past embarrassing affect" which he had "added" to the original affects. However, without any apparent effort to evade the question, he launched into an academic discussion concerning the possibility of transference of learning as applied to emotional responses, which did not appear to yield any pertinent information. Neither did he seem to grasp the significance of the question.

Accordingly, he was asked how he felt about the whole situation as he recalled it. He replied, "Well, I'm glad to know that it was just a lot of suggestion and that it didn't really happen." He added that his hesitant, fearful manner of trying to use the ashtray must have appeared ridiculous, saying, "Let me show you how I did it." He proceeded to imitate his previous conduct in great detail, suddenly interrupting himself to say, "Now, I'll show you how I do it now." Lighting another cigarette, he tossed the match into the tray as he talked, and finally extinguished his cigarette by crushing the tip against the bottom of the tray and shoving it back and forth through the ashes, remarking with a smile, "Now, I can feel satisfied about it."

Following this the patient was thanked for his services and dismissed with the understanding that the experiment had been concluded.

Three days later the patient returned to the author's office in a jubilant frame of mind, declaring excitedly, "I can do it." When asked to explain what he meant, he stated that on the previous evening he had been in the company of a girl who had responded warmly to his advances. As usual, upon kissing her he had experienced an ejaculation, but instead of reacting with his customary sense of shame and depression, his erotic desire had increased, there had been no loss of his erection, and he had been able to consummate the sexual act, prolonging his pleasure greatly and repeating the act during the night. He was permitted to tell about this experience in detail, after which he began to question the author as to the origin and validity of his "cure." Noncommittal replies were made and he was reminded that in the past he had succeeded after a preliminary ejaculation. He protested that no comparison could be drawn between past successes and that of the previous evening, which had given him his first sense of genuine sexual satisfaction. Also, his whole psychic attitude and reaction had been entirely new, since he had not experienced any of his customary feelings of fear, shame, and inferiority, but on the contrary he had felt confident, secure, and free. Nevertheless, the author's disbelieving manner caused him to leave the office in a discouraged, doubtful frame of mind.

Several days later he returned, again jubilant, declaring "You're wrong, doctor, I am cured." His story very briefly was that, after leaving the office, he had been much depressed by the author's doubts, and for two days he had continued in a wretched frame of mind. Finally, in order to know the truth, he had secured a girl and had spent the night with her in his apartment. He had begun his love-making cautiously, and as his partner responded, he had become increasingly ardent. Since no untoward event had occurred, he had lost all doubts and had proceeded to the overt sexual act. During the act a neurotic fear had developed that he might be unable to have an ejaculation, but this fear had been promptly dispelled by an orgasm. After a rest he had repeated his performance satisfactorily. The next night he had obtained another girl and had confirmed his "cure." (Subsequent investigation into the truth of the patient's story confirmed his report.)

At the close of this account the patient was asked what explanation of the change in him he could offer. He declared that he had no explanation, that apparently he had spontaneously resolved his conflicts, and that he was satisfied to let things remain as they were. The author suggested that he sit quietly and think hard, letting his mind wander at will, and as he did so, to recall all the various emotions he had so often experienced in conjunction with his precocious ejaculations. After a few moments he flushed, moved uneasily, then soon, in a low, monotonous tone of voice said, "I see it now—I put my cigarette in the ashtray and it broke—spoiled everything—I felt terrible—just the same way—I see it now—I was afraid to use the ashtray—I'd try to—I'd pat the ashes to be sure there were no sparks—I'd use my trousers." An expression of amusement and understanding appeared on his face. "But I showed you I could do it. Remember? First, I showed you how I acted when I was afraid, and then I showed you when I wasn't afraid. Remember how I put it out by rubbing it around?" He paused, his reminiscent manner disappeared, and in a puzzled tone of voice he said, "Say, that was that complex you suggested to me—say, that explains a hell of a lot to me—I see through a lot of things now—now I know what I meant when I said I could be satisfied." As an amused afterthought he added, "No wonder my feelings were so awful."

An attempt was made to secure an elaboration of these utterances and to elicit an explanation of his apparent identification of the emotions of his neurosis with those aroused by the fabricated story, but he became so ill at ease and appeared to develop such repressive mechanisms against further conscious insight that it was considered unwise to press questions. The only information obtained was the inadequate statement that "the emotions were just the same" for his ejaculatio praecox and the situation of the suggested conflict.

Several months later the patient was asked to read and check the accuracy of this account of his problem. When he reached the paragraph containing his "explanation," he put the page aside, saying, "Do you know, doctor, I can't remember what my explanation was. Let me think." Within a few moments he repeated in toto the scene described above, uttering almost exactly the same words. As he concluded, he picked up the page, read it eagerly, exclaiming repeatedly, "That's it, that's it." Again he seemed unwilling or unable to elaborate further, protesting that he had explained the whole matter previously on the basis of the stimilarity of emotions.

More than a year has elapsed since this experimental procedure. During the first few months the patient indulged freely in sex relations whenever the opportunity offered, with no recurrence of his symptom. Then, after a period of abstinence, he again developed precocious ejaculation, but without the previous emtional concomitants and without loss of his erection, and in each instance he was able to consummate the sexual act satisfactorily. During the last few months he has discovered that a mere recollection of the experimental procedure will suffice to inhibit a precocious ejaculation, and he is able to function normally. He does not feel handicapped in any way and is well satisfied with his sexual life, and he has not developed any other neurotic symptoms.

DISCUSSION

Careful examination of the above report discloses a wealth of complex psychodynamic manifestations which appear to have been elicited as stimulus-response reactions. From these a number of inferences may be drawn which invite discussion.

Concerning the ultimate soundness of the therapeutic result, there may be legitimate doubt, since the origin of the neurosis and its purposes and function for the personality are not known. However, the fact that the patient can function normally now and can obtain personal satisfactions hitherto impossible, indicates definite and significant changes in his personality reactions of clinical validity. Further, the results suggest that the psychoanalytic theory of pregenital fixation in ejaculatio praecox, developed by Abraham (1927), may not be applicable to every case, since in this instance it is difficult to comprehend how the experimental measures utilized could have bridged such a gap in libido development.

Another question concerns the possibility that the previous hypnotic experimentation, by developing suggestibility, capacity for dissociation, and responsiveness to direct or implied suggestions, might have influenced his neurosis by giving him special insights or new methods of expression. During that time, however, no improvement from his neurosis occurred. For the same reason the hypothesis may be excluded that the author's role as combined hypnotist and promised therapist was unconsciously formulated by the patient as one of an authority-surrogate and permissive agent upon whom he could place the responsibility for successful coitus. Further, it may be contended that the mere induction of a strongly emotional state in the hypnotic trance might have constituted a sufficiently vital experience to occasion a reorganization of the psychic economy with a consequent alteration of the neurotic structure. This is negated by the fact that in the previous work he had been subjected to procedures similar to the one used in this investigation which were equally strongly tinged emotionally, though in a different regard. None of these experiences appeared to have had any role other than that of teaching him how to accept suggestions and how to mobilize his affective responses.

An important consideration is the patient's demonstration of the phenomenon of interpolating into a communication one's own feelings, ideas, and experiences. Given a factually baseless communication, he incorporated it into his mental life, reacted appropriately to it emotionally, and apparently transformed it into a vital part of his psychic life. But in doing so, he interpolated into it other and past experiences, ideas and affects of other origin, formulating the admixture into a new emotional constellation of greater inclusiveness and significance, to which he reacted in a new fashion, as judged by his subsequent behavior and explanations. The means by which he achieved this elaboration appears to have been his unconscious response to the equating of the various emotions which were centred around a single object and which were aroused simultaneously by the intentionally devised relationships, connotations and symbolizations contained in the story of the complex. His vague desire to possess the girl and at the same time to please her, and his desire to smoke and at the same time to give her something which would eventuate in his own satisfaction were integral parts of his general emotional state in relation to the girl. Similarly, his admiration for the ashtray constituted part of his admiration for her, and the expression of a part of his emotional reactions served as a vicarious expression of the other part. This composite nature of his affective reactions formed an emotional background against which one object could be substituted for another to evoke one or another aspect of a common emotion. Accordingly, the cigarette could acquire thereby the cathexis of the penis and the ashtray that of the vagina with a symbolic representation of the one by the other. That such symbolic values did obtain is indicated by the concluding part of the experiment in which the patient appeared to develop some form of conscious insight. His fragmentary remarks signify an intermingling of ideas and affects, an equation of the emotions from one source with those of another, and an identification emotionally of the suggested conflict with that of his neurosis. It is indicated further by the record of his speech and behavior during the time that he had the complex, and by his posthypnotic discussion, all of which suggests strongly that deep affects not appropriate to the story of the complex were stimulated. Particularly interesting are his naive descriptions of deep emotions, and the physiological concomitants of strong feeling states which he manifested in the first trance state of this experiment—namely, profuse perspiration, deep sighing, and strained behavior.

In this same regard arises the question of whether or not deep affects are amorphous in character and are dependent upon stimulation for definition and for direction into channels of expression. The patient's extreme emotional response to the content of the artificial complex suggests, figuratively speaking, the attachment of an amorphous mass of affect to the relatively simple ideas it contained with a consequent disruption of the personality reactions.

A final question for discussion is the rationale of the patient's explanation of his recovery in terms of the suggested complex. A plausible inference seems to be that, having verbalized the emotions of his neurosis in terms of the trance events during the experimental situation, he had been conditioned to that method of response. Hence, when asked to recall those same emotions and to explain his recovery, he did so in accordance with the established pattern. But as he did so, a new psychic factor—specifically, the mental perspective derived from his successful experiences—gave his utterances a new significance for him, enabling him to declare, "Why, that was the complex—that explains a lot of things to me—now, I know what I meant when I said I could be satisfied!"

SUGGESTED PROBLEMS FOR FURTHER INVESTIGATION

The author is well aware that, however valid the results are in this one instance, no general conclusions concerning the neurosis of ejaculatio praecox or its therapy can be drawn from a single case subjected to a new experimental approach. Nor has this account been offered as a possible solution to such a problem. Rather, the purpose of this report is to direct attention to the practicability of the use of hypnotism as a possibly fertile technique for the laboratory study of the dynamics of human behavior. Any therapeutic aspects of such study are of secondary value until a better understanding of the processes involved is achieved.

Although used profitably in experimental academic work, there has been a tendency to overlook the feasibility of hypnosis as an investigatory agent in the study of psychodynamic problems. This investigation indicates that hypnotic measures can be used in a significantly productive fashion to elicit dynamic responses and to manipulate psychological processes. Although no absolute conclusions can be drawn from the findings above, certain inferences and hypotheses, previously discussed are warranted concerning the mental mechanisms involved, the dynamic relationships developed, and the methods for determining or influencing behavior and affective responses. These, in turn, suggest a number of definite experimental problems which invite analytical study and of which a few most relevant to this investigation will be presented.

The first of these problems is the practicability of evolving a technique for the development of experimental neuroses in a human subject for laboratory study. The present investigation is not entirely satisfactory experimentally because of some degree of sophistication in the subject. Despite this fact and the crudity of the technique employed, the results obtained suggest significant clinical and experimental possibilities. The study needs to be repeated, however, on a naive subject with a simpler personality problem such as a specific mild phobia, and in connection with a thorough investigation into the genesis of the symptom for the purpose of elucidating the experimental results. By means of this procedure a more comprehensive appreciation of the interrelationships of conflicts and the influence of one complex upon another might conceivably be reached.

A second problem is the possibility of studying the concept of abreaction. An improved technique similar to that used above, but controlled by continuous observation of the subject and by the centering of his behavior around activities less heavily endowed with affective values and social implications, might offer a good approach to an experimental investigation of the nature, mechanisms, and methods of induction of abreactive processes. A counterpart of experimentally induced abreaction may be found in the "living-out" of fantasies in the psychoanalytic procedure, the clinical results of which also suggest the feasibility of studying abreaction in a laboratory setting.

Another investigatory aspect would be that of devising a technique whereby the subject could be induced to select from a communication the material requisite to form a complex. The present experiment indicates that such a selection was made in this study, since the fabricated story symbolized also an Oedipus complex and a sister-incest situation to which the patient apparently did not react. Such a technique might serve materially to disclose natural complexes and to reveal personality trends and types. Huston et al, referred to above, found suggestive evidence that the hypnotic induction of complexes served to reveal natural complexes. Malamud and Linder (1931) have also made an approach to this problem from another angle by showing pictures to patients and then obtaining reports of their subsequent dreams.

The patient's emotional behavior during the experiment gives rise to the conjecture that affective responses may be "conditioned" somewhat like the conditioning of neuromuscular responses. This might conceivably be accomplished by arousing deep affects upon which, as a direct sequence, a second emotional situation could be created. An illustration of this is to be found above in the establishment of an affectively significant heterosexual situation out of which arose a special emotional state. From such experimentation, by noting sequences, direction, methods of expression, and purposes served, information regarding the genesis, attachment, and interrelationships of emotional reactions might possibly be obtained.

An approach to some of the problems of symbolization is also suggested by this report. The role of similarity of affects in producing symbolic values may be inferred from the patient's account of his recovery. Experimentation designed to attach similar affective tones to dissimilar objects or concepts might conceivably yield information regarding the development of symbolic equivalents. To illustrate, the present experiment might be repeated by arousing the affects of the Oedipus complex, followed by a second emotional situation centered around a fabricated role of authority exercised by the subject. Verbalization of the one situation in terms of the other would possibly indicate the establishment of symbolic values. Or, if the patient's symbolization resulted from the connotations and the relationships of the ideas communicated to him, experimental procedures based on temporal contiguity and association of ideas might give pertinent results.

Another problem is concerned with the question of the development of insight, the factors controlling its growth, its influence upon mental structures, and its function in the psychic economy. The patient studied apparently acquired insights, some complete, others partial, presumably as a result both of the sequences and the nature of his behavior. The same technique, but with continuous observation of the subject and an adequate objective record of his behavior before, during, and after the experiment, might serve to give an appreciation of any progressive manifestations of insight. Or, the omission of certain parts of the procedure, the changing of sequences in the experimental behavior, or the introduction of new measures might determine the relative importance of the various experimental steps. For example, what would have been the ultimate result in this case had the patient failed to demonstrate, "how I do it now," or had he been informed of the experimental procedure by the author instead of recalling it himself?

SUMMARY

A patient seeking a therapy for a neurosis of ejaculatio praecox was subjected to an experimental procedure wherein an attempt was made to induce in him a second neurosis by means of a hypnotically implanted complex. This complex had been formulated to symbolize or to parallel his actual neurosis. In consequence of this procedure there appeared to result an identification of the induced conflict with his original neurosis and a fusing of their affective reactions. After the patient had been forced to relive, abreact, and gain insight into the suggested conflict, it was discovered that he had made a clinical recovery from his original neurosis and that he was still able to function normally a year later. A discussion is given in which possible psychological processes and mechanisms underlying the experimental results are elaborated, the ultimate soundness of the therapeutic results is questioned, and emphasis is placed upon the practicability of hypnosis as an experimental procedure in the analysis of personality disturbances. There follows a list of certain specific problems suggested by this study.

29. The Method Employed to Formulate a Complex Story For the Induction of an Experimental Neurosis in a Hypnotic Subject

Milton H. Erickson

In 1935 a report was published on the induction by hypnosis of an experimental neurosis in a patient suffering from ejaculatio praecox (Erickson, 1935). The procedure employed was that of fabricating a story which would parallel and symbolize the patient's actual neurosis in terms of an ordinary, credible, but unpleasant instance of social behavior. This story was then told to him while he was deeply hypnotized in such fashion that he would believe it to be a true account of an actual past experience of his which he had repressed completely.

The patient's profound psychological and neurophysiological reactions and responses to this procedure and the experimental neurosis he developed were reported in the original article. However, for reasons pertinent at the time, no explanation was given of the process by which this artificial complex was fabricated or of the logic that was employed in attempting to make that story uniquely significant to the patient. Instead, the original worksheets, outlines, and rough drafts as well as the final copy were filed away for possible future use.

Recently, discussions with Margaret Mead, Gregory Bateson, Lewis B. Hill, and others on hypnotic techniques of suggestion and methods of interpersonal communications have suggested the possible value of presenting in detail the explanation of how that complex was fabricated. Also, such an analysis seems warranted by the continued experience of the superiority of this general type of technical procedure in inducing extensive changes in the behavior of hypnotized subjects, as contrasted to the less satisfactory results secured from spontaneous, unplanned, haphazard suggestions, or when the same degree of detailed care is not exercised in building up hypnotic suggestions and hypnotic situations.

In considering how to devise or formulate a suitable complex applicable to the subject, the task seemed to be essentially a problem of, "It is not only what you say, but how you say it." Under the proposed experimental conditions "what" was to be said had to be a seemingly innocuous and

---

Reprinted with permission from *The Journal of General Psychology,* 1944, Vol. 31, 67-84.

credible but fictitious story of a past forgotten social error by the subject. The content of such a story was relatively simple to determine and required little imagination, since the patient had been a hypnotic subject of mine for over a year and I knew him intimately, I was well acquainted with his family, and I also had professional knowledge of his neurosis. Hence the content of the story was easily made to center around an imaginary visit at the home of an unidentified prominent man. There he was supposedly greeted by the man's wife and introduced to an attractive only daughter, in whose presence he smoked a cigarette and accidentally broke a prized ashtray.

The "how" of telling this story seemed primarily to be a task of so relating the fictitious account that it would become superimposed upon his actual experiential past in a manner that would cause him to react appropriately to it emotionally, to incorporate it into his real memories, and thus to transform it into a vital part of his psychic life.

This could be done, it was reasoned, by taking the objective items contained in the essential content of the story and so weaving a narrative about them that they would stimulate a wealth and a variety of emotions, memories, and associations that would in turn give the story a second and much greater significance and validity than could its apparent content.

To do this would require a careful choice and use of words which would carry multiple meanings, or which would have various associations, connotations, and nuances of meaning which would serve to build up in a gradual unrecognized, cumulative fashion a second more extensive but unrealized meaningfulness for the story.

Also, the words, by their arrangement into phrases, clauses, and sentences, and even their introductory, transitional, and repetitive uses could be made to serve special purposes for building up emphasis or cutting it short, for establishing contrasts, similarities, parallelisms, identifications, and equations of one idea to another, all of which would build up a series of associations and emotional responses stimulated, but not aroused directly, by the actual content of the complex. Additionally, sharp transitions from one idea to another, sequential relationships of various ideas and objects, shifts of responsibility and action from one character to another, the use of words that threatened, challenged, distracted, or served only to delay the development of the narrative were all employed to formulate a story possessing a significance beyond its formal content.

Additionally, it must be noted that the patient had been a hypnotic subject of mine for a long time and that therefore he had had a wealth of experience in responding to both direct and indirect suggestions. Thus, his experiential background was of a character to enable him to react adequately to the indirect, concealed, and disguised suggestions and significances of the fictitious story.

Supplementary to this is the fact that the hypnotist, in administering the complex to the patient, was fully aware of what he hoped each item of the story might mean to the patient. Hence, the hypnotist's voice in administering that complex to the patient would carry a load of meaningful intonations, inflections, emphases, and pauses, all of which, as common daily experience constantly proves, so often convey more than spoken words.

Essentially, the task, as worked out, was comparable to that of composing music intended to produce a certain effect upon the listener. Words and ideas, rather than notes of music, were employed in selected sequences, patterns, rhythms, and other relationships, and by this composition it was hoped to evoke profound responses in the subject. These responses were to be of a type not only hoped for in terms of what the story could mean but which would be in accord with the established patterns of behavior deriving from the patient's experiential past.

How well this was done, aside from the experimental results secured, is a matter for speculation. No proof can be offered that the explanation of the complex offered is correct, or that someone else, using the same words, could not construct an entirely different explanation. Proof, if there is to be any, can only be inferential at the best. However, continued experience with the greater effectiveness of hypnotic suggestions carefully calculated as to structure, as contrasted to the lesser effectiveness of spontaneous suggestions primarily concerned with an obvious content, indicates that this initial effort at an analysis of an interpersonal communication of a particular type is warranted.

One additional preliminary to the presentation of the explanation of the complex relates to the actual process of composing the story. During a period of several weeks the story was rewritten in various wordings many times before it seemed to be satisfactory. Two colleagues read and discussed the proposed complex story and contributed a number of helpful suggestions for the final wording of it. Other colleagues contributed unwittingly by discussing, upon request, the meaningfulness of sentences worded in slightly different ways. Also, items of fact relating to the patient, such as his attitudes toward his parents, conversational cliches, patterns of behavior, and actual experiences, were all kept in mind and worked directly or indirectly into the story at every opportunity so that it might have a special and unique appeal for the patient.

As a method of presenting the explanation, the story as devised will be given in the first column of Table 1 and the explanation, logic, intended significances, hoped-for reactions and responses will be given in the second column in the form of comments. These are listed as they were formulated for the final draft of the complex. No attempt will be made to show preliminary or partial formulations as they were worked out from one draft to the next. Finally, the reader must bear in mind that these explanatory remarks constitute only preexperimental formulations of what the complex might possibly mean to the subject and that hence they are not necessarily to be taken at face value. They constitute simply a preexperimental effort to determine the possible meanings of an intended specific interpersonal communication in a special situation. In a few instances it was possible to confirm the validity of a number of these comments postexperimentally, but for the most part such confirmation was not actually feasible aside from also being precluded by the experimental situation.

TABLE 1

The complex	*Explanatory remarks*
Now	"Now" relates to the present, the immediate, circumscribed, highly limited present; it will not bear upon the past nor upon the future; it is safe, secure.
as you	"You" is a soft word; the subject is introduced gently.
continue	"Continue" is a most important word, since it carries on into the future, it contradicts "now," which relates to the present, and it introduces an indefinite extension into the future. Hence, the subject unwittingly makes a change from the "now" situation into a continuing future situation.
to sleep	Thus he has the time situation changed and at the same moment is given a command to "continue to sleep," a command based upon the past, including the present and extending into the remote future.
I'm	First-person pronoun, which means that anything done is to be done by the hypnotist and that the subject can be safely passive.
going	"Going" carries on the future connotation of "continue," but enlarges it by bringing both the hypnotist and the subject into the continuation into the future.
to recall	"Recall" signifies the past, and we are both going into the future, taking with us the past.
to your	Second-person pronoun, emphasizing that we are both going into the future and taking the past with us.
mind	"Mind" is a selected, important, most important part of him, a part of him related to the past.
an	"An" means just one, a certain one, and yet is at the same time so indefinite.
event	"Event" is a specific word; just one event, "an event," and yet, despite its seeming specificity, it is

Table 1 (cont.)

The complex	*Explanatory remarks*
	so general that one cannot seize upon it or resist or reject it or do anything but accept "an event."
which occurred	"Occurred" is a narrative word; lots of things occur, especially minor things.
not	If the subject wishes to reject, deny, or contradict, the word "not" gives him full opportunity. He can seize upon it and attach to it all of his resistances to an acceptance of the story; it is literally a decoy word to attract his resistances. The sequences are "occurred not"—in other words, "did not occur"—but, even should his resistances seize upon "not," that decoy is legitimately snatched away by the next two words, and thus his resistances are mustered, mobilized, but left unattached and frustrated.
long ago.	Actually "not long ago,"—"not" now destroys itself as a negative word; it is positive in that sequence. Furthermore, it is highly specific, but in a vague, general way; when is "not long ago"? Yesterday? Last week? Also "not long ago" is real, since we do have a "not long ago" in our lives; thus a weight of truth is given which will radiate.
As I	First person again, assuming responsibility.
recount	Previously, I was going "to recall," but in this phrase I immediately withdraw from that responsiblity. Now I am only going to "recount," and "recount" and "recall" are totally different words. Thus the responsibility for "recall," which was the initial task, is rejected by the hypnotist, who assumes the responsibility only for recounting. Therefore, if the hypnotist recounts, the subject is thereby compelled to recall. Indeed, if the hypnotist can recount, and there can be no doubt about that, then the subject can, actually can, recall; a sophistical but indisputable establishment of the truth of the story to be told.
this	"This," like "an," is a definitive word that cannot be disputed; and readiness to dispute or deny must be held in abeyance.
event	Again a specific word.
to you,	Second person; first it was recalled to "your mind," and now it is recount "to you," that is, to him as a person. Thus he is introduced so that, in his passive acceptance of the recounting, he, as a person, can assume responsibility.
you will	The subject is called upon to act as a person and at the same time is given a command.

Table 1 (cont.)

The complex	*Explanatory remarks*
recall	"Recall" completes the shift of responsibility from first to second person, with a final allocation of responsibility for recounting and for recalling.
fully and completely	These are distraction words since they attract attention not to the task, but to the size or quality of the task. Hence, he must first refuse to do it "fully and completely" before he can refuse to do the task at all, and if he refuses to do it "fully and completely," he is by implication obligating himself to do it at least in part, until he goes through the process of refusing to do it in toto. All this takes so much time that there is no opportunity to go through those mental processes permitting a logical rejection of the entire task. Additionally, if he still has resistances to the hypnotic situation, he can mobilize them against these distraction words.
everything	"Everything" is really a threatening word; to tell everything is something one just does not do. So here is an opportunity to mobilize resistance, since, if he is to accept this story, his resistances must first be mobilized as a preliminary to a dispersion. Also, if he refuses to tell "everything," he is thereby affirming that there is something to tell.
that happened.	The command to tell "everything" is now seemingly qualified, since it is not "everything," but just the bald facts of "what happened," not the meanings or personal implications. Again there is an implication of other things.
You	Second person, reemphasizing the subject's role as someone involved.
have had good reason	There is not only a "reason," but a "good reason," at that! We all like to think we have a "good reason"; it vindicates.
to forget	Now the "good reason" becomes inexplicably transformed into a "bad" reason; "good" no longer is "good," but is really a bad sort of thing; the kind of reason one likes to forget. Also, "to forget" explains the need "to recall," and explains the recounting. But what does one forget? Bad things, especially!
this	Explicit word, intended to reemphasize the feeling of specificity.
occurrence,	"Occurred" was a narrative word, and now the word is "occurrence," so often a euphemism applied to bad things one forgets.
but	"But" always prefaces unpleasant things; "let's

Table 1 (cont.)

The complex	*Explanatory remarks*
	have no 'buts' about it," is so common an expression.
as I recall it,	This phrasing is a reprieve, since the first person assumes the responsibility, but he who can assume responsibility can also assign it. Thus, indirectly, the dominance of the hypnotist is assured, and the next words lead to active work for the subject.
you will remember each and every detail fully.	More than recall is wanted. Previously, it was "you will recall"; now it is more "you will remember"; furthermore, "remember" is in itself a simple, direct, hypnotic suggestion, similar to the suggestion of "sleep" in the opening sentence. Also, what is to be remembered is "each and every detail," so refusal to remember has to be directed to each detail, not to the whole occurrence. Thus, "each" and "every" and "fully" are distraction words, directing refusal or rejection to a quality of performance.
Now	"Now" harks back to the first word of the first sentence, a word that could be fully accepted. Thus, utilization is made of that first attitude.
bear this in mind,	"Mind" harks back to the first sentence again for a similar reason.
that while I repeat	"Repeat" is a word which relates to a factual experience in the past, one that really occurred and is known, since otherwise it could not be repeated by someone. Also, the role of the hypnotist is clearly defined and cannot be disputed.
what I know of this event,	"Repeat" and "know" affirm and establish the truth, but they give an avenue of escape, because the qualification of what "I know" implies that there may be much that "I" don't know, and therefore something additional that he does know.
you will recall fully and completely	This phrasing harks back and reaffirms the original allocation of responsibility to "you." "Fully and completely" is again a repeated distraction, reinforcing the previous use of those words.
everything	That meaningful, even threatening word again.
just as it happened,	A qualification that limits and comforts since it excludes possible personal implications and meanings.
and more	Further threatening since "more," what "more," is wanted.
than that,	Still carrying the threat.
you will	A hypnotic command carrying compulsion.

Table 1 (cont.)

The complex	*Explanatory remarks*
re-experience the various conflicting emotions	The thing is now defined as conflicting and as emotional, of which things he had a plenty, all real and, above all, emotional.
which you had at the time	A specific but unidentified "time" in the past, but a time related to "conflicting emotions."
and you will feel	a hypnotic command that he is to feel, which carries a threat since it follows " conflicting emotions."
exactly as you did while this occurrence was taking place.	The thing is defined and outlined, his course of action indicated to be a revivification, only that, of a past experience—not a confession, just a reexperiencing of something that took place.
Now	Harking back to the opening word, repeated later for its acceptance values immediately after the assignment of a task, and once again repeated here at a similar point.
the particular event	"An event," "an occurrence," now becomes a highly specific item.
of which I am going to tell you is this:	"I" can tell only what little "I know," a casual statement, transitional in its use, reassuring in its implications.
Some time ago	"Not long ago" redefined, but still vague and elusive of contradiction.
you met a man	Indisputably true and acceptable.
prominent	We like to know "prominent" people, an initial appeal to narcissism.
in academic circles	A narrowing of the identification of the man, but safely so!
who manifested an interest in you	A strong appeal to narcissism.
and who was in a position	A tentative threat, because "position," synonym of power, can be used favorably or unfavorably.
to aid you	Narcissism reinforced and reassured, but more than that, the subject now wants to know, to identify, the man, hence is open readily to suggestion.
in securing a certain	Highly specific but not definitive.
research fellowship in which you were much interested.	A true statement in that he was interested in a fellowship, actually any fellowship, but this statement offers no opportunity to take issue or dispute, since each item is progressively qualified, and each qualification requires dispute before the initial premise can be attacked, and his narcissism requires that he accept each time in the suggestions. Thus, resistance is dispersed. Additionally, the man is "interested," the subject is "interested," there is a

Table 1 (cont.)

The complex	*Explanatory remarks*
	common denominator, and the reality of the subject's interest radiates to and substantiates the man's interest.
He	A third person taking all responsibility. Therefore, the subject can listen receptively, since the story is about a third person.
made an appointment with you	This is a disputable statement, hence is to be qualified in more and more detailed and specific fashion, thus to preclude any upsurge of resistance or rejection, and each little item to be added must have a cumulative effect that takes the subject ever farther from the essential point.
to see him at his home	A qualification as to place.
and on that day	A qualification as to a specific day that must be selected out of the past.
you called at the designated	"Designated" is so specific, final, absolute, and yet so indefinite.
hour.	A final specific qualification for the appointment, and it is most important to establish that appointment. Thus the subject is led to a home, to "that day," to a "designated hour." With such detail not even a thought can flash obstructively in his mind, since the only measure open to him in the hypnotic situation is to reject a "designated hour" of a specific day at a home of an interested man who, narcissistically, he wanted. Thus, an idea has been offered, and its acceptance literally forced. Therefore, an opportunity to resist something about this rapidly growing story must be given him in return for being forced to accept some ideas.
When	A challenging word, anything can happen "when."
you	Second-person active, giving opportunity for him to get set for action.
knocked at the door	A brief item of detail, momentarily obstructing action.
you were met	"You" is second-person passive—thus he is forced from the active to the passive role. "Were met" is a dogmatic declaration which is the opening for all resistance and rejection, an opportunity to interpolate from past experience, a wide-open door for dismissal of the entire story, and thus a chance for him to construct his own account.
not	A negative word, emphatically negative.
by this gentleman	Apparently, it is unnecessary to deny, reject, or dispute the story, since the hypnotist is doing that

Table 1 (cont.)

The complex	*Explanatory remarks*
	by the implications of "you were not met." Thus, the subject's resistances have been built up and then lulled into inaction, rendered futile by the negations employed.
but by his wife	"But" used a second time, this time in close association with a woman to reinforce possible previous unpleasant associations, since a wife is a sexualized woman. Also, this is another disputable statement, but before he can remobilize his resistances, the total situation is completely changed by the next words.
who greeted you cordially and was very friendly,	A tremendous appeal is made to his narcissism, already stimulated previously. One likes to be greeted cordially by a "prominent" man's wife.
making you feel	"Feel" means "respond emotionally," a safe, secure situation for responding to narcissism. Also, the word is a direct call for narcissistic response. At the same time there is given the simple direct hypnotic command of "you feel."
that her husband had given a good account of you to her.	Full opportunity offered for unrestricted narcissism in a safe, secure fashion. All that has been told now rests upon secure foundation of narcissistic satisfactions. He needs this story.
She explained apologetically	An indirect attack upon his narcissism—is this gracious woman who flattered him now becoming apologetic? That must not be so, because whatever that cordial woman does must be right, and he will make it so. Apologies and praise in that combination are not good.
that her husband had been called away	A faint, remote realization that he was alone with a woman who was a wife and hence a recognized sexual object.
for a few moments	A limitation of the danger, and hence he is safe, although alone with a woman.
but that he would return shortly,	"Shortly" is so specifically vague and reassuring.
and had asked that you	"You," the person, introduced again.
be made comfortable	Gracious man, gracious woman, narcissistic satisfactions reinforced.
in the library.	A distraction phrase. Yet, to be made comfortable by a lone woman in the safe confines of a library is like inviting a girl to meet you in the sitting room of your hotel suite—a faint suggestive implication.
You	Second-person active.
accompanied her to this	Reduction of possible fear by specificity in mention-

Table 1 (cont.)

The complex	*Explanatory remarks*
room where	ing only this room—but what is to happen?
she	A woman active in his company—something will happen!
introduced you to a charming girl	For him there can be no greater threat in all the world than a charming girl. A terrifying, threatening situation, loaded with tension firmly established by his past.
who was obviously rather shy and reserved	The threat castrated, and he was master. Thus, his fears were aroused and immediately lessened.
and who, she explained,	First she explained apologetically and unacceptably, now she explains in relation to a threat—will these displeasing explanations never end? A direct opportunity for relief of tension, directed against unnecessary social amenities conducted in such a terrifying situation, but serving to introduce another antagonism.
was their only daughter.	A very special kind of daughter, all the more threatening despite the castration. Thus, a useless, only temporary castration was performed, and while it did relieve his tension briefly, that tension has been revived and intensified.
The mother	An immediate shift from the threatening daughter to the displeasing mother, permitting his tension to increase.
then requested your permission	This cordial, gracious, apologetic woman led him into a trap; she was nice, and certainly he would do anything for her, especially since it would change the total situation by letting him deal with the mother and not the daughter.
to go about her work,	Work is a far cry from social pleasures, remote and distant, and thus she was removing herself far from him, leaving him alone with danger.
explaining	That unpleasant word again, first used to rob him of narcissistic pleasure, then to lead him into a danger situation. What now?
that the daughter	Special, precious, only daughter—charming girl. A peculiar threat, challenge, and danger all combined.
would be very happy to entertain you	To be entertained by a charming girl with the mother's connivance!
while you waited.	"Waited" for what? "Waited," a threatening word, expressive of his passive helplessness. He could only wait, and in the past he had so often "waited" in the company of a charming girl.
You assured	"Assured" carries connotations about risks and dangers.

Table 1 (cont.)

The complex	*Explanatory remarks*
the mother	Who led you into a trap, a danger situation—opportunity for intense resentment and tension relief.
that you would be very comfortable	"Comfortable" with a girl? Past history proves the mockery of that.
and even now	Harking back to the first "now" and reutilizing its "present" values.
you can recall	Harking back to the first use of "recall" and thus tying everything tightly together.
the glow of pleasure you experienced	Harking back to "reexperience the various conflicting emotions." If there were conflicting emotions, some were glows of pleasure, and now his situation is one of a conflict, of attractive and shy, of charming and only daughter, of mother coming and not staying and praising and apologizing, pleasure and unpleasure.
at the thought of having the daughter	"Having the daughter," possessing the charming girl—synonymous phrases.
as a hostess.	Dance-hall hostess? He had had hostesses before, and now there is given the suggestion that he have the "daughter as a hostess."
As the mother left the room	A distraction by shifting attention away from the immediate threat of the girl, and hence readily accepted even though it leaves him alone with his danger.
you set about conversing	Second person introduced. "Set about" implies action, doing something. "Conversing" is a safe activity, but it is a euphemism, and what thinking one can do as he converses!
with the girl,	Alone with a dangerous girl brought to full realization.
and despite her shyness and bashfulness,	Despite those qualities, what else? What danger threatens?
you soon found	Continuation of the threat.
that she was	What was she? An only daughter, a charming girl, a daughter as a hostess?
as attractive conversationally as she was pleasing to the eye.	Safe, yet unsafe, physically pleasing, capable of conversation, capable as a hostess.
You	Second person again.
soon learned	He had learned much about her, too much, and now what more was to be learned about this charming girl so pleasing to the eye?
that she was much interested	Repetition of the word "interested." In what could she, in this danger situation, be interested?

Table 1 (cont.)

The complex	*Explanatory remarks*
in painting,	"Painting"? Painting the town red? A euphemism?
had attended art school, and was really profoundly interested in art.	He had done commercial art to pay his way through college, so there was something in common, a common interest—to be profoundly interested in art would mean that she was interested in *his* art, and his art was part of him. A part of him?
She	A shift from him to her.
timidly	A dangerous girl being timid? Girl-boy behavior, coy, luring behavior?
showed you	Presented to you.
some vases she had painted.	A symbol innocuously introduced, and with the word "painted" establishing their common interest in doing something.
Finally	This is a threatening word. It establishes a moment surcharged with finality—a grand finale is about to be!
she showed	Previously, she timidly "showed," but now where is that timidity? The situation has changed!
you a delicate little glass dish	Fragile, precious thing, easily shattered by masculine strength, so like the girl.
which she had painted	Something on which she had lavished attention.
in a very artistic manner,	Lavished care in a special sort of way that he and she together could both appreciate.
explaining	That word of previously unsatisfactory connotations.
that she had decorated it as an ashtray for her father,	Charming girl, precious possession, father's ownership and priority.
to be used	There is something in this danger situation to be used!
more as an ornament	An ornament can decorate a pleasing body.
than as an actual ashtray.	It's not an ashtray! It's something different. Thus, the symbolic value is clearly established. It is just called an ashtray, but it is an ornament belonging to her and over which the father exercises some undetermined undefined authority.
You admired it	"It" was what she had; she was attractive, pleasing to the eye.
very greatly.	Redundant superlative! In other words a special significance is to be attached to this symbol, a significance in relation to admiration in the presence of a physically attractive girl.
This mention	Some things are just "mentioned," hinted at, not said in a forthright manner.

Table 1 (cont.)

The complex	*Explanatory remarks*
of using the dish as an ashtray	But it is not a "dish," it is not a vase, it is not even an ashtray—it is just an ornament that belongs to her and to her father in a peculiar sort of way.
made you desirous	One wishes to smoke but becomes "desirous" in the presence of a pretty girl.
of smoking.	A euphemism, a safe, conventional way of giving expression to the feeling of being "desirous," actually a pattern of behavior taken out of his past, since smoking was used by him in his problem situation as a distraction.
Because of her youth	Not "youth" really, though she was fresh and pretty and youthful, but something that "youth" connoted, something not to be expressed.
you hesitated	One may eye an attractive girl and be "desirous" and "hesitate." Thus, a sexual motif becomes more evident. Besides, one does not hesitate to smoke in the presence of youth.
to give her a cigarette.	A symbolic ashtray, an ornament belonging to her in which both she and he were "interested" in a special way, with a father lurking in the background. The words "desirous," "smoking," "youth," "hesitate" all constitute a background for a symbolic cigarette that fits a symbolic ashtray.
Also,	There is something else left unsaid as yet, an implication repeatedly established by transitional words.
you did not know how her father	Father lurking in the background reinforced.
might feel about such things	What are "such things" in the presence of a youthful girl that might arouse a father's ire?
and yet you wanted	A long history of "wanting," "wanting" in the presence of every pretty girl.
to observe the courtesies of smoking.	A euphemism, since what else can be said?
As you debated	One does not debate about smoking, one debates for deep reasons, one strives against and tries to controvert the forces against him in a debate.
this problem	He had a "problem," a most troublesome problem in relation to girls, and he is "debating" a "problem" in a girl's presence.
you became increasingly impatient.	Not over smoking does one become "increasingly impatient," but only over vital problems.
The girl	"The girl" follows "increasingly impatient," and by that juxtaposition a relationship is established between "the girl" and the feelings described.

Table 1 (cont.)

The complex	*Explanatory remarks*
did not offer you a cigarette and thus solve your problem	She failed him like all other girls he had known, equating her with those other girls who did not solve his "problem."
and you kept wishing	"Wishing," just "wishing" in direct connection with a girl who had failed to solve his "problem," an old, old story for him.
that you might	If only he "might," really "could" do something.
offer her a cigarette.	"They satisfy," was one of his clichés, and he did want satisfaction. The conventional and the sexual motifs intermingled—satisfaction in relation to a girl, a symbolic ashtray, being "desirous" and his "problem."
Finally	Another final moment, with implications of other things.
in desperation	Strong, bitter, frustrated emotions constitute desperation, and it does not derive from being deprived of a cigarette.
you asked her permission	The role of being miserable, a suppliant, incapable of self-determined action.
to smoke,	A long history of smoking in his "problem" situation to cover up and conceal his disability.
which she granted very readily,	A permissive, willing girl, readily granting favors—another item taken out of his past history.
and you took a cigarette	That was all he could do, and which he had so often done in the past.
but did not offer her one.	She had no pleasure, she was unsatisfied. Past history still being utilized.
As you smoked	He couldn't do anything else, as he had proved many times.
you looked about for an ashtray and the girl, noticing your glance,	Did she notice? Did all those girls of the past notice your glance, your look? "For an ashtray and the girl," making them in this juxtaposition a single object to be looked for. Also, another cliché was "ashes hauled."
urged	Not only permissive, but urgent, active, aggressive.
you to use the ashtray she had designed	An "ashtray she had designed" for what? She had only decorated it for father.
for her father.	Father's special thing, unused by him and not intended for his use, but only an ornament over which he exercises an undefined authority.
Hesitantly	Again he "hesitates," but more than that, the word "hesitantly" implies insecurity, uncertainty, even fears.

Table 1 (cont.)

The complex	*Explanatory remarks*
you did so	"Hesitantly, you did so"—in other words, disposed of "ashes" in a forbidden object.
and began talking on various topics.	A technique of self-distraction and of distraction for the girl often employed in the past.
As you talked you became aware of a rapidly mounting impatience	"Mounting" is a word he often used with special significance. He was always "impatient to mount" before "something happened" that meant the end of the attempt to succeed. Incongruous words!
for her father's return.	What choice is there between "father's return" in a seduction situation and ejaculatio praecox? Any ending, however tragic, is needed to bring to a close an impotence situation.
Shortly you became so impatient	This is only another "impatient" situation, thereby it is equated with other "impatient" situations.
that you could not enjoy smoking any longer,	Past history repeated. Was that why the slogan "they satisfy" was his cliché?
and so great was your impatience and distress	Those words can describe only something more vital than smoking. They are pertinent to past experiences.
that instead of carefully putting out your cigarette and then dropping it in the ashtray, you simply dropped the lighted cigarette	The whole performance was of no value—it was futile, useless, hopeless, fraught with distressing emotions. "Lighted cigarette" and ashes just dropped futilely.
into the ashtray and continued to converse with the girl.	Past history, in that he could only conclude by conversing with the girl.
The girl apparently	"Apparently" carries a weight of hope.
took no notice of the act	There are acts, and then there is "the act," and this was an act that preceded his despairing resignation to mere conversation with a girl, a girl who "took no notice," a parallel of many previous instances.
but after a few minutes you suddenly heard a loud crack,	"The crack that never heals" was a paraphrase from a song often employed by him to vent sadistic reactions.
and you immediately realized that the cigarette you had dropped into the ashtray had continued burning and had heated the glass unevenly, with the result that it had cracked in pieces.	He had often bitterly described his repeated efforts and failures on a single occasion as an attempt "to take a crack in pieces."

Table 1 (cont.)

The complex	*Explanatory remarks*
You felt very badly	Redundancy, strained superlative to carry extreme emotional weight.
about this, but the girl	"This" is one thing, "the girl" is another—another juxtaposition of two items that are to be equated.
very kindly and generously	Permissive, granting, urgent, now maternally kind and forgiving—copies from past experiences.
insisted that it	An unnamed "it."
was a matter of small moment,	Past history again, carrying the same load of bitter ironic significance. What he did was of "small moment."
that she had not yet given the ashtray	Further ironic truth.
to her father,	First maternal, now the girl speaks for her father, thus combining maternal and paternal attitudes in her forbearance.
that he would not know anything	"Not anything," a secret was to be kept, a guilty secret.
about it,	Still an unnamed "it."
and that he would not be disappointed.	A seriously tense situation does not warrant such a mild word as "disappointed." "Disappointed" is a euphemism and at the same time signifies that the situation warrants the mockery implied by "small moment."
Nevertheless,	"Nevertheless" implies the existence of certain other facts.
you felt exceedingly guilty	Fitting words, but not for the superficial content.
about your carelessness in breaking the ashtray.	A euphemism, since exceeding guilt does not attach to an ashtray.
And you wondered	How many times had he "wondered" in similarly emotionally charged situations?
about how her father	Man of power, authority, prior rights.
would feel about it	Not think but "feel," since this was a matter for profound emotion.
if he ever learned of it.	"Ever learned"—a continuing threat implied.
Your concern was plainly evident,	How many times in the past had his concern been evident?
and when the mother	Maternal retribution, forgiveness, or what?
came into the room you tried	You really did try, you've always tried, but it always ends the same old way.
to explain, but she graciously	Forgiveness, not retribution, always forgiveness as in the past.

Table 1 (cont.)

The complex	*Explanatory remarks*
reassured you and told you that it really did not matter.	"Small moment" ironically brought home by the one who should be most bitter.
However, you felt most uncomfortable about it,	A conventional way of saying something too vital to be put into words.
and it seemed to you that the girl felt badly too.	Like other unsatisfied girls who masked their disappointment by maternal behavior, who did not reveal that they had been "badly" used.
Shortly after this a telephone call was received from the father stating that he was called away for the rest of the day	A reprieve, a postponement.
and asking your permission to see you on a later day.	"Your permission," when he has been wronged and violated in relation to his only daughter. The whole situation now radiates beyond the room, reaches out into the fabric of the social situation, the educational situation, infringes upon and enters into everything, and continues to a "later day." Hence, it is not ended yet, but reaches indefinitely into the future.
You left the house very gladly, feeling most wretched about the whole situation	That was all it was, a "whole situation." A pun upon another cliché he employed when distressed about his disability.
and realizing at the time that there was really nothing you could do about it.	A final, despairing repetition of the teachings of the past.
Now after you are awakened,	The original "now" situation continuing into the immediate future with the repetition of the word "now" reestablishing the original receptive attitude.
this whole situation	Pun repeated in relation to the immediate future.
will be on your mind. You will not consciously know what it is but, nevertheless, it will be on your mind, it will worry you and govern your actions and your speech although you will not be aware that it is doing so.	Hypnotic suggestions, with careful emphasis upon the second-person pronoun.

Table 1 (cont.)

The complex	*Explanatory remarks*
I have just told you of a recent experience of yours, and as I recounted it to you, you recalled it in detail, realizing the whole time that I gave you a fairly accurate account of the situation, that I gave the essential story.	A brief summary of first- and second-person activities with allocation of responsibilities and definition of roles reiterated.
After you awaken, the whole situation will be on your mind, but you will not be conscious of what it is, you will not even be aware of what it might be, but it will worry you and it will govern your speech and your actions.	A final shifting of all action upon the second person and repetition of hypnotic suggestions.
Do you understand?	A final command, request, and plea that in itself signifies that there is much to be understood.
And you do feel badly about this thing.	A simple statement in the present tense that concludes with the ambiguous reproachful sounding phrase, "this thing" of such utterly unpleasant connotations.

CONCLUDING DISCUSSION

That all of this labor was warranted in devising a complex is, at first thought, questionable. Previous experience (Huston et al, 1934) had disclosed that complexes could be devised easily which would exert significant influences upon the behavior of hypnotic subjects. However, such influences were found to be uncertain, unreliable, and unpredictable. Additionally, that same investigation, as well as other experimental work had shown that hypnotic subjects could reject complexes for even minor reasons or mere whims.

In this particular experiment, however, the total situation made heavy demands. Not only was the subject to accept the complex and to have his behavior influenced by it, but he was also to be induced to develop an artificial neurosis which would in some way parallel his actual neurosis. Thus, the experimental situation required of the subject a highly specific type of behavioral reactions, determinable only by the personality structure of the patient, and which would be expressive of responses at a symbolic level to the implications rather than to the actual content of the story.

Just what forms such responsive symbolic behavior would take was entirely a matter of speculation. For example, phobic reactions about smoking were anticipated, but it was not realized these phobic reactions would lead to a ready acceptance of a cigarette for smoking and then result in a fearful dusting of the ashes into his trousers' cuff, with a subsequent spontaneous equating of this specific behavior with the consequences of a premature ejaculation. Such symbolic equating of two different types of behavior in relation to his trousers can be explained only in terms of the intended special meanings of the complex story, and hence, the results suggest that, at least in this type of interpersonal communication, the method by which a story is told may be even more important than its content.

REFERENCES

Abraham, K. Ejaculatio praecox. In *Selected papers,* L. and V. Woolf (Eds. and Trans.). London: Hogarth Press, 1927, pp. 280-298.

Alexander, F. The psychoanalysis of the total personality. *Nervous & Mental Disease Monographs,* 1930, No. 52.

Barber, T. X. Suggested ("hypnotic") behavior: The trance paradigm versus an alternative paradigm. In E. Fromm and R. E. Shor (Eds.), *Hypnosis: Research developments and perspectives.* Chicago: Aldine-Atherton, 1972, pp. 115-182.

Bass, M. J. Differentiation of the hypnotic trance from normal sleep. *Journal of Experimental Psychology,* 1931, *14,* 382-399.

Beck, L. F. Hypnotic identification of an amnesia victim. *British Journal of Medical Psychology,* 1936, *16,* Part II.

Bramwell, J. M. *Hypnotism* (3rd ed.). London: William Ryder & Son, 1921.

Breuer, J., & Freud, S. Studies in hysteria. I. The psychic mechanism of hysterical phenomena. *Nervous & Mental Disease Monographs,* 1936a, No. 61.

Breuer, J., & Freud, S. Studies in hysteria. III. Theoretical material. *Nervous & Mental Disease Monographs,* 1936b, No. 61.

Brickner, R. M., & Kubie, L. S. A miniature psychotic storm produced by a superego conflict over simple posthypnotic suggestion. *Psychoanalytic Quarterly,* 1936, *5,* 467-487.

Cooper, L. M. Hypnotic amnesia. In E. Fromm and R. E. Shor (Eds.), *Hypnosis: Research developments and perspectives.* Chicago: Aldine-Atherton, 1972, pp. 217-252.

Erickson, M. H. Possible detrimental effects of experimental hypnosis. *Journal of Abnormal and Social Psychology,* 1932, *27,* 321-327.

Erickson, M. H. The investigation of a specific amnesia. *British Journal of Medical Psychology,* 1933, *13,* 143-150.

Erickson, M. H. A brief survey of hypnotism. *Medical Record,* 1934, *140,* 609-613.

Erickson, M. H. A study of an experimental neurosis hypnotically induced in a case of ejaculatio praecox. *British Journal of Medical Psychology,* 1935, *15,* 34-50.

Erickson, M. H. The development of apparent unconsciousness during hypnotic reliving of a traumatic experience. *Archives of Neurology and Psychiatry,* 1937, *38,* 1282-1288. (a)

Erickson, M. H. The experimental demonstration of unconscious mentation by automatic writing. *Psychoanalytic Quarterly,* 1937, *6,* 513-529. (b)

Erickson, M. H. A study of clinical and experimental findings on hypnotic deafness: I. Clinical experimentation and findings. *Journal of General Psychology,* 1938, *19,* 127-150. (a)

Erickson, M. H. A study of clinical and experimental findings on hypnotic deafness: II. Experimental findings with a conditioned response technique. *Journal of General Psychology,* 1938, *19,* 151-167. (b)

Erickson, M. H. An experimental investigation of the possible antisocial use of hypnosis. *Psychiatry,* 1939, *2,* 391-414. (a)

Erickson, M. H. An experimental study of age regression. Address delivered before the American Psychiatric Association, Chicago, 1939. (b)

Erickson, M. H. Experimental demonstration of the psychopathology of everyday life. *Psychoanalytic Quarterly,* 1939, *8,* 338-353. (c)

Erickson, M. H. The applications of hypnosis to psychiatry. *Medical Record,* 1939, *150,* 60-65. (d)

Erickson, M. H. The induction of color blindness by a technique of hypnotic suggestion. *Journal of General Psychology,* 1939, *20,* 61-89. (e)

Erickson, M. H. Hypnotic psychotherapy. *The Medical Clinics of North America,* 1948, 571-583.

Erickson, M. H. Deep hypnosis and its induction. In L. M. LeCron (Ed.), *Experimental hypnosis.* New York: Macmillan, 1952, pp. 70-114.

Erickson, M. H. Pseudo-orientation in time as a hypnotherapeutic procedure. *Journal of Clinical and Experimental Hypnosis,* 1954, *2,* 261-283.

Erickson, M. H. Self-exploration in the hypnotic state. *Journal of Clinical and Experimental Hypnosis,* 1955, *3,* 49-57.

Erickson, M. H. The "surprise" and "my-friend-John" techniques of hypnosis: Minimal cues and natural field experimentation. *American Journal of Clinical Hypnosis,* 1964, *4,* 293-307.

Erickson, M. H. Experiential knowledge of hypnotic phenomenon employed for hypnotherapy. *American Journal of Clinical Hypnosis,* 1966, *8,* 198-209.

Erickson, M. H., & Erickson, E. M. The hypnotic induction of hallucinatory color vision. *Journal of Experimental Psychology,* 1938, *22,* 581-588.

Erickson, M. H., & Erickson, E. M. The nature and character of posthypnotic behavior. *Journal of General Psychology,* 1941, *24,* 95-133.

Erickson, M. H., Haley, J., & Weakland, J. A transcript of a trance induction with commentary. *American Journal of Clinical Hypnosis,* 1959, *2,* 49-84.

Erickson, M. H., & Kubie, L. S. The translation of the cryptic automatic writing of one hypnotic subject by another in a trancelike dissociated state. *Psychoanalytic Quarterly,* 1930, *9,* 51-63.

Erickson, M. H., & Kubie, L. S. The use of automatic drawing in the interpretation and relief of a state of acute obsessional depression. *Psychoanalytic Quarterly,* 1938, *7,* 443-466.

Erickson, M. H., & Kubie, L. S. The permanent relief of an obsessional phobia by means of communications with an unsuspected dual personality. *Psychoanalytic Quarterly,* 1939, *8,* 471-509.

Erickson, M. H., & Rossi, E. L. *Hypnotherapy: An exploratory casebook.* New York: Irvington Publishers, 1979.

Evans, F. J., & Thorn, W. A. F. Two types of posthypnotic amnesia: Recall amnesia and source amnesia. *International Journal of Clinical and Experimental Hypnosis,* 1966, *14,* 162-179.

Fischer, R. A cartography of ecstatic and meditative states. *Science,* 1971, *174,* 897-904.

Freud, A. The ego and the mechanisms of defense. *The International Psychoanalytic Library.* London: Hogarth Press, 1937, No. 30.

Freud, S. Group psychology and analysis of the ego. *The International Psychoanalytic Library.* London and Vienna: International Psychoanalytic Press, German Ed., 1921, English translation, 1922, No. 6.

Freud, S. General remarks on hysterical attacks. In Collected papers, II. *International Psychoanalytical Library.* London: Hogarth Press, 1924, No. 8.

Freud, S. Note on the unconscious in psychoanalysis. In Collected papers, IV. *International Psychoanalytical Library.* London: Hogarth Press, 1925, No. 10.

Grotjohn, M. Dream observations in a two-year-four-month-old baby. *Psychoanalytic Quarterly,* 1938, *7,* 507-513.

Haley, J. *Uncommon therapy: The psychiatric techniques of Milton H. Erickson, M. D.* New York: W. W. Norton, 1973.

Homburger, E. Configurations in play-clinical notes. *Psychoanalytic Quarterly,* 1937, *6,* 139-214.

Huston, P. E., Shakow, D., & Erickson, M. H. A study of hypnotically induced complexes by means of the Luria technique. *Journal of General Psychology,* 1934, *11,* 15-97.

Kent, G. H., & Rosanoff, A. J. A study of association in insanity. *American Journal of Insanity,* 1910, *67,* 317-390.

Kubie, L. S. A critical analysis of the concept of a repetition compulsion. *International Journal of Psychoanalysis,* 1939, *20,* 390-402.

Lebedinski, M. S., & Luria, A. R. Die Methode der abbildenden Motorik in der Untersuchung der Nervenkranken. *Arch. f. Psychiat.,* 1929, *87,* 471-497.

Luria, A. R. Die Methode der abbildenden Motorik bei Kommunikation des Systeme und ihre Anwendung auf die Affektspsychologie. *Psychol. Forsch.,* 1929, *12,* 127-179.

Luria, A. R. Die Methode der abbildenden Motorik in der Tatbestandsdiagnostik. *Zsch. f. angew. Psychol.,* 1930, *35,* 139-183.

Luria, A. R. *The nature of human conflicts.* Trans. W. H. Gantt. New York: Liveright, 1932.

Malamud, W., & Linder, F. E. Dreams and their relationship to recent impressions. *Archives of Neurological Psychology,* 1931, *25,* 1081-1099.

Nicholson, N. C. Notes on muscular work during hypnosis. *Johns Hopkins Hospital Bulletins,* 1920, *31,* 89.

Olson, D. M., & Jones, V. An objective measure of emotionally toned attitudes. *Journal of Genetic Psychology,* 1931, *39,* 174-196.

Platonov, K. I. Experimental age regression. *Journal of Experimental Psychology,* 1933, *9,* 190-210.

Platonov, K. I., & Prikhodivny, E. A. Objective proof of experimental changes of personality. *Psikhoterapia,* 1930, 191-203.

Prince, M. *The dissociation of personality.* New York: Longmans Green & Co., 1908.

Rossi, E. L. *Dreams and the growth of personality.* New York: Pergamon Press, 1972. (a)

Rossi, E. L. Self reflection in dreams. *Psychotherapy: Theory, Research, Practice,* 1972, 290-298. (b)

Schilder, P., & Kauders, O. Hypnosis. *Nervous & Mental Diseases Monograph,* 1927, No. 46.

Sears, R. R. An experimental study of hypnotic anesthesia. *Journal of Experimental Psychology,* 1932, *15,* 1-22.

Wells, F. L. *Mental tests in clinical practice.* Yonkers, N. Y.: World Book Co., 1927.

Whitehorn, J. C., & Zilboorg, G. Present trends in American psychiatric research. *American Journal of Psychiatry,* 1933, *13,* 303-312.

Williams, G. W. The effects of hypnosis on muscular fatigue. *Journal of Abnormal & Social Psychology,* 1929, *24,* 318-329.

Williams, G. W. Comparative study of voluntary and hypnotic catalepsy. *American Journal of Psychology,* 1930, *42,* 83-95.

SUBJECT INDEX

[Page numbers in **bold face** type are major references.]

NAME INDEX